The Hub
of the Gay Universe

Also by Russ Lopez

Boston 1945 – 2015: The Decline and Rebirth of a Great American City

Boston's South End: The Clash of Ideas in a Historic Neighborhood

Building American Public Health: Urban Planning, Architecture, and the Quest for Better Public Health in the United States

The Built Environment

Urban Health: Reading in the Social, Built, and Physical Environment of U.S. Cities (with H. Patricia Hynes)

The Hub of the Gay Universe

An LGBTQ History of Boston, Provincetown, and Beyond

Shawmut Peninsula Press
Boston, Massachusetts

© Russ Lopez, 2019

ISBN: 978-0-578-41086-9

Library of Congress Control Number: 2018914987

To Ann Maguire

Table of Contents

Photo Credits

Preface

WRITING IN *THE Atlantic Monthly* in 1858, Oliver Wendell Holmes, called Boston the Hub of the Solar System. Given the city's propensity for exaggeration, this quickly morphed into the Hub of the Universe, much to the annoyance of just about everyone else in the country (and presumably, the universe). Holmes was being sarcastic, poking fun at Bostonians' provincialism and chauvinism, but over 150 years later, Boston still refers to itself as The Hub.

Until now, no one has called the city The Hub of the Gay Universe. Obviously, Boston is only one important island in the vast archipelago of the LGBTQ world. But as you will read, a lot happened here. And during these events, LGBTQ Bostonians were convinced that the eyes of the country, if not the solar system, were watching them intently. Provincetown also holds a unique place in the country's LGBTQ life: this tiny town on the tip of Cape Cod is about as queer and rambunctious as possible. Together, the country's most historic city and most fabulous resort have been the settings of some of the most tragic, triumphant, and important events in LGBTQ history. If they are not at the hub of the LGBTQ universe, they are at least pretty darn close to the center of it.

Acknowledgements

LIKE MANY EPIC adventures, this book began over wine, conversation, and song. In the summer of 2015, I was struggling through the production process of my South End history book while beginning the research for my post-World War II history of Boston. Gene Nakajima and Howard Rubin had rented the condominium above where my husband and I were staying in Provincetown and invited us up for drinks. There I met Stephen Hemrick and Richard Schneider, the publishers of the *Gay and Lesbian Review*. I told them I wanted to write a Boston LGBTQ history but as no one else had already done so, I was afraid there wouldn't be enough material to produce a book remotely as good as George Chauncey's groundbreaking history of gay New York or John Boswell's comprehensive study of homosexuality and the Catholic Church. They assured me that this book was both possible and necessary. It was just the encouragement I needed and carried away by rowdy toasts, the sultry evening, and a few hearty slaps on the back, the project was on.

This book was only possible because of The History Project, the Boston-based archive of LGBTQ history. I was very familiar with their collections because I frequently consulted their materials for other projects. From the beginning of the research for this book, Joan Ilacqua, Andrew Elder, and Martha Stone were full of ideas. When my energy flagged, Libby Bouvier was there to keep me going–she is a resource that any community would be lucky to have and meeting with her on Saturday mornings has been a high point of the past several years. She is not the only one who has her hand on our history. Mark Krone's encyclopedic knowledge of Boston's LGBTQ community was a blessing to tap into. Week after week, Bill Holden fetched countless boxes of materials with Tom Norris stepping into that role when Bill left for other climes. The rest of the people involved with The History Project deserve thanks as well: Tony Grima, David White, John Kyper, and everyone else who supports this great archive.

Records of Boston's history are scattered in a large number of places. I was fortunate to benefit from the assistance of library and archives staffs at Boston University, Northeastern University Archives, Boston Athenaeum, New York Public Library for the Performing Arts, University of California–San Diego Special Archives, Commonwealth of Massachusetts Archives, Provincetown Monument Museum, Isabella Stuart Gardner Museum, National Archives in Washington, Historic New England, Harvard University, Provincetown Library, and Boston Public Library. The collections at the British Museum, the Museum of Fine Arts–Boston, and the Art Institute of Chicago were great resources. Jeff Peters of East End Books in Provincetown hunted down a number of books for me as well as provided cheerful encouragement for this project. Brad Gooch helped point the way towards Frank O'Hara's unpublished novel and Andrew Lear's knowledge of gay artifacts at the Museum of Fine Arts was a treasure. When I couldn't locate people, Cindy Rizzo helped identify where they had scattered to.

My friends, especially Al Petras, Brian Gokey, and Eric Secoy, have been most supportive, patiently listening to me as I rattled off stories as we walked around Boston and Provincetown. If you write enough history, you become surrounded by ghosts and past events. For years, Eric has graciously let me stay at his Provincetown condo, enabling me to binge on research and writing while sitting on his wonderful deck. My wonderful buddies at the South End Authors and South End History groups were also great in their encouragement in this and other books: Mel King, Alison Barnet, Paul Caizzi, Ann Smart, Lauren Prescott, Ann Hershfang, and Judy Watkins.

I also want to thank the people who took the time to be interviewed by me: Ann Maguire, Steven Tierney, John Meunier, Barbara Burg, Priscilla Golding, George Mansour, Holly Gunner, Ben Klein, and Richard Pillard. Brian McNaught patiently answered questions for hours over the phone while Gary Daffin and Grace Stowell allowed me to pull them aside to ask about key people and events. John Affuso not only spent an entire Boston-Provincetown ferry ride filling me in on his knowledge of LGBTQ history, he also shared his astute political analysis over drinks at Club Cafe. There have been many more who have left their papers, interviews, and oral histories at libraries and archives, and I encourage everyone to put down on paper (or electronically) their knowledge, stories, and experiences.

The photographs for the book were graciously provided by the Library of Congress, the City of Boston Archives, and The History Project. Marilyn Humphries is another Boston treasure. Her decades of photographs provide some of the best documentation of LGBTQ history anywhere and she was kind to grant me the rights to use her work. Janet Ferone, who presented at the wonderful 1984 seminar taught by Eric Rofes on the history of Massachusetts LGBT politics, was kind to lend a photograph for use in this book as well. Nechama Moring transcribed the interviews. Kristof Nelson was a great editor, taking on this project at a time when a health crisis threatened chaos. His calm expertise and sly wit saved the day and kept the book moving forward.

Most important, I have been lucky to have a great family that has encouraged all my book projects. Their support has been priceless. Thank you to Jo Lopez, Steven Lopez, the wonderful late Neil Sherman, Bonnie Sherman, and my tremendously supportive husband, Andrew Sherman.

Introduction

THIS LGBTQ HISTORY includes lavish nightlife and nightmare repression. It is peopled with courageous students, defiant transgender activists, groundbreaking gay and lesbian politicians, and hundreds of thousands who simply wanted to live their lives unmolested by straight cisgender society. This is a story of a community that transformed itself, a historic city, a picturesque seaside town, and a country. The contribution of Boston to LGBTQ history has been out of proportion to its size. New York, Los Angeles, and Chicago have much larger LGBTQ populations while the queer communities of San Francisco, Atlanta, and New Orleans are much more visible. Yet Boston had the first national LGBTQ newspaper, the first elected out lesbian, the first legal same-sex marriages, and the first trans right victory at the ballot box. Boston activists have gone on to run LGBTQ organizations across the country and its political, social, and artistic institutions are the envy of cities across the globe. Why did this staid, conservative city produce all this excitement?

Nearby Provincetown is a premier LGBTQ vacation spot attracting LGBTQ visitors, performers, and residents. For over one hundred years, it has been the home of LGBTQ artists and writers and its one square mile may have the highest concentration of outrageous entertainment in the country. Why here?

This history tries to answer these important questions. In addition to documenting the vibrant history of Boston and Provincetown's lesbian, gay, bisexual, trans, and queer (LGBTQ) people, this book reveals a number of important lessons for everyone regardless of gender or sexuality.

Most important, this history documents that LGBTQ people have existed in Massachusetts from the very beginning of European domination of the region and most likely were here well before the coming of the Pilgrims in 1620. No records of pre-contact attitudes towards LGBTQ people exist, but within a few years of the arrival of English colonists, there were people prosecuted for engaging in same-sex behavior and challenging gender norms, and soon we have records of people describing their attractions to others of the same sex and rejecting their birth-assigned gender. There are accounts of those we would call LGBTQ people (no such self-identities would develop for nearly 250 years or more) in every era. From groups prosecuted for same-sex relations in Plymouth Colony to LGBTQ people socializing together in the nineteenth century, the evidence for a continued, robust LGBTQ society in Boston is strong. Similarly, Provincetown had such a large group of LGBTQ residents and visitors at the beginning of the twentieth century that they must have been in the town decades earlier.

A second lesson is that societies choose to be accepting or repressive. At certain times, Boston has been a very affirming place; at others, it has been a nightmare for LGBTQ people. Similarly, LGBTQ people were central to the history of Provincetown and its vibrant cultural life even though there have been periodic crackdowns by intolerant authorities. At various points in the history of the region, straight people embraced their LGBTQ neighbors, welcomed them into their homes, and supported them in their day-to-day struggles. Conversely, the many episodes of repression, rejection, and violence resulted from conscious decisions to attack LGBTQ people. None of these actions were inevitable or necessary, but their consequences could be helpful or horrific.

Third, there is a long history of LGBTQ political consciousness and advocacy in Boston. LGBTQ people spoke out against repression over a century ago. In the nineteenth century, people challenged conventional thinking about homosexuality and there is evidence of solidarity among LGBTQ people regarding their rights by World War I. A Boston advocate petitioned the legislature to repeal sodomy laws in the 1920s and the modern LGBTQ civil rights movement in Boston predates Stonewall. Similarly, people opposed gender norms in the seventeenth century and trans groups thrived in 1940s Boston. During periods of adversity, LGBTQ people were each other's best friends and provided emotional, social, physical, and other support to each other through good times and bad.

A final lesson is that LGBTQ people were resilient. After every wave of repression, LGBTQ people were soon back and they lived their lives to the best of their abilities while adapting to social environments that could be overwhelmingly negative. They asserted their humanity and dignity when others tried to deny both and they resisted discrimination, violence, and adversity, sometimes with humor, sometimes by filling the State House with boisterous outrage.

A major challenge for any LGBTQ history is who to include in it. Many people, even those who were regularly having relations with people of the same sex, did not consider themselves to be gay or lesbian. At the same time, many who understood their attraction to those of their own sex married the opposite sex while some chose celibacy. Furthermore, the very idea that people who desire to have relations with their own sex are a distinct type of person only began to emerge in the 1890s. In one sense, no one could be gay before that time because the concept of gayness had not yet been invented. Another complication is that for most of the years covered in the book, any attempt to challenge assigned gender roles was met with arrest or violence making it impossible for people to live openly as they really were. How do we uncover those forced to remain invisible? How do we decide who among us is gay, lesbian, bisexual, transgender, or queer?

For this history, I use a preponderance of evidence metric to judge whether an individual should be included. Yet for many people whose lives seem rather queer, the evidence for their sexuality is meager. Given that homosexuality was a crime punishable by death or imprisonment and that people could lose their jobs, families, and housing if their non-conformity was discovered, only a brave few would leave anything behind that might incriminate themselves. For example, over the past 125 years of documented public cruising in Boston, perhaps hundreds of thousands of men participated. Yet only a few dozen or so have given us evidence that they did so in their diaries, letters, or other written materials.

However, there is no need for explicit evidence of sexual acts to conclude people are part of the LGBTQ community. As will be seen, some same-sex couples such as Vida Scudder and Florence Converse and Henry Sleeper and A. Piatt Andrew left behind correspondence full of tenderness and love but devoid of explicit sexuality. Others burned their letters or their heirs purged their holdings of all incriminating evidence in an attempt to hide the truth. Strangely, some scholars and historians have held LGBTQ people to a higher standard of proof than they do straight couples. For example, despite never having children and a lack of explicit sexual content in their voluminous correspondence, no one suggests that George and Martha Washington were celibate or not heterosexual. Yet one scholar, whose reputation will be protected here, stated in her work on F. Holland Day that one of her goals was to prove that this man who never married, mostly socialized with other men, dressed in elaborate robes and Turkish slippers, and photographed naked young men, was straight.

A second major problem for any LGBTQ history is what to call the people in it. This book uses gay, lesbian, transgender, and LGBTQ. I strongly considered using queer to refer to the group as a whole, but though it would be convenient and brief, I rejected it for several reasons. Many, particularly older and cisgender people, find the word offensive though it has been used for over a century. At the same time, many others, particularly younger and genderfluid people, use the word more restrictively. In their opinion, just because an individual might have relations with someone of their own sex doesn't make them sufficiently different to deserve the title queer because the word has greater meaning than just same-sex attraction. Furthermore, though most scholars now use queer, it is rare to find a cisgender binary lesbian or gay man referring to themselves or their friends as queer regardless of age. I also rejected the longer variant of LGBTQIAPK, an expansion that includes people who are intersex, asexual, and questioning, as well as others. These people are important, but some of them, asexuals, for example, are beyond the scope of this history. Others, including those who might be questioning their sexuality or gender, have left such little evidence behind if their existence and struggles that it was too cumbersome to call them out as a separate group. For the most part, in this book lesbian refers to women who are cisgendered (people who agree with their at-birth sexual assignment), gay refers to cisgendered men, and trans is used for people who have challenged their birth gender assignment. However, sometimes gay is used to refer to all LGBTQ people. For example, since just about everyone refers to a drinking establishment that caters to LGBTQ people as a gay bar, I use that term. Also very important, I have tried to use people's preferred pronouns, but we will never know what some people in the past would have wanted if they had a choice.

Unfortunately, this history leans heavily on white upper-class cisgendered men and women and gay men more than lesbians. Given that people who have the most resources are the most likely to leave behind evidence of their private lives, this was unavoidable. But the inequity both saddened and angered me. I did my best to find additional documentation on working class people, women, trans people, and people of color, but the holes in this narrative persist and I hope that future historians are more successful. This is one reason why this book is subtitled *A history* rather than *The history*. My hope is that this story will be expanded by others in the future. The very lack of more information on those who were poor, non-white, non-binary, transgendered, and others reflects the tremendous discrimination they have faced and continue to confront.

Writing a history of one's own people is not easy. Though I have tried to be objective, it is impossible to describe the sorrows and anger of the AIDS years dispassionately and so the narrative might seem strong, but it pales in contrast to the grief and fury of the time. Similarly, anyone who could write about the murder of trans people or the bullying of children without emotion might ask themselves how they could do so. I could not. On the other hand, some of the institutions and people who are otherwise most praiseworthy did not always behave admirably. I hope I was able to assess people, organizations, and events fairly.

As Boston nears its four hundredth anniversary and Stonewall its fiftieth, the time to preserve and report on LGBTQ history is now. My hope is that readers will find this history informative and useful. One important axiom of historical studies is that nothing is inevitable. If we could go back in time and rerun events, perhaps none of the triumphs in this book would have happened. But they occurred here, not elsewhere, and understanding our LGBTQ history may help identify the fertile ground that made these achievements possible. Perhaps this history might help some of the ghosts from out past sleep soundly and assist those confronting bigotry today to have hope for a better future.

Chapter 1

Radicals and Rebels

IN 1620 PROVINCETOWN was a barren strip of land. What would a group of wayfarers, seasick and starving after a two month voyage to escape from what they considered to be a perverse England, have thought if they had known that the sandy cove they were setting foot on would someday feature drag bingo? The group eventually settled in Plymouth on a site abandoned after a terrible plague decimated the Natives who once farmed the area. What would have happened if they had foreseen that their religious commune, known for its draconian anti-sodomy laws, would become part of a state (Massachusetts) that would be the first to legalize same-sex marriage? A few years later the Puritans (whose name would become synonymous with sexual prudishness) established the city of Boston. Could these settlers have dreamed that the Charles Street Meeting House, home of a congregation that was a direct descendant of their religion, would house the first national LGBTQ newspaper?

This history has many such twists and turns as well as many improbable events. It is not a story of continuous progress; there are tragedies as well as triumphs, happy times and desperate years. But it is a portrait of a diverse community that survived adversity, regrouped after bitter repression, and worked together to achieve victories after 1970 that no one could have predicted back in the seventeenth century.

Some Native nations welcomed what we now call LGBTQ people with warmth while others were less supportive, but nothing is known about how pre-contact Boston area tribes treated LGBTQ people. Thus, unfortunately, the history of LGBTQ people in the region begins with the coming of Europeans. This lack of information reflects the horrific enormity of the destruction inflicted on Native peoples in Massachusetts.

European ships began arriving along the coast of North America within a few decades of Columbus reaching land in the Caribbean. These included not only official voyages of exploration, but also fishermen exploiting the bounty of the Grand Banks and other fisheries. Oftentimes, these vessels would land along the shore to pick up fresh water and supplies, with the result that even before Europeans arrived to colonize what is now Massachusetts, the effects on Native people were devastating. A 1617 expedition noted that the coast was heavily settled, but when the English arrived in 1620 they found abandoned villages and the remains of unburied people; a vicious epidemic brought by Europeans killed 90% of the Native population.

English settlement in New England was chaotic, with competing groups simultaneously employing lobbying and political influence to obtain official charters while struggling to secure financing from hastily formed investor partnerships. The politics and disputes between these groups, both in New England and back in Europe, shaped the legal framework for administering laws against homosexuality in the New World for the next 150 years. The most important groups consisted of religious dissenters who referred to themselves as Separatists (also called Pilgrims) and Puritans, with both names derived from their desire to rid the English Protestant church of Catholic influences. The Separatists wanted to leave the Church of England altogether, while the Puritans wished to remain Anglican, albeit in a dramatically reformed version. The English Reformation began when King Henry VIII was unable to have his marriage to Catherine of Aragon annulled in order to marry Anne Boleyn. As a result, the king established a new religious entity with himself as its leader, the Church of England, which refused to recognize the authority of the Pope in Rome. Despite this independence, little was done to strip away Catholic doctrine and ceremonies. Henry VIII mostly concentrated on confiscating church property and rewarding supporters with ecclesiastical offices.

The Separatists and Puritans were unhappy with the ongoing use of Catholic ritual and theology and wanted the independent church to adopt ideas from the Protestant Reformation that was sweeping much of Europe. They were especially against royal control of church doctrine and believed their independent churches should be able to worship as they pleased. The two groups were followers of John Calvin of Geneva, who preached, among other assertions, that the Roman Catholic doctrines of confession being sufficient for the absolution of sins and the practice of selling indulgences for the same purpose were false. In Calvin's view, neither strict observance of religious practices nor simply living a moral life were sufficient for attaining the splendor of heaven. Instead, salvation was only granted by a parsimonious God who knew in advance which lucky few would make it to eternal grace and who belonged to the great mass of humanity that would suffer eternal torment in hell.

Central to these doctrines was a strong disapproval of the rollicking pleasures of seventeenth century England, with its ribald entertainments, sensuous lifestyles, and conspicuous consumption; excesses that guaranteed damnation. The Separatists and Puritans believed that homosexuality was one of the worst sins rife in the population. Though homosexuality was illegal in England and punishable by death, the Separatists believed it was too often overlooked by English society. Thus, it is not surprising that those who were about to emigrate to Massachusetts associated homosexuality with the rich cultural life of the country's capital and despised it and anyone who tolerated it.

These beliefs put Separatists and Puritans in conflict with the prevailing morals of the English political establishment, which in response saw them as threats. Facing increasing repression and unhappy with the sinful state of English society, many Separatists went to Holland. However, once there they grew uneasy with the Dutch who proved to be even more liberal-minded than the English and the exiles feared their children were becoming assimilated and losing their religious ardor. In this context, the New World looked promising.

One group of Separatists planned to establish a settlement in the northern reaches of the Virginia Colony, and working with a group of sympathetic business-men, they purchased and outfitted two ships. Gathering supplies and upgrading the ships for the Atlantic crossing proved time consuming, however, and they missed their late spring sail date. Then when the expedition finally embarked, one of the ships was found to be unseaworthy, forcing the colonists to return to England. The passengers crowded onto the one remaining overloaded ship, the *Mayflower*, which finally sailed on September 6, 1620. It carried 130 people including passengers and crew, of whom about one-third were Separatists, with the rest either hired help or others sent to establish a new colony.

Strong storms hindered the progress of the *Mayflower*. The ship finally reached land on November 9, far north of where the colonists had intended. The Separatists tried to sail south, but the dangerous shoals between Cape Cod and Nantucket cou-pled with unfavorable winds forced them back north to search for a safe harbor along Cape Cod. They found a refuge in a cove created by the hook of the tip of the cape in what is now Provincetown and set foot on shore on November 11.

Realizing that they were beyond the boundaries of where they had been granted permission to settle and out of reach of both English law and the jurisdiction of the Virginia Colony, the group created a new governing document, the Mayflower Compact, to guide them through the coming months. As far as English law was con-cerned, this document had no legal power, but the new colonists accepted it, at least temporarily, because it was based on the self-governing documents created by their congregations in England and Holland.

Unfortunately, Provincetown was not hospitable and the Pilgrims were ill-prepared for the coming winter. The site had little fresh water and its sandy soils were of low fertility. The group had also enraged the local Native people, the Nausets, by raiding stashes of corn that had been put in place at burial sites for the deceased. Search parties were dispatched to find a better place for a settlement.

After a month at Provincetown, the Mayflower sailed across Cape Cod Bay for Plymouth and the group settled on a hill overlooking the water. It had been a prosperous Native village before disease caused its abandonment. The new site was easily defended, surrounded by fields previously cleared by Natives for farming, and near accessible fresh water. Thus, the first permanent European settlement in New England, Plymouth Colony, was born.

The new colony heavily depended on the assistance of the surviving Natives. During the first winter, many of the newly-arrived Europeans died as starvation and cold weather took their toll. Only the assistance of the Natives helped them through these bitter months. The Natives welcomed the newcomers, rather than attacked them, because they were in precarious circumstances themselves. While struggling to reorganize themselves after they had lost a huge percentage of their population, they faced attack from powerful neighboring tribes. To the south, the Narragansetts had grown wealthy from their control of wampum (beads critical for religious ceremonies and trade) and saw an opportunity to expand their influence on their newly-weakened longtime enemies. To the north and west were other tribes who sought to take over the fertile lands surrounding Massachusetts Bay. Thus, the surviving Wampanoag and Massachusetts Natives hoped the Europeans would give them the strength to resist their enemies.

It wasn't long before the colonists began to encroach as well. As more settlers arrived at Plymouth, they began to disperse around the area. Starving but well-armed, many fed themselves by stealing corn. The Natives complained to William Bradford, the governor of the colony, who struggled to enforce discipline among the colonists. Bradford ordered one man hanged for stealing from the Natives, but most thefts were not investigated, and thus most thieves were not punished.

The soldier hired to provide security for the colonists, Miles Standish, further aggravated the situation with blatant aggression. For example, when a few trinkets belonging to some colonists disappeared, he threatened Natives with mass murder despite the lack of evidence that any of them were responsible for the theft. Feeling guilty and unsafe, the colonists became convinced that the Natives were plotting to wipe them out. Several reported hearing plans for an insurrection, but the stories are suspect. The men who reported them waited several days before passing on the warnings, while others made no effort to retreat back to the safety of Plymouth after supposedly learning about the conspiracy.

Seizing on the rumors, however, Bradford sent Standish to murder the Natives suspected of being the ringleaders of the feared rebellion. "Promising a feast of roast pork, Standish lured four of the warriors into a house; on a prearranged signal the door was bolted, and three were stabbed to death with their own knives, but not without a blood-spattered struggle."[1] As news of the massacre spread, many Natives fled west. The Plymouth Colony survived, but its moral authority was compromised and the Europeans' vulnerability increased. If Europeans more sympathetic to Natives established any new settlements in the region, Plymouth would face financial ruin. Unfortunately for the colony, a man was about to arrive who threatened the economic viability of Plymouth and would have to be violently opposed. His name would come to be linked with homosexuality.

Thomas Morton had sailed from England to revive a small, independent camp of traders, Merrymount, in what is now Quincy. Though the evidence that he or his followers engaged in same-sex activity is very weak, his case is the first example of gay baiting (calling an opponent a homosexual in order to defame them) in the New World.

Morton's year of birth is unknown, though he married a forty-year-old widow in 1621. As a younger son, he did not inherit any property or money from his father. Still, he was a member of London's fashionable society. "An aristocrat by birth and a bon vivant by inclination, Morton was educated for the law at the Inns of Court; he was fond of falconry and foppery, bawdy puns and esoteric poetry; in London he might well have devoted his time to finding patrons to further his ambitions and imbibing with Ben Jonson's boisterous tribe at the Mermaid Tavern. He was, in sum, an Elizabethan dandy, a man of the Renaissance, with a smattering of high culture and a hankering for low adventure."[1] The Separatists abhorred him.

Morton and associates established the Wollaston Company in London to finance a settlement of fur traders. There had been an attempt by "sixty lusty men" to create a colony at the site in 1622-23 but the colony foundered in the unrest between Natives and Europeans. Finding conditions too harsh, most colonists quickly left for Virginia. Merrymount was not the only non-Separatist settlement springing up in Eastern Massachusetts. There were also a number of high-profile arrivals in the area, including William Blackstone, who was the first European settler in what is now Boston. However, many of these more mainstream settlers moved to Maine or returned to England as the Separatists consolidated their hold on the area. Meanwhile, Morton took over what remained of Merrymount to see if he might squeeze some money out of the investment. Unlike many of his fellow Europeans, Morton was enamored with the New World and its people. He later wrote that the Natives were descendants of the Trojans. In contrast, the Separatists thought the wilderness and the Natives were hideous. Because of this and other differences, conflict quickly escalated between the two groups of colonists.

Morton profitably traded alcohol and arms to the Natives in return for furs. Consequently, his camp attracted both Natives and Englishmen. "Unlike the starving and defensive Plymouth colony, Merrymount was festive, utopian, diverse, and commercially successful."[2] Thus Morton set off a retail war with Plymouth Colony, which was trying to keep the cost of furs down to a few beads. Adding fuel to the rivalry, Morton purposely antagonized the Separatists. He called Standish "Captain Shrimp" because of Standish's short height. He also accused the Separatists of drunkenness and wanting to eat him. The last straw came when Morton and his men erected a maypole, an old English tradition of revelry that reflected everything the Puritans hated about "corrupt" English society. Morton raised his eighty-foot-tall maypole, sporting a pair of buck horns near its top, in 1627.

The enraged Separatists moved to arrest Morton and drew up a long list of charges, which included selling alcohol, dancing on the sabbath, and promoting the Church of England. Governor Bradford complained about the presence of Native women at the parties around the maypole, but a later account that Nathanial Hawthorne used for a short story about Merrymount implied that only men were present, contributing to the subsequent legend that the dancing was related to same-sex behavior. Different from Plymouth because it did not include families, most likely its male to female sex ratio was highly skewed in the male direction. Men may have danced together simply because they had no one else to dance with.

The Puritans' charges also included hints of homosexuality, but there is no evidence that Morton was gay beyond a single line in Morton's book on the settlement: "There was likewise a merry song made, which (to make their Revells more fashionable) was sung with a chorus, every man bearing his part; which they performed in a dance, hand in hand about the Maypole, whiles one of the Company sung, and filled out the good liquor like gammedes and Jupiter."[3] Most educated people at this time would have known that in Greek and Roman mythology, Gammedes was a young boy who was so good looking that Jupiter kidnapped him to make him his cup bearer. It was a blatant homoerotic fable that inspired much poetry and art, but the myth was also used in a benign way to signify drinking and merrymaking.

Morton had gone too far and the reaction was harsh. "After this they fell to great licentiousness and led a dissolute life, pouring out themselves into all profaneness," complained Bradford as he justified his efforts to wipe out the settlement.[4] Standish ambushed Morton and dropped him on a deserted island off the coast of New Hampshire in 1628. Standish had wanted to execute Morton, but others prevailed, and Morton was exiled instead. Morton later claimed he was stranded in the middle of winter without weapons, spare clothes, or food, and that he was saved by Natives.

In fact, Morton was exiled in summer and Blackstone and his allies provided Morton with supplies for which they billed Morton's business partners. Morton was sent back to England to be tried by his patron, Sir Ferdinando Gorges, but no charges were brought against him. Meanwhile, Morton unsuccessfully tried to get the Massachusetts Bay Colony's land grant nullified and he continued to scheme against the Plymouth colonists, allying himself with anti-Separatist royalists. His efforts ultimately failed.

When Morton returned to Quincy in 1630, he was again arrested, this time for stealing a canoe. Convicted, he was put in stocks, his possessions confiscated, and his house burned to the ground while he watched. He was once more sent back to England where Gorges not only refused to try him, he encouraged Morton to publish his version of the events in the New World. Morton remained in London for the next thirteen years.

Morton and his allies eventually convinced the British government to revoke the charter of the Massachusetts Bay Colony, but it took until 1637 and required the rise of a new political landscape for that to happen. These efforts did not help when Morton went back to Massachusetts in 1643. Briefly tolerated, he was arrested the next year. He was never formally tried but imprisoned until the colony exiled Morton to Maine where he soon died.[1]

Morton was doomed, in part, when a second chartered settlement was established, the Massachusetts Bay Colony. Conditions for those challenging the established church under the reign of Charles I were rapidly deteriorating, and with Plymouth colonists sending propaganda back to England that promoted the success of their colony, more in England were ready to emigrate. Though they were less radical than the Separatists, the Puritans who came to the new colony shared most of the same Calvinist doctrines and were just as eager to leave England. To encourage this second colony, Plymouth convinced the authorities to charter a new company to settle the area between the Charles and Merrimack Rivers. As a result, 100 colonists arrived in Salem in 1628, followed by 300 more the next year. The new colony struggled at first but then took off and within a few years, 30,000 English people flooded into the area. The settlement at Salem was unable to accommodate the large number of newcomers. Thus, in 1630 they established a new settlement on the tip of the Shawmut Peninsula, and Boston was born.

At some point in his 1630 journey to the New World, whether aboard the *Arabella* or shortly before disembarking, future governor John Winthrop delivered what became a famous sermon, "A Model of Christian Charity." Known popularly as the "City on a Hill" speech, Winthrop's words would continue to have implications for LGBTQ people well into the twenty-first century. First, Winthrop declared that "There are two rules whereby we are to walk one towards another: justice and mercy." Ironically, though Winthrop wrote his sermon at a time when his fellow colonists were harshly anti-gay, as Massachusetts grew into one of the most liberal states in the country in the 1970s, these ideals would partly underlie a series of court decisions that established freedoms for LGBTQ people. Winthrop's call for justice and mercy were echoed in Chief Justice Margaret Marshall's famous decision affirming the right to same-sex marriage in the state in 2003.

Second, Winthrop proclaimed, "We shall be as a city upon a hill. The eyes of all people will be upon us." Centuries later, when Massachusetts LGBTQ people were fighting for the right to be foster parents, married to people of the same sex, and for trans people to live in freedom and dignity, they would be very conscious that they were setting examples for other places to follow. They were energized by the words and certainty of Governor Winthrop, and the eyes of other states and countries rested on Massachusetts as it became more inclusive and welcoming of freedom for all.

The Separatists and Puritans faced a number of religious challenges. Anglicans (loyal followers of the Church of England) joined the emigrant stream and were tolerated, but there were also dissidents who openly challenged key Puritan/Separatist doctrines. Roger Williams believed that the colonists were still adhering too closely to Catholic dogma. The Separatists exiled him and Williams established a new colony at Providence. Ann Hutchinson and her associates preached that salvation came to anyone who had the Holy Spirit inside them and that a personal relationship with God had importance and authority equal to that of the Bible. She was also banished.

These controversies helped set the colonial churches on their centuries-long path to liberalism in several ways. First, they established that the Puritans/Separatists were not radical. There were limits to the reforms they were seeking and there were

Protestants more extreme than them. Second, they supported those who believed that good works and a life of avoiding sin were ways to get to heaven. The promotion of alternative paths to salvation helped the Puritans and Separatists question their doctrines and contributed to their evolution over time. Finally, it brought legitimacy to those who maintained that individuals must find their own path to God with individual conscience being a major force for salvation. This softening of Calvinism would have profound impacts on the lives of some LGBTQ people in the nineteenth century and beyond as the harsh religion of the colonists became more tolerant and inclusive.

The new colonies had a difficult time sustaining and paying for themselves. Subsistence farming would not be sufficient, as their sponsoring companies had taken on debt to finance the cost of founding the new settlements. They needed a source of income that could pay down the interest and principal owed to London financial backers. Unfortunately, the area was lacking in gold and other easily exploited natural resources and the colonists needed all the food they could grow for themselves. New England was never self-sufficient and relied on grain from colonies further south to feed its people. During the early colonial years, the main way for European colonists to earn money was through the fur trade; but the colonists were ill equipped to hunt beaver and other animals prized by Europeans. Therefore, they needed to trade with Natives to secure pelts they could send back to England, but the colonists feared and despised the Natives, making it difficult for the colonists to work with them. Eventually, the colonies supported themselves through ship building, fishing, trade, livestock, and cider production, but it took decades of trial and error to establish these new industries.

Unlike other colonies and the American Western frontier where single men detached from families and free from social pressures predominated, New England was mostly settled by extended families and their servants. This enabled a measure of social control not possible elsewhere. Terrified of God, the wilderness, and the increasingly hostile Natives, the colonists created settlements that consisted of houses clustered around a central point in each town. There they built meeting houses where all were required to spend hours at services every Sunday. Families had to be close enough to the meeting house that everyone could easily walk to these marathon religious services. Once a town grew large enough, a group of families moved off together to establish a new town. Another incentive for clustered development was the growing anger of the Natives who soon realized that the newcomers aimed to displace them from their ancestral lands. European aggression would spark two bloody conflicts, the Pequot War of 1636-38 and King Philip's War of 1675-78, which together broke the power of Natives in southern New England.

Each household consisted of a married couple, their children, and servants. A husband presided over the household with everyone else subservient to his rule, establishing a strong patriarchy that further enforced social control. Consumed by the idea that they needed to increase their numbers in order to maintain their hold on the new land, single adults were looked down upon and most children were not allowed to leave home until they married. Connecticut, for example, levied a fine of one pound a week on bachelors. Furthermore, because houses were small and difficult to heat, most people lived in close quarters and slept several to a room. Though it was common for people to share beds with others of the same sex, privacy was impossible.

Because religion was the primary motivation for the founding of the Plymouth and Massachusetts Bay Colonies, religious fervor was intertwined with almost every aspect of life. God and the devil were everywhere, with the newcomers convinced that they were in the middle of a battle between good and evil. "Puritans lived in a constant state of vacillation between fear and hope, often resulting in a persisting anxiety of the status of their salvation. They constantly sought signs of divine approval, while at the same time rooting out and attempting to vanquish the innate depravity of humanity of which they were so acutely aware."[5] As homosexuality was assumed to be the work of the devil, anyone committing a same-sex act was thought to be Satan's agent.

With a biblical condemnation coupled with a fear of any sexual act that was outside of approved relations between husband and wife, the colonists believed that masturbation corrupted the soul, the body, and society as a whole. Masturbation was seen as a threat against conforming to the era's strong gender norms. Gender was thought to be the result of the interaction of the body's four humors. Men were hot and dry while women were cool and wet. One supposed grave danger of masturbation was that it would feminize men by upsetting a man's natural balance of humors. This would result in impotence and a loss of virility making men unable to be adequate husbands. Because the colonists did not conceive of the idea that women masturbated, there was never any formal pressure against them doing so. In European America, women's sexuality often did not exist. In general, these pressures to maintain gender norms permeated all aspects of society and are part of the reason why colonial laws prohibited cross-dressing.

To indulge in illicit sex, even acts that didn't involve another person, had profound moral and spiritual implications; it threatened one with eternal damnation. Therefore, it is not surprising that homosexuality was a great moral offence and people who were attracted to those of their same sex were horrified by their desire. For example, Reverend Michael Wigglesworth, Harvard class of 1651, Puritan preacher, author of Day of Doom, and onetime candidate for President of Harvard, hated himself for being attracted to male Harvard students. "Lord I am vile," he wrote.[6]

The founders of both the Plymouth and Massachusetts Bay Colonies wanted a society built in God's image, but they saw the devil was close at hand and knew humanity was easily corrupted. To counter temptation, they used an intense system of pressure, reflected in their laws, to keep people from straying. "The colony's leaders attempted to create a godly community based on precedents from the Bible. As such, they believed that it was their duty to exterminate the corrupt tendencies inherent in each man and woman, as much as possible within humanity's sinful state."[5] One of the sins that threatened social norms and promised eternal damnation was having carnal relations with a person of the same sex.

That being said, there was no concept of homosexuality at this time and the idea that a person might have a fundamental interest in persons of their own sex was inconceivable. From the perspective of the colonists, a person might commit a sinful act but that did not mean they were different. It merely meant that they had succumbed to temptation. In this world view, anyone might give into sinful lust, and therefore they did not seek to eliminate homosexuals but rather sought to control bad behaviors. With no separation between church and state, this meant they used laws to control sin.

Creating a legal structure to govern themselves proved difficult, however. The colonial charters provided the legal legitimacy for governments to enact and enforce laws. These were granted by kings and parliaments to colonists and their sponsoring business partners but were intentionally vague because the granting authorities wanted to maintain control over the colonies. In addition, the colonists had to tread carefully when creating legal codes that would impose orthodoxy by zealously religious authorities, yet still complied with English legal freedoms fundamentally expected by all.

To further complicate matters, England went through a series of civil wars over much of the seventeenth century as supporters of the monarchy battled champions of Parliament. Three kings, Charles I, Charles II, and James II, would be deposed before Parliament was finally victorious. At one point during these conflicts, there would even be a dictatorship by a Separatist leader, Oliver Cromwell. These battles were tied up with religious conflict as Catholics, Anglicans, and Separatists/Puritans each sought to impose their religious beliefs and political control on the others. Since the kings promoted the Church of England and were hostile to the Separatists and Puritans, they sought to assert their power over the colonies, Cromwell was obviously the colonists' ally and worked to support their efforts to build a new religious utopia. In contrast, Parliament was torn by factions with conflicting goals. These disputes would have repercussions in the New World as kings, Cromwell, and Parliament would grant and revoke charters as they asserted power. This also explains why the colonies adopted several legal codes over the 150 years before independence.

The colonists believed that sodomy was a concept greater than sex. It implied a corruption that permeated society that reflected an inability to control impulses and desires. Thus, sodomy was included in the category of major sins that they criminalized along with adultery, incest, masturbation, and bestiality (also known as buggery). These sex-related crimes threatened the social order and might arouse God's wrath such that He would turn away from His chosen people and perhaps even will the colonies' downfall. Because the punishment for sodomy in the Bible included the complete destruction of the communities of Sodom and Gomorrah that tolerated it, the perversity of any individual member of society threatened the colonies' existence. Given the precariousness of the English's grasp on the land, this imminent destruction was very believable.

There were also practical reasons to be harsh: coming down hard on sodomy highlighted the differences between old and new England. The colonists had left Europe in part because it was besotted by sodomy and in the eyes of its religious leaders, New England had to hold the line against this grave sin. Their conservatism was further reinforced by the idea that the colonies were supposed to be better than England; moral superiority was the rationale for their existence. Thus, when Governor Bradford reacted to a case of sodomy (and one case of bestiality) in Plymouth Colony, the guilty had to be strongly condemned. Similarly, Governor Winthrop blasted all sexual evils in the Massachusetts Bay Colony because otherwise Boston would cease to be the favored city on a hill.[7] Laws had to be harsh.

In general, there were two sources of colonial sodomy laws: a legal code established by King Henry VIII in 1533 and the biblical text in Leviticus. Henry was secularizing English law and his statute represents a change in treating homosexuality from a religious to a civil crime, while the colonists often went back directly to Leviticus, using a new English translation of the Bible that predated the now more well-known King James version in order to integrate biblical law into civil society. Both types of laws called for the death penalty and tended to only apply to male-male sex, but as charters were revoked and reissued, the laws would need to be rewritten over and over again.

As enacted, these laws required that there be two witnesses to sexual acts in order to convict, a legacy of English common law where this requirement for capital cases was the norm. Coupled with a reluctance to sentence anyone to death, prosecutions for sodomy were fairly rare in New England. No one was executed for sodomy in Massachusetts, though several were whipped, branded, or otherwise punished after being convicted of lesser but related crimes. This was also related to the mercy of the Puritans, as there were more executions for sodomy further south in English North America as well as countless sodomy executions in England.

At its founding, Plymouth Colony had no specific law against sodomy. When five "beastly sodomical" boys were found on an incoming ship (the *Talbot*) in 1629, they were sent back to England where their fate is unknown. It wasn't until 1636 that the colony adopted laws against sodomy and buggery, with sodomy vaguely defined as male-male anal sex and buggery as sex with animals. Both were punishable by death as were murder, rape, treason, witchcraft, and arson.[8]

Though some tried to make sexual relations between women illegal including a provision in an unused legal code for Plymouth Colony written by John Cotton, these attempts failed except for a brief period in New Haven Colony. When New Haven was absorbed into the Connecticut Colony, this law disappeared and there would be substantial gender differences in legal codes and enforcement for the next several centuries.

The first recorded trial for same-sex contact in Plymouth Colony was of John Alexander and Thomas Roberts in 1636. They were found guilty of lewd behavior and often "spending their seed on one another", significantly falling short of the legal definition of sodomy which required anal penetration. Both men confessed to the crime (how or why is not known). Alexander was apparently well known for his homosexual behavior and propositioning other men, yet it seems that it was his obnoxious behavior in the non-sexual realm that had sparked the judicial inquiry into his and Roberts' actions. In practice, perhaps, same-sex behavior could sometimes be ignored, but insubordination and heresy never could be tolerated.

In the early decades of English settlement in Massachusetts, the colonies were repeatedly split by religious dissent. Separatists and Puritans harassed Baptists, exiled dissenters to New Hampshire, and hanged Quakers on Boston Common. However, people engaging in same-sex behavior often escaped maximum punishment. Neither man was condemned to death, though Virginia Colony had already executed a man for sodomy. Instead, Alexander was whipped, burned on the shoulder, and exiled. Roberts, a servant, was whipped, forbidden ever to own property, and returned to his master.

In 1641, William Kersley was brought up on charges that he had been unclean with men he had layed with, but the Plymouth County court could find no evidence to pursue the case and it was dropped.[9] Another Plymouth Colony trial occurred in 1642. This was part of a complicated case involving Edward Michell and Edward Preston, who were convicted of lewd and sodominical practices with each other. Michell was also having relations with Lydia Hatch, who at the time was in an incestuous relationship with her brother, Jonathan. Meanwhile, Preston was found to have solicited another man, John Keene, who turned Preston down, though the court was not convinced that Keene was entirely innocent. In the end, Lydia Hatch was whipped once and Michell and Preston twice (at Plymouth and Barnstable), while Jonathan Hatch was declared a vagrant, whipped, and banished to Salem. Together, these complicated relationships demonstrate that there was a network of LGBTQ people from the earliest days of European settlement in Massachusetts.

There were other cases. In 1649 Richard Berry accused Teague Joanes of sodomy as well as "unclean practices" with Sara Norman, just as she was being accused of having lesbian relations with Mary Hammon. Both Berry and Joanes were ordered to stand trial for sodomy, but before legal proceedings could begin Berry recanted his accusations, resulting in his being whipped and the charges dropped. Confusingly, three years later the court ordered Berry and Teague to cease their "uncivil living together" and ten years after that, Berry was referred to in another court proceeding as a convicted scandalous man. There were several other Plymouth Colony prosecutions that may have been for homosexual acts but for which the surviving legal accounts are too ambiguous to draw sound conclusions.

Though there were no laws against lesbian sexual relations, Plymouth Colony records show one prosecution. In Yarmouth, 1649, Mary Hammon and Sara Norman were accused of having lewd relations on a bed, with Hammon charged additionally with lascivious speech. Only Hammon was convicted. Her sentence required making a public speech which acknowledged her unchristian behavior. Strangely, Norman was found innocent but warned not to commit these acts again.

Though the crown granted the charter of the Massachusetts Bay Colony in 1629, the document was immediately challenged by English authorities and this and other conflicts kept the colony from adopting a legal code with a law against sodomy until 1641. When finally enacted, it excluded women from its sodomy laws and exempted boys fourteen and under from the death penalty but otherwise used the language of Leviticus. Yet, the colonists still found ways to punish women for having sex with other women. In 1641 Salem, Elizabeth Johnson was accused of "unseemly practices betwitx her and another maid" as well as other crimes including "stopping her ears with her hands when the Word of God was read," evidence that religious heresy may have been a motivation for sodomy prosecutions.[10] She was severely whipped and fined five pounds.

In 1684 the Massachusetts Bay Colony charter was revoked and the colony reverted to English law regarding sodomy. As far as can be found, nobody was ever put to death for sodomy in the Massachusetts Bay Colony regardless of which law was in force. After a new charter and the merger of Massachusetts Bay, Plymouth, and Maine colonies into one entity, English laws governed sex in the colony until a 1697 sodomy law restored language based on Leviticus: "the detestable and abominable sin of buggery with mankind or beast, which is contrary to the very light of nature." The language again only covered male-male sex, exempting female-female sex which was still technically legal. The law proscribed the death penalty for those convicted of the crime, but the only execution was for sex with animals, not sex between men.

In the nearby Connecticut and New Haven colonies, there were several sodomy cases. These colonies, like those in Massachusetts, based their laws on the Bible, English common law, and Henry VIII's anti-sodomy legislation. Connecticut's legal code, based on a 1638 charter granted by Charles I, did not specifically mention sodomy; thus, in 1642 the colony adopted language from Leviticus to make sodomy a capital crime. Yet again, courts were reluctant to put people to death. The first man to be executed was William Plaine, charged with engaging in sodomy in England as well as masturbating with several young men in Guilford in 1646. However, Connecticut courts would have had no jurisdiction to prosecute sodomy crimes committed in England and masturbation was not defined as sodomy, therefore the prosecution and execution are somewhat mysterious. This may explain why the court hesitated to sentence him to death and consulted magistrates and clergy in Massachusetts for their opinion on Plaine's crimes and punishment. In response, Governor John Winthrop called him a monster in human shape and encouraged the authorities to execute him. Plaine's own words worked against his pleas for mercy. When confronted by the authorities regarding the sinfulness of his crime, Plaine questioned whether God even existed. Once again, the court was as much disturbed with public atheism as it was with gay sex.

In 1653, six young men in New Haven were publicly flogged for filth and wickedness that could not be mentioned in public, most likely some sort of homosexual activity, bringing forth more evidence that there was a same-sex underground at the time. Then in 1655, New Haven Colony resident John Knight was charged with the attempted sodomy of a teenage boy. The charges also included sodomy with a number of both men and women, all of whom appeared to have consented to the encounters. Found guilty, the court cited a previous conviction for child molestation and other evidence of sodomy as justification for the death penalty. As with other cases, the accused's conduct enraged the court enough to sentence him to the gallows. He went to his death with a string of invectives that were lewd, profane, and corrupting.[11]

Interestingly, even some serial sex criminals avoided the death penalty in Connecticut. For thirty years, Nicholas Sension was notorious for his actions toward young men. Despite this, his neighbors in Windsor did not turn him in even as young men complained to their masters when they were compelled to be alone with him. Sension had first been judicially reprimanded for same-sex relations in the late 1640s, but a 1677 prosecution resulted in his being convicted on the lesser charge of attempted sodomy. Still he escaped any serious punishment, even a fine. In contrast with others whose public heresy condemned them, Sension's piety saved him. One witness reported that Sension prayed for deliverance from his life of sin after he had masturbated with one of his servants. Convicted but not punished, he lived for another twelve years in the community without legal problems.

In comparison with sodomy, its sister crime buggery (sex with animals) was more likely to result in the death penalty. Thomas Granger, for example, was found guilty of buggery with a mare, a cow, two goats, diverse sheep, two calves, and a turkey and was hanged in 1642. The crime and its prosecution point out another potential reason for mercy in sodomy cases: the expense of prosecuting them. It cost 2 pounds, 10 shillings for Plymouth to execute him and the "vile beasts" who were his partners in crime. The colonial authorities spent much time and money going after men who had sex with animals, including one investigation where they staged a lineup of sheep and asked the accused man to point out the guilty animal—the sheep involved in the crime was executed as well. The last certain execution for buggery occurred in 1673 and was controversial as it relied on a retracted confession.

In Massachusetts, there may have been a death sentence for buggery imposed on a slave, Mingo of Charlestown. Mingo was convicted of "forcible buggery" in 1712 and may have been hanged shortly thereafter, but the record is not clear as to the exact nature of the crime or whether the death sentence was carried out.

Though there may have been other prosecutions for same-sex relations in court records now lost, it seems that there were few, if any, sodomy cases prosecuted in Massachusetts after 1700. It was not that homosexual relations ceased, of course, but the appetite for prosecuting them ended.[8] In addition, the severity of capital punishment may have helped increase the tolerance of same-sex behavior. Neighbors may have disapproved of homosexuality, but not to the extent that they wished the person dead, making them reluctant to denounce same-sex practitioners in their midst. They may have turned to other ways of showing their disapproval: shunning, threats, or imposing exile, which do not show up in historical records.

At times, authorities could be quite forgiving of same-sex behavior. In 1732, Ebenezer Knight was suspended from his pulpit for long-standing practices of sex with other men. After spending six years in Boston working to overcome his predilection for sin, he was welcomed back to his church in Marblehead.[9] Again this reflects the idea that persons committed same-sex acts but there was no concept of people being homosexual, i.e. having an immutable interest in their own sex. It also suggests that prosecuting same-sex relations was a choice rather than an inescapable duty.

Despite the day to day lack of official action against same-sex behavior, public discourse against it was strong and unequivocally condemning. When Governor Bradford complained about the great prevalence of sin in the colony he paid special attention to same-sex behavior, famously writing, "but that which is even worse, even sodomy and buggery (things fearful to name) [which] have broke[n] forth in this land oftener than once." Bradford at first maintained that sodomy had burst like a dam upon the population. Later, he contradicted his words by saying the presence of sodomy was no greater in Plymouth than elsewhere.

Though anti-sodomy laws were little-enforced, it does not mean they lacked impact. Puritan legal prohibitions against homosexuality were important not only because they placed colonists at risk of capital punishment back in the seventeenth century but also because they helped shape future laws and contributed to the oppression of LGBTQ people for hundreds of years afterwards. For example, in the repressive 1986 *Bowers* decision of the United States Supreme Court, which allowed states to enforce sodomy laws against consenting adults who had sexual contact with people of the same sex in the privacy of their homes, justices cited colonial laws as precedent for their ruling. Further demonstrating their impact, in almost every discussion of LGBTQ rights in the twentieth and twenty-first centuries, opponents would bring up these sex laws as arguments against equality.

The lack of prosecutions for sodomy and the potential acceptance of some gay men did mean that the colonists tolerated people who challenged gender norms. People of southern colonial New England had to be strictly binary, strongly conforming to either female or male roles based on their assigned gender at birth. Conventional masculinity was associated with virility and hairy robust men were thought better able to satisfy their wives and produce sons, while hairless men and those associated with conventional feminine attributes were thought more likely to sire daughters, if they had children at all. Women were advised to avoid these men as husbands if they could as these men were also thought to be dim-witted and prone to sadness. Thus, from an early time, deviance from traditional sex characteristics was associated with illness.[12] Even haircuts were tightly regulated: in 1649, the Massachusetts legislature ordered men to keep their hair cut short with Harvard doing so as well in 1655. The rationale was to prevent effeminacy.[13]

Of course, there were those who did not conform. A 1652 case outlined how "it doth appear that Joseph Davis of Haverhill was presented for putting on women's apparel"[14] Davis was fined forty shillings. Cross-dressing would continue to be illegal until the 1960s. Other colonists challenged the severe pressure to conform. In 1677, Dorothy Hoyt was convicted of wearing men's clothes. Colonial courts prosecuted Deborah Byer in Suffolk County in 1691 and charged Mary Henley in 1692 with wearing men's clothes (though she escaped punishment). A new law in 1695 set forth a fine of five pounds or corporal punishment for cross-dressing and in 1697 Mary Cox was arrested under that law. In all, the number of people who resisted clothing-related laws is not known but these prosecutions demonstrate that there were what we would now call gender non-conforming people in the colonies from the earliest years of their founding.

One of the colonial era's most famous lawyers, John Adams, was involved in defending a man accused of assaulting a cross-dressing man in 1771. His client, Lendall Pitts, had mistaken another colonist, John Gray, for a woman. A witness at the trial recounted, "I saw him dressed in women's cloaths. I saw a couple of young gentlemen gallanting him. Pitts was one…. They appeared to be very loving, she rather coy."[15] Evidently, there were multiple people challenging sex and gender norms in prerevolutionary Boston. This was not the first time the future president had encountered someone we would call LGBTQ. In 1760 he wrote in his diary about a man "discovered to have been the most salacious, rampant, Stallion, in the Universe …, lodging with this and that Boy and Attempting at least the crime of Buggery."[16]

Though carnal relations with people of the same sex were severely condemned, some women had passionate, if unconsummated, relationships with each other. One of these involved Esther Burr (1732-58), the daughter of famed preacher Jonathan Edwards and mother of Vice President Aaron Burr, and Sarah Prince (1728-61), daughter of the pastor of Old South Church.

Several years before Burr died of smallpox, the two women poured out their dreams, hopes, and fears, and accounts of their daily lives to each other through an extensive exchange of letters. Rarely together, the two still shared an intense connection. For example, Burr wrote in one letter "I believe tis true that I love you too much." When news reached Prince that Burr had died, leaving her two children orphans, she was devastated. "My whole dependence for comfort in the world are gone."[17] Sadly, Prince lived only a few years longer. The correspondence suggests that same-sex emotional relationships, if not sexual ones, were acceptable in late colonial

New England as the letters don't seem to indicate that either woman was embarrassed by their closeness.

When the war for independence broke out, a number of women donned male uniforms to fight. According to one of them, the entertainer Deborah Gannet (1760-1824), not only had she dressed as a man to fight in the Revolution, she had also been a combatant in a skirmish with Natives and was so handsome in her uniform that she had to wage an even more dangerous battle to fend off hordes of female admirers. She had ample reason to publicly state she had remained chaste the entire time: to have admitted to sex with men or women would have destroyed her career. As it was, she placed herself at the limits of acceptable social behavior.[18] A popular entertainer in the post-war period, Gannet appeared in her uniform to perform military drills on the stage of the Charles Bulfinch-designed Federal Street Theater, Boston's first legitimate stage after productions were legalized in 1792. According to a 1797 semi-fictitious autobiography, Gannet had grown up in rural Massachusetts and was mostly uneducated. The first time Gannet tried to enlist, she was punished and expelled from her church. A second attempt was also rejected but she finally joined the army on May 20, 1782, sixteen months before the war ended.

Audiences were fascinated by Gannet's gender defiance in a way that reflected both sexual and non-sexual curiosity. Though some later scholars have suggested that Gannet was only following the direction of her male publisher and collaborator, the exquisite timing and calibration of her onstage persona suggest that at a minimum, she was an equal partner in the creation of her character, if not its driving force. By the time she took to the stage, she was beyond forty years old, had four children (including one adopted), and the war had been over for more than a decade. Still, audiences found it believable that she had been a dashing young boy during the war. Gannet was eventually given a pension for her service in the army, in part because of the intervention of friends including her neighbor, Paul Revere, and in 1944 a liberty ship was commissioned in her name. Other cross-dressing women did not fare as well. Ann Bailey, who had enlisted under the name Samuel Gay, was found to be a woman in 1777 and sentenced to two months in jail and a sixteen pound fine.

There is no accurate way to quantify the amount of LGBTQ behavior in colonial Massachusetts. However, LGBTQ people were part of Boston and Massachusetts from the time of the first European settlement and individuals challenged gender norms and behavioral mandates from the founding of the Plymouth and Massachusetts Bay Colonies. These examples demonstrate that even in the face of draconian laws and strong social and religious disapproval, some LGBTQ people courageously lived as they wanted to be. They were part of a community, often largely unknown to heterosexual and gender conforming people, that has existed for almost 400 years.

Chapter 2

The New Republic

I N THE EIGHTY years after independence, Boston grew into a bustling city. It was not the largest in the new republic, but it was one of country's the most important. Economically, it was eclipsed by New York, Philadelphia, and Baltimore—all of which had greater access to the growing western regions of the country. Boston was further held back by poor agriculture; New England soils were incredibly rocky and the climate was harsh enough that many left for the Midwest, where deep soils and abundant farmland allowed farmers to prosper.

The wealth of the city rested on trade and exploiting new technologies. The greater Boston region was one of the first in the country to benefit from the industrial revolution, with mill towns springing up from Pawtucket, Rhode Island to Manchester, New Hampshire. Over time, New England became known for its shoe and textile factories, many of which relied on the labor of young women displaced from failing farms in the countryside. Women who migrated to smaller industrial towns were often housed in dormitories, where they were carefully watched by their employers. If they moved to Boston, they were more likely to live independently in the many lodging houses and tenements crowding the city. Many men also left their family farms with a sizable percentage ending up in Boston's increasingly overburdened lodging houses. The quality of life for these new residents varied immensely. Some lodging houses catered to the middle class and provided meals while others were more humble buildings that packed as many bodies as possible into rooms where lodgers paid by the night. In an age when same-sex relations were unspeakable, we don't know what might have happened in these crowded living quarters but the opportunities for intimate contact between consenting adults were numerous.

Boston saw large scale political change during this time as well. Most important, Massachusetts effectively outlawed slavery in 1781-82 after it adopted a new constitution written by John Adams. Even before it took effect, Massachusetts slaves were people with rights that included the ability to file lawsuits and more than thirty slaves had used the courts to obtain freedom. However, these rulings were based on other points of law, not on the constitutionality of slavery itself. Then, in a series of cases related to Quock Walker, a slave who had been promised his freedom but who was subsequently kept in bondage by his master's heirs, the Supreme Judicial Court (SJC) ended slavery in the Commonwealth.[1] The justices did not directly rule on the constitutionality of slavery but eliminated all of the legal infrastructure that enabled it through rulings that outlawed slavery contracts, banned compensation to owners for freed or escaped slaves, and prohibited authorities from helping owners keep slaves in bondage. In effect, slavery was not formally ended, but no one could own slaves. This principle set a precedent for how the SJC voided anti-sodomy laws after 1980; it issued a series of rulings that ended the ability of the police to arrest people for sexual relations between consenting adults acting in private but did not rule on sodomy itself.

Slavery had never played a large direct role in the regional economy. Few people owned slaves, yet the institution indirectly but majorly contributed to New England's prosperity. Yankee ship captains moved cargo, both inanimate and human, around the Atlantic in the infamous triangle trade. Ships transported molasses from sugar plantations in the tropical Western Hemisphere to Boston and other ports where it was used to make rum. They carried the rum to Africa where it was used to pay for captured people, who were brought to the Caribbean and what is now the southern United States as slaves.

The profits from the slave trade and the products of slave labor fueled Boston's prosperity. Boston banks profited from financing slave purchases, plantation capital expenses, and the cotton trade. Shipbuilders sold vessels to carry slaves and the products of their labor and Massachusetts textile mills used southern cotton raised by exploited slaves to produce textiles. Without slavery, Boston would not have been a maritime powerhouse and a banking success. Despite this dependence, the city became a center of the abolition movement and over time Boston developed a reputation as being hospitable for black freemen and women. By 1800 almost 10 percent of the population was African American.

The first Bostonians who left a record suggesting they might be a same-sex couple were a pair of black men who lived on the unfashionable side of Beacon Hill. One, George Middleton (1735-1815), led the Black Bucks of America, a guard unit, during the Revolutionary War. Middleton was given the rank of colonel and John Hancock presented him with a flag in recognition of the efforts of his regiment to defend the people of Boston.[2]

After the war, Middleton settled down with Louis Clapion (also spelled Glapion), a hairdresser with whom he built a house at 5 Pinckney Street—now one of the oldest buildings on Beacon Hill. Clapion was half-black and half-French and from the West Indies, while Middleton was born in Boston. While we have no direct evidence the two men were gay (note that they would not have considered themselves gay even if they were romantically and sexually linked), the circumstances of their lives indicate that the two were at the very least extremely close friends and partners. They lived together until Clapion's marriage, whereupon they divided their house in two and continued to live side-by-side for the rest of their lives.[3]

Middleton played the violin, worked as a coachman, and was a horse trainer. As a major force in Boston's African American community he promoted civic causes, advocated for the rights of children, established a benevolent society that sought to alleviate poverty among Boston blacks, and published an anti-slavery tract. He also worked with Prince Hall to found Boston's influential black Masonic lodge where Middleton served as Grand Master in 1809.[4]

In 1781 Middleton married Elsie March at Trinity Church. He outlived his wife, had no children, and when he died in 1815, he left his estate to a white sailor, Tristom Babcock, who lived on West Cedar Street.[5] Less is known about Clapion, who ran his hairdressing business out of his home with his wife, whom he married in 1792. She continued the business after Clapion died in 1813, living at 5 Pinckney until 1832.

Many young men in the early 1800s had relationships with other men that were far more intimate and intense than would be considered heteronormative today. For example, Daniel Webster (1782-1852) was eighteen when he called his best friend, James Harvey Bingham, "the partner of my joys, griefs, and affections." The two called each other "Lovely Boy", and "Dearly Beloved" and exchanged many letters that are infused with romance even as they wrote about their relationships with the young women in their lives.

These male-male relationships were very time limited, generally extending from a young man's teens to early twenties only, and the men in them did not feel guilt or shame. They were considered normal by the society of the time. Yet "all together, these friendships inverted usual patterns of male behavior—they were intimate attachments that verged on romance."[6] Young men in New England had many casual male acquaintances. They were surrounded by fellow workers, students, and residents of rooming houses, but they had fewer opportunities for meeting women and relationships developed between men and women had to follow very narrow parameters to avoid social censure.

Bingham and Webster left no record of any physical intimacy, but other men of the time reported touching, kissing, and caressing. For example, young engineer James Blake was in an intense relationship with another man, Wyck Vanderhoef, to the extent that Blake's wife complained he "went about like a widower" when Vanderhoef departed after one visit. When together, the two men shared a bed, slept in each other's arms, and kissed.[6] As long as relationships such as these did not include overt evidence of sex, they did not cross the lines of impropriety. In addition, because there was no concept of homosexuality or a word for being gay, these men did not conceive of themselves as such; nor did sleeping together raise suspicions because severe space constraints made the sharing of beds common and even expected.

Another Boston man who may have been involved in a homosexual relationship was the painter, Washington Allston (1779-1843). Born in North Carolina, Allston met the soon-to-be-famous Washington Irving (1783-1859) in Rome in 1805. The two spent their days visiting galleries and discussing art. Their time together was so enchanting that Irving briefly considered becoming a painter, fantasizing that "we would take an apartment together. He would give me all the instruction and criticism in his power, and was sure I could succeed."[7] But nothing permanent came of this time together and Irving left Rome while Allston stayed behind.

After Allston's first wife died, the two met up again and the relationship was rekindled at "its greatest intensity" in London in 1815-18. The two would "sit up until cock-crowing, and it was hard to break from the charms of his conversation." During

these days, Irving was "all glowing with tender, affectionate enthusiasm" whenever he heard Allston's name.[7] Working closely together, Allston illustrated Irving's Knickerbocker History of New York.

Sadly, Allston abruptly left London, not even taking time to say goodbye to a heartbroken Irving. One scholar thinks the sudden departure was caused by Allston being blackmailed for homosexual activity because of the line (later heavily edited by Allston's nephew) that he was being hounded by "letter and other applications from imposters."[8] At the time, England experienced a spasm of prosecutions for homosexuality resulting in men hanged, with others fleeing into exile. Allston and Irving never met again and Allston moved back to the United States, remarried, and settled in Cambridge. Buried there, he is most known today for giving his name to the neighborhood of Allston-Brighton.

2.1 Washington Allston, Self Portrait

As the city grew, many fashionable young men in Boston gathered in all-male clubs. One, the Anthology Club, had a number of men who seemed to be afraid of women and marriage, or at least treated the opposite sex with sarcasm and humor. Sharing a similar terror of matrimony was the Bachelor Club. Whether these clubs were actually misogynistic or simply full of mirth is not known, but they could have served as covers for men interested in other men.

Boston, closely connected to other US cities as well as Europe, was also home to young men who were part of a major multinational male fashion and lifestyle trend of the time, the Dandies. These men traced their beginning to mid-eighteenth century London where a group referred to as Macaronis became widely known and oftentimes subject to ridicule. In the first decades of the republic, enough young Boston men adopted similarly ostentatious dress and manners to provoke responses that ranged from scorn to imitation. One entertainer, Mr. Price, sang about them:

"Then the beaux that we meet, how they figure in the street,
With their bodies laced in corsets tight and handy, O

Short pantaloons and coats, and their flashy high heel'd boots,
that's all that is required for a Dandy, O."

He also sang:

"They dined at midnight and stayed out all night"[9]

This suggests that Boston may already have had a well-developed gay nightlife by this time. At a minimum, it means that there was a robust, highly fashionable,
all-male society for those with the means to participate in it. This could have provided
a cover for gay men to meet and socialize with other men of similar tastes.

A growing population coupled with a perceived need for better services
prompted Boston to incorporate as a city in 1822. Up to that point it had been governed by town meeting, a direct form of government still popular in much of New
England two hundred years later. Incorporation marked the beginning of new ways
of managing drinking establishments and policing the city, two municipal functions
that had profound impacts on LGBTQ people. Prior to incorporation, maintaining
civil order was the responsibility of Boston's night watch, established in 1634. Suspects were detained by these semi-volunteers (any male citizen had to answer the call
for a term of duty or find a suitable replacement) and went before a justice of the
peace the next day. The watchmen would have been the town officers responsible for
regulating any same-sex activity that was out in public, including any that occurred in
Boston's streets, parks, wharfs, or elsewhere, also bearing the responsibility to arrest
persons found cross-dressing. Usually these arrests would be for disorderly conduct,
however, making them difficult to identify in historical records. After incorporation,
Boston created a standard police force to keep the peace.

Another byproduct of incorporation was that Boston gained the right to
regulate the sale of alcohol. In practice, the city would be a terrible enforcer of liquor
laws and the number of illegal establishments would often approach that of legal
bars. The city enacted strict liquor laws and it was illegal to sell alcohol in lots less
than fifteen gallons unless the business also provided food and lodging. However, the
law had little impact and in 1830 Boston had 700 legal drinking establishments with
another 300 illegal ones.

There were few recorded arrests for same-sex activity in the decades before
the Civil War but this does not mean that LGBTQ people did not exist, or that Boston
was a "wholesome" city. In the early years of the nation, the back of Beacon Hill was
so well-known for its vice that the neighborhood was often called "Mt. Whoredom"
by the city's moral leaders. A large portion of the three hills in the area was leveled
in 1805 to fill in areas along the Charles River and the waterfront, most famously the
flat of Beacon Hill created by the Mt. Vernon Corporation (an organization of the
city's leading businessmen). Yet this early urban renewal project did little to change

the area's reputation. In 1817, for example, the Reverend James Davis complained to members of the Boston Female Society for Missionary Purposes that "hundreds are intoxicated and spend the holy Sabbath in frolicking and gambling, in fighting and blaspheming; and in many scenes of iniquity and debauchery too dreadful to be named."[10] This suggests that either there was significant gay activity going on in the area or more likely, the term, "too dreadful to be named" was a cliché and catchall for any and all vice.

Respectable Bostonians hated the Beacon Hill area. When Josiah Quincy was mayor from 1823-29 one of his priorities was cleaning up the vice thriving on the hill. His focus was on gambling, dancing, alcohol consumption, and prostitution, however, leaving same-sex behavior unmentioned. Thus there were few arrests or court records for sodomy. In his final year in office, Quincy moved against businesses on Southac Street (now Phillips Street) on the back of Beacon Hill that was also the core of Boston's black community. Reports say there were twelve to fourteen establishments in the area where dancing went on all night.[11] Two years later, a crackdown was directed at nearby Ann Street, located at the waterfront, where similar activities were happening. Despite these actions, vice continued, in part because laws were only sporadically enforced.

Southac and Ann Streets catered to poor and working class men and therefore there was a strong consensus among city officials for moving against them. Their entertainments were cheap, anonymous, and full of transients. If there was a place for men to meet working class men for sex indoors, it might have been in these and similar streets nearby. At the time, the city had few formal bordellos as most prostitutes worked independently and brought customers back to buildings that specialized in rentals for an hour or less. Some of these may have been willing to let two men use a room, but there is no evidence regarding this. As most respectable Bostonians avoided these streets, it would have been easy for men who wanted anonymity to find or consummate liaisons there. We also do not know if Boston Common (set aside as public open space in 1634) and the Public Garden (created in 1859 but whose filling began decades earlier), two prime cruising areas by the second half of the nineteenth century, were already popular for men seeking trysts. But their popularity probably started around this time. In this era before outdoor lighting, the opportunities for cruising and meeting in these parks would have been numerous.

For upper-class heterosexual men, there was relative freedom to purchase the services of prostitutes who regularly made the rounds of the city's cafes, oyster bars, and other tony establishments. Boston theatres were major places for finding prostitutes with some having a "third row"–special sections set aside for prostitutes. In 1847 the city cracked down on this practice using their licensing powers, but even afterwards straight men continued to use Boston theatres to meet prostitutes.[12] Again, we don't know when in the nineteenth century gay men started using theatres for meeting others but theaters would continue as meeting places for gay men up through World War II.

Beginning in the 1840s, a dramatic influx of people from Ireland radically changed Boston. The migration began slowly but had already reached levels that inflamed anti-Irish sentiment well before the great famine of 1845 sent a million Irish people to points around the globe. Boston had welcomed native Protestant immigrants from rural New England for decades, but the new Catholic arrivals faced tremendous prejudice. Many existing residents moved away from central Boston or left the city altogether as the Irish moved in, and soon native-born Protestants were clamoring for action to stop the "invasion."

By 1851, many Protestant voters believed their beloved Boston was being overrun by filth and vice brought by the Irish. In response, the city staged a series of dramatic, well publicized raids on houses where prostitution and gambling were allegedly taking place. The most spectacular of these was on April 23 when over one hundred policemen descended on Ann Street to arrest brothel owners, prostitutes, pipers, fiddlers, and other associated hooligans. Public outrage was so strong that the street was eventually renamed North Street.

Despite crackdowns, the area remained a commercial center of vice at least until the end of the century when it shifted to nearby Scollay Square. In 1853 a sensationalized account of the area proclaimed, "Talk of Boston being a moral city! There is villainy, misery and vice enough in Ann Street alone, to deserve for the whole place the fate of Sodom and Gomorrah."[13] Again, there is no way to know if this is a reference to same-sex activity or if it was simply a catchall phrase. In any case, as late as the 1880s Harvard students would go down to the West End (which then included the north slope of Beacon Hill) and North End to drink, gamble, and find heterosexual sex. Others may have found same-sex partners there as well.

Harvard University would play a major role in Boston's LGBTQ history over the next several centuries, and indeed, that of the entire county. Established in 1636, it only admitted men until female Radcliffe students were allowed to attend classes in the twentieth century. As an all-male hermetically sealed institution, Harvard would have all the drama, attraction, and repression that mark homosocial organizations. In addition, in the decades before the Civil War students often entered the college at the age of sixteen or younger. Away from their families and living in boarding houses around Harvard Square, the temptations posed by nearby youths were perhaps extreme for some.

For example, junior Ralph Waldo Emerson (1803-82) developed a strong crush on a Harvard freshman, Martin Gay, in 1819. As indicated in his diaries, the young Emerson was very inept at romance and seduction, he would furtively look at Gay and hope for a glance back as he followed him around Harvard Yard. But they barely exchanged words, which inflamed Emerson's passions but did not lead to any apparent consummation of this longing and most of Emerson's energy was directed instead to his diaries and poetry. These passages were later mostly crossed out in an effort to erase them, perhaps by Emerson, perhaps by his son.[14] For a year and a half, Emerson followed Gay with another eighteen months spent before his interest died "like other romantic crushes, this one finally killed by time and a heavy dose of reality."[6]

Emerson's struggles indicate how young men, adolescents at the time, were confronted by same-sex desire yet lacked the ability to act upon these yearnings. Living in a society that severely frowned on same-sex activity meant that these men had to suppress their desires. Any evidence they might leave regarding these feelings would be destroyed by themselves, their families, or their heirs. In this case, Emerson went on to have other crushes on men as he grew into one of the literary giants of the nineteenth century, while Gay became a prominent physician. There is a strong debate as to whether these crushes suggest Emerson was gay. In any case, Emerson struggled with these feelings and sought to suppress them as he despised vileness and dissipation in himself and others. He would have known from his religion and the laws of the time that same-sex contact was strongly forbidden.

Emerson did not stop with merely suppressing his own same-sex desires; he also tried to talk Walt Whitman (1819-92) into omitting the most homoerotic poems from his 1860 version of *Leaves of Grass* during a two hour walk around Boston Common, arguing that they would be found offensive and could ruin Whitman. He ignored Emerson's advice and went on to publish the poems.

The reaction to *Leaves of Grass* was strong. James Russell Lowell, professor of modern languages at Harvard (he succeeded Henry Wadsworth Longfellow) forbade his students to read the book and the college kept it locked away in the stacks, as did the Boston Public Library. Despite reservations Emerson continued to champion Whitman, even getting him into the Boston Athenaeum, but others often shunned him.[14] Thomas Wentworth Higginson, a Civil War hero and women's rights champion, for example, wrote that he did not have a problem with Whitman writing *Leaves of Grass*. His only complaint was that Whitman didn't go on to burn the manuscript. He said he had read the poems during a voyage to the Azores and that the writing upset his stomach more than the stormy Atlantic.[15] This was the reaction of a man who went before the New England Women's Club to read a paper on Sappho.

Ignoring warnings, Boston publishing house Thayer and Eldridge put out Whitman's 1860 edition but went bankrupt in the process with most of the books printed in Philadelphia. In 1882, the book was banned in Boston courtesy of the agitation of the New England Society for the Suppression of Vice (later called the Watch and Ward Society), greatly increasing sales elsewhere. Despite the reticence of literary Boston, the book of poems is now seen as a landmark of American literature.

Boston also produced one of the most important actresses of the nineteenth century, Charlotte Cushman (1816-76), whose life illustrates the tremendous challenges faced by lesbians in the nineteenth century. Cushman was a celebrity. "At the height of her career she was considered America's greatest actress and one of the best-known women in the English-speaking world." When she held her retirement celebration in New York, thousands attended a ceremony that included a candlelight procession and fireworks.[16]

Along with passionate affairs with a number of women, she challenged contemporary ideas regarding women's sexuality, work, and behavior. She was also an advocate for women's rights. She befriended many people within Boston's establishment, and yet worked hard to support other women who were also opposing strict gender norms.

One of the greatest constraints during this period on all women and lesbians in particular was economic. In Cushman's world, "the only way that two women could make a home together would be for them both be financially independent."[16] If they lived with their birth families or in conventional marriages, a female-female relationship was impossible. Lesbians (again, no one used that term at the time) either had to be wealthy or have some form of independent income, or else their families would control their lives and even their access to other women. So few women had the economic freedom to be in a lesbian relationship.

2.2 Charlotte and Susan Cushman as Romeo and Juliet

Despite these obstacles, Cushman was a successful romantic. While later in the nineteenth century upper class Boston lesbians were discreet to the point of being publicly sexless and tended to mate for life, Charlotte Cushman was a dashingly different type of woman. She took to the stage to support herself, her family, and friends, and while doing so had a series of tempestuous affairs.

Cushman knew she was different from an early age and later "bragged that, rather than play with dolls as a young child, she cracked open their heads so that she could see how they think."[16] Because respectable women were not allowed to work, Cushman had to invent a public story to account for why she took to the stage. She claimed that her father, depressed by bankruptcy, abandoned her family and this forced her to support her mother and three younger siblings. Singing European classics was less morally wrong for women, so she began her career in opera. Even though her mother was ambivalent about her stage career Cushman had already begun her musical education and had her debut at eighteen as the Countess Almaviva in *The Marriage of Figaro* at the Tremont Theatre. She strained her voice and switched to playing Lady Macbeth the next year. Soon she became known for portraying men. Women in male roles were common, particularly in stock companies where everyone had to perform multiple characters, meaning Cushman was not the only woman playing men at the time. Not surprisingly, Cushman's charisma and vitality caused both men and women to want her and her suiters included one young man, three years older than her, who wanted to marry her. She rejected him. She wanted stardom, financial independence, and the love of women.

Her career quickly took off. Playing Lady Macbeth in New Orleans, she transformed the role from meek helpmate to the major force propelling the drama forward. "Appearing as she did, Cushman was playing to her strength. She was not a conventionally beautiful woman. Tall and robust with a square face, lantern jaw and heavy brows, she relied not on feminine prettiness but rather on energy and wit to appeal to spectators."[17] Her perspective on the role continues to shape how actresses play Lady Macbeth even in our own age.

Cushman's younger sister also took to the stage and the two won rave reviews by playing Romeo and Juliet, Cushman taking the male lead. Given the tremendous pressure on women to dress modestly, a woman onstage in pants was much more revealing than even the skimpiest attire allowed at this time. Thus there was a strong male demand for these types of performances, but Cushman also mastered the art of appealing to female theatre goers as well. She exuded a competency and mastery of her fate that women wanted and aspired to.

Now in her mid-twenties, Cushman was a success in New York but left after a dispute over a raise. Again asserting her independence, she moved to Philadelphia to manage as well as act. There, Cushman began a relationship with a woman, but the other woman's brother was so unnerved by the sexual nature of the affair that he prohibited his sister from seeing Cushman. Both women rejected his characterization of them as "wicked" but the relationship ended nonetheless. In 1842, women simply could not dispute the power of male relatives to control their lives. Cushman was heartbroken.

Cushman soon met another woman, a retired actress seven years older than her, with whom she cultivated another affair. But as thrilled as she was by the flowers and companionship Cushman showered on her, the woman was in a precarious position, stuck in an unhappy marriage. She disliked her husband's position on slavery (he came from a prominent southern family that owned many slaves) and his affairs (his carrying on with his children's nanny was an open secret around Philadelphia yet was less of a scandal than a rumor about a relationship with Cushman could ever be). But if she filed for divorce, she would end up penniless and lose her children. She chose her family over Cushman. This demonstrates the difficulty lesbians had in building relationships with other women. They were controlled by their male relatives, had weak legal power, and precious little economic means to be independent. Again, Cushman was devastated. The silver lining was that the woman introduced her to Thomas Sully, who painted a portrait of Cushman and soon she had a new love interest–his daughter Rosalie.

The relationship between Cushman and Rosalie Sully deepened as Cushman's theatrical career blossomed. As much as she was attached to Sully, however, Cushman needed to go to London to cement her position as the leading actress in America. With a heavy heart she said goodbye to her lover and sailed to England. If she had known she would never see Sully again, it would have been even more heart wrenching. As it was, Cushman had learned to be discreet and her farewells focused more on her own brother than on Sully. Because Cushman could not afford a scandal, the relationship had to be kept a secret.

The sexual nature of Cushman's relationship with Sully was undisputed, at least to the two women. For example, after spending the night in bed with Sully, Cushman wrote in her diary that she was married to her. Also significant, before she left for England in 1844, Cushman and Sully burned their letters to each other. Over the next century, LGBTQ couples repeated this ritual of destroying evidence many times. Same-sex lovers would methodically gather their letters, diaries, and any other incriminating items and burn them.

Cushman was extremely ambitious when she sailed to conquer the London stage, the zenith of theatre. Part of her motivation was also seeking money and fame so that she would have the "freedom to live as she chose, with another woman."[16] She worked hard and earned what she had. But as she grew successful in England, her ardor for Sully cooled. By 1847, Cushman was in a relationship with British poet Eliza Cook who was two years Cushman's junior and known for her radical politics as well as her "mannish dress and haircut." Though she knew they had to be discreet, Cushman began to dress like Cook and the two would be seen in public together, looking more or less the same.

Cook was madly in love with Cushman and wrote that a mere glance from the actress caused "a flushing ray into my breast it never felt before." But Cushman never remained faithful to just one woman and she was also interested in an eighteen year old music teacher named Sarah Anderton. Soon there was yet another rival in Cushman's life. In this case, Geraldine Jewsbury was not willing to share Cushman with other women and wrote, "I am not an angel but a wild cat and I'll scratch you if I can't beat you." Cushman would have a similar effect on other women.

Despite their dependence on Cushman for support and their moving to England to be with her, Cushman's mother and sister did not approve of her relationships with women and Cushman had to be almost as circumspect around them as she was with the public. Yet still she carried on with her romantic pursuits, even during tragedy. In 1847, Cushman received word that Rosalie Sully had died.

The year before, Cushman had met Matilda Hays (1820-97), a novelist and journalist determined to use her talents to advance women's rights. By 1848 the two women were romantically involved and living together. When Hays had some financial reversals and Cushman's sister decided to marry and retire from performing,

Cushman encouraged Hays to take up acting and found roles for her. Meanwhile, their contemporaries accepted their relationship. The poet Elizabeth Barrett Browning told her sisters that Cushman and Hays were in a female marriage with each other. At the time there was no word to describe a romantic and sexual relationship between two women, but it was impossible not to see that here were two women who wore masculine clothing and haircuts, went everywhere together, called each other by male nicknames, and lived together. Unfortunately, their passion was not enough to sustain Hays' theatrical career even though it centered on her playing Juliet to Cushman's Romeo. She soon stopped acting but remained in the relationship.

In 1849 Cushman returned to the United States to perform in Eastern and Midwestern theatres, taking Hays with her. The tour received generally good notices, but critics were struck by her off-stage presence that was now decidedly masculine and well outside gender norms of that era. These male critics (female reviewers were rare) did not know how to account for Cushman's masculinity and attributed it to her pro-women's rights activism rather than deviant sexuality. Again, there was no vocabulary these men could use to describe what they were seeing.

It was during this 1849 tour that Cushman and Hays met Hatty Hosmer (1830-1908) in Boston. So stricken was this young aspiring sculptor with the couple that she felt abandoned when they left the city. Fortunately, her spirits brightened when in 1852 Cushman announced her retirement from the stage and her intention to move to Rome. Hosmer decided to go with them.

Born in Watertown, Hosmer's physician father was determined to save her from the tuberculosis that killed her mother and three siblings and he pushed her into outdoor sports and vigorous exercise. As a result, she grew up high-spirited: "[t]o her teachers in school, she was a holy terror."[18] Luckily, next store lived a free thinking woman who regularly hosted famous Transcendentalists including Ralph Waldo Emerson, Bronson Alcott, and Margaret Fuller. She helped convince Hosmer's father to send her to boarding school in the Berkshires, where she blossomed. Returning home, Hosmer declared her desire to become a sculptor. But there was an immediate obstacle: she wanted to go to medical school to study anatomy, but no Boston area school admitted women at the time. Hosmer went off to St. Louis to pursue her studies.

Hosmer eventually became one of the country's most accomplished sculptors. Most of her works are very realistic and romantic and statues grace museums and public locations in Boston, Chicago, and abroad. Yet throughout her career, Hosmer faced biting sexism and most male sculptors ignored or ridiculed her. Similarly, male critics panned her work. But she was sustained by her friends who backed her up when critics were harsh and helped her secure commissions. Without this network of lesbians, there might not have been a number of her most important works that exist today.

Now living mostly abroad, Cushman created a community of women who studied together and supported each other. Cushman and her company settled at 28 Via del Corso, not far from the Spanish Steps in Rome, surrounded by a number of English and American expatriates. Not all outsiders were accepting of Cushman and the other women. Several left letters and other evidence that they felt disgust for this group of women who lived as they wished, free of men and male-imposed constraints on their behavior.

Cushman found she didn't have a taste for retirement and soon returned to London and the stage. Back in Rome, the relationship between Hays and Hosmer deepened and it seemed the two had at least a brief affair that left Cushman dejected. But Hays soon returned to London and with Cushman, set up a household near Berkeley Square that was the scene of much merrymaking.

In 1856-57, the couple decided to return to Rome where there was now another sculptor, Emma Stebbins (1815-82). Stebbins was the never-married daughter of a successful banker. Her best known work is the Bethesda Fountain in New York's Central Park, commissioned to commemorate the opening of the Croton Reservoir. In Boston, her most prominent statue is of the educator Horace Mann.

Stebbins had moved to Rome to study sculpture and found her way into Cushman's colony of independent women. As Cushman and Stebbins spent more time together, Hays grew jealous. Soon Cushman and Hays fought like "cats and dogs" and hurled hairbrushes at each other. Cushman's sister, back living with her, watched the two grow increasingly hostile, so much so that her son had to physically defend Cushman. In a fit of jealousy, Hays chased and hit Cushman as Hosmer watched, horrified. Cushman ended the relationship and Hays, who claimed she had given up her career to support Cushman's, filed for a stipend—one of the first instances anywhere in which a person leaving a same-sex relationship attempted to receive alimony. The lawsuit was settled out of court and in July 1857, Stebbins moved in with Cushman in an apartment at 38 Via Gregoriana near the top of the Spanish Steps.

The new apartment included space for Hosmer as well as Cushman's faithful maid Sallie Mercer, a free black woman who began employment with Cushman when she was just fourteen. It was a domestic arrangement that friends were at a loss on how to describe beyond the vocabulary of heteronormativity, such as "domestic" and "family." Hosmer described the group as being "jolly bachelors" or an "old maids' hell".

Stebbins' family strongly disapproved of the relationship and thought she was "morally, socially, and physically injured by it." Luckily Stebbins and Cushman now had the resources to ignore them. Others were disgusted by two openly-devoted women living together, but regardless their apartment, expanded to include the entire four story building, became a social epicenter of Americans in Rome. The couple were part of a social milieu that also included other female-female couples. Cushman worked to get her female artist friends commissions and her success at this, of course helped by their talent, pulled other ambitious and artistic women into her orbit. Thus came Margaret Foley, a maker of cameos, and Edmonia Lewis, a sculptor, to Rome and Cushman's circle.

Lewis was African American and Native American. Fierce and independent, her art focused on depictions of Native Americans (such as Hiawatha) or images of slaves breaking chains and asserting their humanity. Lewis had attended Oberlin, but she "was targeted for her race" and was accused of poisoning two white students. Abducted, beaten, and left for dead, she returned to class, determined to earn her degree. Forced to leave before graduating, she was helped by Boston abolitionists to start her art career.[19]

Cushman was close friends with the publisher James Fields and when critics charged Hosmer with relying on male craftsmen for her sculpture, she persuaded him to have *The Atlantic* publish a defense of Hosmer's talents. Cushman was also close to Annie Fields, James' wife, frequently writing her and dining with her when she was in Boston. In one letter, Cushman wrote to Annie how lonely she was when Stebbins was not around. Further demonstrating her influence, Cushman was also friends with Elizabeth Peabody and Julia Ward Howe, two central pillars of elite Boston society.

Within months of beginning of her relationship with Stebbins, Cushman returned to America to replenish her finances through further performances. She had entrusted her money to a man who had squandered much of it. After a month of performances in New York, Cushman left Stebbins behind to tour the stages of the Midwest. In St. Louis she met Emma Crow, the impressionable eighteen year old daughter of the man Cushman wanted as her new financial manager. Despite the twenty-four year age difference, Crow fell deeply in love with Cushman after being enthralled by the eroticism of her performance as Romeo. Sixty years later and more than forty years after Cushman's death, Crow could still graphically describe her rapture the first time she saw Cushman on stage. The two exchanged hundreds of passionate letters over the next eighteen years. Crow wanted a full-scale romance and Cushman was tempted, but she was still in love with Stebbins.

Still, she couldn't reject Crow and so invited her to visit Rome. While there, Crow met and married Ned Cushman, a nephew Cushman had adopted as her son. The marriage did nothing to cool the physical relationship between the two women—a letter from Cushman to Crow describes a night of passion between the two in a Paris hotel room—even though Crow genuinely cared for Ned as did Cushman for Stebbins. However, the marriage allowed Cushman and Crow to spend time together without causing scandal. Not surprisingly, the two Emmas were jealous of each other and conditions in the household grew tense, particularly after Cushman's nephew and his growing family moved into the fourth floor of the Rome building upon his being appointed counsel in Rome by Secretary of State William Seward. Ned won the assignment largely because of his aunt's connections, as Cushman had long been close to Seward. During one visit to Washington, Seward even took her to meet Abraham Lincoln. A solid supporter of the Union cause, Cushman returned to the United States during the war to perform a series of benefits for the United States Sanitary Commission.

Despite temptations, Cushman stayed with Stebbins to the end of her life. When Cushman became ill with breast cancer in 1869, Stebbins put aside her career to nurse Cushman and the two women had a number of good years together before the cancer returned. Cushman died in Boston at the Parker House of pneumonia in 1875, with Stebbins at her side.

During these decades, not only did men lack a term to describe their same-sex desires, they also struggled with how to connect with the men they were interested in. One example of this is the affair between Herman Melville (1819-91) and Nathaniel Hawthorne (1804-64). That Melville was at least bisexual and fully aware of same-sex attraction is undeniable. What may have been thinly disguised in *Moby Dick* was fully in the open in *Billy Budd*, a novel so explicit that Melville kept it hidden during his lifetime. *Moby Dick* begins with two characters, Ishmael and Queequog sharing a bed, after which Ishmael considers themselves married. Not only does *Billy Budd* have male-male desire at its center, it also contains long sensuous passages dwelling on the title character's physical attractiveness including one paragraph describing the beauty of his foot. We know much less about Hawthorne's sexual tastes at the time of the affair with Melville, but later (1858) he went to Rome and befriended Cushman and her circle. He also hinted about Thomas Morton's sexuality in the short story he wrote about Merrymount.

Melville and Hawthorne had much in common. Both writers had lost their fathers at an early age and both had New England roots, though Melville was raised in New York City. In 1850, they lived six miles apart in Western Massachusetts: Hawthorne in Lenox, Melville in Pittsfield. Both were in the prime of their literary lives with Melville writing *Moby Dick* and Hawthorne working on *The House of the Seven Gables*.

The two met on August 5 on a group climb up Monument Mountain that included a thunderstorm, drinking champagne out of a silver cup, and Melville sitting on a promontory and pantomiming pulling on ropes as Hawthorne lustily called out that their doom was at hand. Other members of the party that day included James Fields and Oliver Wendell Holmes.

Two days later, Melville visited Hawthorne at his house and the friendship was on, much to the joy of both men, at least at first. Hawthorne wrote a friend, "I met Melville, the other day, and liked him so much that I have asked him to spend a few days with me before leaving these parts."[20] Even before they met, Melville was swooning over Hawthorne. Writing about him in a book review, Melville said that, "He expands and deepens down, the more I contemplate him; and further and further shoots his strong New-England roots into the hot soil in my Southern soul."[21] The first draft of the review had "me" instead of "my Southern soul". Melville also dedicated *Moby Dick* to Hawthorne.

Sadly for Melville, Hawthorne cooled on him. Any possible relationship would have been stymied by logistics as both men were married and most of their time together was spent with other people around. Furthermore, it appears that either Hawthorne did not share Melville's feelings or soon began to regret them. As a result, the relationship ended quickly so that Melville stayed close to his family and lived out the remainder of his life in obscurity. Even *Moby Dick* was almost forgotten before his works were rediscovered and became well known. *Billy Budd* was finally published in 1924 and two British gay men, W. H. Auden and Benjamin Britten, collaborated to turn the story into a popular opera in 1951.

In the middle decades of the nineteenth century, Boston embarked on three important projects that would have a tremendous impact on the city as a whole as well as the LGBTQ community of the twentieth century and beyond. Hemmed in by water on a narrow peninsula, Boston created Bay Village, the South End, and Back Bay. Together, these new neighborhoods would provide housing for hundreds of thousands of LGBTQ people over the next several generations.

Boston began filling in land on the edges of the peninsula decades earlier as hills were pulled down to provide material for projects adjacent to the North End and Beacon Hill. South Cove and Bay Village quickly followed, allowing the city to create new residential blocks as well as facilitate the construction of a bridge to South Boston and a railroad connection to the mainland. The new land around a train station (now long demolished) in Park Square would become a major center of gay night life beginning in the 1930s. Bay Village started attracting LGBTQ people soon after and to this day, its modest federal-style townhouses are known for their quiet interior opulence and their LGBTQ households.

The South End had been the only land connection between the town of Boston and the mainland. The famous "one if by land" line in Longfellow's poem about Paul Revere refers to the narrow neck that also served as a place for brickworks, breweries, executions, and burial grounds. By the end of the 1840s, city officials became alarmed by the growth of Boston's Irish Catholic immigrant population and they sought to create a district that would tempt proper upper-class Protestant Yankee families to remain in the city. Many of these were moving to the suburbs now that they could easily commute by railroad, and thus the city saw a need for elegant townhouses, built for the well-to-do, at a medium distance from downtown. Commencing with the selling of lots on Worcester Square in 1850, the city directly sponsored development in the area generally to the south of Tremont Street while the state-chartered Boston Water Power Corporation (BWPC) was responsible for creating land and selling lots to the north of that street (the actual line between ownership crosses Tremont Street at an angle).[22]

While legend suggests that the area was initially successful and that it was only later that the South End would sink into poverty, in actuality the neighborhood struggled from the beginning. Worcester and Chester Squares, the crown jewels of the new neighborhood, each spent over ten years under development. Throughout the next two decades, the houses became cheaper and less ornate and by the time of the Great Fire of 1872, the neighborhood was complete but mostly occupied by lodgers and modest shop owners. The South End declined for almost a century as maintenance was deferred. Its townhouses decayed such that they were mostly spared from destruction because developers did not dare risk money on new projects in the neighborhood.[23] By 1900 most of its rowhouses had been converted into cheap lodging houses and tenements. Many LGBTQ people would find anonymous and safe housing in the neighborhood over the next century. After 1960, LGBTQ people began moving into these buildings as they were renovated and by 1970 the South End would be the city's gayest neighborhood.

Back Bay was the third great landfill project that would shape Boston's LGBTQ landscape. Originally Back Bay was a tidal flat that provided a rich fishing ground for the region's Native peoples, but in 1814, the city allowed BWPC to build a mill dam along what is now Beacon Street. That unsuccessful development, along with the construction of railroad tracks across the flats and the emptying of sewers into the bay, created a putrid public health crisis. The city, state, and BWPC agreed to fill in Back Bay in 1857.

The new project was much more successful in attracting the wealthy than the South End in part because as it was developed, tastes were shifting from the English style row houses of the South End to the French inspired town homes now iconic in Back Bay. The wealthy built mansions along Beacon Street and Commonwealth Avenue while the city's most important institutions flocked to the area around Copley Square: the Museum of Fine Arts, the Boston Public Library, and Trinity Church.

The city's elite gay men also moved into the neighborhood and entertained each other as well as cruised the Commonwealth Avenue Mall, the Esplanade, the Public Garden, or the bar in the Copley Plaza Hotel. The Back Bay Fens, which would become the prime outdoor cruising ground in the second half of the twentieth century, does not seem to have been an area for nighttime activity before 1950, or even before 1960–perhaps because gay men had yet to move into the Fenway and the park didn't acquire its cover of invasive reeds until the 1930s at the earliest. Back Bay would be a popular residential area for LGBTQ people until the 1980s when rising real estate prices caused most to look elsewhere for housing. In the twenty-first century, Back Bay, like Beacon Hill, no longer has a major LGBTQ presence.

A working-class woman without Cushman's talent or financial resources, Emma Snodgrass (1835-?), also challenged prevailing gender norms in the middle of the nineteenth century and she did so in such an audacious way that the popular press closely followed her story. In a more accepting society, no one would have noticed that some women preferred to dress like men in public (not to mention that the very existence of these gender norms indicates undue rigidity). But nineteenth century Boston did not tolerate cross-dressing and Snodgrass was repeatedly arrested for wearing men's clothes. For unknown reasons, Snodgrass traveled from New York City to Boston in 1852 where she "used to circulate in all the drinking houses, made several violent attempts to talk 'horse,' and do other things for which 'fast' boys are noted." Another account says "Emma had a tobacco-chewing, cigar-smoking friend named

Charley, who was really another teenaged cross dresser, Harriet French. Eventually, Harriet was discovered, too."

At one point, Snodgrass called herself George Green and worked as a clothing store clerk for John Simmons, the founder of Simmons College, until her sex was exposed. Each time she was arrested, Snodgrass was sent back to New York, but the police could not deter her. She would briefly appear in women's clothes, but then would be caught out in public wearing "a neat frock coat, cloth cap, and black broadcloth pants" or other male attire.[24] In one instance she was turned in by a bartender after she had asked him where to find someone to cut her hair short. Fascinated by this challenge to gender norms, the Boston press and even the New York papers enjoyed writing about her with news accounts published as far away as California. Eventually, however, Snodgrass disappeared from public records and her fate is unknown.

There are other examples of women opposing the constraints put on them, sometimes resulting in important works of art. Louisa May Alcott (1832-88) challenged the standard gender roles of her era, never married, and asserted that she had a man's nature inside her body. Her refusal to accept contemporary standards of behavior helped enliven her portrait of Jo in *Little Women*.[25] There is also debate as to whether Emily Dickinson (1830-86) was a lesbian and whether this influenced the course of her life and her poetry. Dickinson never married and spent much of her adulthood as a recluse.

Lesser known now, but famous in her time was Mary Gibson (1835-1906), a popular fiction author before the Civil War who wrote under the pseudonym of Winnie Woodfern in a number of Boston papers. Drawing from her own experiences, her stories had themes of cross-dressing, female-female romantic relationships, masculine behavior by women, and other alternatives to antebellum Boston gender norms.

Born in Woodstock, Vermont, Gibson's mother died when Gibson was two and her father passed away only eighteen months later, leaving four girls to be raised by guardians and in foster homes. Gibson was by her own admission a tomboy, playing with old muskets and makeshift swords while growing up. By seventeen, Gibson lived in Boston and had begun writing fiction for local newspapers when she eloped with a man forty years older. They became engaged the first day they met and the marriage lasted only a few months.

Gibson used her poems and short stories to communicate the details of her romantic life to her fans. She told readers that her life had been a wreck because of the breakup of her marriage and that she felt tortured by her ex-husband. She also wrote of an intense short romance with a young woman named Lulie and described another woman as the "queen of her throbbing heart." She wrote stories about the absurdity of heterosexual courtship and the dulling effects of marriage on women. In several works, she contrasted the acceptability of married men being able to have affairs and debauched relationships with the mandate that wives retreat into the domestic sphere and adhere to strict standards of fidelity.

Gibson took the conventional plot of an orphan woman achieving social success through her talents and added to it same-sex attractions and a strong disdain for mandated gender roles. One of her heroines had muscles as hard as iron and smoked cigaritos. Another traveled to Italy to become an artist, perhaps a reference to Cushman and her set. Also popular, some of Gibson's protagonists wore male clothing and committed gruesome murders of men before escaping back to the safety of their female relationships.

Gibson wrote short stories in a variety of genres and by 1855 had moved to New York to capitalize on her fame. She was less successful there and went to London for a few years, even operating a literary magazine, before returning to Vermont in 1867 where she gradually faded into obscurity.[25]

The charged same-sex atmosphere of Harvard during the Civil War inspired a novel, *Two College Friends*, about undergraduates in a very romantic relationship. One of the boys, Tom, is too young to enlist in the army while the other, Ned, goes off to war, is captured, and executed by Stonewall Jackson. Written by Frederick Wadsworth Loring (1848-71), the novel has not so much as a hint of sex, but no author could be explicit at the time when the book was published (1871). There is very little about the day-to-day relations between the two boys beyond passing references to them living together in rooms in Harvard Yard, but there is constant jealousy and lots of declarations of how much they care for each other. Even in an era where same-sex platonic relationships were common, the attraction between the two is incredibly intense. Both young men intend to marry women and when Tom weds, he names his first born son after Ned. There are few women in the novel other than Tom's mother and a mention of the Ann Street brothels.

We can't know Loring's motivations for writing the story, but it is an example of the nineteenth-century practice of using ancient Greek ideals about male-male attraction between soldiers to advocate for the purity of homosexual relations. Neither Ned nor Tom are apologetic for their desire for each other. On the contrary, as he says his final goodbye to a feverish, unconscious Tom, Ned confesses that he had been passionately obsessed with Tom since they first met.

Loring died in a Native attack on a stagecoach the year his novel came out. He had dedicated the book to a fellow undergraduate from whom he was estranged. The other man was already married (but never named a son after Loring) and eventually had a successful career as a journalist and playwright as well as spending a substantial amount of time in Europe.

We have very little data regarding police actions against LGBTQ people in the decades before the Civil War. There was, however, a slight weakening of the anti-sodomy laws in Massachusetts. In 1785, the anti-sodomy moralizing in the preamble to the statute was eliminated, severing the religious justification from civil law, though the effect on how the law was implemented was modest. Nearly 200 years later, prosecutors would again cite the religious horror of homosexuality during the Revere scandal of 1978 (see Chapter 10).

In 1805, the law was further secularized by removing the paraphrasing of Leviticus. The law still prohibited men from committing a crime against nature with any other man or a male child, but the language represents a further movement away from religious texts. In addition, the punishment for sodomy was reduced from death to up to one year in solitary confinement followed by up to ten years of hard labor. There is no evidence that anyone had been put to death for sodomy after independence, but the possibility of capital punishment must have been chilling. In the revised law, references to lesbian sex were eliminated and the SJC ruled that English common law, which did not prohibit female-female sex, was to be used as the basis for Massachusetts legal actions. As a result, women were free from the possibility of arrest, at least for sodomy, for a few years.

Not everyone was happy with these reforms. An 1828 treatise to guide judges and prosecutors in writing warrants, complaints, and sentencing complained about this new leniency. It outlined the change from death to imprisonment, then almost gleefully described how the traditional sentence for sodomy was usually carried out by burning the guilty alive. The treatise then dramatically restated the severity of the crime and went on to say that in God's judgement, sodomy should have remained a capital crime, presumably punishable by gruesome means.[26]

The treatise also included a standard form for charging men and women with open gross lewdness and lascivious behavior. Interestingly, there was no standard definition of lewdness, it was whatever the arresting police officer decided was lewd making it impossible for the accused to challenge. The model complaint is written for opposite-sex couples with no mention of same-sex couples, however. Significantly, the author points out that the gross lewdness behavior must be public and not private, and similarly the complaint for a lewd and lascivious person stresses the importance of an act or exposure being witnessed by other people. This would be important in the 1980s when the SJC gutted the state's anti-sodomy statutes. The court would then note that there had been a long tradition in the state that heterosexual acts in private between consenting adults were legal and finally rule that if sodomy and other same-sex acts were done in private, they should be legal as well–but this equality would not come for nearly 150 years.

The sodomy statute was again revised in 1835 when the Commonwealth made the law gender neutral, making women once again at risk for sodomy prosecutions. This time, the punishments of solitary confinement and hard labor were eliminated, but the maximum prison sentence was increased to twenty years.[27] It is not known how extensively these new laws were enforced in the first half of the nineteenth century, but at least during the years before the Civil War, it appears that arrests were rare. This does not mean LGBTQ people were not harassed by the police, but rather suggests that the practice of using disorderly conduct charges to arrest people was already well established.

With sodomy rarely prosecuted, the focus on morality fell heavily on women, with the imbalance aggravated by the fact that men looking for prostitutes were rarely arrested. Most single women had a difficult time and even if they were financially independent, they could rarely venture out in public after dark alone without being considered a prostitute. Lesbians may even have been more at risk for prostitution arrests than for sex crimes. Before 1820, lewdness cases did not involve men as they almost exclusively targeted women whose husbands were angered by their adultery or levied against single women who were sexually active. In one case demonstrative of this principle, a father brought lewdness charges against his daughter. But the laws were now on the books, and they would soon be marshalled against gay men.

Looking at the annual published statistics of the Boston Police Department, there certainly were men swept up in lewdness arrests in the first half of the nineteenth century, but these were almost always men involved in running brothels or men involved in heterosexual cross-racial relationships. For the most part, gay men escaped police actions for this particular crime. Though the law was written to be gender neutral, no men were arrested in the decades after 1850 for lewdness.[11] For the women caught up in police crackdowns, no evidence of sexual activity needed to be presented and the judicial system was harsh. Most arrested women were given quick trials and found guilty. Sometimes, five or six were tried and sentenced in a single trial with none given the chance to defend themselves. This practice later had profound negative impacts on gay men once police began to target them. Gay men would frequently be arrested, tried, and sentenced in groups. Similarly, judges would be openly hostile and be unwilling to listen to the defense arguments or pleas of gay men. Thus, while the police and judicial system had not yet targeted gay men in Boston, the infrastructure to destroy them was in place.

Chapter 3

Boston Marriages

BOSTON ACHIEVED A prosperity between 1865 and 1914 that it would not see again until the end of the twentieth century. Part of this wealth flowed from the entrepreneurial spirit of the city as Boston-based families, trusts, and banks funded projects and businesses across the country including transcontinental railroads and new companies now iconic, such as General Electric and American Telephone and Telegraph (AT&T). Locally, there was an explosion of investment in wood and paper products, textiles, ship building, and munitions manufacturing. One enterprising man even figured out a way to sell ice harvested from New England ponds to cities around the world.

The beneficiaries of this prosperity included families who used their fortunes to fund trusts that provided sustenance for thousands of Bostonians. The money supported two generations of people who had the freedom to pursue careers unburdened by the need to earn a living and as a result, there would be poets, artists, writers, and others who would make important contributions to society and the arts. Among these were a number of LGBTQ people (at the beginning of this period, at least, there was no concept of gay identity, nor were transgender or non-binary people able to assert themselves) who created a world of interlocking groups that were closely integrated into the highest levels of Boston society. At least a few enjoyed a freedom and visibility in the city that was unique to Boston and perhaps unmatched anywhere in the United States until the 1980s or beyond.

There are a number of contributing factors to this acceptance of some lesbians and gay men by at least a significant percentage of straight mainstream society. One is that Boston historically had a degree of tolerance for non-heterosexual people. Proper Bostonians might abhor Catholics, Baptists, the Irish, and Marxists, but well-bred gay men and lesbians who belonged to the right churches and clubs and who otherwise conformed to standard gender roles (or had enough money to get away with flaunting social norms) were welcomed into homes, theatres, and other fashionable places.

Perhaps another factor behind this openness was the success of Boston-based abolitionists in overthrowing slavery. Opposition to slavery was controversial in Boston for much of the period before the Civil War, but as the monumental struggle for freedom swept over the country, more people came out in favor of emancipation. By the end of the Civil War, much of Boston's upper crust took credit for leading this successful moral crusade. This did not mean that abolitionist leaders were pro-gay. On the contrary, many remained very conservative and even opposed women's suffrage and other politically progressive ideas. However, it did make them more open to unconventional thought and behavior.

The religious beliefs of the elite had also fundamentally shifted. Their ancestors may have trembled before an angry god who found terrible sin around every corner, but they also bequeathed to their descendants the belief that God was present in their daily lives. Therefore, it was imperative for believers to redefine their relationship to Him. With His people basking in the warmth of political triumph and economic prosperity, the God of the Puritans and Separatists was now a benevolent deity who gazed upon on His worshipers with love. In addition, their religion had split into two denominations: the Congregationalists and the Unitarians, the latter of which were the most liberal in the country and the former almost equally far to the left. Both groups believed that a person's relationship with God was a matter of personal conscience. Though many could still preach a rousing sermon, ministers reduced their reliance on fire, brimstone, and fear to move towards assisting church goers to lead moral, prosperous, and intellectual lives. There was less preaching against sodomy (with many pretending it simply didn't exist), while religious rhetoric increased against alcohol, gambling, Catholics, and immigrants. For example, the most outspoken Boston evangelist of the time, Henry Morgan, used all the virulent anti-Catholic rhetoric of his age as he denounced priests, lotteries, and alcohol, but did not turn his vitriol against sodomy.[1]

Perhaps the final reason that so many lesbians and gay men were welcomed into polite society was that as individuals, they were well-known by their straight neighbors. Many went to Harvard or other similar schools of the elite. Within the city, upper class lesbians and gays worshipped at the same churches that their straight comrades attended: Trinity Church, the Church of the Advent, Old South Church, and the Park Street Church. Everyone knew their families and most were related by blood to straight society. Many also had homes in Back Bay and Beacon Hill where the fashionable people lived, and many wealthy LGBTQ people summered in Newport or the North Shore next door to other members of elite society. They were seen at the theatre, the symphony, the Athenaeum, and at upper-class parties and dinners. Familiarity makes deviance harder to reject, it seems.

For the most part, this tolerance only extended to a lucky few. Low income LGBTQ people were neither accepted nor welcomed into elite social gatherings, Catholics were widely disliked, and most people who were not strictly male or female faced tremendous obstacles. The final decades of the nineteenth century were difficult for people who did not conform to contemporary standards of gender expression. Men were expected to unquestionably accept defined gender roles, marry (though they were allowed to delay marriage until their forties), and only have sex under very controlled parameters: with their wives, mistresses, or prostitutes. Even masturbation was prohibited. In the context of very strict norms of gender expression, people who were non-binary or who questioned the gender assigned at their birth were mostly invisible. This is not to say they did not exist; but rather that their scarcity in records, news accounts, and other items from this era is testimony to the repression of the times.

In addition, all women, not just lower class women, faced tremendous social and economic barriers. They had few educational or occupational options open to them and they were expected to stay with their families until they married, all the while controlled by their male relatives in most aspects of their lives. While women moved about as they pleased, any unescorted woman, particularly at night or lower-class, was considered to be a prostitute. Similarly, places where unmarried lower-class women gathered were suspected to be brothels or somehow facilitating immorality. These prejudices extended to the women who flocked to Boston's South End to live in rooming houses while they worked in the needle trades, as sales clerks, or as house-keepers. Their lodging places were considered to be potential dens of vice and the establishments that employed them along with the locations where they socialized were demonized as well.[2] There was also a sexist underpinning to the acceptance of coupled lesbians. Because they avoided any personal relationships with men, freedom for upper-class lesbians existed, in part, because most of society could not conceive of the reality of same-sex attraction between women. This allowed lesbians to live fairly openly and resulted in few laws against same-sex contact between women.

Over time, however, this freedom from suspicion for women in same-sex couples eroded because the cover of women's lack of sexuality began to thin. First medical professionals and then the public at large began to understand that women were capable of sexual feelings and that the exterior sexlessness of a woman-woman couple could mask passion behind closed doors.

Many late-nineteenth-century relationships between women were called Boston marriages in part because their existence was first popularized in Henry James' book, *The Bostonians*. To this day, there is heated debate over whether these relationships contained a sexual dimension or not, arising, in part, because of the continued reluctance to acknowledge women had sexual desires in addition to the lack of explicit evidence of sexual activity left from this era.[3] But there is no dispute over the strong romantic and emotional bonds between the women in these relationships, making arguments over the frequency of sexual acts inside them irrelevant. Women experienced sadness when they were apart and jealousy when their loved ones caught the eye of others. Over entire lifetimes, these women sacrificed and cared for each other and their grief upon death or the end of a relationship could be overwhelming. Further indication of the sexual dimension of these relationships is the number of women who destroyed correspondence, diaries, and any other materials that might have provided evidence of the sexual component of these partnerships. Whatever chastity these women demonstrated in public was refuted by their shame of the eroticism of their private lives.

As Boston's population grew from 177,000 in 1860 to 670,000 in 1910, the demographics of the city changed as well. The first great wave of immigrants came from Ireland and though the numbers arriving in any given year varied, they would be the city's dominant ethnic group up through our current time. Around 1900, they were among the largest groups in South Boston, the South End, Dorchester, Charlestown, Brighton, and Roxbury. Italians began to arrive in large numbers after 1890, settling in the North End, the West End, East Boston, and Roslindale.[4] Jews, fleeing repression in central and eastern Europe, first moved to the West End and the South End and then to Roxbury and Dorchester.[5] Black people had a complex migration to the city. Up to the Civil War, they were mostly freedmen moving to the city because of its less-hostile racial environment. Later they were joined by immigrants from the Caribbean and additional refugees from the American South. But because Boston had few jobs open to them, their migration numbers were small compared to other northern cities where they could access low-skilled positions such as maids and dock workers. In Boston these jobs were taken by the Irish and were closed off to black workers.[6] As a result, Boston's black population would be small up until World War II. In addition, there was a small Chinatown located near South Station; otherwise the city's Asian population was not large and the Latino population was almost non-existent.

Though there were ample jobs in factories, on the docks, and in other low paying jobs, there was widespread poverty in the city. The poorest neighborhoods were the North End and the Fort Hill area just to the south of downtown. There, new immigrants packed into overcrowded, substandard tenements with housing and environmental conditions deplorable. One step up were the West End and the South End, which had large numbers of tenements, but the housing was better and residents were more likely to have stable jobs.

Religious authorities disliked the South End lodging house district because of its large numbers of young men and women living alone without parental supervision. Officials preaching against the licentious of the neighborhood was a common feature of sermons of the day. Residents took their meals in cheap restaurants and patronized nickel shows, arcades, and "low theatre" productions. Worse, they drank in the area's many unregulated saloons.[7] For many of the city's extensive network of evangelical and mainstream churches, drunkenness was one of the major moral issues of the day, second only to the problem of Catholics gaining political control of Boston.[8] However, the anonymity and transitory population of these lodging houses may have provided cover for LGBTQ people.

Over time, more established immigrants and their children began to move to neighborhoods further from the center of the city as they bought triple-decker houses in Dorchester, Brighton, Roxbury, East Boston, and Jamaica Plain. These neighborhoods were less-dense than the inner wards and often their residents looked down on those who remained behind in tenements.[9] Such neighborhoods offered less privacy and therefore may have had fewer LGBTQ residents–or at least LGBTQ people had to be more discreet.

There were very few outlets for intelligent ambitious women seeking to make their mark in a world where almost every profession was prohibited to them. The arts were one exception and it is from artistic Boston that we find much of what we know about lesbians in the gilded age. One of these talented women was Ann Whitney (1821-1915), who came from old-line Yankee Protestant stock. Her family owned over 100 acres in what is now Belmont and Whitney was as educated as a young affluent Boston woman could be: private tutors followed by a boarding school where she studied Latin, literature, and how to properly entertain young gentlemen callers.

Like many lesbians of her time, she was deeply committed to social justice causes, even ones that might be unpopular with her straight peers. For example, when Whitney was thirteen, anti-Catholic rioters burned down the Ursuline Convent in Charlestown in one of the worst examples of religious bigotry ever to occur in the United States. Unlike many other Protestants, Whitney was angered by such violent prejudice and continuously asked her mother when the rioters would be brought to justice. Her commitment to equality and fighting wrongs grew over time and later she would be close to Boston abolitionists including William Lloyd Garrison.

Early on she found both the roles and future laid out for her constricting. At twenty-four, she took advantage of her brother's marriage and moved to Brooklyn, studying to be a teacher and two years later she opened a school in Salem. Since colonial times, Salem had transitioned from a seaport to a more artistic and relaxed town than Boston. Whitney drew on the growing Transcendental Movement and freethinking preachers flourishing there to solidify her determination to be an independent woman. During these years Whitney decided not to marry, leading some to suspect she was suffering from a broken heart though the nature of this failed romance is unknown. In any case, Whitney turned first to poetry and then to sculpture. She left Salem for Boston, and shortly thereafter moved again to New York to study art in 1848.

The love of Whitney's life was Adeline Manning (1836-1906). Though they met several years before, it seems their romantic relationship began in 1860. At first, the romance troubled both Manning's stepmother and Whitney's mother. In 1862, when Manning moved in with Whitney, Manning's family still had some reservations about the couple. Manning and Whitney were together for more than forty years and as time went on, both women's families grew to approve of the relationship. Eventually, Manning ended her letters by telling Whitney to send her love to her mother and Manning's parents came to visit the couple at their home. The couple's relationship was very passionate. One letter from Whitney to Manning reads, for example, "The pure spark burns amid endless corruptions. Only say, my beloved, this spark is kindred with that fire which arose with my being, which fills me with a great longing to grasp and hold something of its nature in human mould."[10] The romance continues beyond death: the two are buried together in Mt. Auburn Cemetery.

For a time, the couple lived in Rome, part of the group of women centered on Charlotte Cushman. Back in Boston, Whitney's studio was in Louisburg Square at 92 Mt. Vernon St. from 1876-93, while Manning worked nearby at 4 Acorn St. Later, the couple moved to the Charlesgate on Commonwealth Ave. They also had a summer home in Shelburne, New Hampshire where they shared a bedroom.

Despite her considerable talent, Whitney faced daunting prejudice. For example, she won a major competition to create a statue of Charles Sumner, earning the support of the Senator himself and beating the submission of the famous (gay) sculptor, Augustus Saint-Gaudens, but when the selection committee learned the victor of the competition was a woman, they took the commission away from her because the all-male committee thought a woman should not sculpt the legs of a man. Deciding to complete the Sumner statue anyway, it is in Harvard Square.

Whitney left an impressive legacy of art in Boston and elsewhere. Most prominent within the city are her statues of Samuel Adams at Faneuil Hall and Leif Erikson on Commonwealth Ave. outside of Kenmore Square. Though she was also an artist, Manning's work is less-known. She created works depicting strong women such as Lucy Stone, an abolitionist and early suffragette, and Harriet Beecher Stowe, the author of *Uncle Tom's Cabin*. The couple also supported other artists including the poet, Louise Guiney, even helping fund Guiney's move to England.

The acceptance of the couple by Boston society varied. The female leader of literary Boston, Annie Fields, openly entertained a number of female couples, including Manning and Whitney and Cushman and Stebbins, though sometimes partners were not invited. Fields' husband, James, did not always socialize with Manning and she was excluded from certain social events that Whitney was invited to (for example, a ball given in honor of a visit by the Prince of Wales in 1860). Yet, Manning was encouraged to read poetry at the Fields' Beacon Hill townhouse. While this may relate more to Manning's lower social status than to her lesbianism, the couple were very aware of the limits of tolerance. Letters from Whitney to Manning suggest that some people disapproved of their relationship and the couple committed large scale self-censorship when they "spent an entire summer carefully editing their correspondence, cutting here, discarding there."[10] They knew they had to be discreet.

Another way to gauge the depth of the relationship is how others saw it when it ended. Upon hearing of Manning's death, scores wrote to Whitney to express their condolences. Settlement house founder Vida Scudder wrote Whitney from Europe, "[i]n one sense, you will not be lonely, for, as you say, her life is yours." Searching for someone to replace Manning, Whitney settled on Olive Dargan, a married writer and poet who had attended Radcliffe. Whitney passed away in 1915, the same year Dargan's husband drowned off the coast of Cuba.[10]

One of the most celebrated Boston marriages was between Annie Fields

(1834-15) and Sarah Orne Jewett (1849-1909). Annie Fields had married her much older husband, James (1812-81) when she was nineteen. He was the editor of *The Atlantic Monthly* and a giant of the Boston literary scene, being one of the cofounders of the publishing house of Ticknor and Fields. The Fields knew all the Boston mid-nineteenth century literary lions: Emerson, Hawthorne, and Longfellow. Their home was a gathering place for writers and those interested in the arts, and they even opened their home to Charles Dickins on his American tour. While her husband was alive, Fields was a major influence on whom he decided to publish, and she encouraged him to consider new authors. Annie was related to the Alcotts and a confidante of Harriet Beecher Stowe, and later in life she was friends with Amy Lowell, Willa Cather, Jane Addams, and Edith Wharton–a social circle that included many of the leading female intellectuals of the day.

After her husband passed away, Fields became involved with Sarah Orne Jewett, a novelist whose work her husband had published. Then as now, relationships varied. Whitney and Manning seem to have had no other romantic affairs, for example, while Jewett and Fields were involved with other women (though the extent of these affairs is not known). But Fields and Jewett were two strong, intelligent women determined to live their lives as they saw fit and the couple "created a relationship in which roles could be highly flexible and interchangeable, sometimes childlike, or protective; assertive, or yielding; even changing within the same letter, at times so swiftly as to be dizzying, and revealing a relationship both intimate and unconfining."[11] The depth of their love was vast. "Oh my dear darling I had forgotten that we loved each other so much a year ago, for it all seems so new to me every day. There is so much for us to remember already—But a year ago last winter seems a great way off for us to have loved so much since."[10]

It was very difficult for upper-class women to be both married and have careers in the decades around 1900. Men expected their wives to stay home, manage servants, raise children, and be subservient to their needs. In contrast, Boston marriages enabled women to achieve success independent of male support. For the most part these women were not interested in playing out conventional roles inside their relationships, though many did adopt some aspects of heterosexual marriages–it was impossible to totally escape the milieu they were born into. Most were looking for relationships between equals. "What they felt they needed was a mate with whom they could share the happiness and misery of their struggles, who would understand what those struggles were since she was engaged in them too, and who would share on an equal basis the excitement of the new ideas which surrounded them."[3] For many lesbian women of the era, these relationships and their sexual reality were central to the art they produced. Jewett's books featured strong independent women for whom a marriage with a male meant sacrifice. In contrast, Willa Cather (1873-1947), beginning her literary career a generation later as the end of this age of acceptance approached, saw that strong romantic relationships between women were becoming distasteful and made sure all of her heroines were conventionally heterosexual despite being a lesbian herself. LGBTQ people increased their self-censorship as repression grew.

Jewett was socially popular in her own right and one of the select guests at Julia Ward Howe's famed 89th birthday luncheon in 1908, along with Edward Everett Hale and Isabella Stewart Gardner.[12] Fields and Jewett lived at 148 Charles St. in Boston and summered in Manchester-by-the-Sea. They frequently entertained at both locations. The societal acceptance of the couple's relationship did not last past their deaths and soon after they passed, their heirs suppressed any mention of it. Mark Dewolfe Howe, for example, found Fields' relationship with Jewett acceptable while it was ongoing but turned squeamish about it when he was editing her letters to Jewett several decades later. It was no longer respectable and he removed as many references to Jewett as he could.

One woman who was involved in a lesbian relationship and left a lasting legacy of service to Boston's poor was Susan Dimock (1847-75), a physician for whom Boston's Dimock Community Health Center is named after. Born in North Carolina, she moved to Massachusetts after the death of her father in 1864. The next year she met Elizabeth Greene who encouraged her interest in medicine and in 1866 she began taking classes at the New England Hospital for Women and Children. She was denied admission to Harvard Medical School but was allowed to make clinical visits at Massachusetts General Hospital. Wanting more training, she went to medical school in Zurich in 1868 and then returned to Boston in 1872. All the while she remained devoted to Greene.

Dimock was employed by New England Hospital where she quickly became known for her competency and compassion and soon she was one of the most prominent physicians in the city. Afraid she might burn out, the hospital encouraged her to go on vacation. Following that advice, she took a leave of absence to tour Europe with Greene but the two died together when their ship was wrecked off the coast of England. One woman memorialized the couple by stating that "They were lovely in their lives, and in death they were not divided."[13]

Dimock was not the only lesbian who dedicated her life to serving Boston's poor. The poverty and social conditions in the city's slums disturbed Boston's middle and upper classes and they sought ways to make poor people's lives better. Traditional charity in Boston was meagre and harsh, reflecting an attitude that poverty was immoral and the result of sloth or sin. Representatives from city charities would visit a family and deny assistance if they deemed a man or woman lazy, drunk, or a bad housekeeper, and they shared information amongst themselves so that no family might get assistance from more than one charity or turn to another after a first attempt was denied. They might take away children from parents who they thought were neglectful and even families that successfully navigated the relief system were subject to open contempt. These prejudices fell most heavily on Catholic immigrants but even Protestants in need were considered barely redeemable.

Dissatisfied with a system that punished aid recipients and rarely seemed to help the poor, two great social work movements commenced in Boston. One, the Institutional Church movement, was a network of programs sponsored by evangelical and mainstream churches that aimed to assist the poor in gaining the skills needed to escape poverty. Mostly targeting Protestant Boston, churches from throughout the city established programs in the South End and elsewhere that taught work skills, provided day care, and helped newcomers navigate tenement life. This movement peaked in the 1890s and though it most likely would have included LGBTQ people, there is no evidence of specific involvement of them.

The other great social work innovation was the settlement house movement. It had its roots in London's East End as students from Oxford sought to relieve conditions in the city's notorious slums. The idea was simple: young college-educated men and women would live alongside tenement dwellers and by offering programs and their example of healthy upper-class living, they would demonstrate to their neighbors how to avoid moral temptations and get out of poverty. Intrigued by this idea, Robert Archey Woods (1865-1925) went to visit the first settlement house, Toynbee Hall. When he returned from England, Andover Theological Seminary hired Woods to establish Andover House, Boston's first settlement house. It would later change its name to South End House and in the 1960s would merge into what is now United South End Settlements, an asset to the neighborhood to this day.[14]

Woods ran South End House until his death and this straight Pennsylvania native became one of the most prominent civic leaders of both the South End and greater Boston. He was liberal enough to support labor unions and city spending on infrastructure for the poor, yet he advocated for Prohibition and curbs on immigration. He was also a strong supporter of Protestant native James Storrow when he unsuccessfully ran for mayor as the progressive alternative to the growing Irish Catholic political machine in the city. Deeply religious and socially connected, Woods was a pious example of propriety.

Woods also enjoyed a long professional association with Vida Scudder (1861-1954) and her lesbian co-founders of Denison House, another settlement house located just a few blocks from South End House. The two settlements cohosted weekly events, sponsored programs together, and cooperated to promote policies that helped their clients. Records show constant contact between Woods, Scudder, and the many other people associated with both houses. If Woods was ever bothered by the lesbians of Denison House, he kept his discomfort hidden.

Scudder was born in India to Congregationalist missionaries. Sadly, her father drowned there when she was an infant. Her mother took her to Boston where she graduated from Girl's Latin School and then Smith College in 1884. She next went to Oxford, studying under luminaries like John Ruskin and also visited Toynbee Hall before returning to the United States in 1886 to teach at Wellesley College. She was one of the founders of the College Settlement Association and was very involved with Denison House, serving as its administrator for over twenty years.

Scudder was in a lifelong relationship with Florence Converse (1871-1967), a writer and editor (they were ultimately buried together). Both women drew energy from this passionate and intellectual relationship and were part of a network of lesbians based at Wellesley. When Scudder, Katherine Lee Bates (1859-1929), and Katherine Coman (1857-1915) came up with the idea of a settlement house, Coman turned to her friend, Cornelia Warren, for funding to get it up and running. Bates, best known as the lyricist for America the Beautiful, and Coman, professor and founder of the economics department at Wellesley, were another prominent lesbian couple.

The first live-in director of Denison House was another lesbian, Emily Greene Balch (1867-1961), who left after a year to study poverty programs in Paris. She eventually become a professor at Wellesley and by the beginning of World War I, was a friend of Jane Addams and a prominent pacifist. In recognition of her work, Balch was awarded the Nobel Peace Prize in 1946. Balch was replaced at Denison House by Helena Dudley (1852-1932), who would serve as its head worker until 1912. Upon her retirement, Cornelia Warren built her a cottage on her estate in Belmont where Dudley lived until Warren's death in 1921. She subsequently moved in with Scudder.

These prominent women in Boston marriages tended to be deeply religious; sometimes Unitarian, Congregationalists, or Episcopalians, sometimes freethinkers. Scudder, for example, wrote extensively about the role of religion in modern life and has a feast day in her honor in the Episcopal Church. This religiosity has led many to suggest that these relationships were chaste. But rather than promoting chastity or celibacy, the religious fervor seemed to add to the sexual intensity of the relationships as these women considered themselves superior to married women, free to physically love and advance themselves.

Bates and Coman met at Wellesley in 1890 and were together for twenty-five years until Coman's death. They traveled together, encouraged other promising female intellectuals, and built a house for themselves which they named Scarab in honor of their trip to Egypt. Their relationship was passionate, romantic, and intellectual with the two very dependent on each other and their circle of lesbian friends.

As Coman's health worsened as she battled breast cancer, the community of lesbians that surrounded the couple became even more important. The women helped with household tasks, took turns assisting with Coman's care, and provided emotional support at a time when cancer was a disease not discussed or even a diagnosis to be shared with the patient. The importance of this group of women to each other cannot be overstated. Together, they provided the nourishment of good times and support during adversity. "Arguably, it was the very strength of this sisterhood that both motivated Bates and empowered her to become the chronicler of her friend's suffering. Providing every kind of sympathetic care and support, their circle of friends spun a cushioned web of protection around both Bates and Coman."[15] Bates was devastated by Coman's death and wrote a book of poetry dedicated to her, *Yellow Clover*, wherein Bates wrote:

And I must bear this grief night after night,
Day after day, through weeks and months and years,
This grief becomes myself, too dull for tears,
Bewildered beyond all pain, past all desire.

Well liked but of lesser social status was Louise Guiney (1861-1920). Her experience demonstrates the limits of LGBTQ acceptability in gilded age-Boston. Guiney had a Boston marriage with Alice Brown (1857-1948). However, Guiney was Catholic and had been educated in a convent school in Providence which meant she could never move as easily in Boston society as upper-class Protestant lesbians. So deep was the anti-Catholic bigotry of the age that when Guiney took a job as a post-master in Newton, Protestant neighbors boycotted buying stamps from her, a serious move given that her pay depended on her volume of sales. Seeking to prevent her from falling into poverty, Guiney's friends organized a campaign to send people from Boston to Newton to buy stamps from her. Guiney, never wealthy, went on to work at the Boston Public Library and provided part time editorial and secretarial assistance to the publishing house of her friend, F. Holland Day. In time, Guiney began to publish her poetry and developed a small but dedicated following. While she achieved modest success and became friendly with some of the LGBTQ community in Boston and its straight literary social circles, she grew frustrated and moved to England.

3.1 Louise Guiney
(photo by F. Holland Day)

Guiney's lover, Alice Brown, was a prolific writer, publishing over twenty novels in addition to short stories, poems, and magazine articles. She moved to Boston in 1881 where she began her romance with Guiney. When Guiney moved to England, Brown was a frequent visitor and the two collaborated on a biography of Robert Louis Stevenson. She was also very private, ordering her personal papers to be burned upon her death.[16]

Despite their modern ideas regarding women's rights, both Brown and Jewett were deeply nostalgic for the past and rejected the growing chaos of the industrial revolution transforming Boston and New England during their lifetimes. For them and their allies, the Boston Bohemians, the so-called material progress of the industrial age was the enemy. Though she advocated for traditional rural New England values, Brown depicted relationships with men as stunting a women's potential. In her books, marriage ruined women by forcing them to focus on men rather than their own feelings. Though she never wrote about her relationship with Guiney, to Brown a Boston marriage allowed a woman to reach her full potential.[17]

Two other major forces in Boston's settlement house movement were Edith Guerrier (1870-1958) and Edith Brown (1872-1932). Guerrier was born into a poor family in New Bedford. Still a child when her mother died, her father sent her out west in addition to periodically placing her with relatives in Massachusetts and Connecticut. Driven by talent and ambition, she went to college in Vermont, and while attending the Museum of Fine Arts (MFA) School, worked at a day care in the North End. She eventually ran clubhouses for immigrant women and became a noted librarian, even working in Washington, D.C. for a term. Guerrier was a modest woman who constantly apologized for her looks in her autobiography. Yet, photographs of Guerrier suggest a short, dark-haired woman with wise, confident eyes and an attractive appearance.

Guerrier met Brown while taking classes at the MFA. Brown was a "pretty young thing, shy as a fawn."[18] After Guerrier's father moved to Pepperell to tend to his health and Brown's sister moved to Nova Scotia, the two women shared a small room on Massachusetts Ave. that had "a full bed that featured as the wardrobe by day and as a bed by night. The room was furnished, also, with a marble-topped table, several chairs, and a bureau." It cost $3.50 per week. The cheap tenements and lodging houses of the South End would be home to thousands of LGBTQ people over the next century.

Through her work in the North End, Guerrier met one of the most powerful straight couples of fin de siècle Boston: Helen and James Storrow. Both had strong pedigrees in a city where family connections were highly prized. James was a successful lawyer and powerful man. In addition to briefly serving as head of General Motors, he tried unsuccessfully to mediate an end to the Boston Police Strike, and he ran unsuccessfully for Mayor of Boston. He also promoted the construction of the Esplanade along the Charles River which opened in 1910. Soon afterwards, it became a popular cruising ground for gay men. Helen was a beloved supporter of social causes and her work in the North End and on behalf of young people brought her strong admiration. Despite being friendly with same-sex couples, both male and female, the Storrows still labored under the prejudices of the day. When James ran for mayor, for example, he alienated African Americans by announcing he was against hiring black teachers at any school with more than fifty white students.[19] His racism didn't help him–Storrow lost the election to John "Honey Fitz" Fitzgerald, the grandfather of President John Kennedy, by little more than 1,400 votes.

The bond between the two couples was intense. Helen asked Guerrier and Brown to stay in her house while she was in Europe, for example. She also paid for Guerrier and Brown to travel to Europe themselves in 1906, thinking that Guerrier needed a two- to three-month vacation. It was on this trip that they developed the idea of a pottery works to provide jobs to young immigrant women. Not only did the Storrows provide the money to build the facility, they also built an apartment for the couple.

An important base for many lesbians was Wellesley College. Even among women's colleges, Wellesley was unique. It did not use faculty from a closely associated men's school, as did Radcliffe, nor did it hire male professors. Instead, for the first several decades after its founding in 1870 by Henry and Pauline Durant, Wellesley relied on full time female faculty for its instructors.

The Durants were deeply religious (the famous evangelical revival leader, D. L. Moody, stayed with them when he came to Boston for a six-week revival meeting in the South End in 1877, for example). Durant's initial plan for Wellesley was a modification of the women's seminary, Mt. Holyoke College, to create an educational experience on par with that of Harvard. However, his oppressive control over the daily lives of Wellesley's professors along with his close supervision of students sparked mutiny and led to a dramatic change in administration as Durant's health declined in the final years of his life.

Just twenty-six when named his successor, Alice Freeman was born in upstate New York and was one of the first female graduates of the University of Michigan. Taking over from Durant, she thought his strong religious ideology weighed down on Wellesley. She fought to secularize elements of the curriculum while easing some

3.2 Students at Wellesley Collage 1903

of the most onerous restrictions on faculty and students. She even intervened to stop guest clergy from giving sermons that focused on female domesticity, seeing that these were direct assaults on her faculty since they were required to remain unmarried. Despite Freeman's reforms, the controls on the women teaching at the college remained strict.

Freeman stepped down as president so she could marry, but first she reconstituted the Board of Trustees, even appointing Vida Scudder's uncle Horace, to protect her reforms. She remained involved, helping to pick Wellesley's next three presidents. The use of female professors continued and there were fifty-three important women faculty at Wellesley between 1900 and 1910 with their influence lasting into the late 1920s. About half hailed from New England, and the rest from the Midwest and the Mid-Atlantic area. All were white and Protestant, though many rejected conventional religious doctrine.

Coman, Scudder, and the other brilliant Wellesley faculty women shared bookish and socially awkward childhoods. Most grew up in middle class families that welcomed education for their daughters, but felt isolated and different than their peers. Many of the women recalled being tomboys when young and consciously rejected conventional sex roles. Bates, for example, remembered running home crying after being forced to take dancing lessons. For most of them, the tyranny of conventional society was intense. When pursuing their education, these women fought to be admitted to colleges and were often confronted by professors who told them they were incapable of learning or that their education threatened western civilization. Many felt the slightest error would rebound harshly on their entire sex.

Balch recalled that one professor "told an acquaintance that a woman should cross the threshold of his classroom only over his dead body." Another professor, Edith Puffer, remembered being the only woman in the room and being stared at by male students. Yet the women would not be denied an education. Only one of the fifty-three professors (Puffer) married and her experience was a warning to the others. She had to leave Wellesley and no other college would hire her. She wrote a few journal articles but her career was functionally over. Women had to choose between academia and marriage; they were not allowed both.

In contrast, a lifelong relationship with another woman offered freedom and a career. Mary Woolley and Jeannette Marks met at Wellesley in 1895, for example, when Woolley was a biblical history professor and Marks a student. The two were a couple for their entire lives, with Marks writing books while Woolley was president of Mt. Holyoke College. They lived in the President's House and their relationship was accepted as a matter of course by the school.

After 1925, this female-positive community began to erode. The original fifty-three women retired or passed away while new hires, which now included men, did not have their commonality of experiences and purpose. Additionally, it was no longer socially acceptable for women to so openly forsake men.[20] The golden age for women came to an end.

Students still had freedom to explore same-sex behavior, however. As women's colleges were founded in the late-nineteenth century and other colleges began to admit women, crushes and relationships between female college students were thought to be common and even normal–as long as they were eventually discarded and the women turned to heterosexual marriage after graduation. The acceptance of these relationships was strongly based on the belief that they were non-sexual. If women persisted in being enamored with other women, they were considered to be suffering from arrested development and perhaps they could be easily persuaded to grow up and leave this period of childhood crushes behind them. However, after the 1920s, outsiders began to consider that college crushes between women could include sex and society became keen on condemning them. Later, Wellesley was seen as a gateway to lesbianism.[21] The women crushing on their fellow female students were regarded as too feminine, so fragile and ladylike that they could not relate to men. They were over emotional, overly sensitive, and extremely delicate. This prejudice was very class, sex, and race specific, however. Only white middle- and upper-class women could be so pure. Black and working-class women were excluded from this acceptance.

The Wellesley experiment as a whole generated intense criticism; the school was accused of fostering spinsterhood and promoting race suicide. But the strictures on these women were at least partially responsible for their lives' outcomes. Wellesley graduates were more likely to become teachers, and approximately 42 percent of the graduates from 1879-99 did so. Because teachers were forbidden to marry, this contributed to marriage rates well below 50 percent for these women. It was very difficult for these women to escape the social pressures they faced.

The lesbians of Wellesley and the literary crowd of Boston had connections to women across the region and beyond. In June 1896, for example, Mrs. Harriet Purinton held a spinster party at her home in Lynn where no men were admitted. Most of the 100 women at the party were single, as married women "were prominent in their absence". The day was festive and "the spacious lawn was decorated in a profuse manner with all the colors of the rainbow, leaves and shrubs and flowers."[22] At one point, a poem was read:

> The modern poet and the novelist
> Have you ever noticed how they are bemissed?
> Miss Jewett, Miss Wilkins, Miss Guiney, Miss Brown, Miss Addock,
> Miss Field — all maids of renown.

One connection of these women to the literary lesbians of the time may have been through Guiney, who had made a presentation to a group of Lynn women in 1891. Afterwards she wrote to F. Holland Day about the gathering, "250 of 'em in bonnets, solemn as owls."[23]

One of the most admirably unconventional of the nonconforming women of this era was the poet Amy Lowell (1874-1925). A member of one of the most illustrious families in Massachusetts, her paternal grandfather was a prominent industrialist and philanthropist, while her maternal grandfather founded the city of Lawrence and her father was a fifth generation Harvard graduate. Additionally, one brother became a noted astronomer and another became president of Harvard (see Chapter Five). Yet for all her family power and influence and her desire for education, Lowell did not go to college as it was not seen as proper for a woman. Instead, she was mostly self-taught as she read everything from Erasmus to Thackery. As a youngster, Lowell was overweight and didn't conform to standard gender roles. She liked snowball fights and baseball and considered herself fat, unlovable, and half a man. By fourteen, her diaries recorded crushes on other girls, writing of one, "I like her much better than before in fact. I love her very much indeed, she does not pay much attention to me, but perhaps she will like me better by and by."[24] After Lowell's mother died when she was eighteen and her father when she was twenty-three, she was alone, wealthy, and in charge of her Brookline estate, Sevenels. This allowed her great latitude to live and love as she pleased. She took tremendous advantage of this freedom.

Lowell's first major romance was with Bessie Seecomb (1877-1915), the daughter of a captain who sailed for Cunard. The Lowell family may have met the elder Seecomb on a transatlantic crossing or in New Hampshire. Bessie was one of eleven children. Her family was English but settled in Peterborough, New Hampshire—not far from the Lowell summer home in Dublin. Seecomb's father was interested in the literary arts to the point of covering the interior of his house with quotations. Bessie was also very well read and educated. She was a nurse and member of the Boston Athenaeum. By 1905 Lowell and Seecomb were together and the romance helped give Lowell the confidence and drive to become a poet.

Lowell and Seecomb traveled together and hardly spent a night apart. The two women were accepted as a couple by their friends, who entertained them together and served as confidantes. We only know of this intense relationship because of the letters that survived in the archives of Robert Grosvenor Valentine, an MIT poetry professor and Wall Street bond trader who also served as President Taft's director of the Bureau of Indian Affairs. When Valentine married, Seecomb and Lowell sent the newlyweds a joint present.

When the relationship ended abruptly in 1907, Seecomb was devastated, writing the Valentines that "the bottom had dropped out of the universe" and she wondered how she could go on living now that Lowell refused to ever see her again. Lowell was also highly affected by the breakup, and that same autumn she wrote to the Valentines saying she had lost all feelings of "spontaneity and freedom." Seecomb pulled herself together, eventually becoming the primary breadwinner for her family after her father died in 1910. Tragically, she drowned in 1915. She was sailing aboard the *Lusitania* when it was torpedoed by a German submarine off the coast of Ireland. There is no record of Lowell's reaction when she heard the news.

Lowell did not restrict herself to poetry. She had many interests and used her money and influence to advance her goals. For example, she famously fought to save the Boston Athenaeum's venerable Beacon St. building when its trustees sought to move elsewhere. Lowell purchased enough voting shares to tip the balance towards staying and renovating its current quarters.

Lowell was not a recluse, nor was she shunned by proper Boston society. Her parties and literary soirées were eagerly attended and she was a member of many influential boards and clubs. Only her brother, Lawrence, kept his distance. Not surprising as he was very intolerant of homosexuality. There is no evidence that Amy knew about her brother's secret court that expelled gay men from Harvard (see Chapter Five).

Only five feet tall and weighing 200 pounds, Lowell was not shy about her appearance; she dressed in a way that emphasized her bulk. An editor once said she entered a room "ponderous and regal" and when she sat down, "she literally sank into a chair, spreading herself comfortably and quizzing the crowd; doing not more than her share of talk, perhaps, but monopolizing more than her share of attention."[24] Lowell took up cigar smoking when she around thirty during one of her many European trips. She preferred slim panatelas, not the big stogies of public imagination.

Thumbing her nose at respectability, Lowell hosted a production of Oscar Wilde's *An Ideal Husband* in 1907-08 at a time when his name was never mentioned in polite society. Russell Sullivan and Berkeley Updike, two gay men, encouraged and supported her efforts. Lowell also promoted new music by Debussy, Satie, and Stravinsky. These varied interests cemented her reputation as a leading public intellectual. A friend described her as "witty, intensely amusing, enthusiastic and impetuous—but there was nothing superficial about what she said, because her knowledge was deeply rooted, and she never, never made any pretense."[24]

The second great romance of Lowell's life was with Ada Russell Dwyer. Lowell met the actress in 1909 when she came to Boston to perform in a play, but their romance did not blossom until 1912 when Dwyer made a return trip to the city. Though Dwyer was raised a Mormon, eleven years older, and once married, she was also talented, well read, and able to stand up to Lowell. Dwyer was the ideal lover Lowell had wanted all her life. However, Dwyer had to be wooed. Lowell begged her to give up the stage and live full time in Brookline, but Dwyer was reluctant to do so.

In the end, Dwyer and Lowell had a long passionate relationship that inspired Lowell's poetry. Supporting her emotionally, Dwyer calmed Lowell when she had to confront Ezra Pound and a group of male poets at a meeting to argue who best represented the burgeoning Imagist poetry movement which Lowell championed. In return, Lowell rhapsodized about Dwyer's talent with a needle and thread as evidence of the quiet domesticity at the center of their love. In one poem, she compared Dwyer to flowers and church bells. Lowell believed that poetry was essentially an erotic declaration. She was an early proponent of free verse and she worked to liberate poetry from the shackles of rhyme and fixed meter. Yet for all her radical efforts to transform poetry, Lowell was a conservative Republican.

Dwyer was often demure when Lowell was entertaining her poetry friends, but the two created a version of domestic bliss. Lowell had an unconventional work schedule, writing between midnight and 5:00 AM. She often appeared late, even at gatherings she put together, so that Dwyer often played solo hostess at dinners for guests invited by Lowell. Dwyer encouraged Lowell's efforts to stretch her poetry and coached Lowell to become a better presenter, which in turn contributed to her becoming a popular reader. Yet despite all her tremendous passion for Dwyer, Lowell understood that there were limits to how public their relationship might become and even Lowell knew she had to keep some of its details secret. She could look and play the part of a lesbian, even allude to the erotic fire in her life, but there could be no overt evidence that could be used to condemn her.

Ready to make her mark on the world, Lowell published her first poems in *The Atlantic Monthly*, followed by her first book of poems in 1912. At the time, Florence Converse was poetry editor for *The Atlantic*–another example of how lesbians helped each other advance their careers. Lowell was also a childhood friend of Mabel Cabot, who had married Ellery Sedgwick, editor-in-chief of *The Atlantic*. This did not mean he favored Lowell's poetry and as time went on he liked it less and less. He particularly disliked her use of free verse and the way she broke up rhythm, yet he felt compelled to continue publishing her work.

Lowell was controversial in her day. Some attacked her for her theatrical publicity tours, which seemed uncouth for both a poet and a woman. Others criticized her because she was a lesbian, or because of her size and physical appearance. One critic even called her a "hippopoetess", and there were many who simply opposed the idea that a woman could write poetry. Some of her contemporaries and later critics considered her a bombastic, overly pushy woman, but she succeeded in getting the publisher and photographer F. Holland Day to share some of his John Keats memorabilia only through charm and flattery.

Though she was very busy with her poetry, by 1921 her health was deteriorating. Lowell was consumed by writing a biography of Keats, a poet who was an inspiration to many creative LGBTQ people in the decades around 1900. While conducting his own research, Day had gained possession of a collection of thirty-one letters from Fanny Brawne to Keats. Day had long been obsessed with the poet. He began his Keats collection in 1885 and in 1894, he commissioned Anne Whitney to create a bust of Keats for the poet's parish church in Hempstead, England.

However, Day refused to let anyone read the letters. Even his best friend, Louise Guiney, did not know what was in them, and Day put off Lowell's request to examine his treasures. At this point a shut-in who rarely even left his bedroom, Day toyed with Lowell, never saying yes or no to her. Among the obstacles he placed before her was refusing all visits after 4:00 PM, knowing that Lowell slept all day and worked all night and that it would be impossible for her to travel from her home in Brookline to Day's in Norwood in time for her to meet with him. But after a year of torment, Lowell gave in and agreed to Day's terms and she arrived at his house at 3:00 on March 2, 1922. Gleefully aware of her bulk, Day surrounded his bed with books, papers, teapots, and silverware while he had all the other furniture removed from his room except for a small armchair. "If Miss Lowell decides to sit down, she will have to stay seated for the rest of the session."[23] Lowell paced for the entire three hour visit. In the end, Lowell seduced Day with books on his favorite topics and a lock of Brawne's hair. Day allowed her access to some of the letters and the biography was published in 1925. Lowell died three months later.

Many participants in Boston marriages suppressed all public mentions of their sexuality, enabling others to question if they were truly what would now be called lesbians. Not Lowell, whose poetry glistens with sensuality and eroticism. "I have lain with Mistress Moon" she proclaimed in the poem, Fool 'o the Moon. Yet even Lowell saw the limits of her ability to push aside critics of her lesbianism and though she lived very openly, she took pains to ensure that no one would directly read of her romantic liaisons with Dwyer or discover just how much Dwyer served as a muse to her. At Lowell's request, all their letters were burned when she died and the daily notes of her secretaries were destroyed. Within a few years of her death from a stroke, she was savaged by critics and biographers, many of whom thought her works lacked creativity. To them, she was chaotic and out of control, even bewildering.

The Boston lesbian golden age that began in the middle of the nineteenth century was mostly over by 1920. There would be no new openly lesbian poets, sculptors, or artists in the city for decades and though some women from these Boston marriages survived well into the middle of the twentieth century, there would not be any more public relationships of women who intermingled with the most prominent and influential straight people of the city. Instead, couples burned their letters while their descendants carefully scrubbed legacies of any hint of lesbianism.

There are many reasons this era of acceptance ended. Freud and other medical and psychological experts told people that women had sexual feelings and were capable of initiating sexual acts, destroying the fiction that Boston marriages were sexless. Being a lesbian was now seen to be a medical condition, a sickness that prompted many straight people to avoid any possible contagion. Another problem was that Boston was rapidly becoming an artistic backwater as Modernism swept the Western World. Thus the artistically conservative female poets and sculptors of Boston were forgotten. A final cause might have been the decline of Boston's economy. The entrepreneurial class that had financed bold ventures around the world now contented itself with buying municipal bonds or funding modest real estate projects. The money that fueled acceptance was gone.

Chapter 4

The Men of the Gilded Age

S OME GAY MEN in the decades around 1900 experienced the same acceptance that embraced many of the lesbians of that time. Also white, Protestant, and upper-class, these men were able to use their money and social connections to remain part of Boston society even as they pursued love, sex, and friendships with other men. These men did not have the cover of sexlessness that protected some lesbians of their time, yet they were able to appear at social events with their life partners or current love interests.

During these years there were large numbers of gay men associated with Harvard, a visible population noticed by outsiders. Surveying the United States to gauge the extent of gay activity, a German physician and head of that country's first homosexual emancipation organization published an anonymous letter that called 1908 Boston a homosexual capital, with Harvard one of the main venues where gay activity took place. "And how many homosexuals I've come to know! Boston, this good old Puritan city, has them by the hundreds." The author of the letter noted that the gay community included men of all ethnic backgrounds and that "homosexuality extends throughout all classes, from the slums of the North End to the highly fashionable Back Bay."[1] In the middle of all this, Harvard was an environment where gay men could easily interact with each other while safely keeping their sexuality out of the attention of the straight world.

Sturgis Bigelow (1850-1926), for example, was a Harvard educated doctor who had studied for five years under Louis Pasteur in Paris. He threw elaborate, male-only dinners in his Beacon St. home, dazzling the young men who attended with stories and fine wines. Bigelow had traveled to Japan where he had collected thousands of items for the MFA, forming the core of its East Asian collection. During the summers, he invited students to his estate on Tuckernuck, an isolated island off Nantucket. The guests, all men, were required to be naked during the day and then don formal dress for dinner. Both straight and gay men attended these gatherings whose guests included George Cabot Lodge, the son of one senator and the father of another. Lodge's father owned Tuckernuck and when Lodge unexpectedly died there, his body was brought to Bigelow's house for the funeral service. Bigelow was also close to other straight men. Theodore Roosevelt, for example, stayed with Bigelow while visiting the city.[2]

Another gay Harvard man was the famous novelist and social critic, George

Santayana (1863-1952), who was related to the Bigelow family (Boston's prominent families intermarried extensively). He was interested in men as an undergraduate. When a friend brought John Francis Stanley (1866-1931), the second Earl Russell and brother of philosopher Bertrand Russell, to Hollis Hall to meet Santayana during his senior year in 1886, Santayana was "immediately taken with Russell's appearance: tall, tawny hair, clear little steel-blue eyes, and a florid complexion." Russell was adrift; he had recently been thrown out of Oxford for having a young man overnight in his room. Santayana was simultaneously attracted to Russell's intellect and repelled by his hypocrisy. Russell, for example, spoke of becoming a parson though he was "about as spiritual as Attila the Hun."[3] Their love-hate relationship would last thirty years.

Santayana also had an undergraduate crush on seventeen-year-old Ward Thoron who, as a sheltered student educated by Jesuits, had a hard time fitting into Protestant Harvard but eventually married the niece of Henry Adams. Santayana wrote a sonnet about Thoron as he did about Warwick Potter, a student of his who died of cholera in 1893. Santayana's homosexuality was so well known that Harvard President Charles Eliot was reluctant to hire him, though he eventually did so.

Even before he quit his Harvard faculty position in 1912 to move permanently to England, Santayana spent a lot of time with fellow Harvard graduate Ned Warren in Europe, particularly when Santayana was writing *The Last Puritan*. Despite Boston's tolerance, Santayana was frustrated by its conservatism. He "could either stay in the city, pursue a career in business while withering and "folds up his heart" or he could flee to Oxford or Montmartre and save his soul...Santayana chose his soul."[4]

Another reason behind his leaving for England must have been the relative freedom of cousin Howard Sturgis (1855-1920), who lived openly as a gay man in the years between 1890 and World War I. Santayana would later remember how Sturgis's Windsor estate was a mecca of gay life at the time. "It seemed a bower of roses. He played by turns the Fairy Prince and the disconsolate Pierrot, now full of almost tearful affection, now sitting dressed in sky-blue silk at the head of his sparkling table, surrounded by young dandies and distinguished elderly dames."[3]

When Santayana was an undergraduate, one of the high points for gay men was the 1882 visit of Oscar Wilde (1854-1900) to Boston during his tour of the United States. Wilde stayed at the Hotel Vendome at the corner of Commonwealth Ave. and Dartmouth St., which would later host Henry James and John Singer Sargent, as he gave several successful public lectures. Wilde was also a highly-anticipated guest at the St. Botolph Club, founded by a group of wealthy men to promote the arts in the city and host to a number of Boston's gay elite.

Though he denied his sexuality, Wilde was the most famous gay man of this era and reading his books, going to his lectures, and dressing like him was a signal of sexual preference for men in Boston and abroad. In addition to his great wit and ability to skewer social norms, Wilde wore outlandish clothes and was said to be partial to lilies. As a result, many straight men despised him. Then as now, his writings were seen as carefully coded portrayals of gay sensibilities and as time went on and he became increasingly careless about his personal life, rumors spread across the ocean about his dalliances with men.

Even so, many Bostonians fawned over him. During his stay in the city, Wilde socialized with Oliver Wendell Holmes and Henry Wadsworth Longfellow. Julia Ward Howe, by then the presiding doyen of Boston aristocratic society, hosted a brunch in his honor with guests such as Isabella Stewart Gardner. Wilde was so busy during his visit he had to apologize for not having the time to visit with the Alcotts or Nathaniel Hawthorne's daughter.

Wilde spoke at the Music Hall to a packed audience on a night so snowy the street cars shut down. Right before Wilde took the stage, a group of sixty Harvard undergraduates marched down the aisle while waving sunflowers in his honor, two-by-two, with Howe's favorite grandnephew in the lead and all wearing blonde or black wigs, knee breaches, ruffles, and other hallmarks of Wilde's aesthete uniform. Wilde, not missing a beat, begged the audience to "save me from my disciples."[2]

There were critics. Thomas Wentworth Higginson (1823-1911), Civil War hero and prominent women's rights advocate, publicly attacked Howe for hosting Wilde, prompting her to take to the press to defend herself and her guest. Higginson's opposition wasn't because he was straight; he was madly in love with journalist William Hurlburt despite being married. The two had a relationship at Harvard in the 1840s, and it seems that Higginson spent the rest of life trying to rekindle the affair. Higginson's wife was an invalid and as her health deteriorated, he sought out Hurlburt even more. Unfortunately, Hurlburt rejected his advances. To make matters worse, Hurlburt and Wilde hit it off and the two spent private time together. This may have sparked jealousy in Higginson as Hurlburt had a notorious reputation as a womanizer and a flirt with men. Demonstrating that being gay was no obstacle to straight marriage in these years, Hurlburt eventually married at sixty while Higginson married twice.[2]

Boston was also the stateside home base of one of the most important American novelists in the decades around 1900, Henry James (1843-1916). A deeply-closeted gay man, he lived most of his life in England but returned frequently to the United States for family and work reasons. Despite his extremely circumspect lifestyle, he was an intimate part of a circle of friendships among gay men in both Europe and Boston. His attempts to keep his homosexuality private while pursuing a very public literary career highlight the pressures on gay men in this era. Though his friends privately accepted his sexuality, James could not afford a public scandal.

James came from a famous family. His father, Henry James, Sr., was part of Boston's literary and social reform set as well as a prominent proponent of Swedenborgianism, a visionary Christian sect. James' brother, William, taught the first psychology course in the United States at Harvard and is generally regarded as the founder of the discipline of psychology. Among his students were George Santayana, Gertrude Stein, and W.E.B. Dubois.

The James family, based in New York when he was young, traveled extensively with long visits to Europe. On the eve of the Civil War, James was injured in an accident rendering him unfit for the military. Nursing his health, he moved to Boston for a time but soon left for Europe. The reasons for James abandoning the United States are many, but he was part of the exodus of gay men out of Boston that fanned out across England, France, and Italy before and after 1900. James would use his exile to gain perspective on US social conditions and in that sense, his homosexuality and exile contributed to his greatness.

James befriended Gardner in 1879, the year she took her three nephews to Europe. James spent the winter of 1881-82 on Beacon Hill while he administered his mother's estate. He broke his fast at the Parker House and spent evenings with his siblings in Cambridge or at the Gardners' home on Beacon St. During this period he was observing Boston society as both an insider and an outsider.

James brought Boston marriages to the attention of the public in his 1885 novel *The Bostonians*. James knew so many female couples that the model for the relationship in his novel is hard to pin down. James' sister, Alice (1848-92), for example, was in an intense relationship with Katherine Loring (1849-1943). Also from a prominent Boston family, Loring co-founded the famous Saturday Morning Club with Howe in addition to being one of the co-founders of what would eventually become Radcliffe College. Loring was torn between taking care of her own invalid sister and Alice, with her many infirmities, but the relationship was intense enough that when Loring went to England, Alice followed. Loring was everything that Alice wanted: "man and woman, father and mother, nurse and protector, intellectual partner and friend."[5] The two lived together through Alice's final illness and James was grateful for the care that Loring lavished on his sister. Though William's wife found the overt lesbianism distasteful, the rest of the family did not.

In addition to Alice and Loring, James was close to Annie and James Fields, who had mentored him during his early writing career. Fields' burgeoning relationship with Sarah Orne Jewett could also have been the inspiration for the couple in the novel. Through any of these women, he would have met and socialized with other female-female couples as well.

Later in life, James expressed regret for not partaking in romantic relationships in his youth and middle-age. Straight critics have interpreted this introspection to mean that he was completely celibate, but it could just as easily have meant that he had limited himself to quick encounters rather than settling down with one partner in a romantic relationship. He spent most of his life in London, Paris, New York, and Boston (four cities with robust gay activity), suggesting he could have easily found sex, and he mostly socialized with other gay men and their close friends.

James met Edith Wharton (1862-1927) at the Paris home of Edward Darley Boit, whose daughters would be the subject of the marvelous painting by John Singer Sargent at the MFA. They had other connections. Wharton was friends with Howard Sturgis, whom she had met in Newport. James had met Sturgis when he was eighteen and James was thirty. The Sturgises were an old Yankee Boston family and Howard's father had settled in London to run the Barings Bank.

Later, Wharton and James were involved in a triangular relationship with Morton Fullerton (1865-1952), another Harvard graduate. Introduced to James in 1890 by Harvard professor Charles Eliot Norton, Fullerton was a correspondent for the London Times and "well-groomed and extremely well-dressed, Fullerton, from numerous accounts, exuded great charm and had powerfully seductive ways—with a slim build, bushy yet groomed mustache, slicked hair and intense eyes." James was captivated. "I'd do anything for you", he wrote.[6]

James introduced Wharton to Fullerton. The journalist and bon vivant was involved with the gay circles of Paris and London. Fullerton dined with the gay poet, Paul Verlaine, for example, and Wilde turned to him for help when he arrived in Paris bankrupt after being released from jail. At first, James was intrigued by Fullerton's and Wharton's attraction and encouraged it. Then he began to feel like a third wheel as their affair deepened and the two spent increasing amounts of time alone. He grew depressed and left the lovers in France.

Edith Jones Wharton was from a very wealthy New York family. The phrase "keeping up with the Joneses" was said to be a reference to her parents. Her career started off slowly and she was in a very unhappy marriage with an alcoholic husband who eventually squandered much of her money on messy affairs with other women. After Wharton found her writer's voice, with much encouragement by James and her other gay friends, her novels became as much a symbol of the era as James'.

The affair between Wharton and Fullerton did not last long and when Wharton became depressed as it reached the end, Sturgis and the other gay men around her encouraged Wharton to not lose faith in the power of love. Sturgis told her, "Fly your flight— live your romance— drain the cup of pleasure to the dregs."[6]

James settled at Lamb House outside of London in 1897. As closeted as he was in his earlier years, there is greater documentation from his last decades regarding his affairs, or at least his romantic infatuations, with other men. One of these was with an undistinguished sculptor named Hendrik Andersen (1872-1940). They met in Rome at the home of Howe's daughter in 1899 when James was fifty-six and Andersen was twenty-seven. Andersen and his brothers had been poor carpenters and house painters for the wealthy in Newport when Gardner was taken by their talent and sponsored their travels and education. This willingness to support young men was common in Boston society at the time. Andersen and his brothers benefited from scholarships and financial support from Gardner and others, as did many poor and less-advantaged men. A young man did not have to be gay to gain assistance. There is no reason to believe Andersen's brothers had any gay inclinations but being able to confidentially move among gay friendly circles certainly did not hurt.

Andersen also attracted the interest of Lord Ronald Gower (1845-1916). The talented seducer of young men offered to adopt Andersen and make him his heir. Andersen declined. Gower was close to Oscar Wilde, who reportedly used him as a model for Lord Henry Wotton in *The Picture of Dorian Gray*. Gower was also implicated in the notorious Cleveland Street Scandal of 1889, though his name did not come up until the following year. The scandal involved telegraph delivery boys exchanging sex for money from important men including, it was rumored, the Prince of Wales. Gower was never indicted.

James was infatuated with Andersen and he was careful to keep him away from Sturgis and his other gay friends, even disinviting Sturgis when Andersen was visiting Lamb House. Though the two only met a total of six times, they had a robust correspondence up until James' death. There is tenderness and eroticism in the letters. When he learned of the death of Andersen's brother, for example, Janes wrote that he wants to put his "hands on you (oh, how lovingly I should lay them!)" and that he wants to "make you lean on me as on a brother and a lover, and keep you on and on."[7]

James' became closer to Sturgis after 1900 when he developed an intense crush on him. Around the same time, James began to be more open about his sexuality, conducting eroticized correspondence with a number of young men. Sturgis had such an effect on many men of his time. "There were distinct qualities about Howard that greatly appealed to his friends—his penchant for brilliant conversation, his thoughtfulness, his ability as an entertaining host and most of all his way of making everyone around him feel important."[6] Santayana wrote that Sturgis "became, save for the accident of sex, which was not yet a serious encumbrance, a perfect young lady of the Victorian type."[6]

Despite all this attention, Sturgis's life romantic partner was William Haynes-Smith, another distant relative, born in British Guyana. Sturgis dedicated his first book (an anonymous novel about love at a same-sex boarding school) to him. Haynes-Smith was called "the Babe" by the couple's friends. Many did not like him because they thought him unreliable and a burden to Sturgis. They were wrong. Haynes-Smith stayed with Sturgis to the end, nursing him as he succumbed to cancer. In 1924 Haynes-Smith married Sturgis' first cousin, Alice Maud Sturgis (she was related to Ogden Codman, an interior designer and friend of Wharton's).

By 1909, James was in a reciprocated semi-public infatuation with Hugh Walpole, a man forty years his junior. The reactions of his friends, including gay men, ranged from disapproval to bemused acceptance. James soon moved on to another younger (in his thirties) man, Jocelyn Persse.[6] In these final years, James seems to have made peace with his sexuality.

However, his family never did; after James died, they made a great effort to erase his homosexuality, carefully scrubbing out any incriminating information when publishing his papers and refusing Andersen's request to publish his collection of letters. Straight biographers, even twenty-first-century authors, have had a hard time accepting James' and his friend, John Singer Sargent's, sexuality. For example, one book innocently suggests that, "Henry James, *head over heels in civilized admiration* for Sargent, helped convince him that London would be more welcoming than Paris"[8] (emphasis added). It is no accident that we have little information on the sex lives of these men.

Edward "Ned" Warren (1860-1928) was another gay man from a wealthy Boston family who went to Harvard. One of the era's foremost collector of antiquities, he had a major impact on Boston's MFA, New York's Metropolitan Museum of Art, and London's British Museum. He was also one of the most openly gay men of his time. He and his lover, John Marshall, cornered the market for Greek pottery and funneled male-male erotic vases to museums.

Though he grew up in luxury, Warren's mother was a noted art collector in her own right, the Warrens had made their fortune relatively late compared to some of the other first families of the city and Ned often felt that the Boston Yankee establishment looked down on his family. But they were still well connected. One brother, Samuel, was the law partner of Louis Brandeis and chairman of the board of trustees of the MFA. Sister Cornelia, never married and most likely a lesbian, was the treasurer of the College Settlement Association and chair of the board of trustees of Denison House where together with Susan Coman, she sponsored classes for young women in the South End. Brother Fiske was noted for his utopian politics and the naked parties he and his wife liked to host. Fiske's wife was a confidant of Gardner and Sargent painted her portrait at Fenway Court.

Even as a young child, Warren did not conform to gender norms. He led his mother in morning prayers wearing a nightgown and a pale blue Japanese scarf embroidered with little fans. He donned his sister's bronze boots on his first day of school, forever earning him the nickname Tassels. Warren had crushes on other boys while in grade school and his early sexual experiences led him to question his religion.

In the late 1870s Warren attended St. Stephen's Church, then located on Florence St. in the South End. He found it to be a good middle ground between the overwhelming presence of Phillips Brooks (another man who never married and about whom there were whispered questions regarding his sexuality) at Trinity Church and the intensity of services at the Anglican Church of the Advent on Beacon Hill. Warren graduated from Harvard dissatisfied romantically. He was constantly falling in love with his friends, but awkwardness and decorum prevented him from having sustained relationships. He slowly moved up the social ladder, but he shed his faith and had to be persuaded by his father to return to Harvard for his final year.

Warren left to study Classics at Oxford. While there, he dreamed up the life he wanted to live: devoting himself to Greek ideals, establishing a country residence outside of London that would enable him to live in a Greek-enthused lifestyle, and sharing a passionate, intellectual, and emotional life with a like-minded man. Greek civilization was not a distant abstraction for Warren and other upper-class Bostonians. Its values, carefully scrubbed of homosexuality, permeated Boston which styled itself the Athens of America. Young men had to learn Greek and Latin to matriculate at Harvard and they were routinely sent to Athens and Rome. Warren took these classical influences one step further after he read the ancient texts on his own and discovered the extent to which homosexuality was part of classical Greek civilization. To him, rejecting Christianity and reinvigorating Greek ideals into his personal life was a way of reviving an era he had been taught was the pinnacle of human existence. Warren believed that western civilization had taken a wrong turn when it began to emphasize female sensitivity and downplay the male-centric philosophy of Greece.

Warren's great love was John Marshall, who grew up outside of Liverpool in a family of merchants. Showing promise, he won a scholarship to Oxford where he planned on becoming a minister. However, he was nervous and shy and didn't fit in with his fellow students, most of whom had gone to British public schools. Marshall met Warren during his third year at Oxford and over the course of their life together they gradually came to look more and more alike so that it became difficult to tell them apart from behind. By mid-life, Warren was "shortish, stocky, with a pair of heavy shoulders and a torso that seemed too bulky for the waist; the short but well-shapen legs (a trifle slim for the weight that they carried), whose toddling added an incongruously feminine touch to his bodily movement."[9]

Warren and Marshall's major joint activity was buying antiquities, many of them homosexually explicit, in Greece and Italy. Their first purchases were in May of 1892 and by 1895, Warren began negotiations with the MFA to sell their vases and other artifacts. He had to work with Edward Robinson, the curator of ancient art at the time and later the director of the museum. In Warren's view, he was saving the MFA from mediocrity and conservatism. Robinson wasn't so convinced and he visited Warren in England, still skeptical of the "Boston rescue" Warren was proposing. After looking at the collection Warren had already assembled, Robinson decided to back Warren's scheme for collecting which granted him wide latitude in selecting objects for the museum. The standard MFA acquisition policy was to have the director oversee all purchases and the museum had mixed feelings about working with Warren. His collecting methods were irregular even in an era when many brazenly looted artifacts and what he was offering was expensive. Furthermore, Samuel Warren, began to oppose the dealings with his brother and brought in Matthew Pritchard (1865-1936) to be secretary to Robinson to stymie his brother's purchases. Pritchard was soon charmed by Warren, however.

Over the next several years, Warren sold large numbers of artifacts to major museums around the world. Though the MFA turned over authority to Warren for purchasing decisions, they made it clear they wanted fewer vases and more statuary. For example, Robinson wrote in 1897, "I have sometimes been urged to write and tell you not to go on buying vases for us: yet this year you proposed to send us over forty, a considerable proportion of which are distinctly not popular in character."[9] In 1899, the MFA began planning for a new building in the Fenway and could no longer fund Warren's acquisitions.[10]

Warren and Marshall knew they were breaking the law by purchasing artifacts from grave robbers and thieves and they spent as much time avoiding the police as they did negotiating with the locals. Warren's outré homosexuality, though partially hidden from his home town by distance, left him in precarious circumstances as well and a friend warned Warren his unabashed lifestyle was pushing the limits of Boston propriety. The city was tolerant of eccentricities, but not an out gay man, and Sam had long feared for the safety of his brother in an environment that was increasingly hostile to LGBTQ people. Anticipating the gathering repression, Sam Warren and Louis Brandeis had co-written a very influential Harvard Law School Review on the right to privacy in 1890. Perhaps the trigger for the article had been the lurid Cleveland St. scandal and a visit to Boston by Ned around the same time. Sam realized that even a cursory investigation would have exposed Ned to ruin, and perhaps would have destroyed the social-climbing Sam as well.[11] The law article proved very influential, even being cited in the 1973 *Roe v. Wade* Supreme Court decision which legalized abortion in the United States.

Marshall and Warren's base was Lewes House, situated on two and a half acres south of London, which combined a Spartan living style with an Athenian love of the arts. It was meant to support the manly pursuit of scholarship and sports, though Warren was not noted for either activity. The house had a constant stream of young male visitors, mostly from Oxford, Harvard, and other major universities, who stayed for varied times—sometimes a night but some also spent years there.

Sent to keep an eye on Warren, Prichard came to Lewes and quickly became part of the household. He was "over six feet tall, with spare athletic body, a long, rather cadaverous face, and long, thin, nervous hands."[9] He taught many of the men at Lewes how to swim (going into the water naked was de rigueur) and he was an accomplished horse rider. Prichard taught himself Turkish and Arabic by memorizing words while shaving and "in the streets of Lewes he wore a Turkish fez, walked in the middle of the road with an abstracted air, impervious to the jibes and jeers of the locals, salaamed on entering a room, used Turkish or Arabic phrases on greeting and departure, and gave the impression that he had a private working-relationship with Allah."[9] Later he would be hired by Gardner to assist with her museum.

In 1900, Warren traveled to Boston and Sam held a dinner in his honor, inviting prominent benefactors of the MFA. It was the highpoint of his relationship with the museum, which bought his treasures to the extent to which it had the resources to do so. Robinson even joked that he would buy more, if only they could get a patron to die and leave his fortune to the museum. By 1902, however, Warren and Marshall were tiring of the trips to Greece and Italy and Warren wanted to be the trustee for his father's estate, which would have meant his having to spend a significant part of the year in Boston. This effort set Warren up for tragedy as it ended with him suing Sam and his brother committing suicide.

Finished with the MFA, Warren ended his relationship by donating a trove of pottery featuring men and boys having sex with each other. Altogether, Warren and Marshall acquired artifacts that showed a wide variety of sexual practices. All types were sent to Boston and other museums, but Warren specifically wanted his gay artifacts at the MFA. He later wrote, "It was hate of Boston that made me work for

Boston."[12] Warren disliked the city's sexual repression, its equality of women, and its emphasis on domesticity.

The MFA had other problems, most notably what became known as the Battle of the Casts. The controversy was whether the museum should display plaster copies of famous works or only originals. It was a bitter fight. First Robinson was forced to resign, leaving Boston for the Metropolitan Museum of Art and then Sam and Pritchard left the museum the following year. Robinson was in favor of casts while Sam and Pritchard were not, but both sides were taking no prisoners as they forced out their opponents. Sturgis Bigelow, one of the MFA Trustees that Sam and Pritchard conspired against, was also a friend of Ned's, but this didn't stop him from proposing to expose Pritchard as gay and he tried to see if Pritchard was connected to the Oscar Wilde scandal.[12]

Meanwhile, Warren used the large number of erotic antiquities he sent to the MFA to advance his views about homosexuality. First, he suggested the artifacts demonstrated that whatever Plato's high-minded version of chaste same-sex love, in everyday Greek life it included sexual relations. To the Greeks, love wasn't only intellectual–it was carnal, despite what was taught in Boston. Second, Warren said the pottery was evidence that sexual relations between men were central to Greek culture and because Greece was the direct ancestor of upper-class American society, homosexuality should be legal now. Warren argued that the idea that the ancient Greeks were not concerned with sex reflects a Puritan misinterpretation of reality.

Warren's circle was connected to Magnus Hirschfeld, a German scientist developing some of the first modern theories that homosexuality was natural, inborn, and should not be illegal. Thus, Warren's collecting and ideas regarding sexuality were enlisted into the first arguments for the emancipation of homosexuality. Focusing on the masculine images decorating the Greek pottery he was sending to Boston, some of Warren's advocacy was a reaction against the effete aestheticism of Oscar Wilde which had been publicly rejected after Wilde's conviction for sodomy.

Seeking to prove his ideas about homosexuality, in 1928 Warren wrote a 60,000 word essay called *In Defense of Uranian Love* that confidently stated that love between men was better than that between men and women and that there are no legal or moral justifications for prohibiting same-sex relations. Many of his arguments were based on ancient Greek literature and nineteenth century poetry that would be mostly unknown to twenty-first century advocates but would have been familiar to the readers of his time (if anyone read the essay). Warren's book argued that man-man love was the natural outgrowth of the masculinity inherent in ancient Greek philosophy and was a necessary counterbalance to the feminine aesthetic of Christian-based morality. Warren never moved on to assert the right of same-sex marriage, but his writing was a bold argument for embracing same-sex relationships at a time when they were criminal. He published the book in a small self-funded printing, but the book was ignored and had no public impact.

Despite his immersion in a gay-friendly environment, Marshall felt profound pressure to marry. He almost wed in 1904 but Ned's jealousy stopped him. Then in 1907 he married Warren's cousin, Mary Bliss. Meanwhile, Warren had other affairs, most notably with Harry Asa Thomas, who would inherit Lewes House, but he remained loyal to Marshall to the end.

The law suit that Warren filed against Sam over their father's estate was a tremendous tragedy for the Warren family. Brandeis had set up a trust and the legal dispute was used by his enemies when he was nominated to the Supreme Court. Warren believed that Sam was cheating the rest of the family out of their due share of the income from the trust while Sam felt he was just being prudent by limiting withdrawals. As the suit dragged on, Sam's mental health deteriorated and he shot himself at his Dedham home in 1910. Most Bostonians sided with Sam in the dispute and Warren gradually spent more of his time at Lewes, dying there in 1928.

One of the most joyous portraits of late nineteenth century LGBTQ life can be found in the letters between Ogden Codman (1863-1951) and Arthur Little (1852-1925). Codman, like many of his contemporaries, kept nearly every piece of paper he produced or received, but perhaps uniquely, neither he nor his heirs destroyed even the most incriminating materials. In all, ninety-two letters eventually entered the archives of Historic New England due to the generosity of his longest surviving sister, Dorothy. Most were written in the early 1890s, usually when Codman or Little was traveling.

The letters show no guilt regarding same-sex feelings or relations and some are quite explicit. Codman was from a prominent old Yankee family and his father mostly spent his time managing his investments, as did Codman's siblings. Codman, however, was different in that he pursued a career in interior design and today he is most known for the book he co-authored with Edith Wharton, *The Decoration of Houses*.[13] Daniel Berkeley Updike (1860-1941), with whom Codman may have had a relationship, assisted by designing the book.[6]

Little was an architect who had studied at MIT. His style was colonial revival and his best known work is the Larz Anderson mansion in Washington, D.C. Both Little and Codman eventually married, Codman to a wealthy widow in a marriage that lasted five years until her death. Afterwards, Codman kept himself occupied with a string of young male live-in secretaries.

The letters indicate that there was a robust gay world in 1890s Boston. Ogden and Little were not alone and isolated; on the contrary, they were part of an extensive social whirl of men who shared same-sex desires. Inside this world, they evaluated men's attractiveness, boasted of sexual conquests, and talked openly of lust and romance. Both men exhibited masculine gender norms and therefore escaped much of the scrutiny and condemnation that more effeminate men faced. This masculine tendency allowed Codman to easily participate in mainstream Boston society while Warren, who was less able to pass, felt oppression from the start. Codman also came from a more prominent family than Warren, who always felt he was looked down on by his would-be peers.

Codman was not looking for an equal in his relationships. He was interested in men in their late teens or early twenties whom he could dominate. Little and Codman often referred to men by women's names or put their male names in quotation marks or underlined them. The executor of Wharton's estate, Gaillard Lapsley, for example, was referred to as Aunt Mary. Ogden wrote of actively pursuing fifteen young men, all but one upper class. Ogden also whimsically wrote about his interest in "letter boys," the young men who delivered telegraphs and messages. For example, in one letter he talks about a boy who was Jewish and particularly handsome, joking he should attend services at a West End synagogue just to meet him.

Little wrote that he liked effeminate young men. In addition to a Boston house that was a showcase of contemporary interior design, he had a summer house in Swampscott where he held all male dances (gay Bostonians would not be joining other LGBTQ people in Provincetown for another twenty years). Older than Codman, Little lived a quieter life, though both shared a love of post cards that featured nude men, which Little purchased during trips to Italy.

Codman liked going to The Slide, a notorious gay night spot located at 157 Bleeker St. in New York and was disappointed when police shut it down in January of 1892. For all their shared interest in sex at Turkish baths in Europe and New York, Ogden's and Little's favorite sauna was at the Boston Athletic Association, sponsor of the Boston Marathon. Codman jokingly complained to Little that he was spending so much time there his work was suffering. He liked to visit the club with young men to consummate their friendship in the steam room or tubs. The clubhouse, located behind the Copley library, proved immensely popular among the city's elite, quickly acquiring 1,200 members within a month after its opening in December of 1888. Its Turkish baths occupied five rooms in the basement along with a forty-one by thirty-foot swimming tank that had a depth of seven feet. The gymnasium was in the second floor along with the tennis courts, which counted famed equestrian and tennis star Eleonora Sears' uncles as players. The ground and first floors had rooms for dining and socializing as well as the club's offices.[14] The clubhouse closed during the Depression and was torn down a few years later.

Codman and Little were very informed about same-sex desire; thus the lack of LGBTQ literature from this era reflects censorship, not a dearth of knowledge. Both men had a concept that a person might be gay, an innate immutable desire for someone of the same sex, and they often used the word queer to describe such a person, though they also used that word to mean something or someone who was different than the norm.

Distinctly upper class, Codman described himself to Little, "You would scarcely recognize me now I am so smart, single eye glass, Boutonniere, gray or brown waistcoat, varnished boots, top hat and cutaway coat or frock gray or black, the very smartest gloves—everything from the very excellent London people. I constantly see myself in the glass and wonder who it is, pink, blue or mauve shirts, butterfly ties, etc., do make a difference."[15]

One thing that made it easy for Codman to court young men was that upper-crust Boston could not imagine there was anything sexual happening around them and typically, Codman would first see a young man socially through family, friends, at dinner, or the theatre. Then he would make their acquaintance, take them to social events, and then move on to initiate sex. He often had what we would consider dates that included dinner and a Pops concert preceding spending the night together.

Life was not always easy. After Wilde's conviction, the volume of letters between Little and Codman vastly decreased and sexual references mostly ended. In 1902, a friend of theirs named George Griswald was mentally undone by a scandal with reports that Griswald was in a state of near collapse–hands shaking, teeth chattering, insomnia, panic–because of gossip and innuendo. He may have been blackmailed, or perhaps some other exposure was feared. Codman was another gay Bostonian to move to Europe, spending his final decades in France.

The risk of arrest was small but real. In the years 1880-86, Boston police arrested thirteen men for sodomy, with fifteen men arrested in the shorter period between 1887 and 1900. In 1887, oral sex was made illegal, resulting in 98 arrests for that crime by 1900. But though there was always some police activity against gay men, there was no major crackdown. For the most part Boston authorities ignored same-sex activity because they refused to believe that there were gay men in the city. Back in 1871, for example, Police Chief Edmund Savage proclaimed there were no male streetwalkers in Boston and there had been none for years.[16]

Two administrative changes towards the end of the nineteenth century had profound impacts on LGBTQ life through the 1980s and possibly beyond. The first was that the state took over the control of the Boston police department in 1885. As the city grew increasingly Irish, the Yankee establishment's hatred intensified. Many in the legislature did not trust Boston politicians with being able to adequately police the city and the Yankees feared Irish mob violence. In this atmosphere, the legislature voted to give the governor the responsibility to appoint Boston's police commissioners.

The other administrative action was the state takeover of the Boston Licensing Board, the entity responsible for overseeing bars in the city. Many Yankees were supporters of the temperance movement and they distrusted the very lax city oversight that had allowed thousands of legal and illegal venues for selling alcohol to exist. It was part of a crackdown on immorality in the city that was focused on drinking, gambling, and prostitution, but not LGBTQ activity specifically.

Both of these moves affected Boston's LGBTQ community because they separated the control of the police and gay bars from the politics of the city. In New York, San Francisco, and other large cities, crackdowns on gay bars routinely accompanied municipal elections or reflected a mayor's effort to show he was tough on crime. The 1969 raid on the Stonewall Inn, for example, was related to Mayor John

Lindsay's presidential ambitions. Because mayors and councilmen had no control over the police or liquor licenses, this did not happen in Boston. LGBTQ people had bars where they might be harassed by the police but these were otherwise safe places for them to gather. Another result would be that Boston's bars would sometimes last for many decades, whereas elsewhere they barely lasted a year or two.

One interesting group of gay men and lesbians, less socially prominent, lived in and around the north side of Beacon Hill beginning in the 1890s. For the most part this group, sometimes called Bohemians (though that is not how they referred to themselves until decades later), were artistic and consciously lived outré lifestyles. They were aesthetes, devoting their lives to sensuality.

The most prominent member of this circle was Ralph Adams Cram (1863-1942), an architect who championed a gothic revival style that found a market in churches and colleges. Among his most important buildings are the All Saints Church in Dorchester, the Cathedral Church of St. John the Divine in New York City, and college buildings from West Point and Princeton to the University of Southern California. Born in New Hampshire, Cram moved to Boston in 1881, initially living in the South End but soon moving to Beacon Hill to be near his fellow Bohemians.

In contrast to the conservatism of his architecture, Cram's personal life (at least before he married) was filled with wild parties, long dinners at fashionable restaurants, and mystical rituals at private clubs. Drawing on this lifestyle, in 1893 the firm Copeland and Day published his book, *The Decadent*, an anonymous account of opium, Japanese robes, and red fezzes in a country house. Of all the Bohemians, Cram was the most socially connected. He was friends with Bernard Berenson, Gardner's art advisor, and he eventually became a member of many of the city's most important clubs. Second in influence among the Bohemians was Louise Guiney, but she had less access to the elite because she was poor, Catholic, and female. Still another gay member of the aesthetes was Daniel Berkeley Updike. He worked for Houghton Mifflin before starting his own publishing firm, Merrymount Press, an obvious allusion to the notorious colonial settlement. Updike published books for the Warrens and Wharton specifically requested his services for several of her books. Another gay man who was part of this circle was Thomas Meteyard, an artist known for his glistening paintings and prints as well as the wild all-male parties he threw at his estate in Weymouth. Meteyard spent much time in Europe, and after his mother died he moved to London permanently. He purchased a house across the street from Hempstead Heath, then and now London's popular outdoor gay cruising area.

Boston's nascent economic decline coupled with the movement of the best families out to Back Bay and beyond meant that parts of Beacon Hill were being converted into apartments and rooming houses, cheap accommodations for the aesthetes who created a vibrant social world along Pinckney Street and the surrounding blocks. When they weren't going to the theatre or other mainstream entertainment, they preferred restaurants on the shabby side streets along Tremont Street rather than the more downscale entertainments in the North or South Ends—unlike how we picture Bohemians today, these men and women did not idealize poverty, starvation, or tuberculosis. Instead they liked ritual, complex ornamentation, and all night parties. It was a very insular group. "Much of their time was spent being purposefully exotic, medieval, and smugly cliquish."[17]

Of the aesthetes, the one with the most influence today is F. Holland Day (1864-1933) who posthumously inspired photographer Robert Mapplethorpe, among others. The son of a prosperous family that owned several leather companies, the family maintained a Boston address in addition to a large home in the suburbs and Day went to a well-regarded private school but did not attend college. Day never had to work and used his money to support friends and several of the young people he used as models.

Day and his close set of friends were the Boston vanguard of the Aesthetic movement, which sought to incorporate art and beauty into all aspects of everyday life and taking to heart the famous phrase "Art for Art's sake." This was a reaction against the ugly and dehumanizing conditions caused by the industrial revolution and the growing poverty and misery in large cities across the globe including Boston. The group promoted craftsmanship over mass production and naturalism over the man-made. This was distinct from the contemporary progressive movement which sought to use political and social pressure to change cities and society into something more equitable. Though there was some overlap between the two groups, the aesthetes were not political.

Day threw himself into the social whirl of the aesthetes, publishing a literary review which featured the works of his circle and the authors they admired, enjoying long group dinners at Cafe Marliave off Province St., and participating in a private club they established. Much to the club members' amusement, it was raided by the police late one night who found nothing more going on than cigar smoking. Most important to his life, he met Guiney in 1885 with whom he would have a lifelong friendship.

4.1 Songs From Vagabondia

Along with Hebert Copeland, Day founded the publishing firm of Copeland

and Day in 1893 with Cram's book their first title. The firm became known for its high-quality front pieces and illustrations, employing some of the best Boston designers. They published the American edition of Wilde's *Salome* as well as *The Yellow Book*, a literary quarterly based in England that featured luminaries such as John Singer Sargent and Henry James. *The Yellow Book* was cofounded by Aubrey Beardsley, who scandalized London with his over the top gay mannerisms and razor-sharp wit almost as much, if not more, than Wilde, though the young Beardsley repented and turned to Catholicism right before he died of tuberculosis. Copeland and Day also published *Songs from Vagabondia*, a book of poetry by Boston aesthetes Bliss Carmen and Richard Hovey, lavishly illustrated by Meteyard. These works were released just as Wilde was ruined by his trials.

The Boston establishment reacted harshly to these titles. The BPL put Salome into a locked stack and Copeland, an alcoholic with a nervous disposition, feared that he might be arrested for publishing Beardsley's works. In addition to negative reviews of its titles, much of the public was put off by the overwrought typesetting and illustrations. As a result, few of the firm's titles were financial successes and expenses were high. Day, weary of his need to heavily subsidize the press and distracted by his growing work in photography, closed the firm in 1899.[18]

4.2 F. Holland Day (Self Portrait)

Many and perhaps most of the circle of friends that Day and Cram collected were gay. Speaking of his infatuation with one young married man, Copeland wrote Day, "I tried to quit then–but–well, I just didn't, and our intimacy has steadily increased. And now, because I have got what I wanted, I am, as you see, 'leaving 'em.' . . . Why can't we find the right one in all ways?"[19] Copeland often used Day's Boston studio, North Shore estate, and Norwood house to bring back tricks for an hour or day's dalliance.

Day first experimented with photography in 1886. In the beginning, he devoted himself to landscapes and old buildings, but eventually he settled on elaborately staged photographs of young men, and the occasional woman, in fanciful garb and poses. He became most known and infamous for his pictures of naked men and boys. Day volunteered at settlement houses in the North and South End to teach photography (and meet teenagers) and he would roam the streets searching for potential models while wearing a long flowing gown and carpet slippers. His most famous model was the poet-to-be, Kahlil Gibran, who began posing for Day in 1896 when he was thirteen. Gibran had immigrated to the United States the year before and quickly discovered Denison House. Promoting his artistic promise, a social worker wrote to Day asking that he take the youngster under his wing.

Day's interest in adolescents unnerved people in his time.[18] There is no evidence he sexually abused Gibran or any of the other youngsters he photographed and parents often were grateful to Day for helping out with advice, career assistance, and money. Several of the young men he took under his wing remained close to him for his entire life, visiting him in his older years when he became a recluse in Norwood. Some sought friendship, others money. Gibran was one of those who maintained his relationship with Day for the next several decades.

Day's career blossomed in the 1890s and at one point he was one of the premier American photographers. Then his art went into eclipse. His subject matter, naked young men in staged classical poses, proved much less popular than the realism of his great rival, Alfred Stieglitz. To twenty-first century eyes, Day's pictures look unfocused, fake, sentimental, and very dated. Stieglitz, on the other hand, went on to be one of the founders of American Modernism and his work would be tethered to the twentieth century. Furthermore, Day became reluctant to exhibit his work and much of his store of negatives and prints was destroyed when a fire engulfed his studio after he moved his workspace into a building near Copley Square. The fire contributed to Day becoming a recluse. Over time, his associates among Boston Bohemia left him: Cram moved to New York, Guiney went to England, and Copeland drank himself to death. Day lived until 1933, rarely leaving his bedroom.

Cram eventually married, perhaps out of love or maybe because he needed respectability in order to advance his career designing churches and college buildings. Though he had several children, the marriage does not seem to have been a happy one. It may have started off poorly when Cram brought a male friend along on his honeymoon. In any case, matrimony did not stop his pursuit of men. He made frequent trips to England where he was a regular visitor to a friend's summer home known for its week-long parties featuring naked Oxford students.[20]

While today we associate Bohemianism with antiestablishment art or future-oriented expression, the Boston aesthetes had very conservative tastes. Cram championed gothic revival for high church Anglicans—those who sought to reintroduce Catholic ritual into the Church of England, perhaps the most conservative Yankee religion at the time. Similarly, Day preferred neoclassical and religious subject matter and at one time produced a series of photographs of himself as a crucified Christ figure. Though the non-aesthete Amy Lowell was a champion of free verse, Guiney's poetry now seems very conventional and dated. Boston's Bohemians even rejected Impressionism and later had little connection to the great revolution of art that was produced by Picasso and his peers in Europe.

While aestheticism is securely located in the early history of modernism, it would be swept aside by the explosion of modern art and architecture in Paris and New York. First the Armory Show, the exhibit of the best of European and American modern art that traveled to Boston in 1913, and then World War I would render the type of art favored by Boston Bohemians irrelevant. Part of an artistic dead end, today they are mostly forgotten.

It was very easy to live in an all-male world in late nineteenth century Boston. Though women went to parties, the theatre, and social events, men had access to many more venues and private clubs. Many of these were stuffy, conservative places but there was also the St. Botolph Club, noted for its art exhibits. It gave Sargent his first American one-man show in 1888, and the club supported many lectures, events, and debates. It also saw some identifiably gay men become members but there was a club with an even more outré reputation, the Tavern Club.

The Tavern Club was started by a group of well-educated and artistic men, most unmarried and around thirty years old. The club's historian admitted that "many of them [had] the habit of more or less Bohemian habits of living," with "Bohemian" being a code word of the day for homosexuality.[21] The men had dined together regularly at restaurants such as the Carrollton, located on the corner of Church and Providence St. opposite the side entrance to the train station. The club was located at 74 Boylston St. and its members included many gay men such as Sturgis Bigelow, Dennis Miller Bunker, Bertram Goodhue, Henry James, Augustus Saint-Gaudens, George Santayana, and John Singer Sargent. Another gay man, Timothee Adamowski provided much of the lunchtime and afternoon entertainment and performed at the club's first general meeting in September 1884. Women were not allowed in the club, which also included the heterosexual cream of Boston's male high society: Cabots, Lowells, and Oliver Wendell Holmes Senior and Junior

Another gay man, Charles Loeffler, met Adamowski when both were with the Boston Symphony Orchestra in 1885 and the two quickly became friendly rivals. That same year, Loeffler joined the Tavern Club, where he often dined after concerts. On at least one occasion, Loeffler and Adamowski played chamber music at the club in an ensemble that included the painter Dennis Bunker.[22]

As the most public gay man of the last two decades of the nineteenth century, Oscar Wilde's trial and public disgrace in 1895 had a tremendous impact on gay men in Boston. Wilde had grown increasingly reckless in his personal life, purchasing the services of young men and frequenting places where gay men were known to congregate. But it was his affair with Lord Alfred Douglas that caused his downfall. Their relationship was difficult as Douglas gambled, drank too much, and had a mercurial personality. His father, a notorious bully, blamed Wilde for his son's problems and left a card at Wilde's club, accusing him of being a sodomite. Against the counsel of his friends Wilde sued for defamation and lost, which in turn led to a trial for sodomy and gross lewdness. He was convicted and sentenced to two years of hard labor.

Suddenly the men who had publicly admired him feared for their freedom and rumors swirled through gay Boston that there was going to be a series of arrests here. Nothing came of such talk but suddenly aestheticism, dressing up as a dandy, and other signs associated with homosexuality were suspect. Men were counseled to erase any connections to Wilde's writings while his plays were suppressed. Though masculine-acting gay men continued to have wide latitude, those Boston gays who would not or could not conform to prevailing gender norms went underground. City police records do not show any uptick in arrests for gay related sex crimes with just nine in 1895, but many were fearful.

The glamorous, kind-hearted, brilliant, eccentric (the list of possible adjectives is very long) straight woman at the center of upper-class gay life in Boston in the decades around 1900 was Isabella Stewart Gardner (1840-1924). She was an outsider, born in New York and many in Boston never forgave her for marrying one of the city's most eligible bachelors, John Gardner, Jr. She loved art such that her museum is her best-known legacy, and she had a connection to almost every wealthy gay man, and many upper-class lesbians, that lived in Boston.

Underlying her many friendships with LGBTQ people might have been her personal tragedies. After the death of her only child and a miscarriage followed by the suicide of her husband's brother, the couple adopted their orphaned nephews. Later, one of the nephews would commit suicide, perhaps because of a failed love affair with another young man. He was not her only gay relative.

Her nephew's drama had its beginnings at Harvard. Charles Eliot Norton, one of the foremost scholars of archeology in the United States, had four protégés in the 1880s. Three were gay: George Santayana, Charles Loeser (1864-1928), who after a lifetime in Florence bequeathed eight paintings by Cezanne to the White House, and Logan Pearsall Smith (1865-1946). The fourth, Bernard Berenson (1865-1959), was straight but very accommodating to his gay friends. All four were frequent visitors to the Gardners, then located at 152 Beacon St. Also at Harvard was nephew Joe Gardner Jr. (1861-86) who lived across the hall from Ned Warren and was friends with the four protégés. Joe was in love with Smith and after graduating, he bought a retreat in Hamilton, Massachusetts purchased as a place he could spend time with Smith. For a while the relationship was happy and Smith went up to Hamilton quite frequently, often bringing his sister, Mary (who eventually married Berenson, her second husband, in 1900). Smith eventually lost interest in Joe. The lovesick young man, who frequently suffered from depression, committed suicide on October 10, 1886. Isabella and Jack were brokenhearted while Smith departed for Oxford and a career as an essayist and social critic in England.[23]

Gardner had so many LGBTQ friends that it is difficult to keep track of them all. They include Clayton Johns (1857-1932), a composer who taught at the New England Conservatory; William Woodworth, a Harvard professor noted for his Sunday afternoon all-male socials at his house at 149 Brattle St.; Charles Flandrau

(1871-1938), the author of another male-male romantic book, *Harvard Episodes*; and most famously, Henry James and John Singer Sargent.

Gardner was a sympathetic confidant. For example, Theodore Dwight (1846-1917) was a frequent guest of the Gardners. A regular participant in the revels at Tuckernuck, he was in a stormy lifelong relationship with Charles Adams who brought him to Boston to assist with the writing of his history of the United States, and to be librarian of the Adams family papers. During the period of 1892-94 he was the chief librarian of the BPL, overseeing the construction of its wonderful McKim Building. Dwight was also an avid collector of male pornography and enjoyed taking naked pictures of young Boston men. Some were Irish, but he had a preference for Italians and regularly employed his models as live-in valets.[23] Dwight lived at 10 Charles St. in a townhouse that featured the framed portraits of his favorites. He shared the space with Russell Sullivan, a popular playwright at the time–his most well-known production was a stage adaptation of *Dr. Jekyll and Mr. Hyde* in 1887.

At one point, Dwight was despondent over the end of a relationship and sent Gardner an undated postcard that read, "This little scrap is to tell you that the period has come to that little romance in which I was so foolish as to indulge. You were right in your prediction. I seem to come out of it somewhat battered perhaps, & somewhat benumbed but quite patient & resigned."[24] Gardner provided a shoulder to lean on for her broken-hearted gay male friends.

Gardner liked to connect men whom she thought would make a good couple. She introduced Bunker to Sargent in 1887, for example, and the two had a very intimate relationship with Sargent reportedly including an image of Bunker in his Frieze of the Prophets in the BPL as well as producing a picture of Bunker painting in a bucolic country setting in 1888. Gardner was so proud of the couple that she reportedly kept their pictures side by side in her mansion and one of Bunker's paintings hangs in her museum. As they painted together in the French countryside, Bunker stayed with Sargent. He married in October 1890 but tragically died of meningitis only a few months later in December.

Sometimes, when Sargent met a man he was interested in, he would bring him over to the Gardners for a visit. One night, for example, Loeffler was the soloist in a performance where he captured the attention of Sargent. Loeffler recalled, "He came into the Artists room that evening and with that irresistible charm of his said a few words which made one rise in one's self esteem and then arranged for our meeting a few days later at a dinner in a mutual friends house [the Gardner's]."[22] This was the beginning of another intimate relationship that resulted in Sargent's portrait of Loeffler. At the same time, Sargent's relationship with Bunker was heating up and soon Loeffler and Bunker were spending time together, influencing each other's work.[23]

Gardner was not friends with the Bohemians with the exception of Cram and Guiney, but to be part of her circle, or the gay men and lesbians she was close to, was to be part of the social and artistic pinnacle of Boston. One critic wrote that "to have known Amy Lowell, John Singer Sargent, Charles Martin Loeffler, and certain others was to be of the inner temple."[22] Loeffler was best man at Bunker's wedding and Sargent visited Loeffler at his estate in Medford. Loeffler eventually married as well, after a twenty-four year engagement. He was friends with Amy Lowell, who always sent an autographed copy of her latest book to him, and he socialized with other important Bostonians including Sears and Higginsons.

Gardner introduced Gaillard Lapsley (1871-1949) to Henry James. Lapsley, a close friend of Santayana at Harvard and perhaps a one-time love interest of Arthur Little, went on to a distinguished career as an Oxford don. Through these men, Lapsley met Edith Wharton and the two became lifelong close friends. Gardner would only become closer to her gay male friends after her husband died in 1898.

Reflecting the power inequities of that time and ours, we know less about the lives of poorer, potentially gay men as well as those who challenged gender norms. There are, however, a few that left evidence of their lives. One, Julian Eltinge (pronounced to rhyme with sing) was born William Julian Dalton on May 14, 1881, in Newton. His father had been a failed gold prospector in Butte, Montana while his mother had Massachusetts roots. Eltinge was purposely vague about his childhood. One account claims he was raised out west where his mother encouraged him to dress up as a girl to sing before miners in saloons. This was said to have enraged his father who beat him and sent him back to Boston.

Another story has Eltinge stealing the show at the age of ten in a production for the First Corps of Cadets. They were trying to raise money to build their armory (the castle at the corner of Columbus Ave. and Arlington St.). As was common at Harvard (the Hasty Pudding Club only decided to produce co-ed shows in 2018), the Cadet shows were all male affairs with men and boys playing the female parts. According to this story, Eltinge proved so popular that the next year the show was written just for him.

Still another story has a seventeen year old Eltinge working in a dry good store while studying voice and dance. His teacher recommended him to the Cadets where his performance was a success in part because he had beautiful legs and was easy to work with. This led to a performance in a production for a bankers' trade group and more work in shows around Boston.

Regardless of how he got his start, Eltinge was a hit. A producer discovered the young man and brought him to New York to appear on Broadway and at one point he was in George M. Cohen's vaudeville troop. Audiences and reporters alike loved him. He even published magazines where he provided women with beauty tips. But despite a career based on dressing as a woman, Eltinge insisted he was straight. "I'm not gay. I just like pearls," he said.[25] Later, Eltinge was in The Latin Lover with Rudy Valentino and performed in front of King Edward VII.

When he walked out on stage, he knew how to entertain. "As a female, Eltinge was fond of graceful gestures and ultra-feminine coyness. Eltinge was the girl in crinolines or the curvaceous bathing beauty."[26] Off stage, he exaggerated his masculinity, talking roughly to men and playing up his relationships with women; anything to hold off the constant rumors he was gay. He owned race horses, got into fistfights in bars, and had affairs with women that failed spectacularly. He had a deep voice and smoked cigars. "This drag queen sounded like she could eat nails for breakfast."[26] It was a niche, but it was also a career.

Another gay man based in Europe but with a strong Boston connection was John Singer Sargent (1856-1925). Similar to his friend, Henry James, Sargent was extremely circumspect about his private life, enabling biographers to declare him sexless and devoid of any romantic interests whatsoever. However, a trove of expressive works of male nudes and a few hints of close relationships with men suggest that he was gay.

Sargent was born in Florence to Americans with Massachusetts roots. He grew up and studied art in Paris and as a young adult showed signs of artistic genius. He soon became known for his portraits, several of which are at the Gardner Museum. One of his most famous paintings is *The Daughters of Edmund Boit*, which is the pride of the MFA. On the Boits' first trip to Europe, in 1865, they stayed with their cousins, the Sturgises. Then at some point between 1871-73, the Boits met James. In turn, the Boits introduced Wharton to James though that friendship did not blossom until later. Wharton had been in so much awe of him that she could not speak.[27] The Boits met Sargent in the late 1870s. Interestingly, one daughter, Florie Boit, was a lesbian who would eventually settle into a happy Boston marriage with her cousin, Jane Boit Patten.

Sargent took two extended visits to Venice, first in 1880-1881 and again in 1882, and there is an unsubstantiated account that one man called Sargent a "frenzied bugger" during his days in that city.[6] Sargent wrote to the Boits he had to stay there longer than planned because he needed to complete a set of paintings of interiors. James had met Sargent by 1882, the same year Sargent painted the Boit daughters. He was immediately infatuated with the painter and asked the Boits to put in a good word for him. But Sargent was still very attached to his studio mate at the time, Albert de Belleroche (184-1944), whom Sargent painted a very sensuous painting of that year. "Almost androgynous in appearance, Belleroche displays a sultry sexual presence" and the paining would be the center of attention in Sargent's London dining room for the rest of his life. Six years later Sargent would paint another sensual portrait of a man, the singer George Henschel. It was so wonderfully erotic that a friend asked Sargent how he could put so much emotion into a painting. Sargent replied, "I loved him."[28] When Sargent faced scandal and ruin in Paris for painting the now much admired *Portrait of Madame X* in 1884, he took James' suggestion to move to London.

As Gardner was herself about to embark on a trip to Europe in 1886, she asked James to introduce her to Sargent. The painter jumped at the opportunity to meet her and invited Gardner to his London studio, apologizing that his constant afternoon portrait painting obligations would be a distraction. The Gardners spent only a limited number of days in London on this trip, but when Sargent planned an extended American visit in 1887, there was time for a portrait of Gardner. Meanwhile, James wrote a glowing review of Sargent's work in *Harper's Magazine* in October of that year, setting him up for portrait painting in New York and Boston. When Sargent finally arrived in Boston the next month, he stayed with the Boits on Beacon Hill at 65 Mt. Vernon St., next door to Sam Warren, and he painted Fiske Warren's wife and daughter at Fenway Court in 1903.

Sargent stayed at the Copley Plaza during his 1917-20 stay in Boston. In the elevator, he met Thomas McKeller, an African American waiter at the hotel whom Sargent painted nude. Hotels such as the Touraine and the Copley Plaza illustrate how gay culture could coexist unnoticed by straight society. For generations, the bars at both hotels were favored meeting places for Boston's upper-class gay men, yet straight people had no idea. For example, just a few yards away from the frothy action at the Copley Plaza bar, clueless straight Harvard football players held dances in the hotel's ornate ballroom. Similarly, straight celebrities soundly slept at the Touraine Hotel, oblivious as gay men drank and cruised in the lounge downstairs. Sargent belonged to the St. Botolph and Tavern Clubs and Sargent's first solo exhibition was at the St. Botolph club in February 1888. Sargent also was friendly with the manager of the Lenox Hotel in the 1920s—the manager would be implicated as a fellow customer of gay bars with Senator Walsh when a gay spy scandal erupted in New York during World War II.[23]

There were other erotic portraits of men and a large number of sketches of male nudes that Sargent kept hidden so as not to draw attention to his sexuality. Sargent also faced an intense desexualization of his life after he died until decades later when his many sketches of nude men were at last made public.[29] But like his similarly-neutered friend, Henry James, Sargent spent most of his life in cities with vibrant gay life that featured opportunities for everything from anonymous encounters to full blown romances that were both open yet out of sight to straight people. Coupled with Sargent's lustrous portraits of men and the obsessive secrecy of his private life, we can only speculate on his place in these worlds.

There were young men simply looking for love in a world where they felt isolated and lacked an understanding of their feelings. One who left a record of these yearnings is Erich Stern (1879-1969) who grew up in Wisconsin and then went to Harvard, where he lived during his freshman year at 12 Oxford St. in Cambridge. Stern met other young men and developed warm friendships with them. Soon he was spending the night with one fellow student who slept in his bed while he took the couch.

Stern longed for love and he looked to his fellow students for romance. For example, he wrote that "the hope of finding in Sam Thurber the friend I have dreamt of for years forces itself in me frequently."[30] He gushed on each sign of intimacy: a bicycle trip to Roxbury to meet Thurber's family, an invitation to spend Thanksgiving at his home, and the three meals a day they ate together. Yet he could not tell Thurber what was in his heart.

It took him until February of his freshman year to confide in anyone of his feelings for men and when he told the student across the hall, the other man said he should not speak of such things, though his behavior toward him became much friendlier. At first, nothing happened between the two as Stern was still in love with Thurber. A month later, the two ended up together on Stern's couch and "I felt what I had always yearned for: a manly breast beating against mine in love."[30] The two were a couple for six months. Stern had been admitted provisionally and struggled academically at Harvard, particularly in Latin and physics. Sophomore year, now a regular student, was spent at 84 Perkins Hall and he volunteered at Denison House. After graduation, Stern returned to Milwaukee and married an artist.

In Boston and elsewhere, new ideas regarding same-sex attractions were developing that had profound impacts on the lives of LGBTQ people. One trend was that doctors began to believe that homosexuality was an illness. In 1898 the *Boston Medical and Surgical Journal* called for sending "inverts" to jails and mental hospitals. "There is a community not far removed …men of perverted tendencies, men known to each other as such, bound by ties of secrecy and fear and held together by mutual attraction….To themselves they draw boys and young men over whom they have the same jealous bickerings and heart burnings that attend the triumphs of a local belle"[1] Eventually, the effect was that the straight public believed that homosexuality and gender non-conformity were diseases. But rather than creating sympathy, it would spark demands for police to crack down on LGBTQ people.

In England, Havelock Ellis, working in collaboration with John Addington Symonds and others, wrote one of the most well-known early books on homosexuality. Published in German before an English version was released, his 1897 treatise was an effort to prove that same-sex desire was natural and innate and therefore should not be criminalized. Ellis's book would provide comfort to many LGBTQ people over the next several decades, but it would also become a useful method for identifying gay men and lesbians. As will be seen, Ellis' efforts to generate sympathy for LGBTQ people terribly backfired. By openly suggesting homosexuality was a fundamental character trait, not a behavior anyone might engage in, just having read the book or having knowledge of Ellis' work would be used as evidence that a person might be LGBTQ. The stage was set for this golden age of acceptance to end.

Chapter 5

The End of the Golden Age

BETWEEN 1900 AND 1920, a wave of crackdowns ended Boston's golden age of acceptance of gay and lesbian people. The boundaries of this openness had been small, embracing only cisgender upper-class, white Protestants, but it is tempting to speculate how LGBTQ history might have been different if this acceptance had continued and broadened to embrace other segments of the community. Perhaps much of the suffering and repression of the twentieth century might have been avoided and the rights of LGBTQ people established earlier. However, the island of tolerance that characterized Boston around 1900 disappeared under waves of repression that began during World War I. As will be seen, the impetus for some of these crackdowns was the US military inserting itself into local affairs, but homophobic elements in Boston initiated their own anti-gay actions as well.

Isabella Gardner's glittering crowd was one of the last prominent circles of gay life in Boston. She spent even more time with LGBTQ people after her husband's death in 1898. She also became determined to build the grand museum she and her husband dreamed about, and the elaborate Fenway Court opened in 1903. That same year she was introduced to Abram Piatt Andrew, Jr. (1873-1936) by Cecelia Beaux (1855-1942), one of the most popular American painters of the era. Beaux was a native of Philadelphia, where she studied art in addition to taking classes in Paris. Her specialty was portraits and her paintings hang in museums from San Francisco to Florence, though her popularity waned over time. Beaux had been the first of a group of lesbians and gay men to move to Eastern Point in Gloucester. Her next door neighbor was Joanna Davidge, the head of a New York school for girls. The next house down belonged to Andrew.

Gardner and Andrew became instant friends and she started spending ample time in Gloucester. Andrew had been recently appointed a Harvard professor, one of the youngest of his time, and had just moved into his Gloucester mansion, Red Roof, a house "honeycombed with secret rooms, hidden passages, bedchamber peepholes and unexpected mirrors."[1] Gardner had invited Sargent to paint at Fenway Court and Sargent was present for Andrew's first visit. Though the two became friends and Sargent would visit Red Roof, Andrew was not impressed by Sargent's physical appearance. "He is very business-like, unaesthetic-looking person—very large and burly—and with a florid face."[2] Andrew had met Beaux because he was a friend of her nephew, who had also been included in the luncheon at Fenway Court that ended up lasting for hours—an extravagance that Gardner rarely granted.

Andrew met Henry Sleeper (1878-1934) in April 1906, perhaps at the home of George Lee–a noted horse breeder, yachtsman, and scion of one of Boston's grand Yankee families. Sleeper came from prominent Boston Methodist stock and his grandfather co-founded Boston University. There is no record of any formal education for Sleeper, though he was intelligent, well-read, slim, and good looking with one biographer calling him a "soft-faced interior decorator with a hatpin wit".[1] Andrew became devoted to him. Sleeper was no social wall flower; within a few years he was one of Gardner's closest intimates and a designer for Joan Crawford and Frederic March.

Andrew hailed from the Midwest and studied at Princeton and eventually Harvard. After academic excursions to Paris and Berlin, he returned to Harvard to earn his doctorate in economics in 1900. Andrew had "an urbane and rambunctious temperament, cuts a wide social swath, entertains prodigiously, and a spectacularly handsome face. The combination is magnetic."[3] Sleeper was smitten.

5.1 A. Piatt Andrew

When they met, Sleeper was living with his widowed mother at 336 Beacon St. He was previously in a relationship with Guy Wetmore Carryl (1873-1904), a promising humorist and author who died from injuries sustained when his "bachelor cottage" in Swampscott caught fire. Sleeper kept at least three photographs of Carryl in his bedroom and Carryl's posthumous last novel had been dedicated to Sleeper. Carryl was first published in the *New York Times* when he was twenty; his most famous line is "It takes two bodies to make one seduction."[3]

Together, Sleeper and Andrew were the hit of Boston high society–on one date they attended the super-haute Myopia Hunt Club Ball at the Somerset Hotel. After more than a year together, their familial relationships became interesting. Sleeper shared the Christmas gift Andrew gave him (a Napoleon medal) with his mother, who was most enamored with it. Yet Andrew spent Christmas in Indiana with his parents. On the other hand, while staying at Red Roof to oversee the construction of his estate, Beauport, Sleeper was a frequent visitor with Andrew's sister's family who lived nearby, and Andrew's niece begged to stay up late to spend time with him. Meanwhile, Andrew's mother sent Sleeper "the loveliest letter of the season" at

Christmas in 1907.[3]

Soon Andrew, Sleeper, and Gardner were tightly orbiting each other. In January 1908, for example, when Gardner was looking for Andrew, she would call Sleeper. Later, when Andrew was in Europe during World War I and he hadn't heard from Sleeper for several weeks, he sent word to Gardner to see if anything was wrong. The three sat with each other at the Majestic Theatre, the entertainment venue of choice for Boston's elite, and Gardner was a frequent visitor to Red Roof. Andrew kept tamed bears in a cage below the window of Gardner's room and she would sit on a leopard skin couch while listening to music. At one party, Andrew dressed as a Roman emperor with Gardner on a couch next to him and on another occasion, he turned down a visit from his parents because Gardner was staying the entire month. Beaux would later write, "We did not consider any party to be of any note without her."[4] A frequent traveler, Andrew was one of Gardner's most prolific correspondents. She referred to him as "A" and he called her "Y". After her first stroke, the visits ended, and Andrew wrote sweet letters to her to remind her of their happy times together. Sleeper and Andrew frequently socialized with the Storrows while Henry James was a repeat house guest at Red Roof. Sleeper and Andrew entertained most of Boston society including Harry Frick and Archbishop (later Cardinal) O'Connell, who told Sleeper that he wished to visit Red Roof again. Sleeper was also a close friend of Ralph Adams Cram and was a pall bearer at Arthur Little's funeral in 1925.

Despite this openness with Gardner and others, Sleeper and Andrew did not dare live together. Instead, Sleeper built the aforementioned estate, Beauport, two doors away from Red Roof. Even though Andrew was the very first person to sign the Beauport guest book and the two were with each other constantly, their official addresses were always separate. Eventually Davidge, Andrew, Beaux, and Sleeper called their collection of summer homes on Eastern Point Dabsville, an acronym derived from their names.

Andrew's career took off. He wrote an influential paper on monetary policy which led to his appointment to the National Monetary Commission and eventually to him becoming the Director of the U.S. Mint and Assistant Secretary of the Treasury. He also found time to co-author the report which led to the establishment of the Federal Reserve Bank. Meanwhile, Sleeper became a noted interior designer with celebrity clients around the country.

Two close friends of Sleeper and Andrew, John "Jack" Hammond (1888-1965) and Leslie Buswell (1888-1964), met at Red Roof in the fall of 1914. They were immediately a couple. "[Buswell] is very fond of Jack–& fascinated by his genius–& J. is intensely spellbound by him," wrote Sleeper to Andrew. With Europe rushing to begin the slaughter of World War I, Sleeper was worried that the English-born Buswell would have to be separated from Hammond if he was called to serve in his homeland's military. Buswell was an actor who eventually gave up his career to manage Hammond's growing business. He lived with Hammond for several years before building his own estate next door and in 1928 he married and fathered a son. Hammond's father was an associate of Cecil Rhodes and very wealthy while Hammond, a noted inventor, went to Yale and then opened a workshop on his Gloucester estate. He married in 1925.

Andrew was politically ambitious, first running for Congress against Augustus Peabody Gardner, Isabella's nephew, who represented the North Shore. He was also the son-in-law of Senator Henry Cabot Lodge and very well regarded; when Andrew ran against him in the Republican primary of 1914, he lost. Frustrated, Andrew went to France just as the war was heating up.

There, Andrew founded the American Ambulance Field Service, the famed volunteer group that included Ernest Hemingway among its members. Under Andrew's leadership, it operated under the supervision of the French army until the United States entered the war and command was transferred to the U.S. army. At great personal risk to its volunteers, the ambulance service saved the lives of thousands of allied servicemen on the Western Front. Its stateside operations, mainly focused on recruiting volunteers among American college students and fundraising support, was overseen by Sleeper with the close assistance of Buswell and Hammond. For his efforts, Andrew was awarded the Croix de Guerre and other honors.

Augustus Gardner held his congressional seat until he resigned in 1917 in order to join the Army. Andrew gained the seat in 1921 and was in office until he died in 1936. Though newspapers mentioned he was a bachelor, there were never any hints about his personal life.

Though Andrew, Sleeper, and some of their friends could still be somewhat out, repression had already gained steam. In the first sign of what was to come, the Watch and Ward Society turned its attention to fighting signs of LGBTQ behavior in the city. In 1908, the Watch and Ward Society had a special hatred of Oscar Wilde, complaining that "the advent of [Wilde's] *Salome* has been the debauching agent. It has meant the introduction of a new element of indecency on the stage—the uncovered feet and limbs—and has created a vogue of risqué dances which have tended to deprave public taste." They would not mention Wilde by name but said rather that "[f] or seventeen years this dance has gone over this country as vaudeville and side-show to a circus, but now it has risen from its contempt to grand opera with the libretto of a lecher who was imprisoned for his vileness."[5] The city was growing intolerant and soon there would be a series of crackdowns on Boston's LGBTQ people.

During the first two thirds of the twentieth century, when the rest of the United States was convulsed by homophobia and anti-trans bigotry, Provincetown was a sanctuary for LGBTQ people. The Separatists were correct in their assessment of Provincetown's unsuitability for settlement as it was periodically occupied and abandoned until the end of the seventeenth century. It was revived by fishing and for almost a century, it boomed.

LGBTQ people have been a prominent part of Provincetown since at least

1915 and most likely were a significant part of the population well before that time. Up to World War I, there was no popular gay resort in the region. Some, including the Dabsville group, preferred Gloucester while Meteyard and others summered south of the city. The war changed this by making Provincetown the preeminent summer place for LGBTQ people. Prior to the war, Provincetown was an isolated backwater. It was a small fishing village, but that industry was in decline as the twentieth century began. At the same time, Provincetown was transitioning from being predominately Yankee to Portuguese families holding the most influence. The town was also becoming known for its art schools, with thousands of students flocking to paint and draw in the open air—perhaps indicating that LGBTQ people were already tourists there.

Even as Portuguese men took over the fishing industry, Portuguese women began to manage the non-fishing commerce in the town. In addition to staffing its stores and restaurants, many women rented out spare rooms to tourists, including growing numbers of LGBTQ people. LGBTQ visitors were welcome into these homes because owners needed the income, and in some respects, it was less scandalous to rent to them than to heterosexuals and aggressively gender conforming people. In return, the visitors liked their hosts. The landlords were kind and accepting enough that boarders became socially integrated into the fabric of everyday living. "If the accommodations suited them, the 'gay guys' and 'girls' (also known at the time as 'confirmed bachelors' and 'maiden ladies'), who hailed mostly from the Northeast but also from Canada and Europe, often returned annually to the same boarding home."[6]

The catalyst for the transformation of Provincetown from declining fishing village to ostentatious LGBTQ resort was the privations associated with World War I. The American artists and writers who regularly visited or lived for extended periods in France, Italy, and England found the Atlantic crossing too dangerous and the rigors of wartime life in Europe too great. As an alternative, one woman who was connected to the Greenwich Village set that was the American arm of this expatriate group, Mary Heaton Vorse, told everyone she met to spend the summer of 1915 in Provincetown. Cape Cod would never be the same.

A journalist, Vorse first came to Provincetown in 1907 seeking space to write and raise a family. By 1912, her home was a center for left wing writers and activists, with famed author Sinclair Lewis and others stopping at 466 Commercial St. whenever they needed a place to rest or work without interruption. Vorse went to Lawrence later that year to cover the great Bread and Roses strike and then returned to Provincetown to write about it. Seeking investment property, Vorse purchased an old fishing pier, Lewis Wharf (571 Commercial St.), and leased part of it to an art school. In 1914 she briefly went to Europe to cover the war only to return shaken by its deadly brutality.

Her friends came in droves and invited others. There were so many Greenwich Village people in Provincetown in the summer of 1915 that two popular Village restaurants, Polly's (at 484 Commercial St.) and Christine's (at 264A Bradford St.), opened branches in Provincetown's East End. Provincetown was officially dry but unsurprisingly this didn't stop anyone from drinking. There were illegal stills in Truro while Boston stores made regular deliveries to cape residents. In addition, many prominent men were members of a key club that was always well stocked with liquor and the Greenwich Village crowd regularly drank themselves into oblivion after they put their children to bed. Seeking to entertain themselves, the crowd created the famous Provincetown Players, an amateur group of artists, writers, and hangers on who produced plays at Vorse's wharf.

George Cram Cook, Susan Glasspell, and the rest of the founders of the Provincetown Players were far from conventional. The women shunned the corsets and the modest fashions of the day for loose fitting, more revealing wardrobes while the men liked open flannel shirts and corduroy pants. Both sexes were wild about purple, mauve and other similar colors. Their behavior was even more avant-garde; the women smoked and drank, Jig Cook was twice divorced before marrying Susan Glasspell, John Reed was carrying on with Mabel Dodge without bothering with matrimony, and Harry Kemp was trying to seduce all the married women he could with perhaps his most famous conquest being Meta Fuller, Upton Sinclair's wife. Kemp figured prominently in their divorce. "Everyone, it seemed, had a roving eye–Louise for Gene; Mabel for Jack; Hutch for Lucy; Mary for Don; and Jig for all the women."[7]

Reed was already an acclaimed journalist when he first went to Provincetown to write a book on the Mexican civil war between covering a violent strike in Ludlow, Colorado and the opening of war in Europe. The group included the gay but closeted Marsden Hartley who had exhibited at the great Armory Show in 1913 and had been in Paris with Gertrude Stein. While in Europe, he met Charles DeMuth (who spent the summer of 1914 in Provincetown) and back in the United States, the two spread the word in New York that Provincetown was a wide-open place for gay men–additional evidence that Provincetown had a substantial LGBTQ population before 1915.

Vorse's wharf was grandly christened the Provincetown Playhouse. The theater featured seats that were little more than rough wooden benches, the stage was lit by volunteers with lanterns, the sea lapped at the pilings, and the old building barely kept out the elements. But the room, which could seat about 100 people, was full when the curtain went up on the first play performed there. Provincetown had a critical mass of people, many of whom were LGBTQ, that turned out for the event despite the pouring rain on premier night. "People had leaned their umbrellas against one of the big timbers which supported the roof. I noticed an umbrella stirred, then slowly slid down an enormous knothole to the sand thirty feet below. With the stealth of eels, other umbrellas went down the knothole to join their fellows under the wharf."[8] LGBTQ people helped produce the plays and they filled the audience. Hartley and DeMuth had a grand time, with Demuth appearing in the production of *Change Your Style* while Hartley threw himself into creating lavish costumes for the town's many parties.

The next summer, Cook envisioned a more ambitious season and soon the group produced the debut play of a young man named Eugene O'Neill, *Bound East for*

Cardiff. O'Neill was unknown, but the group liked what they heard when they read his work in Cook and Glasspell's living room. O'Neill had come up to New England to attend a play writing class at Harvard but dropped out. He then met Reed and others who convinced him to come to Provincetown.

The party was just getting going. By the summer of 1916, there were twenty illegal "kill-em-quick" liquor dealers and up to 2,000 sailors on leave and visiting Commercial St. at any given time as the Navy anchored many ships just offshore. The streets were filled with brawling sailors and those trying to take advantage of them as the combination of alcohol and easy sex attracted even more visitors. Every summer day, the ferry *Dorothy Bradford* from Boston discharged 1,650 passengers while thousands more drove into town or arrived via the railroad. There were minstrel shows, costume balls, and drunken dances at town hall. The Playhouse added to the excitement.

In 1916, Hartley moved in with Bryant and Reed, the couple wasn't married but acted like they were. Reed was frustrated with his house guest, saying "He doesn't contribute anything intellectually and I don't really like him, but how can we move him out without offending him?"[8] Hartley says that he and Demuth went out at night to pick up tricks in "tiger-like stalking." During the day, Demuth went to the beach with O'Neill, who used Demuth and Hartley as the basis for a character in his play, *Strange Interlude*.

There were also many lesbians in Provincetown. Maud Squire and Ethel Mars were friends of Gertrude Stein, who used the couple as models for her poem, "Miss Furr and Miss Skeene." The couple were just modest Midwesterners when they first went to Paris in 1906. But soon "they colored their hair in flaming colors and wore heavy makeup."[7,8] They did not tone down their appearance in Provincetown where they showed up at bars, parties, plays, and openings.

Provincetown was also home to a group of lesbian artists, the most well-known today being Blanche Lazzell (1878-1956). In contrast to the conservative bohemians in Boston, these women were closely connected to the growing modern art movement in Paris and New York. Eventually becoming a full-time resident of the town, Lazzell took the excitement of cubism and abstraction she found in Europe to help develop what was one of Provincetown's most famous contributions to art history: the white line print. Lazzell and her friends were supporters of the Provincetown Theatre and as well as the town's many galleries.

During the war, Eugene O'Neill lived at the A House, as did the detective assigned to read his mail after O'Neill was suspected of spying for the Germans—it was a time when just walking through the dunes could lead to an arrest for espionage. The detective would brief O'Neill on his mail over breakfast "You got a letter from your mother, Gene, but your girl's forgot you today."[8] O'Neill would often return to Provincetown over the next several decades.

The crackdowns that marked the end of Boston's golden age began in military facilities during World War I. The United States' mobilization for war brought tremendous changes. It also exposed many LGBTQ people to arrest and harassment with a major crackdown on military and civilian gay men and same-sex activity at nearby Newport, Rhode Island with investigations reaching into Boston itself. A complaint about openly gay men at a naval hospital led to a largescale investigation. As a result, there was a court of inquiry followed by arrests and a series of court marshals against navy personnel identified (details of which are discussed below) as having participated in gay sex acts. Then navy prosecutors went after a civilian clergyman, prompting an uproar in the Rhode Island press. This led to yet another court of inquiry, this one focused on the actions of the investigators. The entire affair lasted several years.

After the United States entered World War I, the naval presence at Newport expanded and by the summer of 1918 there were 13,000 men stationed there. With the barracks unable to house them all, Newport underwent drastic change. Many of its old mansions were converted to boarding houses and as more military personnel flooded into the small city, sailors were housed in private homes. Thousands passed through the Army and Navy YMCA while streets were full of young men, many away from home for the first time, looking for excitement. Before, during, and after the war, there were calls to rid Newport of alcohol, prostitution, and homosexuality as all represented "threats" to the general public and national security. Yet Newport did little to crack down on its ribald ways and the Navy did not trust the local police and prosecutors to help keep the city in line.

If Ervin Arnold, a chief machinist mate from San Francisco, had not been assigned to Newport's naval hospital, the homosexual activity in the city might have continued unreported and unhindered. Rabidly anti-gay and a veteran prosecutor, Arnold boasted he could spot the most closeted gay man. He was repulsed and angered by the behaviors he observed in the Newport hospital: men calling each other by women's names, wearing makeup, displaying effeminate behaviors, and talking about the great deal of gay sex in the city.[9] It was the special vulnerability of LGBTQ people at the time that a single man could wreck so much havoc.

Arnold met a sailor, Samuel G. Rogers, 23, who was in the hospital suffering from bronchitis. Rogers possessed powder puffs and make up and shaved his arm pits. Encouraged by Arnold to speak boldly, Rogers told him stories about his ability to satisfy men with large penises and the gay nightlife in Newport. Rogers declined deceptive offers to visit New York City or Boston with Arnold and did not invite him to participate in same-sex relations.

Arnold next met a sailor named Thomas Roland Brunelle, who also spent hours telling him about the sexual practices of his many gay friends, their drag nicknames, and where they lived, met men, and had sex. His stories included how the YMCA was the center of the gay scene in Newport, how men picked each other up for sex or paid for sex there, and how sailors could get their hands on alcohol or cocaine. Brunelle also boasted that he had a "wife," another sailor with whom he regularly had sex.

Arnold took the stories he heard to the hospital welfare officer, Dr. Erastus Hudson, and base commander Edward Campbell as he pushed for arrests. Agreeing that the presence of homosexuals in Newport was an abomination and a threat to national security, Campbell convinced his superiors in Washington to launch a large-scale investigation that eventually involved secret offices, undercover investigators, and special tribunals.

The undercover operation, working out of donated office space, recruited a group of good-looking sailors, mostly in their teens and early twenties. Seven men were given the task of soliciting sex with others providing logistical support. The investigators quickly found evidence of the extensive gay underground in the city. These zealous young men became friends and often went to bed with suspects, but actual sex was not necessary for men to be prosecuted. One seventeen-year-old sailor, for example, was arrested based on evidence that he had a flushed face, had been observed going upstairs at the YMCA with another man after talking with him briefly, and had a reputation for participating in sex with other men.

The operatives were never ordered to have sex. They were to use their own judgement regarding how best to collect evidence, but several reported they did have sex with the accused. Thus, the investigation quickly posed several moral, legal, and logistical issues that would ultimately reflect negatively on the Navy: how far should deputized sailors go during sex with potential suspects? Could they also be charged if they had same-sex conduct? Was the Navy paying men to engage in homosexual conduct? As the investigation progressed, the Navy hierarchy encouraged greater participation by the operatives which created problems for them later.

The investigation confirmed that the center of gay activity was the YMCA. Men met in the first-floor dining facilities and club house and went upstairs to rented rooms or elsewhere for sex. Some men were paid for sex, others offered it for free, and often there was alcohol or cocaine involved–both prohibited to naval personnel. There were also off-base parties where many drank or danced together with some men dressed in drag.

The scandal in Newport revealed several features of gay life and society in this era. It showed there was a group of men who defied conventional masculine gender roles and who were sometimes openly effeminate, even more so when in private or with other gay service members. Many were part-time drag queens or dressed in women's clothes on occasion. Those who were not completely obeying gender norms were most at risk for arrest. In addition to this core of gender non-conforming individuals was a much larger group of men who obeyed contemporary norms as to masculine behavior and appearance. At first glance, evidence seems to indicate that these men only performed the penetrative role in sexual relations, but later testimony suggested that these men enjoyed a wide variety of sexual activities. This group also ranged from men who were closely and almost exclusively involved with the core group to those who possibly only participated in same-sex relations once or very infrequently. There were also class distinctions. Until the Navy went after civilians, all the men caught up in the scandal were working class: cooks, low-level recruits, and so forth. Officers, wealthy or middle-class men, or men with college educations were initially exempt.[10] It was only when the operatives penetrated deep into the gay subculture of the city and began to ensnare men who were masculine in appearance that the large numbers of men involved in Newport's gay subculture became clear.[11]

The men who most transgressed traditional gender roles had categories to identify themselves: fairies, pogues, browns, and so forth. The names helped men form group identities that were distinctly separate from mainstream society. However, men who were traditionally masculine seemed to defy categorization to both those inside the core group and those outside investigating it and even within the group there were those who explored multiple roles and identities.

For the most part, the sailors caught up in the investigation were extremely cautious in their dealings with men they did not know, and operatives had to interact with suspects multiple times before they found evidence. There was a uniformity of behavior among the accused in the reports. First encounters were often guarded. Then as suspects got to know the operatives better, there was a gradual sharing of information. Actual explicit sex talk did not usually begin until people were somewhere private and it could still take additional meetings before operatives were propositioned. Encounters in cruising areas were similarly scaled. The first words were usually asking for a cigarette or a light and only after talking for some time was a sex act proposed.

Some of the accused had simply been boasting of exaggerated sexual histories, which the operatives recorded in great detail to use in court against them. Some of the stories collected appear ludicrous, such as a report that one man was naked and bent over a gravestone in a cemetery for hours to receive rough sex–in the middle of winter. Another story involved a man dressed up as a woman who spent hours dancing and yet still found time to have sex with eight different men that night.

The military inquest began in early April 1918 and five men were quickly jailed, followed by another round of arrests. After weeks of testimony, two men were released, two were ordered to be discharged, and seventeen were ordered to stand trial for sodomy and scandalous activity. Then nothing happened until August 21st, when two more were discharged and the rest recommended for court marshaling. At that point two more men were discharged while another two deserted and were never found.

At first during the trials, the Navy acted on the assumption that "what you did determined what sort of person you were" with many of the accused believing this as well. The operatives repeatedly testified that they received oral sex from the suspects, but always denied initiating it, giving it, or having anal sex.[12] This led to objections by the accused that both parties in a sex act were equally guilty of a crime under the Navy code of justice and that both were equally suspect of being gay. This changed the attitudes of the operatives. At first, the operatives seemed to believe that their orders and the fact that they were not the ones giving oral sex protected them from prosecution or any hint that they themselves might be gay. However, as they listened to the authorities connect any same-sex behavior with the moral horror of being gay, they became increasingly defensive and many claimed they had been unable to sustain erections. Some began to invoke the Fifth Amendment when cross examined.

As the scrutiny on the operatives increased, the distinction between categories blurred; who was gay and who was straight? What was the difference in guilt between the accused and their accusers? For the most part, the operatives tried to say that the suspects maintained strict sex roles, but sometimes their testimony suggested that most men had a variety of preferred practices and would accommodate the tastes and limits of the men they were with. Thus, one accused, David "Beckie" Goldstein, a ship's cook, first wanted to anally penetrate the operator trying to gather evidence against him and when that was refused, suggested the opposite. Another accused said he had never associated with effeminate men until after a sailor (who was also a fairy and noted female impersonator) drugged and performed anal sex on him. At least one man claimed he was now straight since it had been eight months since he had received anal sex.

The prosecutions were sustained by the bias of the man who was simultaneously the head of the inquiry, the judge in the court marshals, and the legal representative of the accused unless they had their own lawyer. In the middle of this major conflict of interest, he tried to protect the operatives but could not overcome the logic of those who were trying to save themselves from prison and dishonorable discharge. Of those court marshalled, five men were found innocent or convicted of lesser crimes and released with time served. Seven were convicted of various crimes, some involving sex only, some drugs only, and were given sentences up to twenty years. The longest time any sailor actually served was seven years.

The trials might have been forgotten except that the Navy, obsessed with stamping out homosexuality, decided to target civilians. However, civilians were beyond the reach of military justice and would need to be prosecuted in state or federal courts. But the people in charge of the investigation thought the city was corrupt and could not be trusted to investigate vice while state agents would be too easily identified. Thus, the Navy decided to use the Office of Naval Intelligence to run the expanded investigation. Though initially charged with collecting foreign information, the federal government gave the office domestic spying authority during the war. On May 5, 1919, Secretary of the Navy Franklin Delano Roosevelt signed orders for an investigation of immorality and drugs in and around Newport.

There was resistance inside the Navy to conducting this kind of investigation, prompting the hiring of a private company to assist the task force. Arnold and the other anti-gay personnel complained about this arrangement and so the investigation was made to report directly to Roosevelt. The new investigation was run out of New York with a local office in Fall River.

A wave of civilian arrests spread across Newport and the surrounding area in late July 1919, with the most prominent man arrested being Samuel Kent. Born into a poor family in Lynn in 1873, he went to the Boston Latin School and then became a successful businessman before being called to the ministry at the age of thirty-five. Kent attended the Episcopal Theological School in Cambridge where he achieved notice for his successful outreach to young men and boys. After the United States entered the First World War, Kent's ability to minister to young men was extremely valuable and he worked at a series of army forts in and around Newport until the influenza epidemic of 1918 resulted in his being stationed at the naval hospital. Kent's standing made him the prime target of the investigation and charges were brought against him in state court for immorality because the Navy did not have the legal authority to try him.

The evidence was weak. The defense claimed entrapment and that many of the reported events and acts didn't happen. There were alibis for several of the times the operatives claimed Kent initiated sexual contacts. When at last challenged by experienced lawyers, the operatives proved to be bad witnesses, flustered and defensive on the witness stand. Kent was acquitted.

To make matters more uncomfortable for the Navy, Kent's trial attracted intense public attention. Most were sympathetic to the minister and many were disgusted by the actions of the operatives and thought them to be morally worse than the accused servicemen. For the most part, Kent's fellow clergy rallied behind him. This was not a defense of homosexuality; most simply believed he was innocent.

Stung by the civilian opposition, the Navy shut down the investigations but was determined to retry Kent. Some of the Navy prosecutors went to see Kent's supervising bishop to persuade him to support a new indictment. Instead the bishop felt the Navy was attacking the reputation of the church and he complained directly to Roosevelt. The Navy Secretary politely listened to the complaints but did nothing to stop the investigation. As knowledge of the charges against Kent became more widely known among the Navy hierarchy, the staff became more convinced of Kent's guilt and the need for a new trial. The Justice Department also became involved because federal civilian law made it a crime to promote immoral acts within ten miles of a military base. The law was primarily aimed at prostitution but was vague enough to include homosexuality. Kent was charged with seven violations of this law.

By now, Kent had been assigned to a parish in Pennsylvania. A new warrant for Kent's arrest was issued on October 19, 1919, and the Navy began an extensive manhunt that included wiretapping, intercepting mail, lying to Kent's mother, and threatening suspected protectors of Kent. Yet the Navy couldn't find him. Finally locating him at a sanitarium in Battle Creek, Michigan, the Navy arrested him and brought him back to Newport where he went on trial a second time, now in federal court, on January 5, 1920. The trial took several days during which the operatives proved even more unreliable regarding what they did, when they did it, and the nature of their orders. The jury took a mere three hours to acquit Kent of all charges.

The *Providence Journal* turned the investigations into a national scandal by denouncing both the Navy's tactics and Roosevelt himself in a thunderous editorial. The piece prompted an investigation into the actions of the operatives and the entire crackdown but was stymied when the operatives refused to cooperate. Now on the defensive and being abandoned by their superiors, the operatives tried to justify their actions, but saw that they were now vulnerable to arrest. When questioned by this later court of inquiry, a large number of the operatives pleaded the Fifth Amendment and refused to answer.[13]

Complaints about the investigation led to a committee of Congress looking into the matter. At the same time, a judge ruled that since there could be no legal order that could compel the young men to engage in gay sex, anything they said could be used as evidence against them. After that point, the operatives refused to give further testimony. As a result, the inquiries ended without any results. The convicted were eventually released, dishonorably discharged, and lost to history while the operatives returned to civilian life and became anonymous. Though the Republicans tried to use the whole affair to discredit Roosevelt, it was a non-issue when he ran for president in 1932.

ELEANOR SEARS 3821-5

5.2 Eleanora Sears

At the same time the Navy trials carried on, a glamorous lesbian heiress from Boston was winning tennis tournaments in Newport. Perhaps the last public lesbian of the early twentieth century, Eleanora Sears (1881-1968) "was glorious—tall and confident in the saddle, her face bronzed by the sun."[14] The Sears were old time Yankees. Her grandfather had built one of the grandest mansions on Beacon St. facing the Common and her parents were married in Trinity Church.

In 1892, Sears' grandfather was appointed minister to France and her mother took her children to Paris for a year to assist him with his social duties. Sears' grandfather was also a cousin by marriage to the Gardners. When they visited Paris to collect art, he entertained them while Sears' mother's best friend was Gretchen Osgood Warren. At one point Warren enlisted Sears' mother help to plan a surprise party for Gardner. Sears' grandfather owned Sargent's famed painting, El Jaleel, which Gardner desperately wanted to buy and a distant relative, Willard T. Sears, was the architect of Fenway Court.

Sears' father is one of many who claimed to be the first to play tennis in the United States and her uncles were early champions. High-society women in Boston were encouraged to be athletic as it was thought to be healthy, but competition was frowned upon because it might lead to mannish behavior. Sears began to attack these conventions and by 1903 she was the top female tennis player on the east coast. Yet she was still careful not to challenge modesty: her athletic uniform included a skirt that went down nearly to her ankles and a special hat she called her granny veil.

As an athletic and attractive young woman, Sears garnered much interest from prominent young Boston men and their sisters. Some thought she would marry a Vanderbilt, others a Lee. A young Ethel Barrymore recalled how robust Sears was, and another young woman wrote in her diary that she "nearly swooned with pleasure" when Sears noticed her. Being wealthy and good looking had its privileges as Sears "shocked propriety by striding along Beacon Street in riding breaches and by turning up, on a dare, on the stage of the Majestic as a matinee extra."[1]

Sears may have avoided marriage, but she was also adventurous. She was one of the first women to drive a car, ventured into a submarine under the Pacific, and enjoyed life with a ferocity that thrilled some and scandalized others. Sears spent more than a decade in a public relationship with the handsome and very rich Mike Vanderbilt and there was constant speculation that the two were on the verge of announcing their engagement. They never did, and he married someone else in 1933.

Sears was always on the safe edge of respectability regarding her wardrobe, wearing men's clothes to sporting events during the day and elegant gowns to social events at night. She managed to keep her reputation intact through the twenties and Sears shrewdly used her public but trivial frolics with men, mostly Harvard graduates, to keep gossip at bay. A public exposure would have ruined her, and so she kept intense relationships with women private. But this did not keep her from several passionate affairs with women.

As she grew older, Boston society became more conservative. Her affair with choreographer George Balanchine's young second wife, Vera Zorina, scandalized many. The prominent actress first caught Sear's attention when she appeared in a play on the Boston stage in 1938. By 1940, the two women were driving twin automobiles and seen together as much as Sears dared. When Zorina was abruptly replaced on the set of *For Whom the Bell Tolls* by Ingrid Bergman, she rushed to find solace from Sears rather than her husband. Still, both denied the affair: "she never even touched my hand'" protested Zorina.[14] Many acquaintances began to pull away despite her protests.

In her last decades, Sears began a relationship with Marie Gendron, her housekeeper who eventually isolated Sears and took over her personal affairs. Longtime friends were frightened and appalled.[14] After Sears died, several institutions that were slated to receive bequests from her estate sued Gendron.

World War I also resulted in the first systematic crackdown on gay men in Boston's history. Prompted by demands from the War Department to eliminate prostitution, the Boston police, assisted by the Watch and Ward Society, launched a series of raids across the city in 1918, with 188 people arrested between June 12th and 22nd. The arrests were not for morality or sex crimes which were time consuming to prove. Instead, those taken into custody faced charges of idle and disorderly conduct, which were much easier to prosecute as there was no need to collect or provide evidence to the courts. At first, the raids only focused on women and over the first two nights, police arrested seventy-four women.

That changed beginning on June 14th, when police began arresting men as well. Many such men were suspected of being pimps or relying on the proceeds of prostitution, but arrest accounts include indications that police began targeting gay men. For example, "These men were found acting in a decidedly effeminate manner," wrote the *Boston Globe*. They had powder puffs, eye liner pencils, and vanity cases; many smelled of perfume. "According to the police officers, some of them wore women's underclothing—silk underwear and long garters, and one had on a pair of corsets. Some confusion arose from the fact that they called each other by women's names. Two were 'Alberta'; one 'Ruth'; another 'Florence Hindley.'"[15] Another paper noted, "There are men who habitually take their stand on street corners and in groups in the parks."[16] These press reports suggest that the police concentrated on men who were nonconforming to standard gender norms.

The geographic scope of the arrests of men helps delineate the boundaries of LGBTQ Boston at the time. Of the forty-six men arrested in the sweeps, the locations of forty arrests were reported. Of these, twenty-one men were arrested in and around the Court St./City Hall station (which included Scollay Square, then the prime gay entertainment area). Another six or so men were arrested in and around the East Dedham St. Station that covered the South End and the Dover St. vice district, suggesting that some gay men were also frequenting establishments in that area. In contrast, women were much more geographically dispersed with the Joy St. and Hanover St. stations having the most arrests. The raids reportedly extended to private homes in Back Bay though the arrest accounts do not confirm this. In any case, as fear gripped the gay community, bars emptied out and many streets saw vast decreases in foot traffic. Triumphant, the police proclaimed the streets were now free of male perverts.

As they were arrested each night, physicians examined the men, who then had to appear before a magistrate the next morning where they were presumed guilty. A judge told two defendants, for example, "Your speech and actions are almost enough to convict you without any testimony."[17] Most were immediately sentenced to jail after which some defendants appealed.

Many of the men were fined, put on probation, and released. Those who were "unemployed," presumably pimps, had their cases dismissed if they proved they had found employment. At least four men were sent to the House of Corrections.

Though these arrests were for disorderly conduct, Boston also recorded the largest number of arrests for same-sex related crimes (lewd and lascivious behavior and sodomy) in the history of the city up to that time, with twenty-seven total arrests in 1918 (including one woman). The average for the period from 1906 to 1917 had been just 15.6 total arrests per year. There would be a legacy from this crackdown. The number of arrests would never fall back to pre-1918 levels and in the years from 1919–30 there would be an average of fifty-six arrests per year. Then during the Great Depression, the number of arrests would increase again. The 1918 crackdown represents the beginning of fifty years of repression.

In another 1918 action that was likely related to the Newport investigation, the Boston police raided a private home at 105 Revere St., located at the foot of Beacon Hill at the corner of Charles St. Again, it was the Navy that prompted the arrests. The military was obsessed with stamping out homosexual behavior; altogether, the Navy spent over a thousand dollars (the equivalent of over $16,000 in 2018) on an investigation that ranged from Newport to Ipswich and included hiring Pinkerton detectives. One of the Navy investigators had been a Boston policeman and had been assigned to be a full-time investigator of prostitution and immorality.

It is not known how the home was first identified but once it became a target, the undercover investigators tried to visit several times but were put off by its owner, Lee Porter. Finally, on the night of October 20th he invited them over, saying he had some friends who would take them out for a drive and show them a very good time.

The investigators testified that they heard civilians were picking up sailors and taking them to the house while others stopped by to meet sailors. A friend, Charles DeMoulin, provided much of the testimony against Porter. DeMoulin had pleaded guilty to an attempt to commit an unnatural act (oral sex) with a sailor he had met on Tremont St. near the Keith Theatre, for which he had paid a $500 fine. After talking with the sailor, who was from New Orleans and stationed at the Charlestown Navy Yard, DeMoulin had telephoned Porter to say he was coming over with him. Arriving, the pair went upstairs to "look at the plaques" where DeMoulin attempted to have sex with the sailor. When the couple arrived, the detectives, dressed as sailors, were sitting in the first-floor parlor.

The parlor conversation indicates that there was already political consciousness and solidarity among gay men in Boston, fifty years before the Stonewall uprising. Porter was angry, referring to a clipping of a newspaper article about two men who had been arrested for having sex in a lodging house. He thought it wrong that lower income men had been targeted while those who could afford hotel rooms were left alone. Midway through the discussion, Porter received DeMoulin's phone call. Meanwhile, two civilians showed up and one said, "My, what a sick girl I am. I have just been over to the doctor, I guess I am going to have kittens."[18] That man and Porter hugged each other several times and held hands a lot. Then Porter took the investigators on a tour of the house and at some point, Porter put his hands on one of the men's pants. The men all went upstairs, and Porter tried to initiate sex, but the investigators kept pushing him away.

Porter's house had been the scene of frequent gay activity. A witness testified he had brought several men to Revere St. There were also stories about a drag party at the house earlier that fall where the men wore silk kimonos and at one point, they held a ceremony with candles to curse the police for harassing gay people–another example of political consciousness but also evidence of homosexuality that the prosecutors used to prove Porter's guilt.

Porter's defense regarding the kimonos was that he was in the antiques business and collected theatre costumes. Born in 1872, the Revere St. house was his in-town residence; his main domicile was in Auburndale and he summered in Maine. He had gone to Harvard and MIT and was an interior furnishings and antique dealer. Other evidence submitted to the court included testimony that Porter had lived with a pianist for eleven years–turn of the century men were capable of long term relationships–and the investigators reported that the men used the terms fairies and queer to describe themselves.[18] One witness told the court that Porter had been to the Golden Rooster, a popular gay bar.

There were two trials. In the first, Porter was accused of sodomy but found not guilty. The authorities tried him again, this time charging him with running a house of ill repute. Found guilty and sentenced to a year at Deer Island, Porter appealed, saying that the second charge made no sense since he had been found not guilty at the first trial and that trying him again represented double jeopardy, but the courts upheld his conviction. By 1922, Porter was living in Europe and further information on him was not available.

A final wave of repression was aimed at stamping out homosexual activity at Harvard in 1920. After the war as Harvard filled with returning servicemen eager to finish their educations, some gay men would be caught up in another witch hunt. Again, this was initiated by one man, in this case a recent graduate distraught over the suicide of his younger brother. Again, once the complaint was heard by the authorities, gay men were vulnerable because those in power were motivated by bigotry.

Harvard had a robust gay scene. There was "a more or less distinct group who were fond of dim lights, patchouli, purple pajamas, and exotic liqueurs, including a few who were not, or who imagined they were not, heterosexual."[19] The group included Cyril Wilcox, who had been on academic probation and had spent the summer after his freshman year taking supplemental course work to avoid suspension. His sophomore year was little better, and the consensus of the faculty was that he was intelligent but didn't like to study. He was warned that if he didn't do well on his April exams, his Harvard career would be over. But Wilcox came down with a bad case of hives the morning of his first exam and as the rash faded, he had a panic attack. Unable to take any tests, officials allowed him to withdraw from Harvard due to ill health.

Back at his parents' house in Fall River, he continued to have emotional problems even as he wrote letters to Harvard begging to be reinstated. Then on the morning of May 13th, his mother smelled gas and when she opened her son's bedroom door, she discovered him dead. Wilcox was twenty-one. Officially, the cause was an accident. Illuminating gas was notoriously unsafe and prone to leaks that asphyxiated victims. But Wilcox's family and friends knew he had committed suicide.

Shortly before he died, Cyril had told his older brother, George, class of 1914, that he was gay and having a relationship with Harry Dreyfus, an older man living on Beacon Hill. George found a letter to Cyril, written a day before his death and which arrived right after his suicide. In it, Ernest Weeks Roberts described detailed gossip about their gay friends. Kenneth Day, for example, was "being sucked foolish by anyone and everybody he can lay hands on."[20] Roberts confessed he had been one of those who had sex with Day and he told Cyril that there had been lots of parties and good times.

Then another letter, from Harold Saxton, a recent graduate, arrived at the house. This letter referred to Cyril as "Salome's child" and "Dot." It also talked about a series of raids on gay bars, including the Golden Rooster and the Cage, though the details of this crackdown were not provided.[21] These may have been related to Prohibition or part of yet another anti-LGBTQ crackdown. Saxton also gossiped about several students who had been to a drag party at the Boston Yacht Club. He also went to Café Dreyfus, owned by Cyril's lover. During this era, saloons were often called cafes, particularly if they were unlicensed.

George exploded and traveled to Boston where he beat up Dreyfus and forced him to reveal the names of several of Cyril's gay friends. George took this information to Harvard Acting Dean Chester Greenough and demanded justice for his brother's death. Greenough consulted with Harvard President A. Lawrence Lowell (Amy's brother) and on Lowell's authority, quickly convened a five-man secret court to gather evidence and decide the fate of all the gay men at Harvard they could identify.

It was a secret tribunal; the university wanted no public acknowledgment of homosexuality at Harvard and no public record of their actions. At first the tribunal was stymied. Of the names they had, one (Cyril) was dead; one had graduated; and two had no Harvard affiliation. Roberts was still at Harvard and as he was the son of a popular former Congressman, the tribunal had to be certain of his guilt. His letter to Cyril sealed his fate.

The court asked the proctor of Roberts' building to compile a list of students and other men seen in Roberts' room. It examined the list and for reasons unknown, immediately removed several students. Then an anonymous letter arrived from someone who had close knowledge of Cyril's social life. The letter blamed Roberts for Cyril's suicide and described parties in his room that included sailors, men picked up on the streets of Boston, and men dressed in women's clothes. The parties included "the most disgusting and disgraceful and revolting acts of degeneracy and depravity took place openly in plain veiw [sic] of all present."[20]

Meanwhile, the proctor had placed Roberts and his room, 28 Perkins Hall, under surveillance, secretly recording visitors and phone calls. Even though the parties in the room were loud and drew lots of visitors, the proctor only gave names that were already suspect, suggesting he tried to protect those students he could. Though he couldn't identify most of the visitors, he reported that more than fifty students attended the various parties there. Furthermore, the events varied greatly and included between eight and twenty guests. Some parties were nothing more than a few students playing cards, drinking, or listening to music. Others were black tie affairs with some men in drag. Sometimes the parties included outsiders from Boston and many ended in sex. The court summoned students in for questioning.

Aware of the investigations, a group of students met and decided they would give complete and accurate testimony, a grave mistake as only students who confessed would be permanently expelled. For example, one student at least, did not realize that even though he told the court he had only taken the active role in sex, this still marked him as gay in the eyes of the tribunal. Kenneth Day had believed that since he had limited his sexual contact, he would be perceived as straight and thus he spoke freely about the sex he had had with men. The Harvard authorities, however, did not share this belief and instead acted on the premise that any male-male sexual contact was evidence a man was gay.[22] The men were always referred to as "perverts" by the court though the men themselves referred to each other as faggots and queer.

The Harvard students had their own ideas of what were signs of homosexuality. These included non-athletic bodies, a lack of muscles, and very youthful appearance. Some shaved their bodies, shaped their eyebrows, bleached their hair blond, attended class in makeup, and wore bright red ties. One student, Edward Say, wore rouge to class while others wore loud suits. The décor of the gay students' room was also suspect. Roberts' room had parrots, goldfish and flowers; others had suspect books such as those written by Freud and Havelock Ellis.

The testimony showed that the goal of attending these gatherings was friendship and support as well as sex. Many Harvard students became acquainted with gay life by attending the Perkins parties, where they first danced with another male or engaged in their first same-sex kiss, or by excursions with others into Boston. The Roberts group was not the only gay clique. There were also other clubs and venues that allowed gay men to find each other, especially the drama club and Sigma Alpha Epsilon fraternity.[22]

Kenneth Day had been Cyril Wilcox's freshman roommate. Day's parents died when he was a child and relatives were paying for him to attend Harvard. Up to this point, he had been a popular and successful student. A boxer and a track enthusiast, he had joined the Sigma Alpha Epsilon fraternity. For a while, Day and Wilcox did not get along. They stopped speaking to each other for several weeks before becoming friends again, shaking hands and attending church together.

In the court's opinion, the evidence against Day was damning. There was the Roberts letter about his sexual activities, the anonymous letter that placed him at the parties in Roberts' room, and he was on the proctor's list. Called before the court as its first witness, Day at first denied any involvement with other gay men or that he was gay himself. Under further questioning, however, he admitted to participating in a homosexual act with two different men. In his defense, he said the only time he had done it this past year was when he was drunk. He also claimed he had not masturbated in seven years (every student who came before the court was questioned about his masturbation habits). Day also implicated other students including several already under suspicion: Harold Saxton, Edward Say, Ned Courtney, Harold Hussey, and Eugene Cummings as well as giving up a new name, Nathaniel Wolff.

The court summoned Roberts to appear. Up to this point, Roberts had successfully lived a double life, romancing a young woman from Brookline as well as having several relationships with men. After initially denying everything, he confessed that he had sexual relations with Cummings, Courtney, Hussey, Saxton, and Wilcox. He would be punished for his honesty as he would be treated as "the ringleader in the homosexual practices in college."[20]

Roberts told the court that Wilcox had first met Dreyfus in the summer, then started dating him after another encounter at a Boston bar that fall. The two had spent most nights at Dreyfus' house at 44 Beacon St. When Wilcox tried to break off the relationship, Dreyfus threatened to tell the authorities at Harvard. Roberts blamed Wilcox for turning Day to homosexuality and told the court he himself had been chaste for the past three months.[21]

Edward Say, a student with little documentation regarding his background, admitted to the court that he had a weekly masturbation habit but denied any homosexual liaisons. But he also confessed to attending one party in Roberts' room back in November, which he had left in disgust. The court was very suspicious about Say, however, finding him effeminate and skeptical about his claim that an injury kept him from playing sports.

When called before the court, Saxton confessed to having gay sex one time. That would be enough for the court to throw him out of Harvard. Cummings admitted he was close to Cyril Wilcox and went to several of Roberts' parties but denied ever having homosexual relations with anyone. George Wilcox sent a letter to the court that Cummings had gone to Fall River to talk with him and that he had beaten him. Trying to save himself, Joseph Lumbard testified against his roommate, Say. He told the court that since the beginning of the year Say had become distant and secretive and started wearing rouge. He had heard rumors that his roommate had sexual relations with Cummings and Courtney; he also admitted to knowing most of the core group of the accused.

Lumbard said the first party they attended in Roberts' room was in December where there were "faggots from the Golden Rooster" dancing and kissing. Lumbard admitted to one dance with another man before he left around 1:30 a.m. Lumbard also admitted he went to other parties at Perkins, though only for a few minutes. He also told the court that he and Say let other men stay in their rooms overnight including Courtney and Cummings and he confessed that he once let a non-Harvard man spend the night in his bed. He denied ever having sex with women but did admit to masturbating once, six years previously.

Wolff told the court about a conversation where Cummings described a large underground gay society at Harvard, with groups of six or seven students often heading into Boston together for the gay nightlife. The most popular destination, in his opinion, was the Golden Rooster. The students often spent time with non-Harvard men who were waiters and workers at other Boston gay establishments. Wolff said he started having sex with males as a child, a practice that peaked when he was at boarding school. He mostly stopped the practice until he met Keith Smerage, with whom he masturbated twice.

The testimony resulted in a summons to Smerage, a transfer student who had come from Tufts. Smerage confessed to having first had gay sex as a child and told the court that he had many affairs since then. He reported he knew the term "queer" and had read Havelock Ellis but had never heard "faggot." He told the court that he had not had sex with men since arriving at Harvard and that he stopped masturbating several months earlier. He then contradicted himself by telling the court he had sex with an unnamed Harvard student and that though he had sex with women the past summer, he preferred sex with men. Smerage gave the court the names of Stanley Gilkey and eight other men he thought were gay but withheld the names of others.

Gilkey admitted to the court that he had an interest in homosexuality but only as part of his studies in criminology. He told the court he had read not only Ellis but also Freud and Jung's work about homosexual attraction. He denied rumors he could spot a gay person but admitted to having conversations about homosexuality with several students. He said he had never had sex with a man but told the court about a romance with a woman the summer before last. He admitted to masturbating, but maintained it was not as horrible a crime as homosexuality.

One student (whose name was redacted) was quickly deemed innocent, but he gave the court the name of Douglas Clark, a doctoral student who was a section leader in psychology. As a teaching assistant, this posed special concerns for the university, so President Lowell called Clark before a subset of the court. Clark at first denied everything but then confessed to being homosexual and propositioning the student who had implicated him. The court ordered Clark to immediately leave the university and set about erasing his existence at Harvard.

After two weeks of testimony, the court condemned fourteen men including seven current undergraduates and four men without any Harvard affiliation. Not only were the Harvard men expelled, they were ordered to leave immediately and then banished from Cambridge—Harvard had no legal authority for these demands but made them anyway. When he was still at Harvard four days later, Roberts' father was sent a letter complaining his son had not yet left. All the students' families were sent letters telling them about why their sons were expelled from Harvard while the university's alumni office was instructed not to respond to any requests regarding the expelled men without consulting the expulsion record. These men were marked for life. One man escaped punishment, however. Eugene Cummings committed suicide in the Harvard infirmary before the court had a chance to expel him.

Though the court concluded he was not gay, Lumbard's guilt included having attended a party for two hours even though no sex was observed. The court said he should have known it was an immoral event. He also was found guilty of taking messages on the dorm's communal phone for some of the gay students and letting his roommate have men sleep overnight in their room. Not content with expulsion, Harvard contacted the deans of other schools to block Lumbard's attempts to transfer. The university eventually relented. He was allowed back at Harvard where he earned bachelor's and law degrees. However, the charges haunted Lumbard's otherwise brilliant law career and whenever asked for a reference, the university explained Lumbard's involvement in the scandal. Lumbard was eventually a member of the Harvard Board of Overseers but never talked about his year off.[23]

Smerage repeatedly tried to return to the college but was refused while his attempts to go elsewhere were stopped by Harvard. Stymied, he turned to the stage, performing under the name Richard Keith. He committed suicide in New York in 1930. Edward Say died in a car crash, also in 1930. Kenneth Day repeatedly tried to return to Harvard but was refused. Greenough thought that Wollf, Day, Gilkey, and Lumbard should be readmitted but was overruled by President Lowell. Eventually three were allowed back in. Day's daughter remembered him as a "skirt chaser" and never heard about his Harvard experience. Donald Clark went to California to teach at Mills College and eventually died of tuberculosis in Colorado. Gilkey became a theatre producer for Martha Graham, Elia Kazan, and others. The first general manager of the theatre at Lincoln Center, he was one of the few Harvard men in the scandal who never married.

Every time Saxton applied for a job and the employer contacted Harvard, the university sent a letter blasting his character. By his twenty-fifth reunion Harvard had lost contact with him and the alumni office suggested eliminating him from the class list. Roberts married his Brookline sweetheart a year after being expelled and his first son was born ten months later. He had a career as an interior designer.[20]

For eighty years, the impromptu court stayed a secret. Then, in 2000 an enterprising *Harvard Crimson* reporter saw a reference to a "secret court" in the Harvard archives and after much effort, heavily redacted copies of the testimony were made public. There were requests that the university award these men degrees posthumously, but Harvard refused.

These crackdowns resulted in fifty years of brutal anti-LGBTQ repression. Boston was no longer an oasis of tolerance, though as will be seen, LGBTQ people were treated better here than elsewhere. LGBTQ people in Boston now knew they had to remain deeply in the closet and keep their sexual and gender non-conformity a secret from mainstream society. As was the situation in the rest of the country, a dark soul-killing bigotry reigned supreme.

Chapter 6

The Dark Years

DESPITE THESE WAVES of repression, gay life persisted, an example of the ability of LGBTQ people to adapt despite efforts to eradicate them and their resilience in times of adversity. The crackdowns in Boston, Newport, and elsewhere were well known in the community. Some were covered in the press and resulted in bars and nightspots emptying out. But though LGBTQ people might have been forced to go temporarily underground, they soon emerged again, returning to their gathering places and restoring ties with each other.

In the aftermath of its secret court, Harvard tried unsuccessfully to have the city shut down its gay bars, but Boston even left Café Dreyfus alone. Another bar frequented by the students, the Green Shutters, also remained open but the bar might have been further protected by its owners. It had received positive publicity in the *Globe* because it was owned by three ex-servicemen, veterans of World War I. One of them was even at Harvard Medical School though he was not caught up in the purge. The Green Shutters was small, just twenty-four seats, but was very popular. Located at 36 Cedar Way off Mt. Vernon St., two of its owners had lived together before the war while the other now lived with them in a nearby apartment.

Just before Prohibition, there was a vibrant gay night life in Boston that attracted an eclectic mix of people. Looking back at the time, Charley Shively (one of the first scholars of Boston LGBTQ history) would report, "[b]efore, during, and after prohibition, the bars on the back of the Hill catered to a miscellaneous crowd of sailors, transvestites, poets, prostitutes, and gay men."[1] With its mix of the wealthy and poor, artists and poets, the area was compared to Paris' Left Bank or New York's Greenwich Village.[2]

There was also a more exclusive gay scene. One of the accused Harvard students told the secret court that "more danger lurked in places like the Copley Plaza and Touraine [Hotels] than at The Shutters." Men went to these places to meet "a higher class of boys."[3] Gay life was stratified by class. The Copley Plaza and the Touraine were meeting places for upper class men. Middle class gays had the Golden Rooster on Carver St. as well as the Green Shutters. For working class men, there was the Moon on Columbus Avenue and the Lighted Lamp. Since women had been prohibited from bars prior to Prohibition, they could only patronize hotel dining rooms and restaurants.

As agents began enforcing Prohibition, all these places were forced to choose their poison: close, become alcohol free, or go underground and continue to serve alcohol at the risk of legal action. The hotel bars remained popular, surreptitiously entertaining their upper-class customers without fear of punishment. Other establishments disappeared within a few years. Dreyfus, for example, moved his café to several locations before opening a restaurant in Chinatown. Meanwhile, one Harvard graduate, Prescott Townsend, opened several "cafes", really speakeasies, in his various properties on Beacon Hill and used bribes to avoid arrest. The Beacon Hill bars included the Brick Oven Tea Room, the Joy Barn, and the March Hare. Around this time, the famous and long-running bar, Napoleon's, opened on a quiet street in Bay Village. While this speakeasy was ostensibly straight, from its beginning it was full of gay men. Other speakeasies welcomed women, setting the stage for women to patronize drinking establishments across the city once Prohibition was lifted.

However, conditions were not easy for these bars. In 1922, the authorities prosecuted the owners of the Lighted Lamp, 168 Myrtle St., for maintaining a nuisance and conducting a house of ill fame. The establishment began as a chess club and a team based there once won a city tournament, but it was always an unlicensed bar catering to LGBTQ people. The owners fought the charges and were acquitted.[4]

Over time, Boston's LGBTQ nightlife learned how to adapt to Prohibition and a new group of bars emerged. The Empty Barrel, for example, was a speakeasy that consisted of tables and chairs made from old barrels that sat on a dirt floor run by the tuxedo clad Evelyn Church. Admission was thirty-five cents, a sandwich and chips included. There was the Tivoli on Washington St., while the Talley Ho in Scollay Square featured gay shows and drag performers. Another bar, the Nest, had a wild reputation.

Despite the nightlife, it was not easy being gay. Stewart Mitchell, the editor of *The Dial* (a major literary magazine) and his friend, the poet Robert Hillyer, struggled with their homosexuality in the early 1920s. In an exchange of letters, they discussed the ability of will to overcome desire. Hillyer believed it was a necessity but Mitchell thought that desire always won and that the "safety valves of those who are used to getting what they want are too fastidious, furtive, or feeble to satisfy themselves in their sexual lives."[5] Mitchell also cited the case of a young catamite in Petronius whose body was "no more than a hilt of the sword" demonstrating that upper class Boston gay men continued to think in terms of classical culture. Finally resolving to move forward, Mitchell told Hillyer he won't restrain himself, but neither will he "be lurking around urinals and water closets."[5]

The secret court finished its business and gay life at Harvard reestablished itself. Some gay Harvard alumni of the 1920s created a bond of friendships and professional relationships that dramatically transformed art and architecture across the United States. Many of them moved to New York where they promoted new artistic ideas, introduced cutting edge artists and architects to the American public, and managed many of the most important cultural institutions in the country.

The groundwork for this influence was laid by Charles Eliot Norton, a straight man who had come to Harvard in 1874 and was one of the pioneers in the new field of art history. Norton strongly believed that there was a moral underpinning to art that had to be championed. He taught that art was meant to elevate the world and educate the masses, a view that dominated Harvard until well into the 1920s. Norton proved very popular; Isabella Stewart Gardner was a follower, and his lectures on John Ruskin were said to attract a thousand attendees.[6]

One influential member of this group was the composer and music critic, Virgil Thomson (1896-1989). A veteran, Thomson entered Harvard at the age of twenty-three in 1919 where, between his above-average age and homosexuality, he was lonely. He knew he was gay but had yet to act on it and he was aware of the secret court. Seventy years later he told a biographer that gay men had to be very careful at Harvard. "I didn't want to be queer. No! No! No! That was another hurdle I didn't want to jump over. Nowadays it's much easier. But in those days if you got caught around Harvard you got kicked out. And the same with instructors."[7]

Eventually he discovered the Liberal Club, an organization for Jews, socialists, and the penniless who did not otherwise fit into the school's social environment. There Thomson met Henry-Russell Hitchcock (1903-87), the great architectural historian, and Maurice Grosser (1903-86), Thomson's lifelong lover, though during their time at the Liberal Club they barely knew each other. For several years, Thomson was entranced by a young Harvard freshman. Despite Thomson's attention, the man put him off; he was more interested in men his own age. He would tease Thomson with descriptions of sex with other Harvard students and wanted Thomson only as a mentor. It took years for Thomson to finally concede that an affair would not happen.[7]

Thomson felt unattractive despite several sexual encounters with men and had no serious relationships. He felt his prospects in Boston and elsewhere were limited and though he was offered several jobs and had already been published as a music critic, there was nothing holding him in the United States. Thus, he joined the great postwar exodus to Paris.

There, Thomson ran into Grosser at the famous Deux Magots café while the latter was in the city on a painting fellowship. The two were opposites. One biographer noted that "Virgil was sharp, Maurice was soft-spoken; Virgil was pudgy, Maurice was sinewy; Virgil delivered opinions ex cathedra, Maurice withheld judgment; Virgil was ordered, Maurice messy; Virgil self-assured, Maurice fidgety and insecure; Virgil homespun, Maurice courtly."[8] Despite their differences, by the end of the year they were madly in love, sharing a double bed in a decrepit Parisian apartment that lacked a bath. The sexual part of their affair lasted twenty-six years, the relationship sixty. Grosser's *New York Times* obituary reports him dying of congestive heart failure, but others say he died of complications from AIDS.

Thomson wanted the regal yet suspicious Gertrude Stein to collaborate with him on an opera. Stein had attended Radcliffe but said she had no idea she was attracted to women while there. Even before they ever met, Thomson had set a poem of hers to music that enabled him to get past the watchful protection of Stein's companion, Alice Toklas. Thomson followed up with another work based on Stein's poetry that thrust him into her inner circle despite the fact that many of her friends disliked him and his music. The opera that resulted from this collaboration, *Four Saints in Three Acts*, would become one of the most acclaimed artistic events of Depression-era New York.

After weeks of discussion regarding the subject and setting of the opera, Stein completed her libretto. Thomson spent his mornings working on the score and then took long afternoon walks with Hitchcock, who was in Paris working on a book on modern architecture. After Stein and Thomson completed *Four Saints*, Grosser developed the scenario that provided the framework for its 1934 production.

The opera was produced by Arthur Everett Austin (1900-57), a bisexual Harvard man who had a major impact on the arts. On the night of the premier, "[t]he slim, graceful figure taking a bow, with his playful blue eyes and brilliantined hair, a gardenia in the lapel of his dinner jacket, was handsome enough to have stepped from the silver screen or out of a Noel Coward play."[9] Nicknamed "Chick," Austin used his looks and charm on both men and women.

His mother met his father in Berlin in 1895-96 while on a European trip and the two traveled to Athens to see the first modern Olympic Games. Though of modest rural roots, the family was well off. Austin's mother had received a hefty inheritance, while his father was a German and Harvard trained physician and founding faculty member of Tufts Medical School, as well as a professor at several universities. The family eventually settled at 110 Marlborough St. and worshipped at Trinity Church while Austin attended the prestigious Noble and Greenough School.

Austin entered Harvard in September 1918, having attended Andover for a second senior year after failing his first Harvard entrance exam. Though he wasn't athletic (his cousin called him a sissy because of his lack of interest in sports) Austin was popular at Harvard because of his money, good looks, wit, and appetite for fun. He lived at home his freshman year and led his classmates into Boston in search of theatre, minstrel shows, movies, vaudeville, bars, and restaurants. "He danced, flirted, and filled his calendar with dinner parties and debutant balls." His first year grades were dismal and he was forced to attend summer school and reapply for admission, which was granted. He lived at 5 Linden St. in Cambridge his second year. Open about his bisexuality, Austin often bragged about his exploits or made them into colorful stories. For example, he turned an incident where an elderly Irish chambermaid walked in on him with one of his classmates into a joke. "You can't spoil a rotten egg, Mr. Austin," he claimed she said.[9]

Austin was not touched by the secret court though he was well known to Acting Dean Greenough because of his academic problems. He lacked sufficient credits to graduate with his class in 1922 and went to Egypt to assist an archeological dig, returning to Harvard to complete his degree in 1924. He finally gained his academic footing and was asked to be a teaching assistant in Harvard's Fine Arts Department. Austin found his life passion and quickly developed a reputation as an art connoisseur. At the recommendation of his Harvard mentors, in 1927 Austin was given the job as head of the Wadsworth Athenaeum in Hartford and for a few years, the institution was at the vanguard of art, architecture, and music, attracting visitors such as painter Fernand Leger and architect Le Corbusier.

Harvard's gay men always seemed to find each other. In 1924, Hitchcock was not good looking but "with his red beard hiding a bad skin condition, Hitchcock was a tall, heavyset, slovenly, long-winded, but somehow endearing young man who spoke rather formally in a booming voice."[9] Hitchcock introduced Austin to the great architect Philip Johnson (1906-2005) in the late 1920s over lunch at the Copley Plaza while Austin met Thomson when the latter was briefly back at Harvard as a teaching assistant in 1925. Together, these men and their gay friends helped each other reach the pinnacle of the New York art scene. Many of these young gay men considered their sexuality to be part of their rebellion against the cultural norms of the era, saying that "the homosexual community was a brotherhood, a secret society with its own loyalties and bonds that greatly helped its members throughout their careers."[9]

Austin transformed the Athenaeum into a cultural powerhouse through a new wing that featured the first Bauhaus-inspired architecture in the United States and the country's first Picasso show. His crowning achievement was producing *Four Saints* in the Athenaeum's theatre. In addition to the collaboration of Thomson and Stein, Frederick Ashton choreographed the show (his American debut) and John Houseman directed (his first time directing). During a 1929 visit to New York, Thomson had gone to Harlem with Hitchcock to see the famous black entertainer, Jimmy Daniels, perform. Inspired, Thomson decided to have an all-black cast for Four Saints. There were other consequences from that night. Daniels would become "the first Mrs. Johnson," Philip's lover.[9]

The production is famous for the celebrities who went to see it. Guests at the premier included Alexander Caldor, Buckminster Fuller, Clare Boothe, and Abby Aldrich Rockefeller. They and other attendees were said to have come by "private railway car, airplane, and Rolls-Royce; even, as one observer suggested, by jeweled pogo stick."

The opera was challenging, bordering on incomprehensibility–it actually featured twenty saints in four acts. Nothing "that followed the opening chorus offer more than a hint of meaning. The libretto told no coherent story, the staging and costumes were deeply eccentric, and most of the lines made no apparent sense."[8] But when it opened in New York, it became the longest running opera in Broadway history. The opera took the city by storm. "Decorated for Easter Sunday, the most prestigious windows along Fifth Avenue evoked Florine's sets: Elizabeth Arden showed Saint Teresa with an Easter egg, Bergdorf Goodman depicted Saint Teresa singing "April Fool's Day a pleasure," and Lord & Taylor and others followed suit. There were even rumors that the Republican Party would incorporate parts of the opera into its next platform."[8]

The excitement of *Four Saints* did not last. Austin's time at the Athenaeum grew difficult when he overreached with his Hartford Festival and Paper Ball in 1936. The Athenaeum's conservative trustees were unnerved by a group of costumed cowboys and Indians in makeup and fake eye lashes. They were even more dismayed by the festival's $1,000 deficit and Austin's relationship with the trustees never recovered (though he lasted at the Athenaeum until 1943).

Austin, always aggressively bisexual, married the beautiful Helen Goodwin, niece of the treasurer of the Athenaeum. They were very complementary of each other and if Austin was a hurricane of activity, Helen was the eye of his storm, a central calming influence. It appears that Austin kept his attraction to men out of view for many years, often by limiting encounters to when he was away from Hartford.

After leaving the Athenaeum, Austin became head of the John and Mabel Ringling Museum in Sarasota, Florida. Austin spent his time there both with and without his wife but almost always in the company of Jim Hellyar, a young man he met in Hartford. Helen and Austin's two children mostly accepted this relationship. Then, as he was in terrible pain from lung cancer that had spread to his spine, he told Helen he never wanted to see Hellyar again.[9] He didn't know the nature of his illness; this was an era when a cancer diagnosis was often kept from patients, but he knew the end was coming. He died in 1957.

Harvard gay men were very involved in the development of the Museum of Modern Art (MOMA) in New York, with the university training some of the most influential men in the propagation of modernism in the United States. Most of these men were gay, including Johnson, who would look back and write, "It was a concatenation of Harvard and the homosexuals and modernism as a creed." These Harvard men referred to themselves as "The Friends" or "The Family". At first glance there is nothing to suggest that Harvard would play such a pivotal role. The university was quiet, staid, and allergic to innovation with "the vast majority of Harvard's student body ... studiously trained to avoid the personal, the radical, and the modern."[8] Modernism at Harvard rested on the tripod of Paul Sachs' museum course, *The Hound & Horn* (a student launched periodical), and the Harvard Society for Contemporary Art.

Lincoln Kierstein, Alfred Barr, and Sachs cofounded the Harvard Society for Contemporary Art. Barr was Kierstein's academic advisor and the two had traveled through Europe looking at the art scene there. Kierstein enlisted other students and they used second floor space in the Harvard Coop building for their exhibits. Barr was straight and the offspring of a family of Presbyterian ministers. Rather than religion, he preached the importance of modern art to the American public. He credited his attraction to modernism to the influence of *The Dial* (edited by Steward Mitchell), an important magazine of the time.[6] Barr also took Johnson to Europe, exposing him to the most famous buildings on the continent. At Harvard, Barr created the first course in modern art in the country which included field trips to the Necco factory in

Cambridge and the Motormart Building in Park Square. With this experience, when Abbey Rockefeller sought Sachs' advice in finding a new director for MOMA, he recommended Barr. At first Barr demurred, but then jumped into the job with all his enthusiasm.

Hitchcock attended Sachs' museum course in 1926 and quickly became part of a group that included Kierstein, Barr, and others. Barr invited Hitchcock to lecture in his class at Wellesley, with Johnson participating on occasion. There are conflicting stories as to how Johnson met Barr at Wellesley in 1929. It could have been at Johnson's sister's graduation or a play; in any case they became close friends. Similarly, there are multiple stories as to how Johnson met Hitchcock. Both Johnson and Hitchcock were at the Barr's Paris wedding in May 1930 and later, the two set off across Europe to research modern architecture.[6]

Barr convinced Hitchcock to head MOMA's Department of Architecture. Hitchcock had grown up in Plymouth and his father, watching his son build elaborate sand castles, assumed he'd become an architect. He entered Harvard in 1921 and completed his degree in three years, taking a fourth year at the School of Architecture. Hitchcock was actually unaware of the birth of modern architecture, having missed the ferment while on his European trips. But he soon caught up with the trend taking over Europe and eventually he published an article on J. J. P. Oud, one of the first prominent modern architects. This caught the attention of Johnson and converted him to modernism as well.

Philip Johnson graduated from high school at sixteen, entering Harvard in 1923. Johnson told his family he was gay when he was twelve and they were very supportive of him. A dashingly handsome young man, "A chiseled cleft chin and intense eyes saved his patrician features from prettiness. He seemed the picture of golden, privileged youth."[8] Harvard provided a rude reality check to him. Though he was given his inheritance early by his father (stock in the Aluminum Corporation of America) that made him very wealthy, Johnson's grades were mediocre and, when during his sophomore year he was smitten by a handsome freshman who did not reciprocate his affections, he became depressed. Because of frequent absences due to periods of depression, it took Johnson seven years to graduate.

Johnson became infatuated with modernism after reading Hitchcock's article and he turned to Barr to get himself further acquainted with the new style of architecture. During their European tour, Johnson drove while Hitchcock provided narrative and instruction and they visited every modern building they could. When Hitchcock went to MOMA, Johnson followed and the two produced the famous International Show, the exhibit that introduced modern architecture to the United States in 1932.

Lincoln Kierstein (1907-96) was the son of the owner of Filene's Department Store. His sister Mina had a dizzying sex life of her own. Twelve years older than Lincoln (in later years their mother explained the gap was caused by their father never having liked sex) she lived for a time in London where she had a torrid affair with Henrietta Bingham, the daughter of the owner of the Louisville Courier Journal. Bingham was also sleeping with John Houseman, who later was a lover of Mina's.

Mina also found time to have a non-sexual affair with David Garnett, a novelist member of the Bloomsbury set. The roadblock to intimacy was not Garnett's many male lovers, but that he was married with a child. Garnett's love life was even more complicated than Mina's: he confessed to her that he had been lovers with the painter Duncan Grant and while the two men were living with Vanessa Bell, the sister of Virginia Wolfe, Bell gave birth to Grant's daughter, Angelica, whom Garnett married years later.[10] The Bloomsbury connection enabled Lincoln to befriend John Maynard Keynes, who took him to art galleries and provided the seventeen year old with much worldly advice.

Kierstein knew he was gay at an early age and had a long affair with a boy at the Berkshire School, which he attended after flunking out of Exeter. The two discussed if they might be homosexuals and neither seemed perturbed by it. When he finally entered Harvard, Kierstein had an active sex life, sleeping mostly with men but also a few women. Once he wrote in his diary that "[a]fter supper [at his parents' mansion on Commonwealth Avenue] went down to the Public Gardens. It was dark and the full beds of tulips, interspersed with pansies, glowed under the lamps, catching light in their cups. A good many marines in pairs. I hunted for a while—became interested in one figure in the ferns."[11] He picked up young men in the Harvard Square subway station and had sex with a fellow student in the stacks of Widener Library. In Harvard Square, he would go to the Athens for dinner until closing time, then he'd patronize the Olympia and he often met men at both places. He wrote that many of the freshman at Harvard considered him queer but he didn't care.

When Lincoln told Mina he was homosexual, she suggested Freudian analysis to cure him. Lincoln was against therapy, however, saying he did not want to change and that if he were to be completely heterosexual he would no longer be himself. Lincoln didn't consider himself queer, but he understood that he overwhelmingly preferred sex with men. To him, queers were fairies, i.e. effeminate men, while masculine men who had gay sex were hard to categorize. Almost any athletic young man caught his eye and he even had sex with his brother (Lincoln was twenty, George was seventeen) in his rooms at Harvard. Lincoln found that encounter emotionally exhausting while George went on to develop a strong heterosexual reputation and married several times.[10]

Lincoln didn't only have casual sex; he also had multiple, if brief, relationships with other men at Harvard. "All of these passionate descriptions were played out over a mere three or four months, sometimes overlapped, were usually not fully reciprocal, and ranged in terms of sexual activity from dreamy talk to holding hands to 'jiggling' to acrobatics all over the bed and floor."[10] But Lincoln wanted romance and lifetime companionship. Many of the young men Lincoln had sex with at Harvard alternated their sexual relations between men and women and most eventually married. One thing that disturbed Lincoln was that his passionate affairs with men would ultimately make a marriage with a woman impossible. Yet his marriage to Fidolma Cadmus, sister of erotic artist Paul Cadmus, lasted fifty years despite his many affairs with men.

Kierstein cofounded *Hound & Horn*, a Harvard literary quarterly, with Varian Fry. In the first issue of *Hound & Horn*, Hitchcock wrote a piece on the decline of architecture and Grosser contributed a homoerotic painting. Hitchcock's good friend, the future historian Ned Arvin, also wrote for the periodical. Kierstein supplied the money and vision for the magazine while Fry did most of the grunt work, such as selling subscriptions. Despite their close friendship, Kierstein couldn't decide if he liked Fry. One night, for example, Kierstein complained of being woken up at 2:00 a.m. by Fry having loud sex with another man in the rooms above his. In his diary, Kierstein described Fry as being a weak effeminate alcoholic always on the brink of being ousted from Harvard due to a combination of violent drunk binges, emotional breakdowns, academic incompetence, and indiscreet homosexuality. Yet after years of this loathing, Kierstein finally had sex with Fry, saying "we always end up by sleeping with or lying with friends."[11]

Suggesting Kierstein was an extremely poor judge of character, Fry went on to become one of the major saviors of Jews, socialists, artists, and other victims being hunted down in Nazi occupied Europe. After France was defeated by the Germans and before the United States entered the war, Fry (working closely with Barr) helped get visas and boat tickets for Marc Chagall, Hannah Arendt, Claude Levi-Straus, and more than a thousand others. His work involved tremendous courage and he was eventually awarded the French *Legion d'honneur* as well as recognition in Israel, the United States, and elsewhere for his bravery.

Kierstein had negative opinions of many of his contemporaries. For example, he labeled Hitchcock "that green dank puss," saying, "he never washes and has a smell of dried wine and cockroaches ever about him."[11] Kierstein also had an assignation at the Touraine Hotel with Jere Abbott, MOMA's first director. Soon after graduation Kierstein moved to New York where he eventually founded the American Ballet Theatre, the most important ballet company in the country, and his contributions to the arts continued for decades.

Upper class men continued to find friends, tricks, and lovers in theatres, clubs, and other social spots during Prohibition. One handsome young man who left information about 1930s gay life was Richard Cowan (1909-39). He grew up in Albany and went to Cornell, where he spent his first three years mostly socializing with fellow students and going to fraternity parties. Just before his nineteenth birthday he met Stewart Mitchell, whom he began to see regularly and who helped him with his college expenses.

For a while, Cowan thought he was the only homosexual at Cornell, but then during the spring of his junior year he went home with two other students after a party. He had a wonderful time, but for the next two weeks he was terrified he might face disciplinary action. That summer, he stayed at Cornell and "lived at the [fraternity] house when I didn't sleep out with someone."[12]

After graduating, Cowan moved to Boston to be with Mitchell in a non-monogamous relationship. He found sex all across the city, meeting a Dartmouth student on the Common one night after symphony, for example. He would go at night to the Public Garden or down to the Charles River near Harvard Square to find men. At one point, he wrote in his diary that he and Stewart walked through the Fens, though there is no mention of sex there.

Right after Christmas 1932, Cowan met a younger man at Symphony Hall and dated him for a short time. Through that man, he met another Dartmouth student, George, and dated him. Cowan loved Mitchell but had no desire to commit to monogamy. George was a friend of Congressman A. Piatt Andrew, who was staying at the Statler Hotel one night when George introduced him to Cowan. George and Andrew wanted to have sex with Cowan, but he declined. Andrew was too old for Cowan's taste, being thirty-six years his senior. It turned out that Mitchell was a distant relative of Andrew and was in Gloucester frequently because he had a house of his own there. Cowan went on to befriend Andrew and he had dinner at Andrew's Gloucester home multiple times. Cowan was introduced to another friend of George's at the Ritz, but again he declined the offer of a tryst as the friend was too old.

Next Cowan met a singer from the Monarch Club, whom Cowan had seen at the Copley Theatre once before. At one point, Cowan got drunk and told the man he loved him. Another time he met a man in the lobby of a theatre. Cowan was staying at the Somerset Hotel that night but because Mitchell was there, he took him back to his apartment on Plympton St. in Cambridge. After decades of suffering from depression, Cowan's life came to a sad end when he committed suicide at Mitchell's Gloucester home. Mitchell was devastated and though he received dozens of condolence letters, he sank into alcoholism.

Once Prohibition ended there was an explosion of places for LGBTQ people, including the Kit Kat Club on Melrose St. and the Black Cat on Beacon Hill. Also popular were the Touraine Café, later renamed the Chess Club, the Old Champagne Lounge, and the Petty Gay Lounge. After the College Inn moved to the Mayfair Hotel, there were lines to get in.[13]

As previously mentioned, some of these bars had a longevity unmatched in other cities. Napoleon's in Bay Village, for example, began as a speakeasy in 1929. At first it was not officially gay (though it was mostly patronized by gay men), but eventually its straight owners embraced their gay clientele and the bar remained open for eighty years.

The first gay bar to go public after Prohibition ended was the Pen and Pencil on Cornhill St. in Scollay Square. Prescott Townsend said that because it was owned by the head of the liquor dealers association and his wife, the Pen and Pencil and thus other gay bars were mostly not subject to police harassment as they were in other cities.[14] Since he hardly drank, Townsend was often assigned door duty at the bar and claimed that one night the mayor and governor came in together. "Don't mind us, boys. We just wanted to see what it was like," reported Townsend.[15] The Pen and Pencil was crowded in the years before World War II in part because it had a female piano player who liked to sing bawdy songs.[16] It too, was open for decades.

The Silver Dollar, run by a gay man named Al Shack, was another favorite. Located in the Combat Zone, "the Silver Dollar Bar was opened shortly after repeal and was featured by singing waiters and performing cigarette girls. The bar is fully 40 feet in length and Silver dollars are imbedded in it."[17] It was said to be one of the most popular bars at the time.

In addition, cross-dressing entertainers often played straight clubs–until the Boston Licensing Board put a stop to men wearing women's clothes. Boston, New York and other cities had a brief "pansy fad" in the early 1930s that featured openly gay and very effeminate men. Gene Malin (1908-33), for example, was a famed pansy entertainer in New York and Los Angeles who even had a brief movie career–most of which was cut out of released films. Malin, however, did not dress in drag. Rather, the six foot tall husky man with blonde hair and blue eyes would act as a master of ceremonies for other acts and entertain audiences with flamboyant lisps and bawdy jokes. But he was tough, and once when heckled he punched the man, prompting Ed Sullivan to quip, "all that twitters isn't pansy." After a shootout in a New York club between rival gangs (including, it was rumored, Dutch Schultz), Malin spent time in Boston headlining at the Coconut Grove. He soon went on to Hollywood, but he tragically died when he lost control of his car and plunged onto the ocean at Venice Beach.

In the wake of the 1942 Coconut Grove fire that killed 492, the city initiated an inspection of all drinking and entertainment establishments. They found the Silver Dollar was under construction at the time while "an unexpected crowd of merrymaking service men crammed every nook of the establishment" at Playland.[18] This would be another bar that would cater to LGBTQ people for over fifty years.

One of the first gay rights activists in the United States, Townsend partied with Bohemians in Paris, visited communists in Russia, and worked with Wobblies out west but was a lifelong Republican. He cherished his lineage, including one ancestor who signed the Declaration of Independence, the Articles of Confederation, and the US Constitution. Using his wealth to buy real estate on the back of Beacon Hill, Townsend began advocating for repeal of the state's sodomy laws in the 1920s. He would fearlessly go to the State House by himself and try in vain to get a representative to introduce his bills. No one else had the courage and resources to be so public, but Townsend persevered and the idea that LGBTQ people deserved equal rights became embedded in the fabric of the community.

By now Townsend and the Beacon Hill bohemians were more known for their behavior and dress than the art they produced. One of them, Eliot Paul, from

Malden but having met Townsend in Paris, distinguished himself with a Van Dyke beard, shiny black suit and a black felt hat while Townsend preferred a raccoon skin overcoat. Another companion was the lesbian Catherine Huntington, with whom Townsend founded the Barn Experimental Theatre.[19] Townsend began summering in Provincetown in the mid-1920s, the first sign that gay men from Boston were visiting that burgeoning LGBTQ mecca.

Women faced tremendous discrimination and lesbians were forced to be extremely discrete about their private lives in the middle decades of the twentieth century, yet many persevered and had successful careers while maintaining lifelong relationships. One couple, Martha May Eliot (1891-1978) and Ethel Dunham (1883-1969), managed the difficulties of these years together as they devoted their lives to protecting the health of children in the United States and around the world.

6.1 Martha May Eliot

Eliot was from a prestigious Boston family. Her relatives included the poet T. S. Eliot and a president of Harvard University. Yet these connections could not help her in the face of the anti-woman customs of the time and Eliot was forced to go elsewhere for an education. Dunham was also from a wealthy family; both her father and uncle served as president of the Hartford Electric Company. Eliot attended Radcliffe but spent a year at Bryn Mawr, where she met Dunham. After graduating, Eliot and Dunham went to medical school at Johns Hopkins. The two lived together their entire adult lives.[20] Dunham was accepted into the internship program at Hopkins, but the school would only allow one woman per class, so Eliot had to look elsewhere and was only able to secure an internship at Peter Bent Brigham Hospital because, she later said, so many men were off at war.

Both women's passion was maternal and child health, a vital field at a time when some neighborhoods had an infant mortality rate of 25 percent or more. Almost always working side by side, the women devoted themselves to research, advocacy, and education, focusing not just on infectious agents but also the need for clean air, water, and food. For many years, their home base was in New Haven, Connecticut, where Dunham joined the faculty of the Yale Medical School in 1920 and Eliot in 1921. Dunham was called "gentle in manner, with a quick sense of humor."[21] She needed these traits, along with her superior knowledge of public health, to convince the overwhelmingly male medical profession to adopt new practices to better address children's health issues. Her work with rickets, for example, revolutionized how doctors treated this then prevalent disease by boosting children's diets.

Both women worked at the Children's Bureau, a Progressive-era program to focus the US government's attention on reducing infant mortality and the burden of childhood disease. Eliot was its director of child and maternal health from 1924-34 and helped write the portions of the Social Security Act that provided for maternal and child welfare. After World War II, she worked to help restore public health infrastructure in areas destroyed by the conflict. By then she had become the chair of the Department of Maternal and Child Health at the School of Public Health at Harvard, ironic given that she had applied to medical school at Harvard but had been rejected because she was a woman.

Though Dunham and Eliot had a lifelong romance, much of their personal correspondence has been lost. Additionally, the couple spent so much time together they didn't need to put their feelings for each other in writing. What remains shows that they loved each other deeply and missed each other when they were apart.

Both spent time in Geneva, working for the World Health Organization before returning to Cambridge in 1957. Later in life, both women were recognized for their achievements by organizations such as the American Pediatric Association. Eliot's legacies include the Martha May Eliot Award given each year by the American Public Health Association for outstanding work in maternal and child health (Eliot was the association's first female president) and the health center in Jamaica Plain named after her.

Beacon Hill was the setting for another long term same-sex romance in the years between the wars. F. O. Mathiessen (1902-50) and Russell Cheney (1881-1945) met aboard an ocean liner on the way to England in 1924 and were lovers until Cheney's death in 1945. Mathiessen affectionately nicknamed Cheney, a painter, "Rat" while Cheney called Mathiessen, a master of literary criticism who has influenced generations of scholars, "Devil". The two exchanged over 3,000 letters during their years together.

Cheney was the youngest of five boys and four girls. His family owned silk mills with the boys sent to Yale and the girls unschooled. Cheney, a handsome man with dark knowing eyes, startled his family when he announced he wanted to be a painter. Though the family was mystified by his relationship with Mathiessen, they were more disturbed that Cheney had left the mill town of Manchester, Connecticut, for a career in the arts than that he was openly involved with another man. Though they never stopped loving their son, at his funeral the animosity towards Mathiessen came out and they treated the grieving man coldly.

Cheney always suffered from poor health. He struggled with tuberculosis, alcoholism, asthma, and several other ailments; yet Mathiessen wrote a friend that their "two lives and personalities have blended into a harmony of understanding affection which brings us closer to the other then we have ever been to anyone else. I did not know that life contained anything so rich and deep."[22]

Talking about sex or bringing up the subject of homosexuality, even to one who seemed to have reciprocal feelings towards oneself, was not easy in those years; thus both were very reticent during their first meeting. After days of intense personal conversation on the boat where they shared some of their innermost secrets as well as laughter and camaraderie, Mathiessen was still afraid to say he was gay. At one point he steered the conversation towards Havelock Ellis but again shrank from coming out to Cheney. Finally, at some point after 2 a.m. on the fourth day of the voyage and back in Mathiessen's cabin with Cheney safely biting into a pear, Mathiessen awkwardly said, "I know it won't make any difference to our friendship, but there's one thing I've got to tell you: before my senior year at Yale I was sexually inverted. Of course I controlled it since."[22] After a moment of silence that to Mathiessen was one of the most frightening of his life, Cheney confessed he too was gay. There followed two hours of even more intense conversation. Later, Cheney asked if a Bartlett pear was the antidote for the apple in the Garden of Eden.

Mathiessen wrote he did not realize he was in love in the beginning, but "I had attained complete harmony with another spirit for the first time in my life. Rat had shown me new visions of beauty. I had shown him fresh fountains of simplicity and peace." After they separated upon landing in Europe, Mathiessen wrote Cheney five letters that first week. In their earliest letters, they discussed the possibility of same-sex marriage. "Marriage! What a strange word to be applied to bed! Can't you hear the hell-hounds of society baying full pursuit behind us? But that's just the point. We are beyond society."[22] They did not pledge monogamy to each other, though they knew from the beginning that they would be life partners.

A trip to Europe in the 1920s offered lots of sexual temptations for gay men. Mathiessen was struck by an attractive red head with a white boutonnière in his suit at Hyde Park Corner in London and Cheney wrote about a man who looked like a Greek god while he was in Venice. Both were very experienced at cruising and picking up men and this was not Cheney's first relationship (he had several before he met Mathiessen as well as many fleeting encounters). Mathiessen even had liaisons with Oxford undergraduates in the first year he was with Cheney.

Both Cheney and Mathiessen were careful who they told about their relationship, of course, but those they did trust with the news were overwhelmingly supportive and happy for them. Yet Mathiessen had to hide his homosexuality from his colleagues at Harvard lest they throw him out of the university and destroy his booming academic career. It angered him. "But damn it! I hate to have to hide when what I thrive on is absolute directness."[22]

The relationship spurred both men to reach new heights of productivity. Returning to the United States, Mathiessen completed his education at Harvard and began teaching at Yale. Within a few years he was back at Harvard and published his first book, a biography of Sarah Orne Jewett. Meanwhile, Cheney had a series of one man shows of his paintings.

Mathiessen suffered from depression. Feeling suicidal, he checked himself into McLean Hospital just after Christmas 1938. When he was released three weeks later, he and Cheney rented an apartment at 87 Pinckney St. to establish an in-town base. Mathiessen eventually bought the entire Pinckney St. building. Mathiessen was short, and when he tried to enlist in the marines after Pearl Harbor he was rejected because he was half an inch under the minimum height. He had a high forehead, floppy brown hair and prominent ears, yet he was handsome with a devilish smile. Cheney was taller, darker, and could have played the part of a rakish businessman.

Mathiessen slowly became more radical. He joined the ACLU, helped raise money to defend the socialist labor leader, Harry Bridges, and fought the censorship of Lady Chatterley's Lover. But he never worked for gay rights. Indeed, he was always careful to avoid public appearances with other gay men at Harvard, though he knew many there including Kierstein and Ned Arvin.

Cheney died suddenly in May 1945, leaving Mathiessen adrift. He no longer felt at home at Harvard, which he felt was turning away from arts and humanities towards baser studies in science, technologies, and business. Some of his best books were published in his final years and he lectured at colleges across the US and Europe, but his isolation increased as longtime friends and colleagues died or moved away. There were other stressors, such as when the House Un-American Activities Committee subpoenaed him, that began to push him over the edge. Mathiessen took his own life while renting a room at the old Manger Hotel next to North Station. After dinner with friends, who found him stiff and tense, he jumped out of a twelfth story window. Today, there is an endowed visiting professorship in gender and sexuality studies at Harvard in his name. Using funds donated in 2009 by what was then called the Harvard Gay and Lesbian Caucus, it was one of the first such chairs in the country.

There were other prominent gay men associated with Cambridge and Harvard in the years between the wars. Henry Dana (1881-1950), for example, was the grandson of Henry Wadsworth Longfellow and son of Richard Henry Dana, the author of Two Years Before the Mast. Because of his family legacy, Dana was granted the lifelong right to live in the fabled Longfellow House on Brattle St. in Cambridge. Having been in Europe at the outbreak of the First World War, Dana was a passionate pacifist who was fired from Columbia University for his anti-war activities. He was a supporter of the new Soviet Union, becoming a leading expert on theatre there, and boasted he had seen over 600 Soviet plays.

Dana was also open about his homosexuality, which got him in trouble with the law in 1935. One night, four teenagers were arrested in Concord when they were joyriding in a car that belonged to Dana's nephew. This led one youth, a messenger boy of sixteen, to tell police about his relationship with Dana. Evidence was presented before a grand jury and Dana was arrested and arraigned. He was acquitted several months later but the charge was extensively reported in the press and led to the trustees of the Longfellow House to attempt eviction. They failed.

Another gay man from an old Yankee family was the architect, Nathaniel

Saltonstall (1903-71), who designed the interior of the Napoleon Club ("Napoleon's"). Saltonstall threw a "boy party" at the Ritz Hotel in 1938 (heavily attended by Harvard students) for Cole Porter to celebrate the opening of Porter's play, Jubilee. Saltonstall also designed a number of architecturally significant houses on Cape Cod. Even very successful men lived with daily anxiety that their homosexuality might be discovered and they would lose everything. Stewart Mitchell (1892-1957), for example, was educated at Harvard and Oxford and eventually named director of the Massachusetts Historical Society (MHS). Yet he lived in constant fear and turned to alcohol to get him through the problems of dealing with the disapproval of society. Mitchell was forced out as head of MHS after he had an emotional breakdown following the suicide of Cowan. Ostensibly he was let go because of his extensive drinking, but privately the directors complained he was aggressively homosexual.

One of the last of the bohemians was John Cheever (1912-82) who lived on Beacon Hill for several years in the 1930s. Cheever was cagey about his homosexuality, often discussing it in the guise of jokes because he had a hard time accepting his attraction to other men. He was born in Quincy to a family that was middle class but grew increasingly poor as he grew up. He attended Thayer Academy and Quincy High School but had a troubled childhood. His father lost his job and drank heavily while his mother became a small store owner, a career that humiliated Cheever because at the time women were not supposed to work.

Cheever's parents divorced in 1930 so he spent much of his time with his brother who was living on Beacon Hill, moving in with him in 1932. They lived at 6 Pinckney St., then moved to 46 Cedar Lane Way. Cheever and a friend rented Townsend's Provincetown home in the offseason. Cheever attended bohemian parties on the Hill that were held in small apartments filled with athletic young men and a few older foreign women. There, he befriended older gay men including the poet, Jack Wheelwright (1897-1940), and Henry Dana. The latter tried to bed Cheever, chasing him down the hall at the Longfellow House shouting, "how can you be so cruel?" when Cheever turned him down.[23] Cheever also met Lincoln Kierstein, who published one of his short stories in *Hound & Horn* in 1931. Kierstein took him to lunch where the drunk Cheever got into a fight regarding Henry James and hurled insults at Kierstein. A friendship with e e cummings resulted in the poet telling Cheever to move to New York.

The popularity of gay bars does not mean that society outside their doors was open and accepting. LGBTQ people knew they had to be extremely careful. "Learning to keep your mouth shut and to talk of everything except what may be on your mind is the first lesson. This may seem hypocrisy but is actually tact. It is a silent self-defense. What you don't say can't be held against you," cautioned Allen Bernstein (1913-2008) in an unpublished book on gay Boston written in 1940.[24] Bernstein had lived in the city in the late 1930s before entering the army, working for the federal writer's project. In addition to leaving one of the most vivid accounts of gay life anywhere before the war, Bernstein also demonstrated that pre-Stonewall LGBTQ people were actively questioning the repression of their time. He denounced the police for their seemingly random arrests in public cruising areas and put forth the idea that it was anti-gay prejudice, not something innate to homosexuality that was at the root of most LGBTQ people's psychological distress.

Bernstein carefully documented the public cruising areas of Boston. One was around the statue of George Washington in the Public Garden, while many men also met up on the benches scattered around the park. At night, male prostitutes stood under the bridge over the pond and pretended to urinate so that customers could examine their penises before making a deal. Prostitutes aside, many men maintained that the Public Garden attracted a better class of men than those who cruised on the Common, though some thought the opposite was true. Some men went looking for trysts in the colonnade at the library while others preferred the Esplanade.

Like other rural New England men, Bernstein moved to Boston to escape from his hometown and meet other gays. He reported that one way to meet men and women interested in same-sex encounters was to place personal ads in magazines. These had to be so discreet and coded that occasionally someone ignorant of the subtext showed up, but mostly they were understood to be signals of people looking for likeminded others. In one intriguing passage in a *Boston Globe* article on South End rooming houses, where a landlady reported that though most of her tenants preferred single rooms, if "two chums" wanted to live together, she did not ask questions.[25]

Altogether, Boston had an extensive social network of LGBTQ people. They met each other at "dinner parties, bridge games, dances, club meetings, concerts, hotel lobbies, summer beaches–everywhere."[24] These chance meetings could result in lifelong friendships, one night stands, or long term relationships. By now, going to Provincetown was an established pastime for Boston gay men. Provincetown's artists' balls, which were filled with men in drag, were particularly popular.

Bernstein thought that male couples were commonplace, but that they rarely lasted for more than a year or two and that five-year relationships were very rare. His pessimism was not limited to same-sex couples, however. He also thought that heterosexual ardor always cooled within a year. Because the anti-sodomy laws in Boston were haphazardly enforced and often a vehicle for abuse and payoffs, it could be dangerous to cruise the parks and other open areas. LGBTQ people patronized Boston bars because they were safe from arrest there. In Bernstein's view, the bars were sanctuaries because of payoffs and the police would walk in, look around the room and then leave, ignoring same sex couples and drag queens alike.

The police often harassed LGBTQ people by making up and enforcing arbitrary rules. For example, men out cruising would be arrested for disorderly conduct simply for sitting on benches in the Common or Public Garden supposedly reserved for the exclusive use of women and children. Despite uncountable numbers of men arrested for this crime, no such law existed. As World War II loomed, police repression increased. Back in 1931, there was an explosion in police actions, with 370 arrests for lewd and lascivious conduct and sodomy with nothing to explain this large increase. After that year, arrest levels remained high and from 1932-45 there were an average of 246 arrests per year. Police actions reached a peak in the years around the end of World War II and 1945 and 1947 had the two highest numbers of arrests in city history with 459 arrests (241 for sodomy, of which 218 were men and twenty-three were women, the highest count for sodomy in Boston history) in 1945 and 487 in 1947.

The criminality of gay sex made men and women vulnerable to violence. Any encounter, no matter how intimate, could end in mayhem or robbery. Because the victims were unable to go to the police, they could not seek justice. Thefts and beatings were taken as a given risk of their way of life.[24]

Transgender people asserted their right to be non-conforming despite the risks. It was illegal to cross dress in public, so gender non-conforming people were careful, but they organized parties that allowed them freedom (if only for a few hours). One man recalled playing piano at a series of Saturday afternoon parties in Newton. Guests would arrive in male clothing and change into women's attire once they were safely inside the house.[26]

Another prominent but closeted lesbian was Miriam Van Waters (1887-1971). Her diaries tell of both a childhood in a warm supportive family and "nameless shadows and yearnings." Her parents were solidly middle class and her father was a minister with the liberal Evangelical Episcopal Church. Born in Pennsylvania, when she was four her father was appointed rector of a church in Portland, Oregon. Her father was a strong believer in social gospel activism and was a supporter of the settlement house movement, while both parents believed that girls should be educated and that making the world a better place was an obligation for all good Christians.

Van Waters was a strong swimmer, an accomplished horseback rider, and she could hitch a team of horses to a wagon by herself. Her upbringing kept her secluded from boys unless they were part of her parents' social and religious world. Thus, she had many close relationships with girls. Her first crush was at fifteen, a girl named Genevieve, who she declared was her soulmate. Genevieve eventually moved to Greenwich Village.

Van Waters entered the University of Oregon in 1905 and though she did not directly challenge the strict sex roles of the time, she was determined to advance as far as she could. At Oregon, Van Waters had a mostly female circle of friends and at least one of these blossomed into a romantic relationship. The outward parameters of the relationship were still innocent enough that Van Waters could entrust their letters to the care of her mother.

Van Waters was a year ahead of Louise Bryant, whom she regarded as much too modern with her rouge wearing and openly carrying on with male students, though the two were close enough to collaborate on a literary magazine. Van Waters did very well at school and armed with the recommendation of a professor, was accepted into a doctoral program at Clark University. Moving to Worcester in 1910, she visited Boston and tried to socialize with the Bohemian crowd that hung out at the English Tea Room. Van Waters did not like the women there, however, some of whom she considered "mannish in the extreme."[27]

Like many LGBTQ people, Van Waters' sexuality helped guide and inform her career. Though she never publicly disclosed her lesbianism, Van Waters developed a questionnaire in her dissertation work for delinquent girls, never distributed, that included questions on same-sex attraction and gender identity. Later, her connections with other lesbians would sustain her during adversity. She received her doctorate in 1913 and worked for a time in the Boston juvenile courts but longed for the west coast.

Recovering from tuberculosis, Van Waters moved to Los Angeles where she lived in all women coops including one called the Colony. It was not exclusively lesbian. Van Waters' younger sister lived there before she married, their mother spent time at the coop, and male visitors were welcomed. Van Waters spent more than a decade in Los Angeles, running a correctional facility for girls, becoming a judge in the juvenile courts, and establishing a national reputation in the fields of social work and criminal justice. In 1931, she moved to Cambridge to devote more time to writing and research. By then she had adopted a daughter.

In 1925 or 1926, Van Waters met Geraldine Livingston Thompson (née Morgan), a New Jersey philanthropist who would become her lifelong partner with each pledging friendship and love to each other. Thompson (1872-1967) was born into a wealthy family that was dedicated to helping the poor and sick of New York. In 1896 she married Lewis Thompson, son of the treasurer of Standard Oil and the couple had nine children, including five adopted orphans. Despite her commitment to Van Waters, she stayed married to her husband, who died in 1936. Though a lifelong Republican, Thompson was a close intimate of Eleanor Roosevelt.

Initially, Van Waters struggled with how to accommodate Thompson into her life and was reluctant to let Thompson live with her full time. Van Waters felt a rush of enjoyment and peace when the two were together and Thompson would become her closest confidant. Van Waters admitted to thinking about images of justices of the peace and wedding bells when she thought of Thompson and in her mind, the two were on a lifelong journey together to "beyond the timberline."[27]

Just as difficult as dodging social pressures was navigating the internal dynamics of their relationship. As both were powerful, headstrong women, they wondered how they could maintain their individuality while forging a coupledom. How could they be supportive of one another without being controlling? They had no role models to follow, and they had to be discreet. Ultimately, Van Waters chose not to live openly with Thompson, who learned to accept her decision.

Long before Thompson became a widow, the two were establishing their partnership. Van Waters met Lewis Thompson and the children, while Geraldine visited the Van Waters family. They exchanged letters when they were apart and the mail was the high point of Thompson's day. "She eagerly awaited each delivery, making frequent visits to the front door to check for the mail. If the presence of relatives or servants prevented her from reading the letters at once, Geraldine felt thwarted." She found Van Waters bewitching, radiant, and beautiful. Van Waters was of medium height with short but stylish hair and as she aged, she kept her good looks with a face that conveyed intelligence, comfort, and openness.

In 1932 Van Waters was appointed the director of the Framingham women's prison, an opportunity to implement her progressive ideas regarding crime and rehabilitation. She spent most of her professional life fighting against conservatives who thought the only role of the legal system was to punish. In contrast, she believed that many of the crimes her inmates were imprisoned for (prostitution, adultery, and drunkenness) were social ills rather than moral sins. Van Waters had other problems. She was a Yankee Republican in a state that was yielding control to Catholic Democrats and many, including politicians such as James Michael Curley and clergy such as Cardinal William O'Connell, strongly disagreed with her policy initiatives.

For years, however, Van Waters successfully fought off political obstacles through her reluctant embrace of Democratic politicians and careful attention to detail. That she was the national expert on women's prison issues helped as well. In addition, the commissioners over the first twelve years of her posting were supportive. But there were ominous omens. The head of the men's prison at Norfolk, for example, launched a purge of homosexuals in his employ in the late 1930s. In 1936 Governor Curley attacked her internship program which placed soon to be released women in jobs. She persevered, but her critics were strong. Through it all, Van Waters successfully kept her lesbianism hidden. Her family ties, with a minister father and a troubled but loyal daughter helped provide cover, and she was very careful to keep her relationship with Thompson quiet. Such protection would not last.

When the United States entered World War II, everything changed for LGBTQ people. Young men and women left home to join the service or to work in war industries. Many who had been isolated now met other LGBTQ people for the first time and in the context of imminent death, relationships and one-night stands blossomed. At the same time, so did paranoia about LGBTQ people. Being both gay and German proved particularly dangerous for New Yorker Gustave Beekman. He had told people he was a florist or a gardener; in reality, he ran an establishment for gay men in Manhattan on West 43rd St. which then reopened on Warren St. in Brooklyn before finally moving to nearby Pacific St.

The house was not a brothel. It was a private club where Beekman provided food and drink as well as a place for men to socialize in return for paying an admission fee, and there was no evidence that anyone paid for sex. If the opportunity arose, however, for $2 men could use one of the upstairs bedrooms. "The House provided a safe, private locale where like-minded men could make acquaintances, enjoy informal get-togethers in the garden, and perhaps engage in intimate activities."[28] It was popular with soldiers, sailors, and their admirers.

Neighbors became suspicious of the activities at the house and reported it to the police, who in turn notified naval investigators. They carried on an intensive investigation using a perch in the Catholic hospital across the street to secretly photograph men entering and leaving the house. They traced the license plates of patrons as well.[29]

Officers arrested several men during a raid on the evening of March 14, 1942, including Virgil Thomson, though no charges were ever filed against him. Most of the people arrested in the raid were released, but two servicemen were pressured to provide evidence against Beekman for a sodomy trial. The judge was Samuel S. Leibowitz, who as a defense attorney had been retained by the American Communist Party to defend the Scottsboro boys in their appeal of rape charges. Beekman was convicted after a two-day trial. Leibowitz's harsh treatment of Beekman shows the lack of compassion for LGBTQ people by many on the left extreme of the political spectrum at the time that would continue for the next thirty years even as repression ebbed and flowed.

Leibowitz appeared to be acting on information provided by federal agents when he threatened Beekman before sentencing: "[i]f there be any wretches who are stabbing at the heart of our country in these perilous times, whether in high or low stations, they must be brought speedily to the bar of justice."[28] Leibowitz promised either "extreme leniency" or "maximum punishment" depending on whether Beekman cooperated or not. Beekman gave the court detailed information that included drag names and the assorted sexual practices of his guests. In the end, this did not earn him any mercy. He was sentenced to more than twenty years in jail.

At least two German nationals who visited the house were found and imprisoned for the duration of the war. The case exploded into scandal when Beekman reported that a US Senator had visited the house a dozen times, preferring the uniformed guests to the civilians.

There had been of rumors about Massachusetts Senator David Walsh in the gay community. Decades later, Gore Vidal reported that the Senator was "trying to make my father when my father was a West Point cadet." He picked him and his roommate up when they were in Washington for the Woodrow Wilson inauguration and "chased them around the room."[30] Vidal also said that when Walsh was in Boston, the Senator was known for blowing boys at the Vendome Hotel and picking up sailors. Walsh and a friend, the manager of the Lenox Hotel, were said to frequent Boston gay bars together.

Walsh often stopped at Pacific St. on his trips between Boston and Washington. It appears the connections from his position on the Naval Affairs Committee tipped Walsh off regarding the investigation and his last trip to Pacific St. occurred two days before the surveillance began. Even so, several witnesses identified Walsh as the mysterious Doc or Senator X with their descriptions matching the senator down to his ruddy complexion, limp, and the distribution of his ripples of fat. After weeks of innuendo, The *New York Post* publicly named Walsh on May 7. Walsh vigorously denied the rumors and a special report by J. Edgar Hoover exonerated him. Despite Hoover's seal of approval and a Senate resolution supporting him, Walsh never recovered from the scandal and lost his seat in 1946. He died the next year.

The war also transformed Provincetown as the Navy based a large number of ships directly offshore with the sailors adding to the party atmosphere. The great playwright Tennessee Williams (1911-83) first lived in Provincetown in summer of 1940. He had been searching for a place to write where he could swim during the day and find men for sex at night. Asking around, friends suggested Provincetown. After trying out a few places, he settled on Number 6 Captain Jack's Wharf at 73A Commercial St. It had been converted into living spaces two decades earlier and in the 1940s, the rooms (all without heat or plumbing) could be rented by the week. Williams moved into the old smokehouse with two other men, the heterosexual Joe Hazan, a handsome model for the painter, Hans Hoffman, and Kip Kiernan (real name Bernard Dubowski) whom Williams would fall passionately and tempestuously in love. The three split the rent ($20 per week) between them.[31]

6.2 Captain Jack's Wharf, 1940 (Williams was in residence at the time of the photo)

Williams had a Rockefeller scholarship that paid him $100 per month. After paying for his New York sublet, he was left with just $2 per day for expenses. But living was cheap in Provincetown that summer. Williams often was given food by fisherman and when he had to buy provisions, they cost pennies. He rented a bicycle so he could ride to Race Point and Herring Cove, then called New Beach. Williams and Hazan liked the naked stretches beyond the tourist parts of the beach and there are a number of photographs of Williams in the nude. But the main attraction was sex. "Offering a glimpse of Provincetown's 1940 summer options, Williams noted that he was enamored with a ballet dancer; courted by a musician, a dancing instructor, and a language professor."[32]

Williams found Provincetown "dominated by a platinum blond Hollywood belle named Doug and a bull-dike named Wanda who is a well-known writer under a male pen-name, the most raffish and fantastic crew that I have met yet and even I—excessively broad minded as I am—feel somewhat shocked by the goings-on."[33] After fighting over a Yale freshman, Williams and the belle spent the night together. Williams thrived on a combination of alcohol, the beach, and writing while the large numbers of gay men helped his mood. He wrote a friend that "[t]he town is screaming with creatures not all of whom are seagulls."[33] Sometimes, however, he would turn bitter. "Pox on all of them—their Lord & Taylor T-shirts, flowered sarongs, baby-blue silk shorts! Portuguese natives have been beating them up on the streets at night lately and I am not sure which side I am on." Yet he would return to Provincetown several more times.

Even before the war, Provincetown was known (at least in some circles) for its LGBTQ drag balls. In 1928, for example, Eugene O'Neil remarked that Provincetown was full of gays, and drag queens were big later in the 1930s. Thus, it is not surprising that Williams attended a drag party, though he went in men's clothing.

During the war the entire town was blacked out at night, so when going into the A House, one entered through two sets of curtains. Inside there was dancing, sometimes to live music. Heavily gay but not yet officially so, both men and women went. "Sometimes the first thing that greeted you was the sight of Madame Pumpernickel, the elderly midget who occasionally played piano for the house band."[31] In a later visit, Williams lived in Mayflower Heights and in order to avoid a jealous lover, he would take men he picked up at the A House to the beach for sex. This was how he first met Frank Merlo, the love of his life. Williams wrote *The Glass Menagerie* and *A Streetcar Named Desire* in Provincetown but not (as rumored) at the A House. Rather, he wrote on the outskirts of town. Williams finished *The Glass Menagerie* in the Harvard Law School dormitory room of a man he met in Provincetown. The student was tall, gangly, dark-haired and a beatnik before the trend took off. He said he was straight but easily succumbed to Williams's attentions and by the time the play was finished he was full-on gay.[34] By the end of World War II, there were four main groups of LGBTQ people in Provincetown: the partying visitors, the artists, the outsiders who moved in year round, and the born-in-town group.[32] All got along just fine.

By World War II, the Boston's notorious Watch and Ward Society was losing its power and for the most part ignored LGBTQ issues. Its focus was on the media of the era: books, movies, and plays, but there was such strong self-censorship of any mention of LGBTQ people that there was no need for the society to step in. But the society did briefly go after gay men. In 1943 it targeted gays, placing the homes of suspected homosexuals under surveillance and they summoned the police who were more than happy to arrest the LGBTQ people gathered at house parties. A January 1944 raid on 126 Commonwealth Ave. resulted in the arrest of nine men with another raid the following year. But the arrested men escaped with nothing more than probation, prompting complaints from the society that judges were insufficiently hostile to gays. Frustrated, the society went back to book banning.[35]

This did not mean that the raids had no impact on people's lives. One man, Robert Reed, was at the Commonwealth Ave. house when it was raided. The Watch and Ward Society had placed the house under surveillance because there had been several previous parties there. When the police arrived, people "were just dancing and mingling, kissing and so forth, nothing specifically serious." There had been twenty people there including a "young lady who danced in veils on a big giant coffee table."[36] But there was no alcohol or marijuana, just soft drinks and people smoking tobacco; thus, there was no reason for the police to barge in except for the presence of LGBTQ people having a good time. The house was owned by Robert Milne who bailed everyone out of jail the next day. But because of the raid, Reed lost his job as an accounts clerk with an advertising company. "The aftermath of the raid at 126 Commonwealth was very, very devastating. People all over the city just would not go to parties. They would not go anywhere. It reverberated throughout the bars."

The large number of military men passing through Boston gave ample opportunities for meeting other men and having sex. The bar at the Statler Hotel, for example, was "packed with servicemen, several rows deep, standing against the long, crescent-shaped bar, too many to count, 100 maybe, maybe 150, most of them drinking beer from the bottle, loud with flighty talk and piercing laughter."[37] There were no women and few civilians among the crowd and all were gay. The Statler was busy at five, Napoleon's after nine.

There were formal parties in the Back Bay where one could discretely go into a bedroom with a new friend, or for the more adventurous, there were regularly scheduled orgies in a townhouse on Commonwealth Ave. near Boston University. On Boston Common was Buddies, a club for servicemen where straight men could meet local women who would show them a good time while those seeking men could meet others with similar interests. The straight world had no idea.

Women also flocked to the city to work in war industries. Many were housed in the Franklin House in the South End where there was a lesbian underground. Other women used their new freedom to explore their lesbianism, all part of the country's great new freedom temporarily available to LGBTQ people.

Yet there were limits. Townsend later told friends he was caught by a homeowner having sex in a doorway on Mount Vernon St. on Beacon Hill. He arrogantly refused to pay a $15 bribe to the arresting officer and was sentenced to the Deer Island Jail. The *Midtown Journal* (of dubious reliability) says Townsend was found guilty of "seducing a handsome boy of 18" who gave his testimony after extensive police questioning.[38] Released on VJ Day, Townsend coyly said he thought the jubilation in the streets was in honor of his release.[19]

Chapter 7

Post War

THE POSTWAR ERA created new opportunities for many LGBTQ people. The Montgomery GI Bill enabled millions of veterans to attend college. This in turn helped establish the acceptability that young people might live apart from families, unmarried, from high school graduation into at least their early twenties, after which they were still expected to marry. Thus, a single twenty-two year old did not arouse suspicions and some LGBTQ people had the time and space to explore living with their non-conforming gender and sexuality. Many of these people clustered in big cities and Boston, with its large numbers of colleges and universities, quickly became a magnet for young LGBTQ people.

Soon there would be another great shift in social norms: the sexual revolution. Kinsey's reports on sexual behavior rocked society's understanding of how people behaved as they revealed a wide range of sexual practices. These new observations regarding sexual activity among straight people led heterosexuals to reach out to each other in ways unimaginable to previous generations. Yet LGBTQ people could not participate in this new world of sex. Even as straight men and women asserted their right to be sexually active, the laws and social condemnations against same-sex activity remained strong as society continued to hate and despise LGBTQ people. If anything, the sexual revolution made them even more at risk as they lost their cover of celibacy created by sexual modesty. If everyone else was openly looking for heterosexual sex, those not actively involved in hooking up began to stick out. In addition, there was a growing disconnect between the personal freedom inside big city gay ghettos with their archipelagos of bars, cruising areas, and safe houses, and the horrific repression in straight society. The freedom inside certain areas actually put LGBTQ people at increased risk outside as there were now greater opportunities to slip up and reveal their outlaw sexuality and more potential witnesses to denounce them. The situation was unstable.

As they made their way into the hostile world and began to hear about other like-minded people, LGBTQ people had to make bleak choices regarding how to live their lives. They could try to suppress their same-sex desires and follow the standard heterosexual path mandated for them by marrying and having children, or they throw themselves as deep into the urban ghettos as they dared, living there fulltime or only entering in occasional furtive visits. Rejecting oppression across New England and beyond, some LGBTQ people moved to Boston to find others like themselves. Some married or tried to cure themselves by undergoing the horrific range of treatments (psychoanalysis, hospitalization, therapy, drugs, and electroshock treatments) offered to them by doctors who were more or less quacks. Powered by stress and the bigotry of straight society, many turned to alcohol and drugs, some turned to religion, and others fled to New York or Europe.

The growing red scare created further repression. As the nation sought to purge itself of communists and their sympathizers, LGBTQ people were a close second on the list of undesirables. The same tactics of overzealous law enforcement, dubious investigations, and extreme repression honed during the prosecution of suspected communists were used on gay men, lesbians, and gender non-conforming people. First society forced LGBTQ people deep into the closet, then it cited their secrecy as evidence of their perversion and untrustworthiness.

Homosexuality was morally repugnant according to mainstream religious thought at the time and medical authorities considered homosexuals sick, while law enforcement personnel maintained they were criminals. As the hysteria increased, society decided homosexuals needed to be found, shunned, arrested, and fired. In addition, the moral turpitude of homosexuals meant that the presence of just one could corrupt the strength and morals of the many around them. Homosexuals were rotting the backbone of the country, it was declared, just as it was locked in mortal combat with the international communist conspiracy. Add the risk of blackmail that could also lead to security breaches, and the panic only increased. The oppression of the 1950s was different than the past. It was organized, systematic, and rooted in a fundamental national policy of intolerance. Like their counterparts elsewhere in the country, Boston LGBTQ people suffered intensely as a result.

Encouraged by the national witch hunt, local police departments carried out waves of raids on bars, cruising areas, and parties at private homes with a national survey indicating that one in five gay men and lesbians had experienced police harassment.1 Fortunately, Boston escaped the worst of these law enforcement crackdowns and while there were raids on bars, these were mostly shakedowns of bar owners and though the patrons had their IDs checked, they were generally left alone. Those found without IDs, however, were arrested while others were shaken down for bribes, so the harassment was oppressive. Furthermore, bar patrons must have been aware of the mass arrests in other cities and never knew if that night's raid might be the beginning of a process that would result in lost jobs and social ruin. These raids were so traumatizing that decades later they were vividly recalled by the people caught up in them.

The Boston bar raids this time around focused on stopping same-sex couples from dancing. This was a new concept. Before World War II, few same-sex couples dared dance in public, though it happened on occasion. But the newfound sexual freedoms enjoyed by straight society emboldened those inside the LGBTQ world and a few Boston bars began to feature dancing, bringing on the raids. This disconnect would grow over time and contribute to the explosion of activism in the late 1960s.

Facing overwhelming repression on nearly every level, some LGBTQ people began to organize a resistance. It was small, even timid by the standards of today, but in fact it took tremendous courage within the context of the times. The largest organization of gay men (the Mattachine Society) was born in November 1950 out of meetings at the Los Angeles home of Harry Hay. The group sought to use education to challenge prevailing social norms and ideas regarding homosexuality. Contrary to what most people then believed, they asserted that homosexuality was not a moral, medical, or criminal problem. It was simply something different than the majority. The laws that sent men and women to jail and the distaste that resulted in people being fired and shunned by their families were unjust ways of maintaining unnecessary social norms.

The Mattachine Society was founded by former Communist Party members and other leftists. By 1953 the organization had several thousand members and expanded geographically, including a Boston chapter. Then a reporter raised questions about the very existence of a gay organization and uncovered the communist associations of several of its founders. Members demanded an end to the secrecy and instituted a loyalty oath to assure members and outsiders that the society was not a communist organization.

The Daughters of Bilitis (DOB), a group for lesbians, was organized in San Francisco in 1955. Less overtly communist that the Mattachine Society, it was a middle-class white organization that emphasized its conformity to straight social values. Both organizations appealed to only a sliver of the population. DOB openly disliked bars and sought to convince women to leave the working class for better jobs while it criticized women who adopted masculine dress. Similarly, as the Mattachine Society transformed itself into a conformist group, it blasted men who were effeminate and wanted nothing to do with people who might be transgender.[1]

The Mattachine Society did not last. Its magazine, One, was seized as an obscene publication in 1956. This was overturned by the Supreme Court in 1958, the first national LGBTQ civil rights victory but this success came at the cost of sapping much of the society's strength. After the national organization dissolved, each local chapter was forced to rely on its own resources and the Boston chapter collapsed a few years later. DOB survived, but it had less of a national reach and its Boston chapter withered by the beginning of the 1960s.

As a closeted lesbian with progressive ideas about prison administration and as head of Massachusetts's women's prison, Miriam Van Waters was in a precarious position after World War II. For a while she managed to avoid too much attention, but her luck didn't last. She dodged a commissioner who was openly hostile to her progressive ideas. There was also an unsuccessful attempt in the legislature to end her internship program and a dispute with the parole board distracted her attention. Van Waters' critics were relentless and they pivoted to another line of attack: she was tolerating lesbian activity at the Framingham prison. The accusations filled the newspapers.

A new commissioner, Elliot McDowell, appointed Frank Dwyer to investigate Framingham and Van Waters. Dwyer was particularly homophobic, boasting of his horror of homosexuals and that he had once beaten a man because he was gay. His power was based on his political connections; he had once been the driver for Governor Hurley.

The trigger for the investigation was the suicide of an inmate. Van Waters' opponents suggested the prisoner was murdered because she was part of a lesbian sex ring. Although Dwyer quickly concluded that the death was indeed a suicide unconnected to sex, he uncovered rumors of inmates sleeping together and lesbians among the staff. Once McDowell told Dwyer to investigate these new allegations, the witch hunt was on.

Dwyer grilled Van Waters for five hours while current and former employees were questioned about their personal lives. Van Waters' policy of hiring former inmates, a key part of her agenda to both give ex-convicts jobs and make prison conditions humane, was accused of contributing to the rampant immorality. The smallest detail was suspect. Employees were asked which women wore flat shoes or other evidence of mannish behavior, for example, and damning evidence included the habit of one female deputy superintendent to wear a coat and tie to church. Dwyer also asked employees to indicate which female employees acted like queens, confusing gay male terminology with lesbian stereotypes.

Rumors circulated that Van Waters was a lesbian, but the press did not report them. Dwyer tried to find evidence to use against her, even questioning former household employees, but no one assisted him and as much as he tried to tie Van Waters to Thompson, nothing he found was explicit enough to get her fired.

Van Waters defended herself and her institution by saying that while there may have been female-female relationships going on, none were predatory or pathological and that unconventional behaviors were irrelevant. For the most part, she relied on her cool, unemotional professional expertise but to protect herself, she burned her letters and purged her diaries, scrubbing her past of all incriminating information. She knew the immense emotional cost of destroying nearly twenty-two years of love letters to and from Thompson and that she was annihilating part of herself. But she had no choice.

A panel was established to investigate the conditions at Framingham. The governor's members were sympathetic to Van Waters while those appointed by the legislature were divided, giving Van Waters the upper hand. Meanwhile, McDowell did his best to undercut Van Waters' authority and the two were at a stalemate. Then, State Senator Michael Lo Presti added another dimension to the attacks by trying to tie Van Waters and her allies to communism. Van Waters, a lifelong conservative Republican found herself being accused of being a communist just as the red scare was at its height.[2]

Van Waters and Thompson, in the fight of their lives, pulled in every ally they could find including clergy, former inmates, penal experts, and academics. They formed the Friends of the Framingham Reformatory that included Felix Frankfurter and Claude Cross, who would later defend Alger Hiss. The group couldn't stop the attacks and on January 7, 1949 Van Waters was fired. The nine page dismissal letter outlined twenty-seven accusations including letting inmates attend school, allowing inmates to work at jobs ranging from domestics to auto mechanics, and giving inmates movie passes. More serious charges included hiring relatives and former inmates to work at the prison.

Van Waters was prepared. With Governor Paul Dever now in office, she had Eleanor Roosevelt persuade newly elected Senator John F. Kennedy to lobby him. In addition, Roosevelt helped Van Waters become a national cause for liberals with her case compared to the Sacco-Vanzetti and Scopes trials. The inquest dragged on with public hearings so large they were moved to Gardner Auditorium in the Massachusetts State House. Van Waters was masterful and coolly competent when discussing policy, sometimes in tears when the credibility of allies was questioned. She dressed in attire that was both feminine and businesslike and she impressed the audience and reporters with her poise and stamina. The hearing, including testimony and cross examinations, took eighteen long days.

Part of Van Waters' defense rested on her use of medical and psychiatric personnel to diagnose homosexuality rather than relying on lay people assessing mannerisms or dress. She refused to classify a woman as lesbian simply because she did not conform to gender norms and even same-sex behavior was dismissed as being situational or transitory. Unless a woman was diagnosed by a doctor as a lesbian, she didn't classify a woman as such. At the time, the prime tool to diagnose lesbianism was a Rorschach test, which was worthless, of course. But this scientific approach enabled many straight middle-class allies to support her even as they remained anti-gay.[2]

Not surprisingly, Commissioner McDowell upheld the dismissal. Governor Dever then set up a three person panel to decide Van Waters' appeal. More hearings followed including one full day of testimony regarding what was homosexuality. The tide was turning to Van Waters' favor, however, with the opponents' case severely undermined when Dwyer had to physically restrain McDowell when he tried to attack his own attorney. On March 11, 1949, the panel voted to overturn Van Waters' firing while focusing on minor infractions rather than on the accusations of immorality.

Her worst opponent, McDowell, retired in 1951 and though Van Waters faced mandatory retirement in 1952, she was allowed to stay on for five more years. Despite surviving the attempt to fire her, she continued to face pressure from conservative opponents. Later, Van Waters began a relationship with another woman, a former convict turned prison reformer. She received permission to hire her in a temporary position at Framingham but was then forced to let her go when it was revealed the woman was a communist sympathizer. The woman moved to New York where she and Van Waters wrote love letters to each other nearly every day. To escape scrutiny, Van Waters rented a post office box but unknown to her, the FBI intercepted the letters and concluded the two were in a lesbian relationship. They did not pursue the matter, however.

In July 1957, an escaped prisoner claimed she had run away to avoid being forced to have lesbian sex and again there were lurid stories in the press. Another state commission agreed with the accusations stating further that homosexuality was a disease that could be spread by close contact. Therefore, it was a vice that had to be rigorously suppressed. Her health deteriorating, Van Waters retired in October 1957.

With the war over and veterans flooding back to Cambridge, 1940s Harvard provided mixed opportunities for gay men; some found the climate exciting while others were miserable. One man, Prescott Clarridge, would later boast that he "found a very active underground homosexual life. We had gay cocktail parties and late-night orgies, cruised the many gay bars of Boston as well as the gay-friendly Club 100 and Casablanca in the Square. Some of us cruised the Lamont Library bathroom. We had affairs and breakups and did a lot of gossiping—just like today."[3]

His gay world extended across the region. Bernard Heyl, head of the Art Department at Wellesley, used to have Sunday afternoon tea dances at his suburban home where no tea was served, but there was lots of scotch and dancing. The parties were full of servicemen and college students, including Clarridge, as well as older men. Most of the servicemen were only interested in older men who could pay them for sex.

Clarridge visited Stewart Mitchell at the Harvard Club, where he was paid $5 for an evening, and he went out with Henry-Russell Hitchcock. "When he'd take me to dinner when in Boston, being slightly deaf, his conversation, spoken in such loud sotto voce that it could be heard several tables away, included his amorous conquests in his worldly travels as well as a description of what he'd like to do with me. Bearded, imperious and physically impressive, he seemed to get away with it."[4] Hitchcock took Clarridge to visit Philip Johnson at his famous glass house in New Canaan, Connecticut where as much as Hitchcock tried to steer the conversation to gay sex, Johnson resisted.

According to Clarridge, at night half of the clientele at Locke Ober's (one of the city's poshest and stodgiest restaurants) was gay as older wealthy men chose to dine there with their young male dates. Many gay Harvard students liked to go to dinner or the theatre with older gentlemen such as Nat Saltonstall, Prescott Townsend, Mitchell, and Heyl. One man who lived on Beacon Hill was known for not only collecting Harvard students, but also sailors and marines. Another man threw a party for men from the USS Baltimore at the Sheraton Plaza where fifteen to twenty sailors showed up.

Not every sailor was gay friendly. On the night of December 9, 1953, John Effner, twenty-two, of Lawrence, Michigan met John Borland, twenty-six, at a Boston bar. After a couple of drinks together, Borland invited Effner, who was stationed on the Baltimore, back to his rooming house at 337 Marlborough St. where around 1:30 in the morning Borland, according to Effner, made "improper advances" to him. Described by the Globe as tall, blonde, and handsome, Effner confessed he was so outraged that he bludgeoned Borland several times and fled the apartment but not before stealing Borland's watch, ring, and $2 from his wallet. Borland's body was found by his landlady the next day and his watch was traced to a Charlestown pawn shop which led the police to Effner. He confessed to the murder, telling the police he struck Borland two or three times with a homemade blackjack "fashioned from wire, sheet metal, and lead."[5]

There were other dangers. A black Harvard student was expelled after being found necking with another student in the Eliot House library while another Eliot House student was thrown out of the college after a similar scandal around the same time. One killed himself.[6]

Another postwar gay Harvard man was the poet and influential art critic Frank O'Hara (1927-66). He was raised in a comfortable Irish Catholic home in Grafton, just outside of Worcester. The Depression had barely been noticed by his family, which lived in a prosperous part of town and vacationed on Cape Cod every summer. Though his parents were uneducated, O'Hara grew up playing Beethoven, Gershwin, and Shostakovich while reading Joyce, Hemingway, and Stein, and learning enough about art to favor Picasso over Braque.

Like many young LGBTQ people in that era, he was profoundly isolated from others with similar interests. O'Hara organized activities and arranged outings for his friends, yet he rarely dated girls. Instead, he was a loner, always apart from his peers. In this case, the isolation was made greater because other than prowess at swimming, O'Hara was very unathletic and he attended a Catholic boy's high school in Worcester rather than the local high school in Grafton. There was a price for this repression. Though later O'Hara would be known for his wit and sparkling personality, his childhood classmates remember him as reserved and quiet. Mostly he retreated to the studio space where he read, wrote poetry, and from what his writings at the time seem to indicate, frequently masturbated. O'Hara's first sexual experience was with a stable boy in a barn on his family's farm.[7]

Serving in the war helped liberate O'Hara mentally. He spent less than two years in the navy and by the end he was determined to remain apart from Grafton and his family. Sexually, it was less liberating and though he was stationed at times in Key West and San Francisco, he had little sex beyond a few furtive encounters. There were crushes and platonic relationships but none he considered to be full-fledged love affairs. At the time, O'Hara successfully maintained a mask of bland two dimensionality with those who saw through his disguise not inclined to bring up the subject.

Once at Harvard, the twenty-year old O'Hara kept the private screen around himself and though many began to sense he was different, no one called him out during his freshman or sophomore year. His Grafton friends came to realize that O'Hara had no sexual interest in girls, but the subject remained unmentioned.

Then O'Hara began to reveal himself under the friendship of Edward Gorey, who would later gain fame as a macabre illustrator. Another freshman veteran, Gorey was tall and dressed flamboyantly in black. Becoming roommates, they decorated their Eliot House suite with lawn furniture and a tombstone used as a table. Gorey often fell asleep in the living room after all-nighters spent designing wall paper and drawing ghoulish Edwardian cartoons using India ink. Some of O'Hara's music department friends thought that Gorey had corrupted him.

O'Hara and Gorey were not lovers but they consciously adopted the highly stylized manners of an Oscar Wilde-era couple.[7] Becoming more socially comfortable, O'Hara began to use his ability to dominate a conversation and his animated Irish background to charm people. O'Hara was finally dropping his mask, but he could not come out of the closet entirely. His poetry professor suggested that O'Hara was using his brilliant talent as a disguise rather than a vehicle to convey who he was.

O'Hara began to carefully construct a supportive environment of close friends and admirers. In his senior year O'Hara moved away from Gorey and was finally able to come out. He had several discrete liaisons with other students and began to enjoy seducing men. That year, O'Hara had a relationship with a non-veteran student from the class of 1950, Laurence Osgood. A native of Buffalo, Osgood had dropped out for a year for psychoanalysis in Philadelphia and then continued to see a therapist to deal with his homosexuality. After a night of drinking that ended with them back in O'Hara's room with a bottle of Southern Comfort, O'Hara and Osgood were dancing to Marlena Dietrich records when O'Hara decided he wanted Osgood. It was Osgood's first time with a man and O'Hara kept asking him if he was okay. Osgood saw the evening as the beginning of a relationship, while O'Hara just wanted a one night stand.

Growing bolder, O'Hara began to sample Boston's nightlife. After graduation, O'Hara lived in an apartment on Myrtle St. in Beacon Hill where he threw himself into Boston's gay scene. Not yet settling on a career in poetry, O'Hara wrote a first draft of a novel about gay men in Boston. In the book, these men drank at the Silver Dollar, breathing in air heavy with cigarette smoke while listening to music. They went to the beach in Revere to relax, Scollay Square for fast pickups (one character loses his virginity there), and the back of the hill to drink with friends in private apartments.[8]

Also attending Harvard at the time was the future poet, John Ashbery (1927-2007). He did not have any relationships at Harvard until his sophomore year when he heard a man refer to himself as gay and decided to meet him. Then, an affair with another student resulted in Ashbery learning about gay nightlife in Boston. His favorite bar was the Chess Room in the Hotel Touraine because he liked its old-style decorations. He had several sexual encounters with men he met in Harvard Square. But throughout this period, he was careful to keep his sexuality secret from his straight friends. He was not the only one being secretive; a gay student couple that Ashbery was friends with moved to Beacon Hill so they could live together.[9] Ashbery began an affair with a sailor he met at the Silver Dollar, but because overnight guests were not allowed in the dorms and homosexuality was grounds for expulsion, the sailor had to sneak out the window of Ashbery's first floor room each night.

There were late night parties at Harvard after the bars closed, with people coming in from Boston for the action. If the party grew too loud the police would show up, but they were polite and didn't pry, even if the door was answered by a young man in nothing but a towel. Since girls weren't allowed in the Harvard houses after seven, it wasn't unusual for there to be male only parties, sometimes with as many as thirty men present. The unspoken rule at gay Harvard cocktail gatherings was that there would be no sex, no making out. That was reserved for late night parties. These parties ended in 1949 after several gay men were forced to leave Harvard.

Though most accounts of this era are from middle- or upper-class men, there is one story about two poor men living together in the New York Streets area of the South End. Charles Gautreau, known by his drag name, Thelma, shared a room with Peter Seifried, better known as May. They were so poor that there were rumors they had captured a swan in the Public Garden and were about to cook it when their landlady stopped them. From their room, it was a short walk to their favorite bar, Playland, where they were in their element. "If life was not easy, it could be glamorous with just the right touch of make-up and attitude," recalled Thelma.[10] One night, May was arrested on suspicion of solicitation, and when she got to the station house, she was charged with armed robbery. But May had an alibi and was released though she could have been prosecuted for being in full drag.

Boston had a thriving gay-for-pay scene as evidenced by the histories of two famous men who were young in the postwar era. One of them, Malcolm X (1925-65), born Malcom Little, first arrived in Boston for a short stay when he was fourteen. He later lived in various locations in and around the South End and Roxbury while also spending time in Harlem and elsewhere. In October 1944, he became involved with a wealthy gay white man, William Paul Lennon, who maintained a house at 5 Arlington St. overlooking the public garden. Malcom worked briefly as a butler for Lennon. In his autobiography, Malcom tells of a man named Rudy but thought to be himself, Malcolm wrote that "Once a week, Rudy went to the home of this old, rich Boston blueblood, pillar-of-society aristocrat. He paid Rudy to undress them both, then pick up the old man like a baby, lay him on his bed, then stand over him and sprinkle him all over with talcum powder."[11]

Lennon was the son of a wealthy Rhode Island family. Born in 1888, he was a veteran and had managed hotels. In 1938, he married a wealthy divorced socialite, Jeanne Marie Scott, with whom he maintained houses in Florida and Sandwich. Scott was famous for her World War I romance with Hobey Baker, the Princeton football and hockey star for whom the annual award for best college hockey player is named. Lennon and Scott separated in 1948. Years later, Lennon made the news when police responded to his Cape Cod home to find him and two naked twenty-something male servants tied up and robbed.

There is no reason to believe that Malcolm was gay or bisexual or that these and other same-sex encounters in his youth meant that he was drawn to sex with men.

Malcolm made it very clear this was strictly a business transaction done to support himself. Keeping his "two lives separate from each other was never easy, due to his unstable material circumstances. But Malcolm had the intelligence and ingenuity to mask his most illegal and potentially upsetting activities from his family and friends."[12]

Another man later famous who hustled in his early years was James "Whitey" Bulger. A product of the South Boston projects, the blonde, good looking Bulger liked to frequent bars around Park Square, particularly the Punch Bowl and Mario's, and pick up tricks and at least once he was arrested for robbing them.[13] Years later, he would be known as the region's most notorious mobster and when he fled after receiving a tip that his arrest was imminent, was on the FBI's ten most wanted list. Bulger kept his gay adventures quiet; few knew that he also frequently visited Provincetown as late as the 1970s, staying at the Crown and Anchor.

Mark Krone, the respected chronicler of Boston gay history, assessed 1950s LGBTQ Boston as "risky and certainly underground. But for those who went to bars, nightclubs and restaurants that attracted a gay clientele, Boston gay nightlife was rich, varied and even glamorous."[14] One neighborhood that had attracted LGBTQ people for decades by the time World War II ended, Scollay Square, continued to a place for men to cruise, particularly those in the service. The area, close to Beacon Hill and downtown, featured bars, restaurants, and cheap rooms as well as all-night movie houses that were patronized by gay men looking for sex.

Another area with LGBTQ nightlife was Lower Washington St., the few tawdry blocks already known as the Combat Zone (though it would not be formally established as an adult entertainment district until several decades later). Though the Chess Room at the Touraine Hotel continued to have a crowd and Playland had been around for years, the Silver Dollar was the most popular bar as it attracted everyone from Harvard students to sailors to Boston bluebloods. Whenever Prescott Townsend walked through its doors "the piano player would strike up 'As Time Goes By.'"[15]

By then, the bar had lost had any glamour it once had. "There was no denying the Silver Dollar was a bucket of blood, plain and simple. Lots of sailors and lots of fights. Cheap liquor and loud music 13 hours per day. But some of the music played at the Silver Dollar Bar, at Washington and Essex Streets, was pretty good, even if it was hard to hear it."[16] Decades later, the great entertainer Sylvia Sydney recalled "[o]h, the Silver Dollar? It was fab-u-lous, my dear, longest bar in Boston. Sailors galore. Whores galore. Gay people galore."[17] Too young to enter, Sydney would stand across the street and invite sailors back to his apartment for a drink after midnight when the bars closed.

In the postwar Silver Dollar, "[t]he uniform as a rule was penny loafers, gabardine slacks, sometimes sweaters, sometimes tweed jackets and colored shirts had just come in, colored sports shirts." One man remembers how the dress code finally fell apart. "I was the first one who came in with Levi jeans, skin tight with a jacket to match, I had 16 sets of them and I had them all numbered and each set would be washed at the same time."[18]

Before World War II, the Silver Dollar had been relatively tame, most noted for hosting Evelyn Nesbitt whose husband, Harry Kendall Thaw, had murdered Stanford White, the famous architect, because of the couple's affair. After the bar featured Nesbitt and other faded stars in its nightclub acts, it showcased jazz. When the bar was sold in 1955, it was renamed the Palace though it attracted the same crowd. Over time the bar declined and gays went elsewhere. It had several more names before the building burned down in 1983.

The most popular bar between the end of World War II and 1968 was the Punch Bowl in Park Square, a neighborhood that increased its number of gay bars as they left the increasingly run down Scollay Square area. "Park Square was where all the sissies would go," recalled T.J., a former librarian who frequented the area's bars and baths in the 1950s and '60s.[19] The Punch Bowl was impossible to miss; it had a large sign outside and a long line of people eager to enter. Originally called Phil Silver's, the Punch Bowl was opened by Henry Vara in 1946. Initially featuring mixed clientele, Vara (who was straight) quickly made it into a major place for LGBTQ nightlife and among the people who showed up over the years were Robert Mitchum and Rudolph Nureyev. In its most popular years there could be 700 people inside with another 200 in line to get in. It expanded over time so one side was a lesbian bar, in the middle was a bar for gay men and on the other side was a lounge for people to sit and talk, while the basement was for dancing. Ellie played on a broken down piano in one room with Freddie in the quieter lounge.[20]

Jacques, on Broadway in Bay Village, opened in the late 1940s and is now one of the oldest gay bars in the country. The longevity of these bars demonstrates the difference between Boston and other cities. Elsewhere, gay bars were mostly transitory as it was illegal to serve alcohol to homosexuals or allow them in a drinking establishment. In Boston by contrast, as long as the patrons conformed to strict standards of behavior, the bars' licenses were safe.

The bars specialized according to which type of crowd patronized them. The Napoleon Club, for example, was a coat and tie establishment that attracted older men; the Punch Bowl was a place where people went to hook up; and Mario's and Jacques were more diverse. Napoleon's decor was plush and grand with its lighting soft and indirect, the better to flatter faded complexions. Guests found hours of enjoyment around a baby grand piano in communal sing-alongs and occasional virtuoso performances. For example, Judy Garland reportedly sang there after downtown engagements, and Liberace, Noel Coward, Vladimir Horowitz, and Leonard Bernstein took turns at Napoleon's baby grand. The entire cast of *La Cage aux Folles* showed up after their opening-night performance and composer Jerry Herman banged out the show's edgy, defiant tunes–*I Am What I Am* was long a crowd favorite.[21] In the fifties Napoleon's "possessed the world's oldest hat-check girl, a beldame who would snatch off Batman's mask and cape, a yarmulke, a sultan's turban or the head-bandages of a man who had just undergone brain surgery."[15] All paid a quarter to retrieve their items. Not everyone liked the bar. The poet, Steve Jonas, complained it was full of shop clerks and decorators.

On the northern edge of Beacon Hill, Sporters was a dirty dingy bar that dated back to 1939. In the mid-1950s, when Harvard Gardens began to discourage LGBTQ people from drinking there, they began frequenting Sporters. Sylvia Sydney said it was a "broken bar, with a broken down piano, and sawdust on the floor—a real dump." It was a favorite of LGBTQ college students.

The Beacon Hill bars were also divided by class: the Sevens was like the Napoleon's, mostly for upscale older men; Harvard Gardens was similar to Mario's or Jacques, catering to working class men; and Sporters was like the Punch Bowl, the place to go to hook up.[20] All Boston bars closed at 1 a.m. on weeknights and midnight on Saturdays because of the city's strict blue laws, so there was a robust post-bar scene in nearby restaurants. The Waldorf Cafeteria was nicknamed the gay apple, while the nearby Hayes Bickford was called the gay Hayes. The Hayes was full of drag queens and had a reputation that anything might happen. For example, one night a man came into the restaurant "with a basket of roses, flinging them in his path as he went."[22] After they left the bars, men would walk home across the Public Garden and Common, some still cruising as they made the trek home. The area of the Public Garden along Beacon St. was known as Queens Row as men sat on benches and eyed those walking by.

There were also bars, not openly LGBTQ but full of gay men, in Harvard Square. There was the Oxford Grill in the 1940s and the Casablanca from the late 1940s to the 1960s (though it was open for decades longer). Neither admitted they were gay gathering spots or that their clientele was mixed. Harvard students liked Casablanca because it had a dress code.[23]

There were many colorful people working in these bars. Sylvia Sydney was an entertainment mainstay who performed in the city's gay bars for over forty years. Sydney's first gay experience came after he was invited to join a group of gay men while at a concert on the Esplanade in 1946. This led to him going to a party and then having sex. The self-styled "mess in a dress" started in show business in July 1947. He was not a drag queen and referred to himself using male pronouns. "I look more like a hardcore madam, sort of a Mae West caricature." He was very proud of his stage persona. "My act is being me. Being loud, vulgar, coarse. I use every word you can imagine—filthy, dirty."[17] Sydney was also known for his roaring hijinks offstage. Decades later, one man couldn't stop laughing as he recalled being chased around the Eagle by Sydney, who had taken out his false teeth to bite him.

There were also bars for women. In 1950 or 1951, a male date took Alice Foley, who decades later would be the town nurse in Provincetown during the AIDS crisis, to a bar located on Warrenton St. under what later became the Charles Theatre. The women called it the Midtown, the men the Cha Cha Palace. "Once the men discovered it, we lost it," lamented Foley.[24] The Midtown attracted a large range of lesbians in the early 1950s, from college educated women to high-school dropouts. It had women from South Boston as well as black and Latina women. On nearby Tremont St., Cavana's "had a piano player there, Nan, who looked like a man. She looked like a little man, little short hair, little hands and little fat fingers on the piano. And she always wore a skirt, a black skirt, and pumps and nylons. And a black tuxedo jacket and a shirt with a bow tie."[24] These bars were not necessarily friendly. Cavana's "was a perfect example of Fifties-oppressive: the bar-side was full of pseudo-macho men, who would sit and make jokes about dykes, who were all in the back."[25] It was demolished for the Castle Square renewal project.

7.1 Queens Row (2018)

To enter the Midtown "[y]ou came into The Rio Casino [a strip bar] and there was a door that matched the paneling on the wall. And Nick was its mafia controller, Nick sat on this bar stool and I don't mean that in an ethnic thing."[24] Nick would warn about the police and patrons knew to keep their driver's license and $5 for the police during a raid or else the police might arrest them for vagrancy. If taken away by the police, the men might be beat up, the women raped, and if the person was prominent,

The Hub of the Gay Universe

these ID checks could lead to blackmail. Yet the bars were safer than socializing outdoors.

There was another attraction. "Ah, the Cha Cha, it was the only place you could dance, boys with boys," one man remembered fondly of the days before the Punch Bowl opened a dance floor, and "[g]irls with girls. Of course, girls didn't have trouble dancing together, as long as it was innocent. But this was real dancing, with lots of grinding and smoochy face stuff as we jokingly called it."[26]

Dancing only happened on Thursday nights and the police raided the bar about once a month. "In a twinkling of an eye all the queer boys changed partners with the dykes and it looked like a normal sock hop, only the girls had shorter hair, and the men often wore mascara."[26] Another man recalled, "[s]ome of the funniest sights were of Fifties-style dykes in leather and denim and D.A.-type slick Fifties faggots like myself pairing up like it was junior prom night."[22]

The rules against drag were very strictly enforced and bars were temporarily shut down for men wearing more women's clothing than allowed. The College Inn, for example, wasn't completely drag as that was against the law. Still, it had to give up its license for a month in January 1952 following a city-wide crackdown on establishments with female impersonators that began when Cardinal Cushing complained about how wild the scene in bars was becoming. This crackdown also prompted a number of non-gender conforming people to leave Boston for other cities. The Collage Inn was owned by Rocco "Rocky" Palladino, a small-time mobster who also owned race horses and the Latin Quarter club in Bay Village. The Boston Licensing Board had made female impersonators on stage illegal in 1948, but defiantly, the College Inn's performers and waiters went as close to the legal limit as possible. "They used to wear makeup and have their hair bleached and teased up, but they weren't allowed to wear dresses or heels. They would wear women's slacks and a frilly blouse, lots of makeup, and maybe earrings or something, rings, and paint their nails."[18] Sylvia Sydney also remembered the laws against dressing up in the 1950s: "[w]e never went out on the street in drag; that was a sure way to get arrested."[27]

Getting arrested could be devastating. "Careers were destroyed, lives were ruined. It was harassment, plain and simple and it was hard for many people to venture out of their lifelong closets."[26] The repression sparked a need for release, "I've seen people sitting on the subway all closed in on themselves not speaking to anyone. Then they get off the train and go into a bar and go crazy: they're basket-cruising, drinking up a storm, and acting outrageous from the start."[27]

In 1954, the Latin Quarter hired Christine Jorgensen, famous for being the first person in the United States to have her sex changed, to perform for a week in February. She never made it on stage. "Mary Driscoll, chair of the Boston Licensing Board, said she'd 'move heaven and earth' to prevent the show on the grounds that Jorgensen was a female impersonator. Upon being told Jorgensen wasn't impersonating anybody, the Boston City Council passed an order essentially forcing Jorgensen to submit to a medical examination."[28] Jorgensen sued but the show was cancelled. She only was permitted to go on stage in Boston in the 1960s.

Though she was tough and uncompromising, Driscoll could also be surprisingly protective of gay bars in the city. In January 1955, for example, the military announced a crackdown on LGBTQ Boston by declaring a number of bars off limits to military personnel. The publicity around the ban did not say these were gay places, but the eleven bars included the LGBTQ establishments of the Midtown Café, Playland, the Silver Dollar, the Touraine Café, and the Punch Bowl as well as the 411 Club (predominately a straight bar catering to African Americans but also patronized by trans people of color) and four other South End bars. In addition, servicemen were prohibited from being on the Esplanade or in the Public Garden and Common after 10:00 p.m. (note that this did not include the Fens, perhaps indicating that it was not yet a popular cruising area). The ban on servicemen in parks was first implemented in 1942 but hadn't been reissued since that time. The stated reason for declaring the bars off limits was to prevent interactions between military men and teenaged girls as well as because the bars were serving underage soldiers.

The military demanded Boston shut down these bars but the city refused to be bullied. Driscoll announced that the Licensing Board would look into the allegations. After an investigation, the Midtown was temporarily suspended for having two women tending bar (illegal in Boston at the time) and a man in a woman's hat and shawl singing an obscene version of *A Good Man is Hard to Find*.[29] The era of tight regulation was nearly finished, however. By 1960, though it was still a misdemeanor to appear publicly in drag, the police let professional entertainers cross dress even if they would still arrest people so dressed in the audience. Sydney began to bill himself as "the mess in a dress." After 1965, people could safely cross dress anywhere in Boston, though trans prostitutes are still sometimes harassed by the police to this day.

Since many men could not take partners home, there were other places to have sex in private. The Broadway Hotel at the corner of Tremont and Broadway was not an LGBTQ hotel, but it was a place to rent a room if someone picked up a friend for the night. The Essex Hotel was not LGBTQ, either, but it attracted a lot of gay men. There were rooming houses in Bay Village that served as places for temporary relations and there are stories about an "orgy-pad" in an "unfashionable part of Cambridge" frequented by Harvard athletes in search of cash and no-strings-attached sex. It was said that Nat Saltonstall and Ed Hood (who would later star in Andy Warhol movies) patronized the festivities.[15]

There were also bathhouses. Lundine's Turkish Baths on Carver Street could hold 150 people. It had Moorish arches and tile work to make it look like a hammam, prompting gay nightlife impresario, Phil Bayone, to call it the "Turkish embassy."[15] It closed in the 1960s but never attracted city notice because it didn't serve alcohol. On "Friday and Saturday nights, there'd be a whole line of people going from the steps down, down along Carver Street, to get into the place." One man remembered that "[i]t was filthy, it was sordid inside, but yet it was campy, too."[30] Some people looked down on the men who went there because there was no hiding that it was just for anonymous sex.

In the Back Bay, where the luxurious Copley Place Mall now straddles the Massachusetts Turnpike maze of exit ramps, was the Irvington Hotel. Some men lived there full time while cruising was on just two of its ten floors. It was noted for its dinginess. "[T]hat was another place that was dirty, but they had sheets on the beds and they had these mangy old World War I blankets, some were khaki and some were grey and scratchy, probably never cleaned at all."[30] Men could meet men in the halls, the bathrooms, or just leave their room door open.

Charley Shively, who would become a prominent gay activist in the 1970s, entered Harvard in 1955. He went most of his freshman year without sex, but then discovered there was lots of gay action in the newly opened Lamont Library bathrooms and he met other men down by the riverbank.[31] He also cruised the Public Garden in 1961 and noted that other men liked to check out the Esplanade on summer nights. Gay men were already moving into the South End by the 1950s, though the highest concentrations of gay men still lived in Back Bay and Beacon Hill. Throughout these gay neighborhoods there were many house parties, some with a dozen or more men and though occasionally a couple would slip away to a bedroom, these weren't orgies. Some parties "were very elegant and they had nice dinners, beautiful tablecloths and crystal and China."[18] By now, there were many man and women in couples openly together, even buying houses together. Still, large numbers of LGBTQ people in Boston were married or deep in the closet.

The city was full of places to cruise. Men met in the bars, on the street, or at the movies. The Stuart Theatre was known for being gay and there was the Rialto in Scollay Square as well as the Cobb Theatre on Washington St. near Dover St. Taking advantage of the many men looking for sex, Townsend kept his rooms at Phillips St. stocked with boys of every variety. "What they all had in common was a waist size of 30" or under."[15] One of his favorite places to pick them up was at Brimstone corner, specifically the sidewalk in front of the Park Street Church but in popular usage also including the plaza around the entrance to the Park Street subway station. This area had been a place to pick up men even as far back as the 1890s and was one location in Boston that seemed to attract men of all socio-economic levels. The genteel Charlie Gibson, (who left the legacy of the wonderful Gibson House Museum in Back Bay) liked to pick up shoe shine boys there.

Another popular place was closer to the action around Park Square. "On the north side of Boylston there once was an entrance to the Arlington Street station inside the Public Garden; but, despite vigorous sweeps by the police, each night after the station would close, the steps descending to it would be jammed with men and boys who could not have been tighter-packed had they been engaged in stuffing telephone booths, a popular sport of the period."[15] After the entrance was demolished, the action moved to the Fiedler Memorial Bridge over Storrow Drive.

Some found the cruising and quick sex rewarding. Film booker George Mansour met his lover of forty years in the Harvard Square subway bathroom and still went cruising when he was in his eighties. Others were less thrilled. When he was fifteen and still living in upstate New York, the future Pulitzer Prize winning poet, John Ashbery, met a twenty-year-old sailor with whom he had sex in a bathroom stall. He was enraptured by the touch of the stranger and he wanted to experience it again, but the serviceman wanted nothing more to do with him and Ashbery became depressed. The sex ultimately left him dissatisfied and he felt guilty about being gay, yet he went on to seduce a boy a year older whom he met while working at a summer job canning cherries. The feelings were reciprocated and the two spent three weeks working side by side, going to the beach, seeing movies, and consummating their relationship. The romance helped Ashbery understand that being gay was not a sickness that would wreck his life but was central to making him a happy adult.[9]

7.2 Arlington Street Subway Entrance (1937)

Another Boston gay poet was John Wieners (1934-2002). He went to Catholic School at St. Gregory's in Dorchester and Boston College High School in the South End. Having skipped a grade, he entered Boston College in 1950 at sixteen. Wieners had his first sexual experience while a youngster in Milton with another boy. At Boston College, he was open about his sexuality and his classmates didn't seem to be bothered by it. Braver than many of his generation, when he registered for the draft, he told the authorities he was gay and was excused from service.

In 1952, Wieners fell in love with a man five years his senior. Tall with a blond crewcut, Russell Dana Durkee was a former high school football star from Swampscott, returning to Boston after four years in the navy. Durkee was reluctan to be open about their relationship. However, Wieners persuaded him to use his G.I. benefits to go to Boston College and the two began an on-and-off six-year relationship.

In 1954, Durkee and Wieners moved into an apartment at 38 Grove St. on the north slope of Beacon Hill. The area was popular with artists, gays, and the down-and-out. A pivotal event in Wiener's life was a poetry reading by Charles Olsen on the night of September 11, 1954, at the Charles Street Meeting House. Wieners braved the remnants of Hurricane Edna to attend the event, which included a poem about the execution of Thomas Granger in Puritan New England. Despite the ferocious wind and rain outside, three people walked out during the poem.

Wieners befriended another poet, Stephan Jonas, from the Beacon Hill gay scene. The mixed-race Jonas was tall and muscular, with a face that could exhibit a range of emotions and feelings from "sympathetic interest to screaming terror". Jonas purposely obscured his origins, telling people he was from New York, but he was born Rufus Jones in Georgia. Living on the back of Beacon Hill with a military disability pension, Jonas was a self-taught poet.[32]

Wieners worked as a clerk at the Lahey Clinic, then located in Mission Hill, and hosted Sunday night poetry meetings in his apartment. These were showcases for Rhode Island School of Design students who covered every square inch of the apartment walls with murals, which Wieners would then cover up and offer as fresh space for more decorations. The meetings attracted art students, poets, and neighbors.

In 1955, Wieners left Boston to attend Black Mountain College for a semester. Returning, Wieners and Durkee rented an apartment at 17 Irving St. where they lived off of Durkee's unemployment check of $19 per week. Wieners worked on a production of *Finnegan's Wake* at the Cambridge Poets' Theatre in December. There, Wieners met Frank O'Hara while an understudy for O'Hara's role in a play and the two bonded. They hung out at Cronin's on Dunster St. and on the banks of the Charles. O'Hara was staying in an apartment over the Wursthaus in Harvard Square at the time.

Wieners went back to Black Mountain College in June 1956 just as the school was disintegrating into bankruptcy. At the end of August, Wieners returned to Boston, this time renting an apartment with Durkee at 33 South Russell St. Fueled by amphetamines, Wieners published the poetry magazine *Measure* in 1957. Sometimes so high he couldn't sleep, he would go out and cruise the streets at 1:00 a.m. He frequented the city's jazz bars and hung out with its junkies—which must have taken him to the South End as it was the center for both. At the end of summer he was preparing to move to San Francisco when word reached him that the first issue of *Measure* was facing bad reviews for being too gay themed. He then left Boston for three years.

In San Francisco, Wieners broke up with Durkee for the last time and bounced between friends' apartments, slowly sinking further into depression and drugs. Soon he was addicted to heroin. Strung out, friends recall him babbling to fire hydrants or wandering the streets glassy eyed. Wieners returned to Massachusetts (O'Hara helped pay his way back) and in January 1960, his parents had him committed to Medfield State Psychiatric Hospital. Hospitalized until July, he received all the near-medieval treatments of the time: electroshock treatments, insulin induced comas, and intense but irrelevant therapy sessions designed to elicit oedipal feelings. He also had several teeth, damaged by his methadrine habit, pulled. He was released through the frantic efforts of friends and went to New York, but when he visited his family over the holidays, they had him committed to the Metropolitan State Hospital in Waltham. He would be there until August 1961, when he returned to his parents' house in Milton. For over a decade Wieners, often in the fog of mental illness and drugs, lived with his parents, attended school in Buffalo and New York City, and spent time in various mental institutions. Finally, in 1972 he settled at 44 Joy St. for the remainder of his life. Charley Shively introduced Wieners to the thriving radical gay scene in the city that blossomed in the fifteen years since he had moved out. Around this time, Wieners also became friendly with John Mitzel, who had been the manager of the South Station Cinema since its opening. Wieners would go to the gay porn theatre to cash the weekly allowance checks provided by his sister. Mitzel would later boast "I was John's banker."[32]

Fellow poet Steven Jonas had spent time in New York before moving to Boston. He led a hard scrabble life, with only a disability pension for support, illegally tapping power lines to get electricity and dumpster diving at Haymarket and Quincy Market for food. He was also generous, feeding one and all despite his own poverty, sheltering friends who were homeless, and sharing what little he had.

Biracial, Jonas experienced prejudice from both blacks and whites. Reciprocated love eluded him and he was often falling for straight men, addicts, and runaways. He had learned poetry in 1948-49 at the West End library where he was as likely to steal a book as check it out. As a result, Jonas was much more read in modern poetry than Wieners and he taught the other Beacon Hill poets how to write.

Wieners met Jack Spicer when he returned from Black Mountain College in 1955. Spicer was working at the Copley Library and skeptical that anyone was writing decent poetry in Boston. But he soon became fascinated by Jonas' work. In the summer of 1956, this group of poets (most of whom were gay) was living on the back of Beacon Hill where they produced a newsletter devoted to their writing. In September they gave a public reading but only eight people showed up. Disgusted, Spicer left Boston in November. Once in San Francisco, he published Jonas' poetry and Wieners included one of Spicer's poems in his first issue of *Measure*.

In 1957, Jonas became involved in a larceny ring that ordered books and records from mail order clubs using fake names and then sold them. He was arrested and convicted of forty-seven counts of mail fraud and served four months in the federal prison in Danbury, Connecticut. Released in 1958, he made friends with a group of new poets. Unfortunately, Jonas' mental health, never great, began to deteriorate as he combined prescribed psychiatric medications with street drugs. He was hospitalized several times while his poetry was now often directed at dark government conspiracies and heavily anti-Semitic. "These poems are angry, dogmatic treatises which can become tiresome, repetitive, ugly, and hateful," said one critic.[33] Yet his fame was spreading and a book of his poetry was published. His better poems have a jazz like quality, full of riffs and dramatic runs and though most of his poems are not overtly sexual, several mention gay and bisexual men on Beacon Hill and the Esplanade. At least three are set in the South End, but in Jonas' time the neighborhood was known for its winos rather than its gay residents. One poem read thus:

> "she" only wanted to
> get up in female attire:
> sequin'd spangled gown
> high spiked heels
>
> threw 'er in the sex tank
> & all for trying to
>
> live it up like a
> real white woman[33]

As the 1960s drew to a close, Jonas continued to deteriorate. He lost all his teeth and his binges on amphetamines increased. Though he hosted poetry evenings in his apartment, he wrote less and less. In 1968, Jonas declared the Beacon Hill bohemian scene over, full of people merely posing as artists and he believed Townsend was the last of the old breed. He died on February 10, 1970.

If the Boston gay bar scene was robust but tightly controlled, Provincetown may have been the most flamboyant LGBTQ community in the country in the post-war years. There are reports of men dancing together at the A House as early as the late 1940s, but no Provincetown venue was explicitly gay until the 1950s. Some say the first openly gay bar was Weathering Heights, while others claim it was the bar at the Townhouse or the Ace of Spades.[34] In any case, LGBTQ nightlife now broke into the open.

1950s LGBTQ Provincetown took on a rhythm: a day at the beach ended by four so that everyone could go to happy hour at the Moors restaurant, which featured entertainment that might include a singalong to popular tunes. A late afternoon cabaret show was a tradition that would last until the 1970s. A couple times each week, "fellow members of the staff or patrons hoisted [piano player Roger] Kent to the top of his piano where he donned a wide-brimmed straw hat, held a long cigarette holder, and sang torch songs in soprano."[35] At five, the action shifted to Phil Bayone's Weathering Heights where "a number of cross-dressing men and women waited on tables and performed as Bayone's Weathering Knights, while Alice King, described as a short, stout, Italian butch, managed the club and at times acted as the emcee." After dinner, the scene moved to a number of other clubs and bars. There were also opportunities for sex in the dunes, near the Pilgrim Monument, and down at the harbor side.

Weathering Heights was on the edge of the town, the last structure on Shank Painter Road to have a connection to town water when it was built as a barn. The building was converted into a night club in the 1940s but failed until it was bought by Bayone and Robert Amero in 1951. Becoming wildly popular, one of the weekly high points during the summer was when the Weathering Knights hoisted Bayone in the air and carried him to the beach, dumping him in the water.[35]

The clubs were full of drag queens, cross dressers, and others who found these spaces safe to ignore gender norms. For the most part, the LGBTQ scene was tolerated by the town, particularly when contained in places not seen by the general public. There were occasional crackdowns, however. One 1949 round of repression began with newspaper accounts of the gay goings on in town and culminated three years later with a ban on cross dressing, female impersonators entertaining in clubs, and other public non-gender conforming behavior. The new regulations even prohibited bars and restaurants from becoming LGBTQ gathering places. But the town was not uniformly anti-gay, and by this time there was a profound split between conservative elements and a broad coalition of businesses that catered to LGBTQ tourists, LGBTQ residents, and the many straight people who were sympathetic and supportive of LGBTQ people. The regulations were largely ignored and soon the town tried promoting heterosexual tourism and moralizing against LGBTQ people. That approach eventually failed as well.

One man who brightened the era for many during these dark times was the legendary Phil Bayone (spelled multiple ways). His fabled Weathering Heights was a cabaret with band numbers, comedy acts, and drinks and food and its reopening each year, covered in the local press, signaled the start of the summer season. Harry Kemp and Nathaniel Saltonstall liked to drink there as Bayone took to the stage to sing songs such as *I Could Have Danced All Night*. Very generous, Bayone was always ready to help out with charities. He performed at fundraisers for the Art Association and a scholarship fund for town residents. When the Moors burned down, he held a party in which attendees were requested to bring old nautical knick knacks to replace those lost in the fire.

He was popular in Boston as well. On May 25, 1955, a banquet was held at the old Boston Sheraton Hotel to honor Bayone on his twenty-fifth year in show business. Mayor Curley showed up to give an oration in his honor, as did former Senator Joseph Langone. The tributes also extended to his mother, who joined 250 others to celebrate his career.[36] Senator Langone's son Freddy was a long-time Boston city councilor who was not as supportive of gay bars. He once went on a tirade, calling on the Boston Redevelopment Authority to use its power of eminent domain to condemn the buildings that housed them.

Bayone inspired others to have fun as well. In late August 1958, a birthday party was held for him at the Sea Urchin on Commercial St. in Provincetown. "The cottage was decorated with red and white carnations and multicolored gladioli. A revolving silver punchbowl was placed on the table which had a gauzy cover, underneath were vari-colored lights."[37] After a feast that included lobster and a special cake Bayone, overcome with emotion, grabbed a hand mirror and sang, *I Feel Pretty* from *West Side Story*.

7.3 Phil Bayone

Back in Boston, Bayone opened 12 Carver in November 1958. It mostly avoided trouble but was shut down for a week for public lewdness and obscene gestures: two men had flexed their hips at each other. It became a piano bar in 1968 after Bayone died and slid into disrepute soon after.[38]

Though Boston lesbians had few places to go to, at least they were safer than some lesbian venues in nearby cities. In 1950s Worcester by contrast, the raids on gay and lesbian bars were constant, almost routine Friday and Saturday night occurrences. "We'd make a joke of it. 'Hurry up and finish your beer,' we'd say, 'cause we're goin' for a ride," recalled one woman.[39]

For many lesbians, particularly working-class women, postwar lesbian society included strict behavior roles for butch v. femme women. These tended to be exaggerated social norms that paralleled the rigid sex roles of heterosexual relationships. Butch women were expected to hide their emotions and control and protect their femme girlfriends. An acceptable lesbian couple was between a butch and a femme.

When a butch woman entered a relationship with another butch or two femmes coupled, some of their lesbian contemporaries struggled to accept them.

Many lesbians did not conform to these expected behavioral norms, of course, and they were often treated harshly by their peers. Neither butch nor femme, these women (often called "kikis") were sometimes treated suspiciously—some thought they might be undercover police. Others were openly hostile to them, even threatening one kiki with violence.

The well-known LGBTQ activist Barbara Hoffman (1933-2015) recalled the tremendous stereotyping within the lesbian community in the 1950s. She had friends who were a "young college crowd who ran around in our Bermuda shorts and big fuzzy, long, loose, sweaters to the utter horror of the butch/fem crowd."[40] Most LGBTQ people tried to keep their status secret, even from their families. "We were so far in the closet then that there was this invisible gay world behind the straight world," recalled Hoffman.

The connection to mainstream society's repression of women in the development of butch/femme roles is very important. Adopting male stereotypical behavior was one of the few ways a woman could be free. One woman, a working-class teenager in early 1960s Springfield remembered that, "[a]s a girl in an Italian immigrant family I wasn't allowed to have a will. I envied [my brothers] fucking freedom so bad. That's what being a boy represented—power and freedom. You could walk through the park at midnight or down the street at any hour. So of course we all wanted to pass."[39]

Conforming to these stereotypes helped create a sense of group identity among the small beleaguered lesbian community of the day. By adopting these standards of dress, speech, and behavior they were able to become part of a nurturing accepting group that protected them from the hostile straight world. Middle-class and wealthy women were much less likely to adopt the butch/femme role. To have done so would've meant jeopardizing their social and economic positions as they had few alternatives to the strict gender roles of this era. The class and behavior rifts created conflicts as working class lesbians ridiculed kikis, while middle class lesbians complained that the butch/femme behaviors and dress reinforced negative stereotypes

The high point of the Boston LGBTQ social calendar was the Beaux Arts Ball. With a cover charge of $2, the first ball was held at the Glass Hat on Newbury St in 1951. The event wasn't publicized except for handmade posters at select bars and engraved invitations. Demonstrating the power of LGBTQ social networks, within a few years the ball attracted people from as far away as Chicago and Florida.

Hotels knew they could make money off the event and worked to make their facilities safe for visitors and attendees. Even so, the crowds outside the balls sometimes grew boisterous, perhaps energized by the search lights, red carpets, and limousines. Not everyone who showed up to watch was sympathetic. Sometimes the crowd threw apples and eggs and some costumed people had their wigs torn off while mounted police struggled to keep the peace.

The costumes were elaborate and included Marie Antoinette with a head-dress of live canaries, Aladdin pulling a giant smoking lamp, a young man riding a turtle, and a southern belle who "had to be tipped upside down and onto her side when her hoop skirt proved too huge to squeeze over the threshold."[41] One year, the ball was at the Somerset where first prize for best costume went to a butterfly with a sequined bathing suit, bra, and eyelashes. That event provoked outlandish behavior inside the ballroom as "boys were dancing with each other quite uninhibitedly with or without the disguise of a costume."[4] Some used the events to make political statements: at another ball, a man dressed up as Mary Driscoll. Sydney later recalled that "I used to make costumes out of waste paper baskets. I made a costume—a gorgeous—wig—out of string! String, steel wool, toilet seats, curtain rods for cigarette holders, lamp shades."[17] By then, tickets were $5, no small amount for some people. Sadly, the last ball was in 1961.

The Boston police were unpredictable. Each postwar year until the publication of arrest statistics ended in 1958 showed that hundreds of men were arrested for lewd and lascivious conduct and sodomy, but there were large variations in the number arrested with no discernable pattern or set of reasons (elections, new commissioners, and so forth) to explain the differences. The worst year was 1945 with 241 sodomy arrests, but there would be just nine in 1951. These fluctuations can also be seen for lewd and lascivious conduct arrests. These periodic crackdowns must have kept LGBTQ people on edge as an arrest could bring jail, commitment to a mental hospital, or other ruin.

The police still raided private houses and it was rarely clear who tipped them off. But these raids had serious consequences that could impact the arrested person's life. In 1953, nineteen-year-old George Mansour was at a party in Bay Village where he met a sailor. The two went up to a bedroom, but they were soon interrupted by a squad of Boston policemen. Mansour and three other men were convicted of lewd and lascivious conduct and were given six-month suspended sentences and two years of probation. The owner of the house went to jail for nine months. Though his parents were supportive, Mansour's life was greatly affected by the arrest. He lost any chance of going to college and his employment possibilities were strongly limited. His friends just accepted it as one of the risks of being gay in those years.[42]

The raid made Mansour determined to live his life as openly as possible. "The arrest really gave me the courage to face down people in charge and see through their completely bankrupt rules. I guess it turned me into even more of a rebel than I was before."[43] Four years later he met the love of his life and the two would be together for forty-four years. Mansour became a film booker and went on to found the Boston Gay and Lesbian Film Festival.

Lesbians were less likely to come to the attention of the courts, but they were more likely to be victims of police abuse as there were widespread rumors that police routinely raped the lesbians they arrested during bar raids. The offenses that gay men were charged with (lewdness, unnatural acts, and sodomy) were considered to be minor felonies and heard in district courts. However, in addition to exposing a man to being fired or his being disowned by his family, an arrest for lewdness or sodomy also put him at risk for being committed indefinitely to a mental hospital. The working definition for being considered a sexual psychopath and sent away was for a person to have no ability to control their sexual impulses and who was likely to attack or injure others. However, many judges and district courts committed men who had just been unlucky enough to have been arrested more than once.

The Cambridge District Court screened all people charged with sex crimes and sent those who were "more serious, aggressive offenders to a mental hospital for a period of observation before disposition is made of a criminal complaint."[44] In 1947, the Cambridge court saw about 10,000 criminal complaints, half of which were vehicle violations, considered criminal at the time. Altogether, there were 100 sex crime arrests of which thirty-nine were for lewdness and fourteen for unnatural acts. The doctor who conducted the screenings was surprised by how few of the men expressed any dissatisfaction or shame for being gay. His advice was for them to "restrict his sex life to his own home with other homosexuals and keep out of public places and avoid seducing boys."[44]

Collectively, the postwar years were a complex mixture of riotous nightlife and deplorable repression. In one sense, Boston was a better place for LGBTQ people because of the small amount of freedom allowed to their bars and most could avoid trouble during the methodical shakedowns. However, the effects of intolerance were everywhere to be seen and just about all LGBTQ people instinctively knew they had to act straight around family, employers, neighbors, and at church. The walls around LGBTQ life must have seemed immovable to most people, but in the 1960s, those conditions would rapidly change.

Chapter 8

Pressure Builds

A S THE 1960S began, the economic decline of Boston accelerated. The city bulldozed entire neighborhoods (the West End and New York Streets area); it had thrown out the old Irish politicians (choosing John Hynes over James Michael Curly for mayor); and it constructed massive new highways (the Southeast Expressway, the Central Artery, and other roads). Yet, Boston was poorer at the end of the 1950s than it was in the beginning. Middle-class families were still leaving as fast as they could buy houses in the suburbs, no new major office building had been constructed for decades, and the city budget was dancing on the edge of bankruptcy.[1] The public schools, providing a terrible education for all students, were on a path towards the tragedy of the anti-busing debacle and nearly a third of the city's housing stock lacked bathrooms, kitchens, or central heat.

Despite these problems, LGBTQ people poured into Boston. Having filled the tenements on the back of Beacon Hill, they overflowed into Back Bay, the Fenway, and the South End. Many were taking advantage of the cheap rents they found in these neighborhoods while those with sufficient resources began to buy buildings and renovate them, the only demographic investing in Boston at the time. The change was most noted in the South End where a trickle of gay men in the late 1950s became a flood after 1964 when the Prudential Center opened. For almost a century the neighborhood had been one of the city's poorest; parents would warn their children that if they didn't do well in school, they would end up on Dover St., skid row. But the old row houses were solid, beautiful, and cheap. The multicultural South End had no dominant demographic group, LGBTQ people could live there and avoid the prejudices of ethnic Boston and the prying eyes of families and hostile straight neighbors. Long ignored by respectable LGBTQ Boston as too shabby, the South End prompted a flurry of interest in exposed brick walls, hanging plants, and antiques.[2] At the beginning of this influx of LGBTQ people, it looked like there was ample room in the neighborhood for everyone including its many low-income, elderly, and nonwhite residents. That would quickly change.

City government actively ignored these newcomers. When working with the South End to implement an urban renewal plan, for example, LGBTQ people were lumped with drug addicts, prostitutes, and other undesirables to be shunned by the Boston Redevelopment Authority.[3] The city wanted straight, middle-class families, not LGBTQ people. In these same years, two LGBTQ entertainment districts were targeted for destruction by urban renewal: Scollay Square was to be replaced by the gleaming new Government Center project and Park Square demolished in favor of a new hotel and office complex. The third, Lower Washington St., would be used as the dumping ground for unwanted adult entertainment venues later in the decade as Mayor Kevin White legalized the Combat Zone.

One last (but especially tragic) episode of systematic police repression of gay men in Massachusetts is the case of Newton (Ned) Arvin (1900-63) and his friends in 1960. He was a Smith College professor and a respected literary critic and biographer. Isolated in Northampton, Arvin collected what we now consider tame, soft-core magazines and postcards. He often invited select friends over for dinner, drinks, and a group viewing of his "pornography." He also sometimes had sex with these men who were mostly younger than him. Having recently turned sixty, Arvin was gradually becoming a recluse, rarely venturing further than a bicycle ride from his apartment. His great works of literary criticism were behind him (though he read for hours each day) and he rarely did any writing other than in his journals as he was constantly tired.

Growing up in Valparaiso, Indiana, Arvin was thin, bookish, and frail. Because he was not athletic with poor eyesight, he was taunted for being effeminate. He decided at an early age he'd be a lifelong bachelor, unloved and alone. During his junior year at Harvard he fell in love with his roommate, though the object of his attention was unaware of Arvin's crush. Arvin fantasized about a life with him, even marriage, though he knew it would never happen. But he did not consider himself gay as he wasn't what he considered to be a pansy or a fairy.

While at Harvard, Arvin decided to take up a career in literary criticism, a field just coming into its own. First he taught in Detroit where the pressures of concealing his sexuality weighed heavily on him. He feared that the slightest effeminate gesture or improperly accented word would give him away. Maintaining a straight façade was too difficult and he resigned his position before the end of the year.

Arvin secured a job teaching at Smith where he found that being immersed at an all-women's college easier to handle. Arvin had a relationship with another Smith faculty member in 1930, but the pressures on the two men caused it to quickly end leaving both feeling depressed and isolated. On the rebound, Arvin married a young woman in 1932 hoping desperately that it might cure him of his homosexuality. Though he managed to have sexual relations with his wife, the marriage was a disaster and by 1935 they were living apart. It was only after his 1940 divorce that Arvin came to understand that he was gay and he found the revelation agonizing, feeling that he was sick and disgusting.[4]

On the verge of mental collapse, a friend drove him to Boston to see Ives Hendricks, one of the city's most prominent psychiatrists and eventually the president of the American Psychiatric Association. Hendricks thought that homosexuality could be cured and convinced Arvin to check himself into MacLean Hospital, but psychoanalysis and bed rest failed to dampen Arvin's sexuality and he was soon back in Northampton. Now deeply alcoholic, his mental state deteriorated and within a few weeks he was committed to Northampton State Hospital. He stayed there for eight days and then went to an asylum in Westchester, New York before returning to Smith.

In the summer of 1946 Arvin met Truman Capote and the two began a passionate relationship which was very public within the private confines of Yaddo, a writer's retreat. Capote was twenty-five years younger but the two reveled in each other's attentions, strongly suggesting that Arvin's mental problems were highly influenced by the brutal repression of his era. The two years they were a couple were the happiest of Arvin's life.

Capote was energized by his relationship with Arvin who he felt gave him the education he lacked. The two were completely opposite in regard to personality. Capote was a vivacious flamboyant lover of parties and glitter, whereas Arvin was a confirmed recluse. This made a permanent home for the two impossible as Arvin couldn't face New York while Capote felt buried in Northampton. But while the affair lasted both felt wonderful and Capote dedicated his first novel, *Other Voices, Other Rooms*, to Arvin. This public outing made Arvin very uncomfortable and contributed to the end of the relationship. Yet it was the most intense love of either's life and Arvin kept a number of items that reminded him of the now cooled relationship: a nude photo of Capote, assorted letters, and a number of erotic postcards that Capote had sent him from Europe. These would be seized and used as evidence against Arvin.

Arvin attempted suicide several times during the 1950s, was hospitalized, and received electroshock treatments that aimed to treat both his depression and his homosexuality, but no treatment was effective. Arvin feared that just being seen in public with other homosexuals would be damning. He hated and envied others who could be out including, for example, a young graduate student who was handsome, flamboyant, and openly flirtatious. The student had also captivated poet W.H. Auden to the point that during their sexual relationship Auden dedicated a book of poems to him. Though Arvin was scared to be seen in public with the student, the two had sex every month or so.

Arvin was appalled by the recklessness of some of his friends and colleagues as they went after sex. One was fond of picking up men in the bathroom of Northampton City Hall and bringing them back to his nearby apartment for sex, for example, and Arvin feared disaster. He was also uneasy with how some of the younger gay faculty freely associated with each other in public and he worried they were too campy. Yet Arvin began to open up, visiting the Everard Baths in New York City for several nights in a row on occasion, frequenting Springfield's gay bars, hosting all night parties for his gay friends that often ended in men pairing off with each other, and collecting pornography.

With same-sex relations illegal, however, the social and legal repression had the potential to warp all intimacy. Casual sex was easier, leading Arvin and his friends to approach romance cautiously. In the world of one of Arvin's friends (Ned Spoffard), "to open oneself emotionally to a sexual contact was to risk becoming vulnerable: to exposure, rejection, blackmail, violence, or worse. To have sex with a friend might jeopardize the friendship and put each partner in the position of possibly betraying the other." They soon found out how much these relationships could harm them.

Foster Furcolo was a Springfield politician who served two terms as governor. He is remembered today for initiating payroll withholding for state income taxes. Under his leadership, the state decided to crack down on pornography, passing a law in 1960 that made its possession and showing it to others a felony, and the state police created a special unit to identify people who owned or watched it. The action against Arvin began with a warrantless search of his apartment, making the entire series of arrests that followed illegal. The police were very vague as to how they first heard of Arvin. They hinted they had been tipped off by a postal agent who found pornography addressed to Arvin when the package accidentally broke open but most likely the police had been notified that Arvin was on the mailing list of *One*. The legality of how postal inspectors had acquired that list is extremely dubious. The case could also have started when a casual acquaintance of Arvin was picked up for an unrelated sex crime and then implicated Arvin as a way of getting the charges reduced. Several men, most of whom barely knew Arvin, were indicted before Arvin's apartment was searched. Still, many of the people involved in the case thought it was Arvin who implicated everyone else.

Five state policemen raided Arvin's apartment. The arresting officer, John Regan, was "forty-two, six feet tall, weighed 220 pounds, and exuded toughness—lumbering, bullnecked, bulging under his suit, up in the balls of his overburdened feet."[4] He had made over forty pornography arrests since May. Arvin was terrified as his apartment was searched, pornography was found, and the interrogation began. As they went through Arvin's diaries and personal papers, overturning file cabinets and pulling the mattress off the bed, the police found out who he had had sex with and who had come to the parties where he showed his pornography. Arrest warrants soon followed.

A wave of fear rippled out from Arvin as first his friends and then their friends wondered if they might be arrested. The fear would have been worse if they had known that the police were methodically going through Arvin's diaries, looking for more people to bring in. Henry-Russell Hitchcock was a major target. He was in Europe at the time and only escaped arrest because the man who was house sitting for Hitchcock was able to find his stash of pornography and throw it into the Westfield River. The house sitter also burned incriminating letters, including valuable correspondence from composer Virgil Thomson. Fearing arrest, another man burned Goya prints while others went into hiding. Panic gripped the small gay community of Northampton and its connections from Boston to Washington, D.C. and beyond. Heterosexuals were also brought in for questioning as anyone whose name was in Arvin's journals was a suspect.[4]

Soon the police had a half dozen men in custody. Spofford was arrested in Cambridge, and the others were mostly in Western Massachusetts. One friend

Joel Dorius, was in Provincetown when Arvin was arrested. Hearing that Arvin had implicated others, he tried to get back to his apartment to destroy his small stash of pornography before the police got to it but he was too late and by the time he reached Boston there was a warrant out for his arrest.

While the press had a great time writing about the scandal, for the most part it did not mention that the pornography and sex acts being investigated were gay. Thus, the prudishness of the time kept that part of the story out of the papers. There was also some support for the men; for example, historian Arthur Schlesinger helped Dorius get a civil liberties lawyer. In Dorius' case, the vagueness of the newspapers helped as some of those who offered assistance were unaware of the gay aspect of the cases.

In 1960s Boston, being publicly identified as a homosexual was worse than being known as a communist sympathizer, and men such as Arvin who were accused of both feared being outed more. When the Northampton men went before the judge, their goal was to keep the charges focused on illegal possession of pornography rather than being gay in order to maintain a public veneer of respectability. But the state police also knew that the men feared public exposure and the investigators used these fears to force men to cooperate even though the men were not charged with sodomy or any sex act violations.

Arvin, whose mental health had been fragile for decades, was broken by the pressure and went from jail to Northampton State Hospital. The court sentenced Arvin to six months probation. Smith offered him early retirement at half his salary as his mental state had become so poor that he could not return to the classroom. Though their departments, the faculty senate, and president of Smith argued to keep Dorius and Spofford on staff, the trustees demanded that they be terminated. Ultimately, the issue that sealed their fate was that they were gay, not the arrests.

Dorius also entered a mental hospital; he felt his life was over and that he was a ruined man because of the exposure. Both Dorius and Spoffard had their cases overturned on appeal, but it made no difference to Smith and neither visited Northampton again. Thus they went abroad, but both eventually made their way to California and resumed academic careers while Arvin died a few years later of cancer. Ironically, the last two years of his life were liberating for him and he even began working on his memoirs.

The case demonstrates the complexity and limits of gay male social networks at the time. In addition to the academics, the seven arrested men included an auto mechanic, sales clerk, and aluminum siding installer. These were working class men, demonstrating that gay social and sexual networks transcended class. Though these networks were large (Arvin was friends with gay men across the Eastern seaboard) they were also fragile, often more dangerous than supportive. Though other gay men throughout the region feared arrest, there was no coming together to protest and no LGBTQ social support network to help the accused through the crisis. Each man faced the authorities with whatever resources they could gather on their own.[5]

LGBTQ life was a series of challenges and opportunities. Lois Johnson first realized she was a lesbian in 1957-58 when she had moved to California but felt compelled to keep communicating with a woman she had known. She quickly moved back to the east coast to become lovers with the woman she initially left behind and they were in a relationship for five years. Both had religious backgrounds and they didn't know any other lesbians, perhaps because they never went to bars. They knew lots of gay men, however. Because her lover was a vocalist and Johnson played the organ, they knew the entire Organ Guild, which was primarily gay men. Still, they were very closeted and feared the stereotypes facing lesbians and felt it much safer to keep to themselves.

Johnson came out to her brother and sister-in-law, very devout Unitarians, through a ten-page letter in 1963. She had been miserable after her lover left her and the family had sensed something was wrong. Fortunately, when she told them she was a lesbian, they were very kind and accepting.

Then in 1964, Johnson's male friends introduced her to Shari Barden. When Barden was in the army in the 1950s, it seemed to her that all the women around her were gay, but she never connected with them. Though she hadn't yet considered herself to be a lesbian, she strongly liked these women. But once she was out of the army and ready to act upon her desire to be with women, the logistics of meeting one of her persuasion were daunting and she feared never encountering another lesbian. Then a gay friend took her out to the Boston bars, where she met a woman and had her first real romance. When it ended, she was devastated.

Barden told her parents she was a lesbian, but her father never understood what she was saying. Her mother tried, but the two were never close. Furthermore, her mother had never liked anyone Barden went out with until Johnson. Then, "she felt she had gained a daughter. We got along fine," recalled Johnson.[6]

The night they met, Shari was dressed up while Johnson was all in black. Barden thought Johnson was haughty and aloof but when Johnson played the piano, she knew they would spend the rest of their lives together. Both played hard to get, however, even while scheming to meet again. The relationship deepened and after forty-nine consecutive nights together, Barden took Johnson into a closet at a party and asked, "will you go with me?"

Johnson replied, "[w]ell, I really don't want to be tied down." Three days later, they were a couple and they moved in together at the end of the summer. Johnson worked at WGBH and despite its liberal atmosphere, she was careful to tell no one about Barden even as she brimmed with the excitement of new love.

The couple had heard of the Daughters of Bilitis, the Mattachine Society, and other homophile groups but they were not members of any LGBTQ organization. Though the couple was friendly with Jan Chase, who restarted the Boston chapter of the DOB in 1968, the two were reluctant to get involved because they worried about their jobs and the type of women they'd meet there. The first meeting the couple went to in 1969 confirmed their reluctance. With a group of older lesbians to the side talking loudly and a discussion group focusing on coming out issues in the front of the room, the two found it very unwelcoming.

LGBTQ people moved to Boston because the city was at the confluence of two important social trends. One was the role of a college education in providing a socially acceptable means of getting away from family. When young people sexually awoke and realized they were not straight or cisgender, oftentimes their first reaction was to believe they were the only one of their kind. Once they found like-minded people, they knew they were not alone, but living with their families made acting on their desires impossible and one of the easiest ways to escape the oppression inside one's family was to leave for college. Straight people would simply think they were leaving to get a better education and move up the middle-class ladder of success, but by going away, LGBTQ people were grasping at the chance for a more open life. The Boston region, with its hundreds of colleges and universities and many of them among the best in the world, was a natural place for anyone to want to expand their "education".

Similarly, young LGBTQ people quickly understood that the opportunities to find others like them were vastly greater in cities. They heard of bars, restaurants, cruising areas, and other attractions not readily found in the suburbs or in rural areas. Boston (though it was in a free fall economic decline) was in a unique position to benefit from both these trends with its many colleges and universities and a robust LGBTQ scene. In the years between 1950 and 1980 when most Americans shunned cities, LGBTQ people kept Boston and other urban areas alive.

Another reason for Boston's growing LGBTQ population was that it had less oppression than many other places, making it a safer, if less energetic, alternative to other cities. The reasons for Boston's relative safety are complex. First, Mayor James Michael Curley, who dominated Boston politics from the early 1900s through 1950, didn't prioritize antigay action. He preferred to bait Yankee businessmen. Second, most Boston politicians were caught up in a battle between middle-class and working-class Irish for control of city hall and neither side cared about LGBTQ people, nor did they use them as weapons in their political fights. Third, the police were taking payoffs and didn't want to stop the flow of cash from gay bars. Fourth, the Yankee suburban establishment didn't care about LGBTQ people either as they were obsessed with containing the Irish in the city. Finally, LGBTQ people were simply ignored in a city tearing itself apart over race and class divisions and grappling with economic decline. As a result, Boston became a magnet for people who would form the first great generation of LGBTQ advocates. For the most part, they moved to Boston first as students, then turned to activism. Their successes and their strategies for addressing the terrible challenges posed by homophobia in these years set the stage for political triumphs into the twenty-first century.

Prejudice weighed on Boston's lesbian artists. Maxine Feldman (1943-2007) was an out and proud lesbian and a fixture on Boston's vibrant coffee house circuit. She had come to Boston to attend Emerson College but had been expelled for being a lesbian. "In 1964 Max had a shoulder length mane of fierce yellow blond hair (which she soon got rid of) and a beautiful Martin guitar, a powerful voice, a giant life force, great humor, a booming laugh, a smile that could melt your heart, and an unconquerable spirit."[7] She was actually too popular as club managers were fearful of the large boisterous LGBTQ crowds she attracted to her performances and her bookings declined.

Fed up with the problems of being an openly lesbian performer in Boston, Feldman moved to California and over the next several years wrote songs that fueled the growing lesbian music movement. Her performances in front of enthusiastic crowds inspired other women to come out and live as out lesbians. Feldman returned to Boston in the early 1980s and founded the Oasis Coffeehouse at the Arlington Street Church, a major center for folk music and LGBTQ performers. One important lesbian who took to the stage there was the comedian Kate Clinton. She also sponsored poetry readings and once produced an all-lesbian version of the biblical story of Esther.

Feldman gradually changed how she thought about his gender and most who knew him later in life recalled that he preferred masculine pronouns or sometimes used both male and female terms to describe himself. In the 1990s, Feldman began to identify as a "transgender butch lesbian". He wished he was younger so he could have transitioned, but felt he was too old to begin that process. He never lost his lesbian fans and "in the transgender community, Feldman finally found the validation and support for his masculinity that had been missing all his life. It was a great thing and a comfort."[8]

In the mid to late 1960s, many women went to Vicki's and Cavana's, two lesbian bars on Tremont St. in the South End with tough reputations. "Vicki would sit on a high stool and survey the crowd for troublemakers. The customers could get out of hand in a hurry. At the drop of a hat, they'd throw a beer bottle." Jacques hosted women's nights, but the conditions there were horrendous with dirty bathrooms, surly bartenders, and an overall oppressive atmosphere.

Given the way bars treated women, it was not surprising that house parties were important venues for socializing for lesbians in the 1960s. They offered fun without the scrutiny and potential danger of bars. There were parties hosted by women in Dorchester, Jamaica Plain, and Cambridge. One woman recalled a friend saying, "'I'm having a party with all the fags and the dykes...' and we'd just dance and it was hilarious. There was a real camaraderie ...there wasn't a separation between the men and the women. I loved it."[9]

There had been raid on a house party back in 1957 where a number of women were arrested and jailed overnight. But when the women appeared before a judge, no one, including prosecutors and the police, could think of an actual crime that had been committed. All of the women were released.[10] Though large gatherings that included cover charges could still bring police to shut things down and loud parties might draw the police to quiet the crowd, this may have been one of the last raids on a private LGBTQ house party.

8.1 Carver Street in the 1960s

The US military continued to be concerned about gays in Boston and issued annual reports on prostitutes and homosexuals. In 1960, the survey noted that the Punch Bowl, Touraine Café, Playland, Jacques, Mario's, and Jo-Bet (59 Broadway) were crowded with men who "hobnob with each other."[11] The report noted that the 411 Lounge on Columbus Ave. was not only full of prostitutes but also "present was a male Negro homosexual in 'drag' (female) attire." The next year, the Revere Lounge at 428 Tremont St. was added to the list. "Most of the alleged 'homos' were white. Some were young. Others appeared to be reaching middle age. Practically all were aggressive types who were striving to make contacts."[12] No action was taken against any of these establishments, however.

Pressured by the relentlessness of urban renewal, the city's LGBTQ nightlife moved west. In 1959, the Gainsborough opened. A beer and wine bar catering to students, it lasted until 1963. The Shed opened in 1961 at 272 Huntington Ave. Near the end of its days in 1977, The Shed's music included The Beach Boys and disco while it featured a notorious backroom. It also claimed to be the third oldest leather and Levi's bar in the country. According to the Shed's manager, when a man walked into Sporters wearing a leather jacket, the bartenders refused to serve him. But the newly opened Shed welcomed him and its clientele was set.[13]

During the 1960s, the harassment of bars by police gradually stopped and there were no more raids. By the last wild days of the Punch Bowl, which closed in 1968 when its building was taken for urban renewal, "men would be dancing with their shirts off in the windows and sailors would walk by and laugh at them."[14] The crowds continued with long lines on the weekends, in part because the people who worked there were friendly. For example, Tex, the famed Punch Bowl waitress, liked to play matchmaker, fixing up people she thought would make good couples.

Nearby Playland and 12 Carver attracted a more relaxed clientele. Blue-collar truck drivers mingled with Harvard students at these bars and Playland even had a few regular black patrons, unusual in Boston gay bars at this time. By now Boston nightlife was becoming absolutely giddy. Phil Bayone, the owner of 12 Carver (replaced by the Transportation Building in 1981), was a large man who liked to mount a swing and glide over the crowd on Saturday nights. Recalled one man, "He'd get all juiced up and get in his swing and say, 'Now it's time for Papa to swing.' And she would sing "Summertime" and she'd wear a big straw picture hat with ribbons and bows and the ribbons hanging down and they would fly out and here she is, 300 pounds with this great big straw picture hat on… If she fell, she'd kill 300 people."[15]

The glittering bar scene didn't mean life was easy for LGBTQ people, however. In 1962, sixteen-year-old Robert Dole told his Exeter roommate he was gay and the two made love prompting the roommate to flee to the infirmary for help. As a result, Dole was allowed to stay at school only if he saw a psychiatrist every week. The psychiatrist told Dole he was sick and made it his mission to cure him. The antidote was to tell Dole how bad his life was going to be: no one would ever love him, he would have no friends, no job. "All homosexuals end up as bums in the Bowery," the doctor said. The therapy contributed to Dole's first psychotic breakdown.[16]

Navigating Harvard as a gay freshman in 1962 was difficult and isolating, even for men who would go on to be pillars of the national LGBTQ community later in life. The great novelist Andrew Holleran, for example, "stopped dating altogether, and freshman year came to an end in utter isolation."[17] He would not venture into the Freshman Union until three minutes before it closed to avoid having to eat with others. As smart as he was, Holleran had a hard time determining the gayness of others. There were two fellow Lowell House boys who talked in code and seemed inseparable yet distant from all others and a professor who produced Wilde's plays and wrote on Emily Dickinson, yet Holleran hesitated to reach out to them, unsure. Even graffiti in Lamont on nude wrestling seemed promising but inconclusive. In contrast, the straight men around him were obvious and open about their sexuality: debating which women were virgins, complaining about the need to rent cheap motel rooms for sex with girlfriends, and posting a red tie on the door to warn roommates not to come in when they were having sex—these heterosexual men had never heard that a red tie was once a sign of homosexuality and wearing one got students expelled for being gay. At the same time, gay men had to hide any sign of their sexuality out of fear they might be expelled, ostracized from their families, and forever denied employment.

Harvard was aggressively heterosexual in its final years of being all male. As author Philip Gambone recalled, "I felt isolated, friendless, anonymous. Sex—heterosexual sex—was everywhere, in the music that blared from dorm windows on any given weekend, in the stories guys brought back of dates at Radcliffe and Wellesley and Smith, in the trashy popular books that circulated like contraband (Candy was especially popular my freshman year, 1967.) worse still, my hormones were raging and could not stop thinking about boys."[18] The problem was finding someone with whom to act out these desires.

Holleran vividly recalled the trauma of the decade years later. "When you are coming out, you do not spend much time thinking of what you are doing—you want simply to live, to have a personal life—an approximation at first of the dreams one was brought up with: domestic happiness, fidelity, affection, trust."[17] The effects lingered with the result that for Holleran's generation, "[h]omosexual desire isn't easy. It takes, for all its romanticism, an unending ability to face facts over and over again. Sometimes painful facts. What to tell parents, if anything. What to tell friends, people you work for. Where to work, how to integrate sex with other parts of your life and personality."[17]

Another Harvard student, the future congressman Barney Frank, knew and accepted the fact he was gay at an early age. "In 1954 I was a fairly normal fourteen-year-old, enjoying sports, unhealthy food, and loud music. But even then I realized that there were two ways in which I was different from the other guys: I was attracted to the idea of serving in government and I was attracted to the other guys."[19] He vowed to keep his homosexuality a secret for the rest of his life. One member of the class of 1967 remembered thus: "I was always having to hide something about myself because I thought that if people knew the truth, I would be ridiculed and ostracized."[20] Even families were unsafe spaces. Upon being told he was gay, one man's father called his boss to get him fired. His mother was ashamed, his brother angry.

For many, sex was furtive, something done in out of the way places. Men had sex in a bathroom in the basement of Lamont and in Burr Hall, for example. Sex in bathrooms allowed men who were afraid of exposure to not only hide their identities but even their faces. It enabled them to act on their desires while staying deeply in the closet. Many of the men reported that they were unclear how to have sex with another man and as a result, their first sexual encounters were often fast and awkward. One remembered that "[a]t least in my case, it took sleeping with a lot of different people and trying lots of different things to learn how to have sex, how to enjoy it."[20]

Even as straight people were surfing the euphoria of the sexual revolution, gay men remained terribly ashamed of their sexuality. The famous financial expert Andrew Tobias spent his four years at Harvard with "one central mission: namely, never to have anyone to find out the horrific truth" that he was gay. "After all, most of us grew up knowing homosexuality was simply too shameful to discuss. Murder and mayhem can be regularly televised, but two men or women holding hands? Decency has its limits."[21]

Like many extremely conflicted and closeted gay men, Tobias took on the mask of an intense homophobe, mocking the sexuality and masculinity of the one student who might have been gay. Others internalized their hatred and at least two men thought to be gay committed suicide. Some, though later successful and out, could never get over the repression of these years. "There is a deep-seated shame, inculcated over a lifetime, that these relatively accepting, liberated last few years simply can't remove,"[21] said one man who wanted to remain anonymous.

Filmmaker Marlon Riggs remembered that being gay "condemned me with unspoken contempt: misfit, freak, faggot." As a result, he "withdrew into the shadows of my soul; chained my tongue; attempted, as best as I could, to snuff out the flame of my sexuality; assumed the impassive face and stiff pose of Silent Black Macho. I wore the mask. I was serving time. For what crime I didn't know."[21]

Tobias also dealt with his sexuality by becoming a driven overachiever, striving to become "the best little boy in the world". Like many young LGBTQ people, he compensated for having a secret by excelling at academics and striving to be the leader of every club and organization he belonged to. Expending great emotional and physical energy, he took on extra duties and used his extreme busyness to hide the fact he was romantically detached from everyone.[22] When he finally walked into a gay bar (Sporters) for the first time, Tobias would be paralyzed with fear and desire, terrified of the people he saw there yet unable to stop himself from returning. It would take him years to relax, and when Tobias wrote a book in 1973 about his experiences he used a pseudonym.

Many men were simultaneously desperate to hide all traces of their homosexual existence from everyone, and to connect with another man. Thus it was possible to have close friends or students living next door who were experiencing similar pressures yet be unaware of each other's struggles and to have gay parties and gay sex going on in the same building and yet have no idea that they existed.

Some men, after great internal turmoil, finally found the courage to go out to find others. One graduate student recalled, "I was at Harvard getting my Ph.D. and I remember I found a place in Boston opposite the bus station, a gay bar called the Punch Bowl, a big place with flashing lights. I was sort of wide-eyed and hesitant, and when I got to the door, the bouncer looked at me and said, 'Yeah, this is the place.'"[21] Harvard and Cambridge attracted a lot of people not affiliated with the university but often hanging out and partying with the students. Edie Sedgwick, who went on to fame as a member of Andy Warhol's group, frequented gay parties and Casablanca's. She was beautiful but suffered from a variety of mental health and substance abuse issues and died in 1971 from an overdose of barbiturates and alcohol. Sedgwick liked going out with gay Harvard students; they used her to attract other men and she used them because she liked the attention. Yet even some gay men were afraid to go to Casablanca's and some avoided it because they didn't want to be associated with its gay taint.

There was at least one young man at the time, Ed Hennessey, who was flamboyant, speaking in elaborate witticisms, wearing wild clothes, and exaggeratedly smoking cigarettes to attract attention, "a deliberately outrageous dandy at a time Harvard was not producing many dandies".[23] He had a crush on a freshman whom he followed to Harvard Yard, looked him up in the freshman directory, and eventually convinced him to go to Casablanca's, where he immediately fell for Sedgwick.

Another notorious Harvard graduate student was Cloke Dosset. Older and balding, he threw elaborate parties that featured drinks such as the Columbine Street-walker and the Halloween Pederast. He used Sedgwick and other good-looking women to attract handsome young Harvard men. He had a thing for the young and vulnerable, and his attentions eventually seemed to reach the wrong person because it was said that Harvard barred him from the Yard.

Even accepting you were gay didn't make finding others easy. Thom Nichols, nineteen and newly arrived in Boston to perform alternative service rather than going into the military, knew that the city was full of gay people, but he didn't know where they might be. He had read John Rechy's books on public cruising in Los Angeles and figured there had to be a similar scene in Boston. But where was it?

To find other gay people, he walked all around the city, finally spotting a man who he thought had to be gay in the Public Garden. "The park was nearly deserted, but suddenly there he was, a tall, blond guy in a cape. The cape took me by surprise. I'd never seen anyone wear a cape in Philadelphia, but here was a definite throwback to the 19th century, only it was not worn by an old, paunchy, Victorian gentleman with sideburns and a pocket watch but by an attractive man who had just left an exclusive social event, like an opera."[24]

His next thought was that the man could be a homicidal maniac and images of the Boston strangler, in the headlines only a few years before, filled his head. Even so, he followed the man to "the Block," an outdoor cruising area in Back Bay. He was reassured by the number of men hanging out on the sidewalk and leaning against the neat cast iron railings, but Nichols was confused when a man in a car rolled down his window and asked Nichols how much he was charging. When he said he was not a hustler, the man shouted at him that he was in the wrong place and drove off before Nichols could ask where he should go.[24]

The next Saturday, Nichols left his Harvard Square room and went to the Combat Zone to ask a peep show clerk where there was gay nightlife. The man directed him to the Punch Bowl. There, he "bought a Miller beer and pretty much walked around in a daze, going downstairs to inspect the room that was sometimes used as a dance floor, and then walking upstairs again, where I took in the clientele, some of them flamboyant queens, while the majority seemed to be quiet, masculine types in V-neck sweaters and white Levi's or black leather jackets."[24]

At the Punch Bowl he met the man in a cape who told him, in a heavy French accent, that he was a graduate student from Paris. Later, on the way back to Cambridge the caped man confessed he was a Harvard Law student from the U.S. "During the ride we were careful not to hold hands or sit too close to one another, because in 1969, the year of Stonewall, you never knew who might be looking."[24]

Though many were successful at it, picking up men in Harvard Square was not easy, either. Dermot Maegher, who would later become the first openly gay man appointed judge in Massachusetts, remembers that "[t]he protocol of cruising is very serious—with geisha-like moves."[25]

Provincetown had had a well-established public gay sex scene for decades—a jealous lover once tried to run over Tennessee Williams while he was in a tryst on the beach back in 1944. But the action shifted to the middle of town during the 1960s. "The gatherings began after one a. m. as the bars closed and the cruising rituals moved to the streets, eventually congregating at the bronze plaque at the foot of Monument Hill." There were dozens of men there late at night. Police Chief James Mead, then a patrolman remembers nightly raids back in the sixties, though records don't show more than a half dozen arrests each week for public sex in the entire town including heterosexual couples. The town eventually cut down the bushes and put in lights, moving the action back to the beaches.[26]

8.2 Weathering Heights

There was a famous party in Provincetown in the mid-1960s, the buggers' bash, which featured a naked young man covered in whipped cream who was brought in under an enormous silver dome. He had a prize hidden in the whipped cream that guests were invited to find. As the party became more boisterous, two handsome young cops showed up in response to a noise complaint and ended up joining in the fun.[27] Most residents enjoyed or tolerated the LGBTQ scene. Some were even proud that it was a place where people were free to ignore the oppressive sex and gender norms of the decade, but there were periodic crackdowns. Though serious, they never dented the town's allure to LGBTQ people. In 1960, for example, concerned that Provincetown was acquiring a reputation for being gay, Chief Francis Marshall "visited all the restaurants, announcing that all waiters were to be fingerprinted and photographed, their records circulated throughout the country, and if any of the men in question had been arrested for sodomy they would not be allowed to work in Provincetown." Seventeen people lost their jobs.[28] LGBTQ people had no ability to defend themselves from this type of abuse.

The most public targets of that moral crusade were Phil Bayone and Weathering Heights. He was vulnerable because he was not a native, mostly used Boston suppliers, and was one of the most flamboyant men on the street and beach. Unfortunately, because he had neglected to renew the license for his nightclub, the town was able to it shut down.

In another bizarre attempt to enforce propriety, in 1965 the wearing of bathing suits on Commercial St. was prohibited and woman could not wear cutoffs. "Provincetown really had Fashion Police," quipped one gay man.[27] But nothing could stop the onslaught of the partying straight and LGBTQ visitors. By the next summer, some residents felt besieged by young people who appeared dirty, unemployed, and very different from the natives. The *New York Times* decided the town was very much like Greenwich Village and thought many of its summer residents were the same people who hung around the Village in the cooler months. Some in the town called on the police to arrest the people they thought were vagrants, but the police chief said they were not breaking any law. Many blamed the establishment of the National Seashore five years earlier for the invasion.[29]

Business owners were not happy, but felt they had to adapt to the new clientele. Staniford Sorrentino, who had opened the Crown and Anchor in 1962, converted one of the complex's clubs to rock and roll, much to the displeasure of the theatre next door. Sorrentino sold part of his business to the Vara brothers and soon it was a raucous gay entertainment complex with first three then four different bars. The complex wasn't officially gay, but it added to the fun for LGBTQ visitors to the city.

This was the era that one of Provincetown's most famous gay residents, John Waters, first visited the cape. "I was in Baltimore in the summer of 1965, and that had been a bizarre year for me. I'd been expelled from NYU for pot, and they told my parents I needed extensive psychiatry. I'd come home to Baltimore and made this movie, Roman Candles. I was very confused, and somebody said to me, 'Have you ever been to P-Town? It's a very weird place.'"[30] He worked at a bookstore and spent his time partying and having sex. The town was filled with LGBTQ people out for a good time. "And I remember the funniest thing, seeing Judy Garland walking down the street with ten thousand gay people following her like the Pied Piper. She went into the little A-House. She was dead drunk, in bad shape, having fun, wearing a big hat. It was like the Virgin Mary appearing, a Miracle."[30] Almost anything could happen and Waters happily brought a number of Baltimore friends. "Swimming on acid and pumped up on speed and dead drunk at the Foc'sle, the Baltimorians shoplifted, stole bicycles. Some fucked everyone in town, sold drugs, failed invariably at menial jobs, and skipped out on the rent."[30]

People were wild in the streets, on the beaches, in the bars, and in the many guest houses. "The crazy people came to Provincetown, the people who didn't fit in Cleveland, or wherever else they were from. This was like a dumping ground for the ne'er-do-wells. And we all got along quite well there."[31]

Boston LGBTQ activism began to grow in the late 1950s. But the repression and hostility of straight society made these years difficult for organizing. In 1957, for example, the Mattachine Society complained that no Boston store would sell *One* because of fear that the Watch and Ward Society would arrest its employees and Prescott Townsend bought copies directly from the Mattachine Society to distribute them to friends and activists. By now, Townsend had paid a price for his decades of activism: he was erased by straight Boston society. Townsend "would have done less damage to his reputation by making a pass at a hostess's son than by waving a banner and tooting his one note," noted his biographer.[27]

Activists met in Townsend's basement at 75 Phillips St. on Sundays. Later, these gatherings moved to the Parker House. Though the focus was on civil rights, many went there to meet others, which annoyed the more political-minded attendees. "The purpose of the group was for public education, not for assignations," complained one.[32] These gatherings evolved into the Boston chapter of the Mattachine Society. Within a few years, the group was asked to stop meeting at the Parker House "because each and every meeting would turn into…well, I won't say an orgy, but we'll stop just short of that."[32] Another man joked that the gatherings gave "a new meaning to the term Parker House roll."[27] After complaints from the management, the meetings shifted back to Townsend's Beacon Hill mansion where they were more noted for their conflicts than their socializing. Unfortunately, the flamboyant Townsend was disliked by many activists because he didn't fit in with their goal of proving to the world they were next door neighbor types. Most were trying to gain acceptance by fitting in, not by shouting for their rights. Boston activists were not the only ones who were reluctant to push straight society. Compared to Townsend, the national Mattachine Society was timid. When asked by Townsend to cosponsor his sodomy legislation in late 1959, for example, it declined.[33] It was afraid to openly challenge homophobic laws. But Townsend was fearless, going on radio programs to advocate for the repeal of sodomy laws.

Fed up with the Mattachine's unwillingness to take political action, Townsend resigned from the Boston chapter. It continued without Townsend's participation until 1961. Meanwhile, Townsend started a new group, the Boston Demophile Society.[34] Its meetings were held on Thursday nights in Townsend's home on Lindell Court (his two residences were connected to each other by a tunnel). This group spanned much of the mid-1960s, but over time, many turned against Townsend, complaining how he dominated the various groups he founded and the unconscious manner with which he lived his life. Most other men had far too much to lose by being so open at the time.

Later in the 1960s, activism increased with the strong beginnings of a movement as LGBTQ people met to strategize on how to advance their rights. There were meetings in the South End at the Piano Factory and at communes on Massachusett Avenue and Prospect St. in Cambridge.[35] In the years before Stonewall, many in Boston were turning to activism and advocacy.

Boston and Cambridge, like San Francisco and New York, became filled with young men and women looking for drugs, sex, and good times. Townsend welcomed male hippies and runaways to his Beacon Hill buildings and his house made of drift wood in Provincetown, called "Provincetownsend." There were always people coming and going there. In the final years of the 1960s, however, Townsend was in a deep decline. He no longer was surrounded by artists and filmmakers, and his guests were mostly hustlers, drug addicts, and others trying to take advantage of him. His houses were fire traps as they became crammed with everyone from long-retired servants to underage runaways. Stuffed with oriental rugs, archeological artifacts, and piles of newspapers, the rooms were dusty, the smell of the kitchen became legendary.[36] Provincetownsend burned down in 1968 and his Beacon Hill buildings were similarly destroyed within a few years, taking countless treasures of Boston LGBTQ history with them. Now homeless (his will would reveal that his fortune had long been spent), he moved in with a friend and died in 1973.[37]

By late 1968, LGBTQ politics had moved past Townsend as several gay men restarted a Boston Mattachine Society chapter. One man had heard about a New York chapter from a television documentary and contacted them. They provided a few names, including Townsend's. Forced to use their own resources to find allies, the Boston men pooled their contacts and reached out to others. Then with Frank Morgan as its first leader, the Boston Chapter of the New York Mattachine Society was founded in January 1969 at the Arlington Street Church. It soon changed its name to the Homophile Union of Boston (HUB), one of the first explicitly political LGBTQ organizations anywhere. Morgan began regular radio broadcasts to reach out to others with its membership growth also fueled by word of mouth. HUB also recruited members from an informal group known as the Breakfast Club which had been meeting weekly at a restaurant called Zara's, at the corner of St. Botolph and West Newton Streets as well as people who had been attending other meetings around the area.

Lesbian activism was boosted after a female liberation conference was held at Emmanuel College in May 1969. Some were out lesbians who had been part of the bar scene, while others were still in the closet but were motivated by the women's rights ideology they heard at the conference and at other gatherings. Within weeks, there was an extensive network of women excitedly working to develop an agenda to advance women's and lesbian rights.

Meanwhile, across the river at MIT, college students began to organize themselves with Stan Tillotson in the lead. Born in New York, while still in high school Tillotson read in the Village Voice about a gay group at Columbia. Going to MIT, he assumed there would be a similar group there as well, but was surprised when no such group existed. Not liking bars and finding HUB to be unfriendly, in May 1969 he placed an ad in the MIT newspaper for an organizing meeting. He had thought the paper would reject the ad and was relieved to find that it appeared in print.

Recruiting members wasn't easy, as his fellow students were cautious and nervous. His roommate, not wanting to be associated with the group, asked for a separate phone line. Others were hesitant to leave their names and still more called but were afraid to be associated with other homosexuals. Meanwhile Tillotson and his fellow students simply wanted to dance. But when students asked MIT for permission to hold an event on school property in May 1969, the dean's reaction was "[t]he faggots want to have a dance on campus!" The request was denied because the dean wanted to "protect young gay people who may later change their mind about their sexuality."[38] The group didn't back down and it kept pressing to simply have the right to dance.

Though outwardly Boston's LGBTQ community might have seemed placid and accepting of the repression weighing down on it, a network of activists was growing. LGBTQ people were attending meetings, strategizing on how to advocate for their rights, and reaching out to one another to provide support in anti-LGBTQ times. It was a powder keg where injustice combined with resistance created a potentially explosive situation that needed the smallest spark to set it off. By 1969, Boston was not the only city where conditions had become tense. Three hours south, a group of LGBTQ people would finally be pushed too far and fight back.

Chapter 9

Revolution

EARLY IN THE morning of June 28, 1969, the police marched into a gay bar in New York City's Greenwich Village to shut it down, scattering and cornering the drag queens, people of color, and others who made the bar their own. As elsewhere, raids on gay bars in New York were easy for the law enforcement personnel involved. Unlike the protestors at anti-war or civil rights demonstrations, no one fought back, asserted their rights, or protested harassment, while anyone who so much as looked the police in the eye or didn't have identification was beaten, arrested, or both.

Thus, the police were shocked when the raid quickly faced opposition that grew loud and violent and soon they were barricaded inside the bar, calling for help. Officers responding to the scene must have been similarly surprised as the blocks around the bar filled with LGBTQ people chanting slogans and hurling projectiles at the police; first pennies and then rocks, bottles, and anything else they could grab. The protestors, led by trans and gender non-conforming people, refused to back down when ordered to disperse and demanded the same rights any other person had.

The protests continued over the next several nights as word spread across the city of the riots. The modern gay rights movement was born from this uprising as drag queens, transgender people, preppy gays and lipstick lesbians, dykes and leather men (and others from across the broad spectrum of New York's LGBTQ community) refused to accept harassment and discrimination, filled the streets, and fought back. The brave actions at the Stonewall Inn became a symbol of resistance and of the need to act against bigotry for LGBTQ people around the world.

It took a while for word of what happened in New York to get to Boston, however. The *Boston Globe* did not mention the Stonewall riot until 1972, for example. Ann Maguire remembered reading about the riot in the *New York Times* and worrying that the authorities might send in the army to quash the rebellion at any moment.[1] She did not know that her life's course was about to be forever altered. Others heard about the resistance but were not motivated by it, at least at first. Stonewall made very little impression on John Graves, for example, as he read about it at his summer home on Long Island. Yet within a year Graves would be a member of several Boston LGBTQ organizations, beginning decades of service to the community.[2]

Brian McNaught, then a student at Marquette University in Milwaukee, didn't hear about Stonewall when it was happening and thinks it was some time before word spread to the Midwest.[3] Already heavily involved in the Catholic Church, his life would also be profoundly influenced by the events in New York. Even many people who were working to organize Boston's LGBTQ community didn't find out about the riots for several weeks. HUB cofounder Frank Morgan, for example, first heard about the riots when he read Dick Leitsch's article in the New York Mattachine Society's July 1969 newsletter, "The Hairpin Drop Heard Round The World." But within a few months almost all LGBTQ people who were connected to the community knew that resistance was possible and Morgan says that by 1970, everyone in Boston knew about those New York nights.[4]

9.1 Charley Shively (left) and John Mitzel

Boston's LGBTQ community was poised to leap into the forefront of the gay rights movement because it included many people who were ready to devote their lives to the cause. One activist was Charley Shively (1937-2017). Born to a poor family in Ohio, Shively moved to Cambridge to attend Harvard. After briefly returning to the Midwest to earn his master's degree, he came back to Harvard for a doctorate. He went on to teach for many years at Boston State College and then when it merged with the University of Massachusetts–Boston, he was a professor there. He developed one of the first classes on LGBTQ history and became very well known for his advancement of what is now called queer theory. During the '60s and '70s he helped publish LGBTQ papers including *Lavender Vision*, *Fag Rag*, and *Gay Community News* (GCN).

Like many Boston LGBTQ advocates of the 1970s, he was a radical in both his politics and his personal life. "Shively and many others of his generation fundamentally rejected the pillars of American society—religion, capitalism, and the family."[5] He also strongly believed that being gay was much more than just sexual activity. Shively sought to educate gay men about their bodies, sex, and their relationships with other men. "History books tend to lionize gay men in sweaty street protests fighting for legal recognition as the epitome of liberation, but Shively interrogated the sex that propelled them to become political in the first place. He shed light on the taboos that many gay men were too uneasy to discuss in public: the mechanics of sex, intimacy between men, the question of promiscuity."[5]

Shively's writings celebrated sex. His first article in *Fag Rag* was titled, "Cocksucking as a Political Act" and he believed that gay men had an obligation to enjoy sex and share its wonders with everyone, regardless of their personal attributes. No one should be ashamed of sex, he argued, on the contrary they should celebrate it. Nor was he afraid to challenge gay men. In one essay, "Shively threw a hand grenade at Gay America by challenging the premium the community placed on physical beauty. For Shively praised random promiscuity" and considered anything else bigotry.[6] And so he promoted orgies, believing they built community, and he was in favor of sex with the elderly and underaged, arguing that everyone deserved the right to enjoy physical relations. For the next ten years, Shively would be the intellectual face of the Boston LGBTQ community.

New groups quickly emerged all over the Boston area so that in 1971, the *Boston Globe* called the city, "a center of the gay movement in America." It reported that eight organizations collectively had 300-400 members.[7] Already growing rapidly before Stonewall, HUB attracted new members as the news of Stonewall spread and by the beginning of 1970 it had 65 members, mostly men. By the end of the year it had 120 members as it opened an office, staffed a telephone hotline, and produced a newsletter. Early on, HUB found allies at progressive churches and synagogues. Morgan and other activists aided these attempts to organize by going on radio programs targeting progressives and the gay community. In addition, news of the group spread by word of mouth in gay bars and in conversations wherever LGBTQ people gathered. Outreach wasn't easy. While the *Boston Phoenix* and *Harvard Crimson* accepted ads for HUB, the *Globe* did not.

Inside HUB, there were disputes as to how it should carry out its mission. Some feared it was too radical, wanting it to slow down and keep a low profile. Others argued that it was not radical enough and pushed it to move aggressively to promote rights. Deciding that now was the time for action, HUB organized two protests. Members picketed the *Herald* for not running ads for HUB and they organized a July 4, 1970 march in Provincetown, the first in-the-streets pride celebration in the state. The march demonstrated the broad support for action as HUB brought fifty to seventy-five people from Boston with hundreds joining them on Commercial St. in a joyous and defiant display of LGBTQ power. The gay rights movement was energizing the community.

The Student Homophile League (SHL), also founded at this time, was similarly split by tensions over its role. These prompted a group of men to start another organization in March 1970, the Gay Liberation Front (GLF), in order to take part in the April antiwar demonstration that was one of the largest ever held in the city. Walking through the crowd, GLF passed out pamphlets and held signs saying "Bring Our Boys Home" but straight anti-war demonstrators did not like these and while most ignored the small band of gay protestors, a few were hostile. Though many of the first-generation gay rights activists were already veterans of the anti-war movement, they quickly learned that mainstream peace activists were not necessarily allies. Next, GLF picketed Ken's, a popular late-night restaurant in Copley Square, for ejecting two men for kissing. Around the same time, SHL held a dance in Harvard Square in the fourth floor of a condemned building. There was no electricity—but there were nude men dancing.[4] A gay group quietly formed at Boston University and within a few years there were a dozen college-based organizations as well as a high school group. Meanwhile, with the support of the student government, MIT gay students finally held their dance in 1970, the first in a series that happened without incident. Soon there were regular meetings between gays and the MIT administration and what became Gays at MIT (GAMIT) was chartered on February 23, 1970.

Just forming an LGBTQ group at some colleges was controversial and difficult, however. New Hampshire Governor Meldrim Thomson, for example, complained about a gay dance at the University of New Hampshire in the fall of 1973 and so university trustees banned the school's gay student association from holding social functions. When students performed a play, *Coming Out*, the Governor threatened to cut off all funds to the university unless the gay group was outlawed. "Moral filth will no longer be allowed on our campuses," he declared.[8] The students refused to back down. Taking the case to federal court, a judge affirmed their right to have a campus group.

The tensions inside HUB, SHL, and other organizations resulted from a fundamental argument inside the LGBTQ community of Boston that emerged in the 1970s and formed the background for disputes around Pride, same-sex marriage, and other issues through the first decades of the next century. Novelist Edmund White in his 1980 groundbreaking survey of gay life in the United States, saw a split between those he called radicals and those he considered assimilationists. White thought that Washington was the center of the assimilationists while Boston was the home of the radicals.[9] But even in Boston the assimilationists were in the majority and most gay men and lesbians believed that they were no different than anyone else. The mentality of assimilationists was that if one took away their same-sex desires and activities they were just like straight people. Thus their aim was to achieve liberation from legal repression and social disapproval, a goal that they thought could be achieved through education and mainstream political activism. Some took their urge for conformity to an extreme and opposed drag queens, leather men, or anyone else that potentially compromised their carefully cultivated, clean-cut middle-class image. The assimilationists powered the efforts for a gay rights bill, pushed for same-sex marriage, and funded AIDS work at a time when straight society ignored the LGBTQ people dying around them, but the assimilationists never considered that their ideas might be hurtful to trans and non-binary people. The assimilationists would spend the next several decades marginalizing a significant portion of the community.

There was also a small, but very zealous, group of radicals who wanted to shatter all norms regarding gender and sex. Providing much of the momentum for LGBTQ rights groups in the 1970s, they argued that conventional heterosexuality denigrated women and demonized homosexuality and so must be overthrown. Already challenging gender norms, they were laying the groundwork for others who would contend that being binary (strictly conventionally male or female) was unnatural and that gender fluidity should be celebrated. Most of the radicals believed that it was vital to defend all those outside the mainstream because that was a method homophobes used to oppress all LGBTQ people. An attack on any one LGBTQ person was an attack on all, they argued. Furthermore, the radicals asserted that, "gays can serve as the vanguard of a liberation movement that might transform America society into something better, more humane, more equitable, less repressed."[9] Over time, however, many radicals would end up isolating themselves from the majority of LGBTQ people who were unwilling to reject capitalism, religion, and other mainstream institutions. Some would become hostile to cisgender lesbians and gay men who they believed were as privileged as heterosexuals, even denying the discrimination the community experienced. As shown later in this book, the radicals' rejection of the assimilationists would sadly lead to their failure to respond to the emerging AIDS epidemic in the early 1980s.

The radicals also had a problem connecting to straight left-wing movements. Many straight activists were homophobic and as likely to reject LGBTQ people as were conservatives of the time. "At the mention of homosexuality, they form ugly facial contortions and unleash streams of misinformed hyperbole," one disappointed gay man remembered. "They talk about repression and oppression, but their romantic vision of revolution seems to end with the prospect of accepting faggots."[10] In addition, leftists were dismayed by the anti-gay policies of Cuba and other international socialist movements and as a consequence, many began to explore feminism and other liberation perspectives that were informed by, but not direct followers of, Marxism.

Many decided to try to live in new ways that emphasized the freedom to be open about their sexuality and soon there were LGBTQ communes, group homes, and gathering places not involving bars across Boston and Cambridge. The most famous residential group was the Fort Hill Faggots for Freedom, based in the Highland Park section of Roxbury. A collective of about twenty gay men, the group bought a cluster of tax foreclosed buildings from the city around 1975 or 1976 where they dwelled "communally in glorious living filth, in what amounts to a self-conscious rejection of about every middle-class value you could think of."[11] They ran around in dresses or half naked, which disturbed their straight black neighbors. Many were poets and writers, contributing to *Fag Rag, GCN,* and other LGBTQ publications and all of them were dedicated to the political act of living as radical gay men. To protest its inhospitality to women, for example, the collective once wore dresses to a demonstration at Sporters.[12]

Women, energized by the burgeoning feminist movement as well as LGBTQ politics, also created new institutions. One of the most well remembered was Bread and Roses in Cambridge. Run by women, the coffee house and restaurant sponsored lesbian poetry readings and hosted meetings of women dedicated to countering the patriarchal society around them. These spaces had to work out their relationships with men. Some banned men and straight women altogether, but when a server made men feel unwelcome at Bread and Roses, she was fired, sparking a series of meetings regarding the purposes and guiding principles of feminism and lesbians.[13] Cambridge, particularly the area around Central and Inman Squares, became noted for its women- and lesbian-run institutions with a credit union, bookstores, and (perhaps the most influential) the Boston Women's Health Book Collective, which published *Our Bodies, Ourselves.*

Another influential member of the radicals was John Mitzel (1948-2014). Also from the Midwest, he moved to Boston in 1965 to go to Boston University, graduating in 1971. In his younger days he went to the Punch Bowl, the Other Side, Sporters, and Jacques. Later he frequented the Shed and the Eagle. Soft spoken at times but always a profound intellectual force, Mitzel also liked to dress up in a police uniform to cruise the bars and the Fens.

Mitzel met Shively at a SHL meeting at BU in 1970 or 1971 and the two began decades of collaboration that helped shape the ideology of the community. One of their first collaborations was *Lavender Vision,* a short-lived paper that focused on political issues. Even though it had one section for women and another for men, the women left to publish their own paper. Shively, Mitzel and others thus started *Fag Rag,* which would be one of the most influential radical LGBTQ periodicals of the 1970s. It featured poetry, art, interviews, and political commentary that aimed to create a new world, one that liberated gay men (though it had some, but not extensive, trans or lesbian coverage) from the personal and social oppression that had constrained their early lives.

Mitzel worked at the South Station Cinema from the day it opened in 1972 until it closed in 1983. Later he managed Glad Day bookstore from 1984 to 2000 before opening Calamus Bookstore in the Leather District. Suffering from depression and alcoholism, Mitzel was a prolific author with his work appearing in *GCN, Fag Rag,* and other publications. From this position at the center of LGBTQ literary Boston, he promoted new authors, sponsored readings and books signings, and enthusiastically suggested books to anyone who walked into his bookstores. Sadly, Calamus closed in 2016, two years after Mitzel died, and Boston no longer has an LGBTQ bookstore. He also helped organize the early pride marches and he would be a major force in the effort to fight the Revere crackdown of 1978. His biting wit and extreme knowledge of issues meant he could win any argument, yet he was kind to those he thought were merely clueless.

The divisions within the Boston LGBTQ community were minor compared to the oppression on the outside and nearly everyone connected within LGBTQ life worked together to achieve common goals. A whole generation of both assimilationist and radical lesbians, for example, empowered each other to come out through their association with the Cambridge Women Center (founded as part of a 1971 protest against Harvard and its real estate practices). The Center traced its roots to the occupation of a Harvard-owned building at 888 Memorial Dr. on March 6.

The takeover was not spontaneous; rather, it was meticulously planned and efficiently carried out. For several months, local women's groups had discussed issues and possible actions. One group, meeting at Bread and Roses, proposed occupying a building and turning it into a women's center. Together with others, these discussions led to a list of demands: safe spaces for women, reproductive rights, equal pay, an end to the incarceration of non-violent offenders, childcare, and medical care.[14]

Expertly executing their plan, a small group of women quietly entered the building (then used by the Graduate School of Design) earlier in the morning to prepare for the arrival of marchers participating in a rally on Boston Common to celebrate International Women's Day. Soon there were 150 women in the building ready to take on Harvard, the police, or anyone else who might oppose them. Before long, Mary Bunting, president of Radcliffe College, and Harvard crisis manager, Archibald Cox, (later of Watergate fame) became involved. Harvard, like other colleges and universities across the country, had just come through a tumultuous period of demonstrations and the administration wanted to avoid violence and the media coverage that accompanied it. In addition, Cox sympathized with some of the goals, if not the methods, of the protestors.[14]

As the hours went by, the women organized working groups for planning, cleaning, skills-building, and so forth. According to Libby Bouvier, a member of the 888 Memorial Drive Women's History Project, the Harvard police may have been reluctant to use force because Radcliffe students were inside the building. They also may have deferred to the Cambridge police, waiting for them to act. But the police were reluctant to get involved in a Harvard-owned property dispute.

Harvard did not make it easy for the occupiers, however. Cox reminded them via bullhorn that they were trespassing and risked arrest. The electricity was turned off but the women were prepared. Supporters had brought in space heaters and food. Some Harvard-associated women visited the building, seeking common ground, while the University was granted an injunction ordering the women to leave. They refused.

Inside the building, the protestors enthusiastically implemented a social structure that empowered women. The women reached decisions by consensus, which took time but meant that all had an equal voice. The atmosphere inside the building was electrifying; for the first time in their lives, some lesbians were able to express affection openly.

The women left after ten days but plans for a permanent center on Pearl St. were in the works. Over the years, this woman-controlled space featured countless classes and seminars led by women to educate women regarding their priority issues. It also became a place where many found the space and the encouragement to come out and an entire generation of Boston-area lesbians would mark the takeover as one of the most important moments of their lives.

Though there was a broad range of incomes with some demographics of LGBTQ people, (particularly those who were young, female, and trans) being very poor, by the mid-1970s Boston had a large number of middle-class LGBTQ people who held professional jobs, were in long term relationships, and open about their preferred sexuality and gender, at least while inside the community. These people marched in pride parades, attended rallies, supported LGBTQ groups, patronized the growing arts and theatre movement, and made Boston a vibrant community for all.[15] As time went on, they would be the base of support for LGBTQ businesses, political groups, and service organizations and it was from this strong infrastructure that some of the greatest political successes of the community would be achieved.

Because the city was poor with many abandoned buildings, it featured large numbers of cheap apartments for rent. This enabled lower income LGBTQ people not only to live in the city, but also gave them the economic freedom to live independently and openly as sexual and gender non-conformists. Many used this freedom to attend rallies, volunteer for LGBTQ organizations, and create works of art and literature. This explosion of culture contributed to the feeling that something important was going on in LGBTQ Boston.

In the 1970s, LGBTQ people still had major concentrations in Bay Village and the back of Beacon Hill but as the numbers of out LGBTQ people rapidly expanded, the community moved west. Many lived in Back Bay and the Fenway, but the South End was now the center of gay life as single men and couples moved into renovated townhouses. Many LGBTQ people also lived in Cambridge, Jamaica Plain, and Allston with smaller numbers scattered across the region. Bars and nightlife began to move away from Park Square as the city's urban renewal program sought to redevelop the area. Boston's LGBTQ community became known around the country for its intellectualism as well as a place for those interested in politics, social issues, and art.[9]

Though there was a mixture of different LGBTQ people in each neighborhood, some were known for certain types of residents. More prosperous lesbians settled in Jamaica Plain, while working-class lesbians seemed to prefer Somerville. Old timers of every description lived on the back of Beacon Hill and Back Bay gays were thought to be the richest and haughtiest. South End gays were younger, more adventurous, more likely to party, and most fixated on personal attractiveness. LGBTQ students lived in the Fenway, Allston-Brighton, and Cambridge.

Charles St. on Beacon Hill was the center of day-to-day gay life even though the bars were elsewhere. Many gay men and lesbians lived on the hill, particularly on its north slope. There was little outward sign of LGBTQ life in other neighborhoods because there were few stores or restaurants that openly catered to them. However, on Charles St. life was different. There was a small store, Esplanade Books, that sold gay and lesbian themed books and magazines and it was on Charles St. that one could see occasional same-sex couples strolling arm in arm.

On the other hand, the freedom inside Boston's gay ghettos was rigidly hemmed in by the continued extreme discrimination outside. For the most part, police harassment in gay bars was over, house raids were a thing of the past, and there were few state or local laws enforced against LGBTQ people in the city. But people still could be fired, thrown out of their homes, and harassed. Any sexual or gender non-conformity could be met by violence and victims feared calling the police as much as they feared injury. Therefore, LGBTQ people routinely lived double lives, one out of the closet while amongst friends or inside this welcoming, increasingly vibrant community, and one extremely closeted for time spent with their families, at work, or in any other situation where they might meet discrimination or violence.

A doctoral dissertation from the early 1970s provides an important glimpse into daily living at this time (though it was based on data gathered from young cis-gender gay men who frequented bars). Using interviews with twenty-five men from Boston, Springfield, and New York, the study illustrates how they navigated dual realities.[16] The study documented how the LGBTQ community was essential to personal and emotional well-being. Inside the metaphorical walls of the gay ghetto there was a strong belief that being gay was good. LGBTQ society provided friends and sex partners, protected individuals from arrest and harassment, and informed people about social events. The men believed there was a general progression of personal growth: first came same-sex fantasies, then sex with another male, next the realization that he was gay, and finally participation in gay society. Despite the hostility from the straight world, attitudes towards straight individuals were quite benign and unless they were harassing gays, straights were ignored. In contrast, attitudes toward straight society as a whole were very negative. Many were wary and unless they were forced to participate and pass, they tried to avoid and ignore it.

Among the men interviewed, views of sexuality were relaxed. Some preferences tended to be more set off than others (sadomasochism, for example), but there was little condemnation of anyone for their tastes. Casual sex was not frowned upon, nor was participating in open sexual activity. In fact, promiscuity was generally applauded and men who had lots of sex were often admired, especially if their partners were thought to be attractive. There was a hierarchy of male physical beauty and the most prized sexual partners were those who were young and at least somewhat masculine. In this world there were some near universal rules governing behavior.

Men did not have sexual relations within their close circle of friends or they could do so only if they were a couple. Relations with a friend's lover was thought to be very wrong.

The dissertation further related how many men assumed that a romantic relationship was not permanent and if it lasted for more than two or three years they were surprised (however, this was a young sample). There were many pressures against long-term romantic relationships. Tensions created by the constant opportunities for sex with others along with infidelity brought down many couples. Adding to their difficulties was the fact that no entrenched social norms existed for addressing common issues. For example, if one partner had to leave town for a new job, there was no expectation that the other partner would move to be with him and so a job move almost always meant a gay couple broke up.[9] In addition, the burden of homophobia on same-sex couples was tremendous. One man, not part of the study, put it bluntly: "[w]alk down the street together holding hands. Kiss when you meet each other at the airport after a long separation. Lie together in the sun. Dance together anyplace you please. Can you? We can't."[17] Yet many relationships endured and thrived.

In this study sample, almost everyone wanted a lover. The motivation was not economic; most of the sample had stable jobs and there was little sharing of finances between men in a couple. Mostly it reflected a desire for companionship, a hedge against loneliness, and a means to avoid having to find new sex partners. Furthermore, men who were in relationships had a higher status among their peer gays. They were seen as more stable, more sexually attractive, and more successful. At the same time, there was a high degree of acceptance of non-monogamy if these out-of-relationship encounters were limited to sexual contact only. An emotional or more personal encounter or relationship was seen as a deal-breaker.

It was common for men in relationships not to live with each other (though of course a few did). Much rarer was economic co-mingling and though they might share rent and household expenses, few merged finances beyond that. In fact, many men seemed to actively avoid depending on their partners economically. Therefore, it should not be surprising that the economic status or social class of a lover was less important. Instead, men tended to sort themselves based on physical attractiveness. Very good-looking men paired up with other very handsome men and others similarly ended up with men of similar physical attractiveness, creating a hierarchy that marginalized some.

Sexual intimacy almost always preceded a couple becoming lovers. Typically a couple would meet, have sex, and then spend increasing amounts of time together before deciding to be a couple. It was taken for granted that casual sex encounters sometimes turned into relationships. Though men with partners were proud of their relationships, couples found it necessary to hide their relationship from families and neighbors.[16]

In the post-Stonewall world, many were looking to be more involved in help ing other LGBTQ people navigate the intense pressures that kept them in the closet. In 1971, Lois Johnson and Shari Barden saw a poster for a dance sponsored by HUB and DOB at the Charles Street Meeting House. The dance was mainly men, but it included some women and they felt energized. The couple would spend the next several decades working with DOB, devoting their time to helping other lesbians face coming out and other issues affecting their lives. Growing rapidly in the early 1970s, DOB rented offices at 419 Boylston St. along with HUB and the Homophile Community Health Service. Rent was just $60 per month. In 1975 when they moved to the old Cambridge Baptist Church they paid $75 per month.

Boston's chapter of DOB had the same split between radicals and assimilationists that affected other organizations. Some women grew unhappy with DOB, wanting it to be more political and radical like the Cambridge Women's Center. Others wanted it to remain safe for those just coming out and a place for women to talk about their feelings and concerns. Though other organizations split, over time DOB focused on helping members address personal and emotional issues, leaving political action to other organizations.

This apolitical outlook did not spare it from police surveillance, however. At one point, authorities became convinced that DOB was hiding Susan Saxe and Katherine Powers, two radical antiwar activists who had come out as lesbians after participating in a bank robbery where a policeman was murdered, and the FBI and the State Police started investigating many Boston area LGBTQ organizations. They tapped phones and rifled through the DOB office.[18] Ironically, DOB was always a middle-class mainstream organization with a median age in the mid-thirties. It was predominantly (though not exclusively) white and few if any members had connections to radical organizations. But none of that mattered to law enforcement because LGBTQ groups were all suspected of being tied to left wing violence despite the lack of specific evidence.

While the Boston chapter seemed more resilient, nationally DOB was split by the same forces that rocked the Boston group and many chapters fell apart as conflicts between radicals who wanted a more political organization and assimilationists who saw DOB as providing a safe place for women to come out proved irreconcilable. By 1989, Boston was the only DOB chapter left. Even though at any time it had as many as 250 members, the Boston chapter did not get the radical influx others did and it continued to be a safe place for women.[19]

In the summer of 1969 "Provincetown was the gay Disneyland. Instead of hippies, gaggles of gay men, hugging and holding hands, dressed in colorful Hawaiian shirts (or colorful dresses with perfect hair and makeup) packed the streets. Provincetown was a full-time gay pride parade."[20] A small minority of the town fumed but for the most part summertime Commercial St. was filled with LGBTQ people, many basking in the sun and freedom to be who they wanted to be.

But there were bouts of repression. For example, town police raided Piggy's, the premier dance club of the early 1970s, in order to put a stop to same-sex danc-ing, one of the last such raids anywhere in Massachusetts. The largest controversy centered on the benches in front of Town Hall, known as the meat rack because they were a place for LGBTQ people to get together at night. The benches were not used exclusively by LGBTQ people, of course; young homeless straight people slept there and many townsfolks and visitors liked to sit and watch the crowds walk by. "The life cycle of the town is repeated there every 24 hours. Everyone takes care of business on or about the benches. Dates made, debts paid, dealables dealt, rumors mongered, ankles rested, continuous remarks on the passers-by."[21] Without telling anyone of their plan, the town pulled the benches out, angering almost everyone.

Suddenly the town was in an uproar and the Board of Selectmen was con-fronted by an angry crowd that included long time permanent residents, summer visi-tors, and everyone in between. The town was forced to relent after a vote revealed 103 people in favor of the benches with only 34 in favor of their removal. Provincetown liked its LGBTQ people.

Lesbians also came to town for the nightlife. In the years after it opened in 1971, the Pied Piper was one of the most popular lesbian bars in the country with lines down the block on the weekends. Owned by the cabaret singer Linda Gerard and her girlfriend, Pam Genevrino, the club had a door person who had a front tooth capped in gold and a strict door policy: in theory men could get in–if they had six pieces of identification. Genevrino had short hair, aviator glasses, bell bottomed jeans, and gold chains while Gerard performed her torch songs in gowns and jewels. The two made a fortune from the club, and then sold it for more than a million dol-lars.[22]

In 1974, Boston made history when Elaine Noble became the first openly LGBTQ person to be elected to state-level public office in the United States. She represented the Fenway, where she had grown up, at a time when the Massachusetts House of Representatives had 640 members–around 10,000 residents per district. Noble had been encouraged to run by Ann Lewis, Barney Frank's sister, with whom she founded the Massachusetts Women's Political Caucus. Noble thought she couldn't be elected but Lewis believed that the newly-redrawn district would be a good fit for her as it was mostly the home of the elderly, students, and LGBTQ people. It was also a poor district with a large arson problem and decaying housing.

Noble was an activist. She led a group of about 200 LGBTQ people at a march against racism organized by the NAACP in early 1974–Boston LGBTQ activ-ists were strong supporters of desegregation in the years the city was torn apart by anti-busing riots. The marchers had a banner that read "One Struggle–Many Fronts." Similarly, African-American politicians were the strongest supporters of LGBTQ rights. City Councilor Thomas Atkins, for example, spoke out for a Boston gay rights ordinance in 1971, State Representative Doris Bunte successfully incorporated a gay antidiscrimination clause in the South End urban renewal advisory board's bylaws, and Representative Mel King was on the board of the Gay United Way, a funding organization that provided grants to LGBTQ groups. In contrast, some of the most rabid anti-busing politicians were also very anti-gay. Racist School Committee Chairman John Kerrigan, for example, complained "How come the fags can get a hearing when the people of Boston can't?" during the run-up to the busing crisis.[23]

9.2 Ann Maguire 1976

Noble's campaign manager was Ann Maguire (1943-). A dynamic redhead from Worcester, Maguire would be the steady political mastermind inside almost every LGBTQ movement up to the twenty-first century. In the 1970s, her radio program reached thousands and many praised her for her calm reassurance to those suffering from bigotry and her feisty resistance to oppression. She would also become known for her charity work. As manager of the lesbian bar Somewhere Else, she made the venue a center of support for LGBTQ causes and in the 1980s, Maguire cofounded the Massachusetts Breast Cancer Coalition. Even in retirement in Provincetown (where her prowess at bingo was legendary), she could be seen on summer afternoons on Commercial St., raising funds for the town's organization that assists women facing health issues. One friend and colleague said of her, "Ann will go down in history as one of the greatest activists of all time. Ann has the courage and commitment to change the world for the better for future generations."[24] Her efforts to elect Noble were just the beginning of her political work.

Being one of the few out public officials was not easy for Noble. "In addition to being the target of bomb threats and vandalism, she was spit on by constituents and had excrement left on her desk."[25] Noble found herself helping LGBTQ people from across the country as they flooded her office with pleas for help with employment, housing, and other discrimination. Because they needed assistance dealing with violence, police harassment, and many other issues, Noble was forced to work long hours and her lover at the time, author Rita Mae Brown, couldn't take the pressure and eventually broke up with her.

Noble's legislative priority was a bill banning discrimination against LGBTQ people. Because the community was constantly bombarded with discrimination, the potential of the bill energized LGBTQ people. But Noble over-promised, saying she thought it would pass in 1975. She might have been optimistic because in 1974, Democratic gubernatorial candidate Michael Dukakis told HUB he would sign a gay rights bill. Additionally, an aide to sitting governor Francis Sargent told Barney Frank that the governor might sign the bill as well, though when pressed Sargent at first said he would take no position on the bill. While getting ready to run against Dukakis, he sent a letter to HUB opposing oppressive sexual behavior laws and saying he would sign a law outlawing discrimination. Of those running for governor, only Attorney General Robert Quinn opposed the bill, but he lost to Dukakis in the 1974 primary.[26] Therefore, when the bill failed to even come to a vote within the Massachusetts legislature, LGBTQ people were bitter with some of their anger directed at Noble.

Another rift came would come when Noble condemned the men caught up in the Revere scandal of 1978. She was not alone in her opposition to the intergenerational sex at the center of their cases as almost all lesbians and the vast majority of gay men felt the same way.[27] But Mitzel, Shively, and GCN were fully in support of the Revere men and never forgave her for her position. Crossing the radicals could be dangerous.

Noble was reelected in 1976 and a high point of her political career was a meeting in Washington with President Jimmy Carter. But overall, being a representative was wearying. She declined to run again in 1978 when another legislative redistricting put her in the same district as Frank. She unsuccessfully ran for US Senator and the Cambridge City Council, eventually leaving politics to move to Florida.

By the 1970s, the Boston police had mostly stopped routine harassment of white cisgender gay men and lesbians, but the relationship between the police and LGBTQ people remained strained. Part of this tension was because contact with the police still often resulted in harassment, arrest, abuse, or worse (police still freely arrested anybody associated with an incident involving LGBTQ people). In 1974, for example, an altercation between two women outside Jacques resulted in nine women being arrested, including some who had just been watching the fight and others who had simply had the bad luck of walking up to the front door of the club when the police arrived. The police assumed all LGBTQ people were guilty of something.

There was some progress. As previously mentioned, routine raids on bars or shakedowns of patrons had largely ceased. There were several reasons the end of these raids. The police, busy battling anti-war protestors, civil rights advocates, anti-busing radicals, and neighborhood residents opposed to urban renewal, lacked the manpower to harass LGBTQ people in bars. Another reason was that by now, same-sex dancing seemed tame. In the early 1970s, Boston had created the Combat Zone, a special zoning district where tawdry heterosexual strip shows and prostitution flourished. In a city where naked women were writhing in simulated ecstasy on stage, two middle-aged men in suits awkwardly disco dancing with each other at Napoleon's did not rate a second glance and the Licensing Board no longer considered same-sex dancing a violation. In addition, Boston Mayor Kevin White, closely in touch with the police department now that control of it had been returned to the city, did not want a scandal that an anti-gay crackdown would have caused, and the police chief would not have dared to do anything to rouse the mayor's fiery temper. Overall, the city was becoming more tolerant of LGBTQ people.

In Frank's eyes, which he focused on his middle- and upper-class cisgender gay and lesbian constituents in the mid- to late-1970s, the law enforcement problem in Boston was not so much police harassment of LGBTQ people as the difficulty in engaging with the police when a crime against them had been committed. Because they could be fired, LGBTQ people needed extreme discretion and though the police department's leadership said they would help victims, in practice most people were afraid to report a crime out of fear they would be further traumatized by the police response.[28]

GCN journalist David Brill had a different view and he documented several ways in which the Boston Police targeted poor, transgender, and non-white LGBTQ people. Perhaps the most egregious day-to-day harassment was a reporting system targeting members of the community. It asked if the person was a criminal, prostitute, or homosexual. Another question had a checkoff for "homosexuals in drag" (apparently heterosexuals in drag were not noteworthy).[29] These questions were dangerous to those who might lose their jobs or housing if word got out they were LGBTQ and they potentially exposed people to violence.

The program began in 1962 when the Boston Police Department created a system for collecting information that had gay men and transvestites in its sights. Called the Field Investigation and/or Observation Reports or FIOS for short, these were three-by-four file cards that were used to keep information on anyone a policeman wanted to target. By the mid-1970s, the police had files on thousands of people despite having said they destroyed the cards predating 1969.[30] The system was used to harass gay men, drag queens, and trans people. If stopped by a policeman in a cruising area, outside a gay bar, or if the person appeared gay, the officer filled out a card. Police especially targeted drag queens in Bay Village and Park Square while several men were approached by police in the Copley Library, the cards already partially filled out. The police said it was a tactic used in lieu of arresting a man for masturbating in public, but the men approached were simply reading or looking for books. After the policy of collecting information was exposed by GCN, it was quietly ended.

Religions had a variety of reactions toward their LGBTQ members. Unitarians were almost unanimously welcoming, and the Charles Street Meeting House and Arlington Street Church would host many meetings, dances, and other gatherings. Other churches and synagogues were quietly accepting while maintaining their official disapproval of LGBTQ people. Being LGBTQ and Catholic, however, could be a wrenching experience. One man recalled being told by a priest that he was living in mortal sin, so he stopped going to church and receiving sacraments. Feeling like outcasts and misfits, gay Catholics were forced to choose between being authentic to themselves and practicing their faith, and many left the church as a result of this conflict. One sympathetic priest noted, "Most gays throw away the church because of the guilt drilled into them."[31]

Some priests and lay people tried to reconcile homosexuality and Catholic teaching. One of the most popular alternatives that emerged in the 1970s was a Sunday mass in the South End. In addition to spiritual nourishment, there were other reasons to go to the Jesuit Urban Center at the Church of the Immaculate Conception on Harrison Avenue. "Known for its gay-friendliness and a theology focused on social justice, Immaculate Conception hosted an after-mass doughnut social every Sunday, where you could score if you'd been unlucky Saturday night."[32]

The congregation had a lot of energy, combining some of the most progressive elements of contemporary Catholicism with the exuberance of newly-out LGBTQ people. One man remembered that "[t]he palpable gayness of the place knocked me off my feet. It felt as if my skin was sloughing off in great waves. The seats were brimming with sophisticated men thin as a pair of folding spectacles. Bearded bears served as acolytes. Rainbow banners streamed from the ceiling. The preferred sign of peace was a same-sex kiss."[32] The masses were held weekly for nearly twenty years before they were stopped by the implacably anti-LGBTQ Archdiocese of Boston.

Another important LGBTQ Catholic association was Dignity, an organization that established its national headquarters in Boston in the 1970s. The local group emerged when a group of men, including Father Tom Oddo and some former Holy Cross seminarians, helped start another organization called Interfaith. This led to a series of masses for LGBTQ people held in private homes. From these gatherings Dignity Boston began in 1972 with its first masses celebrated at the Randolph Country Club.

The effects on observant gay Catholics were electric. Lourdes Rodriguez, for example, had moved to Boston from Puerto Rico to attend graduate school. At first, she was nervous about attending a mass at Dignity but soon she felt it was her home parish and eventually she went on to become president of the national organization. Some felt Dignity was a buffer between a hostile institution and the people who were attached to it by tradition and faith. It softened the harsh rhetoric of a difficult time. The group was also closely related to the effort to advance LGBTQ rights, in part because of the political and moral values of Brian McNaught and other Catholic activists. One man recalled that "Dignity represented—for those of us who were Catholic—our political family, because [secular gays wanted] nothing to do with the religious crowd. Boston was one of the most politicized gay cities in the country and one of the most Catholic." In such an environment, "Dignity gave voice to the political piece that people of faith were trying to get into the public square."[33] McNaught tiring of controversies in his Midwestern home, moved to Boston to work for Dignity. Because of his books, lectures, and newspaper columns, he became one of the most prominent LGBTQ Catholics in the country.

The Catholic Church hierarchy intensely disliked Dignity and the Archdiocese expelled the group from its meeting place in St. Gregory's Church in 1977. Then it prohibited priests from saying masses for Dignity in 1979. Similarly, the Archdiocese shut down the Jesuit services and decreed that no priest could give communion or other sacraments to LGBTQ people. Though the Catholic Church provided some services to gay men dying of AIDS in the 1980s and 1990s, its opposition to LGBTQ people would reach a homophobic climax during the fight over same-sex marriage in 2004.

Until the late 1960s, there was no gay press and no mention of LGBTQ people in mainstream newspapers except perhaps when someone was arrested. Toward the end of that decade, "alternative" publications such as *Avatar* and *The Boston Phoenix* had sporadic LGBTQ coverage, but it was random and limited to the extent that simply communicating with others in the community was difficult. Then HUB started a newsletter in 1969, renamed *Gayline* in June 1972. Meanwhile, DOB also put out a newsletter, *Maiden Voyage*, later renamed *Focus*. HUB's newsletter was dedicated to news and current events, while DOB's preferred features.[34]

After the collapse of *Lavender Vision*, another radical male publication was started by the Gay Male Liberation Front, GML Newsletter, in the Summer of 1971. By now it seemed that every LGBTQ organization had its own newsletter while sometimes an individual such as Shively would put out one as well. With each new publication, there would be a small flurry of interest, but without consistent help, people burned out and the haphazard publication schedule of these newsletters slowed and stopped. It occurred to one GLF activist, David Peterson, that if he could get everyone together, they could harness their energy for a sustained publication; thus he put out a proposal for a newspaper and called for a meeting at the Charles Street Meeting House in June 1973. Twenty people showed up, including many who were not activists, and a committee formed to produce a newsletter.[35] The newsletter became *Gay Community News* (GCN), the foremost LGBTQ paper in the country for the next two decades.

The early days of the paper were chaotic. For one thing, the atmosphere of the Meeting House was frenetic. The building also housed a café as well as church functions and employees from the café had to pass by the offices on the way to the kitchen. People would come down to the basement to use the pay phone and if there was an event at the church there would be dozens milling around. Meanwhile, a family lived in the building as well and they wandered by the paper's offices to get snacks from the kitchen. However, the tumult contributed to the excitement of the new venture and some of the people visiting the building eventually became volunteers. That's how John Kyper became involved, for example. The longtime activist was in the café but wandered into *GCN's* offices, and subsequently worked at the paper for years.[35]

GCN quickly transformed into a radical paper because the people willing and able to work on it were not mainstream. Many who were conventionally employed couldn't be publicly involved because they'd lose their jobs. It was only people with nothing to lose who could regularly contribute. The paper was famously run as a collective and sometimes strategy and editorial meetings would last for hours until a consensus was reached, a structure that burned out many but energized others. In addition to the fact it had grown out of Boston's radical LGBTQ community, this structure contributed to the paper's sustained radicalism as only those who could devote their time and energy participated. Though it often told outsiders it was politically neutral, the staff was proudly and unapologetically devoted to advancing what they considered the paper's radical agenda. They strongly believed there was a need for an alternative LGBTQ viewpoint.[27]

Because it was dangerous for many people to be seen with gay papers—as with any association with LGBTQ culture it could cause them to lose their jobs, apartments, or be cast out of their families—*GCN* had to mail its papers out in plain brown wrappers. But this distribution system still left people uneasy as it had only been a few years since the United States Post Office refused the Mattachine Society's mailings and *GCN* feared government repression and prosecution. When it sought to incorporate as a non-profit, members feared that the IRS would reject their application because it was an LGBTQ organization and so it used the name Bromfield Street Educational Association to hide its sexuality.

The paper, covering local and national issues, lasted until the 1990s and even survived an arson fire in 1982, one of a string of crimes committed by a ring of former police and firemen who were angry at being fired because of city budget cuts. The Bromfield St. building housing *GCN* was the only downtown building they targeted; the other 200 or so torched structures were scattered across Boston's low-income neighborhoods. Despite the total destruction of its offices, the paper did not skip an edition. The only time it failed to put out a paper was during the great blizzard of 1978 when staffers could not get to the office.

GCN greatly contributed to both the Boston and national LGBTQ community. It was the only national LGBTQ newspaper and even after the development of a constellation of local weeklies across the country, it was the only paper available for many LGBTQ people at a time when so many were struggling with their identity in solitude. Furthermore, it covered hard news when many other papers were more concerned with keeping their advertisers (mostly bars) happy. *GCN* had the courage to report on people and issues that the mainstream press would not and from its earliest years, there were articles on police harassment, the concerns of LGBTQ people of color, women, and those who would come to call themselves trans or non-binary. It had a special outreach program for people in prison and it was never afraid to cover controversial issues.

Very significantly, the paper served as a training ground for a large number of activists who were influential in the 1970s, 1980s, and beyond. One well known LGBTQ activist who got her start at GCN was Amy Hoffman, a writer and editor. Other important writers and activists include Cindy Rizzo, Sue Hyde, Cindy Patton, and Urvashi Vaid (an influential author and activist whose career started at *GCN* before she went on to work at the National Gay and Lesbian Task Force). Another staffer was Laura McMurry, who had moved to Boston to go to graduate school at Harvard. By 1969, McMurry was in therapy with a woman who claimed to be able to cure homosexuality, but McMurry learned to come to terms with being a lesbian and started going to DOB meetings at the Arlington Street Church. Then she became an activist, speaking on the radio and elsewhere. One of the organizers of the first Boston Pride March in 1971, McMurry read a speech when the parade paused in front of the State House to denounce the state's draconian sex laws. She also pushed for a stronger gay rights bill and opposed exempting teachers from gay employment laws even as Barney Frank was in favor of doing so because he thought it was practical.

Author Neil Miller was a *GCN* contributor as was Kevin Cathcart, who would be head of GLAD during some of its most important years. Eric Rofes worked at the paper, first under a pseudonym and then under his own name. Later, Rofes would run the Shanti Project in San Francisco and then become a professor and the author of a number of influential books on gay issues. Michael Bronski, the great critic and writer, was a *GCN* reporter and Richard Burns, who later became the Executive Director at the Lesbian, Gay, Bisexual and Transgender Community Center of New York, was once *GCN's* managing editor. Burns later recalled that after an interview by thirty or forty people, he was hired at $70 a week with no benefits. With ten paid staffers and a circulation in the thousands, *GCN* may have been the largest LGBTQ institution in the country at the time.[36]

By 1970, nighttime outdoor cruising had moved away from the Common and the Public Garden to concentrate on the Esplanade and the Fens. Shrubbery along the Esplanade sheltered an area known as "Faggot Flats" that was popular late in the evening.[37] On summer days, gay men and a few female friends sunbathed on one stretch of the chain of islands along the Esplanade and a warm weekend afternoon would find the area almost completely covered with men baking themselves on towels. It was a very social scene.

The Fens were extremely popular on summer nights and even attracted a few men cruising for sex during the coldest days of winter. Up until the early 1980s, the carriage road and parking area along Park Drive were on the Fens side of the street (after which it was moved to its present position on the neighborhood side). On a Saturday night in the summer, there might be a thousand men in the area as some opened their car doors to loudly blast KISS-108, a radio known for its disco music, while others socialized and danced. Just a hundred feet into the park, there might be large groups of men rubbing against each other; still another hundred feet in down near the river in the maze of reeds, there would be men pairing off for sex. One man remembered, "It was this little maze. It was crazy! There were these little rooms in the reeds."[38]

The Fens had an international reputation. In 1981, actor/director Frank Ripploh was in Boston for the premier of his movie *Taxi Zum Klo*, a German film about cruising in Berlin. He was scheduled to take part in a question and answer session when the movie ended, but he asked George Mansour, the booking manager of the theatre, to point him towards the Fens on the way to the screening. When the movie was almost over and the director had still not made it to the theatre, Mansour began to panic until at last, "he comes staggering out of the reeds with mud on his knees."[39] The show went on.

The Fens could be dangerous as well. A string of murders of gay men prompted the formation of a group to work against gay bashing in the Fens. In June 1980, for example, Charles Kimball of Beacon Hill was found shot to death in the Fens early one morning. His slaying followed two other murders of gay men earlier in the month and though the police said the three deaths were unrelated, many feared a serial killer was on the loose.[40]

Gay men were also victimized elsewhere in the city. Some of the most vicious murders were a series of homicides across the city committed by four men from

9.3 The Block - Marlborough St. (2018)

South Boston between 1973 and 1975. They were caught after they picked up two gay men hitchhiking home to MIT and took them to a back alley where they stabbed them multiple times and then beat one man's head in with a tire iron. The other man survived by playing dead and he later identified two of the men. It took a national manhunt to find one of the murderers with many in the community alarmed that the police had taken so long to arrest the suspect, he had time to leave the state.

In the absence of records, it is difficult to assess the level of violence against the LGBTQ community. Judging from articles in *GCN*, it appears that there were three to five murders of gay men each year across the region, though the actual number may be higher.[41] Assaults, muggings, and threats must have been several orders of magnitude greater. The violence didn't stop people from going out, but almost everyone quickly learned to be on guard whether on the street or in a situation where they might be alone.

One controversial cruising area was the Block, the area formed by Marlborough St., Arlington St., Commonwealth Ave., and Berkeley St. During the day it was a quiet, mostly residential area with a few offices (The *Atlantic Monthly* was published there in the 1970s). But at night, along with an extended area out to the bus station in Park Square, the block was noted for its young male hustlers. Men in cars would circle the Block, stopping to pick up a hustler who caught their eye. Waiting for tricks, young men (some barely teenagers) would walk, stand, or lean against railings and light posts to sell their wares.

Hustlers frequented the block for many reasons. Popular lore suggested that most of these young men had no choice because they had been abandoned by their families. However, a detailed survey of hustlers revealed that in reality only a fraction of the boys on the Block were homeless with as many as two thirds being high-school and college students looking for extra money, excitement, and sex. There was also a small subset of men who were there to rob or beat johns.[42] These young men prone to violence were more likely to only be on the Block temporarily. It is still true that a significant minority had been abandoned by their families and were using the Block to survive. "Many of these [teenagers] become runaways and take to the streets. They cannot go to bars to meet other gays because of their age, and find the only way to engage in gay sex is through experimenting on the streets."[43] In addition, the Block and the area around Park Square were more than just a place to hustle, it provided a place for LGBTQ street people to meet and socialize as well.

Every so often the Boston police cracked down on the area, arresting dozens for disorderly conduct, public drunkenness or more rarely, soliciting sex. Though HUB tried to get arrested individuals legal assistance, they ran into extreme prejudice from the local magistrate Judge Adlow. "They don't call it queen's row after Queen Elizabeth, ya know." He mocked one defendant. "It is well known that this section, once considered to be the finest in the city—it's a shame what you people have done to the area—is now a gathering place for homosexuals and those who prey upon them, and, therefore, such a wholesale gathering is automatically a public nuisance and the conduct of those present is to be construed as disorderly."[44] Adlow was not only homophobic, he was wrong. Queens Row was located several hundred yards away from the Block and hadn't been a cruising area for a decade. He routinely convicted anyone accused of being in a known gay cruising area anyway.

Many LGBTQ people strongly disapproved of the action on the Block as they disliked prostitution and abhorred sex with minors, looking down on the men who stalked those streets and finding the interest in young men very distasteful. Most thought the johns were mostly men from the suburbs, deeply in the closet and deeply in denial about their sexuality. Thus, they were further scorned as closet cases. GCN estimated that ninety percent of the clientele were closeted men who did not identify as gay.[45]

Residents of the area (one of the most expensive in the city) especially opposed the nocturnal action and called on the authorities to stop it. In May 1974, residents of the Block "complained of traffic jams, persons sleeping and/or urinating in their doorways, and an extremely noisy situation at all hours of the night allegedly caused by the presence of hustlers, those who would be looking for them, and their friends."[46] Barney Frank, the representative for the area and a resident on the Block defended cruising in nonresidential areas such as Park Square, the Fens, or along the Charles but was against the activity in residential areas. The cruising was finally stopped by changing the direction of Marlborough St. so cars could no longer circle the Block. The hustlers then moved closer to Park Square, where their numbers, and the complaints against the action, diminished.

In the Spring of 1970, Boston activists (many of whom where members of HUB) began to think of ways to mark Stonewall as well as celebrate LGBTQ people. The Boston commemoration that year did not include a parade. Instead, there was a weeklong series of panel discussions and other events while others, including Prescott Townsend, went to New York to celebrate the anniversary there.

The first Pride Parade in Boston was held in 1971. It kept to the sidewalks and though it had a heavy police presence to protect the marchers, many participants were terrified of exposure.[47] With only 150 marchers (estimates of the number of participants range from 25 to 200), there was no need to secure a permit. It stopped four times. The first stop was in front of Jacques to protest its treatment of women, the control of bars by members of organized crime, and the horrible conditions inside the club, particularly its bathrooms. The second stop was in front of police headquarters on Berkeley St. to protest police harassment of LGBTQ people and the lack of attention to crimes against them. The marchers stopped a third time in front of the State House in support of legalization of sodomy and the repeal of other repressive laws. Stop four was in front of St. Paul's Church in protest of most religions' condemnation of LGBTQ people.

More than just a protest, the parade was also a celebration of being LGBTQ with the day's march finishing off with a nighttime dance at the Charles Street Meeting House. The 1971 marchers carried yellow balloons with the word GAY on them. "It was more of a stroll, really, with men and women walking arm-in-arm along the sidewalks two and three abreast."[48] At the end of the first parade, there was a sheet cake for marchers and their supporters with a cake in 1972 as well. By the third march, there were too many people to have a shared dessert.

The 1974 march saw the beginning of a controversy that would still mark pride events over forty years later, all revolving around the questions "are the marches and other events essentially political? Or are they at heart celebrations of being gay?" As part of the controversy that year, there were complaints that Pride organizers had set a Mardi Gras theme for the parade. In addition, some women complained that men in drag were demeaning. All these early Pride commemorations in Boston had two important elements. Firstly, there was celebration. LGBTQ people asserted they were not sick or evil and that they had a right to live joyously, freely, and openly, and from its first years the parade attracted drag queens, teachers, office workers, and activists with some marchers dancing in the streets. Secondly, there were protests and politics. Discrimination and repression were so intense that the parades and rallies aimed to create lasting political change. In addition, by 1974 politicians were marching in the parade and many of its banners and buttons reflected issues at the State House and City Hall. These tensions inside Pride were not resolved, however; they only grew stronger over time.

Chapter 10

Good Times, Bad Times

I N THE POST-STONEWALL years, many in the gay male community associated sexual activity with freedom, an attitude that had its roots in the decades in which all public homosexual desire had to be completely covered up. Thus Boston, like other big cities at the time, had a robust street cruising scene dating back decades, if not centuries. Anonymous sex had several advantages. It was quick, inexpensive, exhilarating, didn't require any commitment, and left men sexually satisfied. For many men, the experience of abundant sex was life-affirming. Men openly discussed the best places for cruising at bars or over dinner. Meeting gay men, whether for sex or camaraderie, was a socially acceptable activity and the South End (with its large numbers of gay men) was ground zero. Later, longtime disc jockey and respected activist Barry Scott remembered just how easy it was: "[y]ou could just sit on your stoop and reach out and there would be a handsome gay guy in your hand."[1] Another South End resident, John Meunier, recalled that "if you saw a good-looking guy in the South End, you knew he was gay."[2]

The disadvantages were relatively small. As long as there was no public sex involved, there was no risk of arrest, but casual anonymous hook ups didn't address loneliness or the need for companionship and there was always the possibility of running into a straight acquaintance, potentially embarrassing all involved. The greatest risk, small but catastrophic, was getting attacked; this was a time when straight men felt they could violently assault gay men with impunity. Therefore, gay men developed elaborate rules to protect themselves from attack or rejection. Cruising men would signal interest in each other, gradually increasing their show of interest depending on how the other responded. The goal would be to reach negotiations of where to have relations and what said relations might entail.[3]

The period from the early 1970s to the mid-1990s represents the apogee of gay bars in Boston; counting establishments that were gay just one night a week, there were over twenty bars catering to LGBTQ people at any given time. These were places to relax, catch up on gossip, see friends, and find sex partners, making bars "the central gathering place of the gay community."[3] Before there was a gay press, most gay men first heard about bars from a sex partner, a few stumbled on them accidentally, and still others were introduced to the scenes by friends who suspected they might be interested. As the number of gay papers grew in the later 1970s, most featured large ads for nightspots along with bar guides for the newly arrived or interested.

To those who were not part of the scene of the 1970s, the excitement and exhilaration of entering a gay bar is impossible to imagine. Outside, one had to be careful lest someone, anyone, suspect they might be gay; for though violence and discrimination were not every day occurrences, they were common enough to weigh on almost every LGBTQ person's conscience at a time when the pressure for sexual and gender conformity was heavy and deadening. But stepping into a bar, with its loud music, dim corners combined with bright lights, and up to a thousand or more LGBTQ people dancing, talking, and laughing, was to breathe free (if terribly smoky) air. Many had spent their adolescence never going to a dance or a party or had thought they were fundamentally unattractive or unlovable because of who they were. Now there was a place where they could be looked at and admired. Some became giddy, almost euphoric.

For the young, attractive, and extroverted, the bars were fun and easy places to quickly find friends and sex partners. As one man said, "it's exciting. I feel a real thrill when I go to bed with someone new. It's really exciting to cruise someone to see if you can pick them up."[3] But for others, the bars could be very difficult and intimidating because of the strong emphasis on physical attractiveness. A customer of a Boston bar contrasted the euphoric element, saying "it's the most incredibly competitive thing you can imagine. I feel like I am being judged in some kind of perverted beauty contest where the winner gets a trick for the night." Even the good-looking could have self-doubt: "I always wondered whether someone really liked me or just the way I looked."

There were many ways to pick up a partner in a bar. One of the most popular was an ornate, purposely nonchalant social ballet that allowed each person to save face if they were rejected. Several decades later, one man described his first meeting his lover at a bar called Manray, located a block behind Central Square in Cambridge. "I slipped up to him. I pretended to survey the dance floor as I inched closer, until I could've taken Scott's pulse with my elbow. From time to time, I stared at the side of his head until he looked at me. Then I looked away. 45 minutes of this courtship technique left me with a back cramp, a full bladder, and a bald patch on my forearm from frantic "casual" brushing against his skin."[4]

In contrast to New York and San Francisco where they were popular up until the AIDS crisis, "the Boston bathhouse culture of the 1970s seemed to die a natural death." By 1980 the Regency and Club baths were empty, while a bathhouse on Franklin St. never caught on and closed after a fire. In all, Boston's nightlife and sex scene was tame compared to other major cities and except for intermittent periods which were quickly shut down, none of the Boston bars had backrooms.[5]

For a while in the 1960s and 1970s, Sporters was the most popular bar for younger LGBTQ people. One man who worked there remembered that it was "packed seven days a week. We were the closest gay bar at the time to all the colleges on the Red Line, so we had a huge collegiate crowd."[6] Chester Wolfe owned the Eagle, Sporters, and the 1270. Straight, he died in 1979 in a tragic accident. He had picked up two female prostitutes and the three died of carbon monoxide poisoning overnight.

His bars survived without him.

Soon there were rivals. Chaps, just outside of Copley Square, opened in 1977 and then merged with the bar next door (Styx) in 1979. Together, the night club was the closest venue to what other regions referred to as clone bars (men who wore a hypermasculine outfit of short haircuts, tight jeans, tee shirts, and mustaches) and its major demographic was men in their thirties and forties. It was the first gay bar in Boston to add lasers to its dancefloor lights. More hardcore was Herbies' Ramrod Room, upstairs from 12 Carver before urban renewal took the entire block and forced it to move to Boylston St. in the Fenway. In its heyday, the Ramrod had a room with a strictly enforced dress code: leather, jeans, and no shirts. Boots were demanded and those who dared to try to walk in with sneakers were turned away. The 1270, occupying three floors and a roof deck on Boylston Street near Fenway Park, catered to working class LGBTQ people and was also one of the few bars that welcomed blacks. It had a piano bar and a very popular summertime rooftop bar illuminated by the lights of Fenway Park when the Red Sox were in town. Some noted the significant numbers of both very young and very old clientele who contributed to the bar's nickname, under 12 and over 70.

Napoleon's was still going strong; it and Jacques were the only two bars to survive the large-scale urban renewal project that rebuilt much of Park Square. Napoleon's opened a disco upstairs called Josephine's, which would pack in men, usually older but often including a younger crowd in search of a classier place to dance on weekend nights. A cavernous bar on Lansdowne St. behind Fenway Park dominated Sunday nights. Known by a variety of names over the years (the Boston Tea Party, Boston-Boston, Metro, and Avalon), there would be lines of young men waiting

10.1 Mayor Kevin White campaigning at Buddies, 1979

atiently to get into a mammoth ballroom that could easy accommodate close to a thousand dancers. Later the club expanded to include a room called Spit that featured new wave rock and was open to LGBTQ people on both Sundays and Tuesdays. Spit was more welcoming to non-binary people than many of Boston's other clubs.

Buddies pulled away Sporters collegiate crowd after it opened in 1979. The new bar's opening attracted Mayor Kevin White, perhaps the first time in any city in the United States that a sitting mayor openly went into a gay bar. He was there because he was friends with the bar's manager, Robin McCormack, whom he would soon appoint to be his liaison to the gay and lesbian community. Located in a basement on Boylston St. in the Back Bay, on Friday and Saturday nights there would be hundreds lined up on the brick edge of the sidewalk, sometimes for an hour or more, to get into an energetic bar filled with young men who wore fashionable jeans, tight polo shirts showing off their chests, and lots of product in their hair. For those into men in their twenties, it may have been the most attractive bar in the country. The club had two rooms: a cabaret that featured torch singers, drag queens, and comedians, and a disco that included a sunken dance floor and a DJ booth that was built inside a large Ford truck cab.

By the end of the 1970s there were two women's bars, Saints and Somewhere Else. Somewhere Else had its beginnings when a nightclub owner asked Ann Maguire, who was a teacher at the time, to manage a basement bar in Provincetown. That led to the opening of Somewhere Else on Franklin St. in downtown Boston. It had two floors, with dancing upstairs and a pool table downstairs. It was bright, welcoming, and "women felt safe here," recalled Maguire.[7] It sponsored sports teams, supported charities, and held a Thanksgiving dinner each year for those who had no families to go home to. Even first-time patrons felt the warmth of its staff and decades later, many women would smile as they remembered the good times there. Saints was run by a collective and it had a fanatic group of patrons who were thrilled with its politics and welcoming atmosphere. It inspired a whole generation of lesbian activists.

None of this night life meant that repression was over. The pressure to cover up one's sexuality was immense, and some of the most out and flamboyant people on Saturday night were rigidly heterosexual come Sunday dinner with their families and work on Monday. This could cause severe emotional distress. "Well, I have a lover. In some ways it's like being married. But can you imagine being married and never being able to touch in public, never being able to say I love you?" reported one man. Another said, "[i]f you are gay you have to hide it. That's all there is to it."[3] In the mid-1970s, some men in couples were afraid to be seen with each other lest their sexuality be discovered. Even men living on Beacon Hill, now several decades into being a gay neighborhood, felt pressure to hide their feelings for their loved ones.[8]

It the context of this split between wide-open and extremely-closeted behavior, the freedom inside certain parts of Boston felt like a trap. One man remembered that atmosphere as "a psychological ghetto. A prison."[3] Most said they felt guilty about being gay or lesbian before coming out and though few feel that way in contemporary life, most reported that their parents did not know they were gay and many men said their parents were pressuring them to find a woman and get married. Of those whose parents knew they were gay, most reported their parents were hostile or did not approve. As a result, many reduced their contact with their families and felt they could not socialize with straights because the pressure to act like a heterosexual was too strong and uncomfortable.[3]

Attorney John Ward, soon to found one of the most important LGBTQ public-interest law organizations in the country, had a different take on this. "Precisely because Boston is two-faced, it is possible for many gays to stay in the closet in their big offices, then enjoy a gay lifestyle from supper time to breakfast, and put on the mask once again."[9] Elaine Noble asserted that there was a group of 200 gay business-women, none of them out publicly.

In 1976, the ferment of activism inside Boston's radical LGBTQ community could be quickly cut off by the strong walls of bigotry. The intense social norms outside the LGBTQ world constrained even the most committed activists. Eric Rofes (1954-2005), for example, spent his nights and weekends volunteering for *GCN*, organizing new institutions to serve the LGBTQ community, and socializing with other men out for a good time. Yet even Rofes found that he had to be intensely closeted while at his day job at a private school in the suburbs and wrote for *GCN* under a pseudonym. A first-year teacher and recent Harvard graduate, Rofes felt isolated by the intense pressure to conform while in heterosexual society and saw deep hypocrisy in the idea. "[H]aving no one at school with whom to talk about the compromises and deceptions was the most difficult part of the experience. Yet I still felt the daily fear of being 'caught' and yanked from my school."[10] A tall burly man with an imposing physical presence, he had to bring female friends to school functions in order to pass as straight. Rofes was not paranoid; he would soon be fired when his workplace discovered that he was gay.

However, the boundaries of the closet in the 1970s were much larger than they had been before World War II. In 1940, the walls were snug against the inner world of just about all LGBTQ people with few straight people aware of their sexuality or gender non-conformity. Friends, neighbors, and family were carefully kept in the dark. In contrast, Rofes, like others who hailed from progressive places, told his parents he was gay while he was still in college and though they initially had a hard time taking the news, within a few months they were supportive. Rofes was out to his classmates and lived openly as a gay man with five straight roommates. The women he took to school affairs also knew he was gay.

The limits of the closet depended on the individual's circumstances. Rofes came from a middle-class Jewish family and Harvard in the 1970s was a very liberal place when it came to sexuality. But if Rofes had been born in a conservative Christian family and attended a different university or lived in a different neighborhood, he might have lived in a closet almost as small as in the 1930s. People who were questioning their birth-assigned gender faced enormous pressures and almost all LGBTQ young people were very at risk of violence or abandonment.

Illustrative of the lingering effects of repression were interviews conducted in 2000 by French sociologist Sylvie Tissot with gay men in the South End regarding their experiences in the early 1970s. These men had been afraid to bring their same-sex partners to the South End Historical Society's formal fundraisers in those years and would instead dance with female dates.[11] Though the South End was already well into its trajectory of being Boston's primary gay neighborhood and the white middle-class residents who made up the bulk of the historical society's membership represented some of the most progressive elements of the city at the time, these gay men (conditioned by their experiences of coming out in the two previous decades) could not undo the effects of decades of repression of that era.

Some felt cheated by the growing openness. For some LGBTQ people who came of age well before Stonewall, there was a wistfulness, a sense that life would have been different for them if they had been able to come out in a more supportive era. The great blossoming of gay night life in the 1970s left some older men feeling neglected by more youthful gays and some thought they were ignored, invisible, and perhaps even scorned and despised.[8]

By the end of the 1970s, coming out at Harvard was becoming easier as fewer people cared about others' sexuality, but that took away some of its uniqueness. Gays at the university were Harvard students first and their sexuality was secondary such that one man complained "the way to make a gay dance a Harvard gay dance would be to invite lots of straight people."[12]

This welcoming atmosphere was only possible because of a decade of work. In the years leading up to 1981, "a political movement has arisen out of silence, consolidated a large following, dominated campus headlines, and outpaced the other student movements in numbers and staying power." The Gay Students Association (GSA), once a small group of white males, expanded to a membership of more than 300 with women and people of color joining as well. Another group, devoted to activism, held events and demonstrations that sometimes attracted more than a thousand. There were gay alumni groups in several big cities and talk of a scholarship targeted to LGBTQ students.

The university adopted an informal policy prohibiting discrimination in undergraduate admissions but did not address ongoing harassment of LGBTQ students. On the positive side, the student medical services became open to serving the needs of lesbian and gay students, though trans students were still ignored and forced to use their assigned gender. On the other hand, some faculty would routinely make anti-gay comments in class or denigrate LGBTQ related projects and the school took no action against them. When gay students showed up at straight Harvard parties and started to dance with each other, they would often be asked to leave, and homophobic comments even ended up in student publications. The faculty refused to adopt an anti-discrimination policy and stalled proposals by the GSA to implement one. Even in 1981, the fear of publicly outing oneself paralyzed many students as they realized it might lead to employment, housing, or other discrimination after graduation. Forming the GSA, for example, had been difficult because Harvard's rules for student groups required organizations to file membership lists with the Dean. Students feared that an official record that they were gay left them potentially exposed to discrimination.[13] Similarly, some students were afraid of being photographed at GSA events. For many, the fear of discrimination and the scars of anti-gay bullying in high school were still fresh.

Importantly, tolerance inside the university could not counteract the tremendous obstacles to LGBTQ people outside it. For example, two gay students were assaulted on the Red Line for holding hands, and when a leader of the GSA was quoted in a *Globe* article about gays at Harvard, he received a letter threatening him with death. However, illustrating how times were changing among both gay and straight progressives, he was a hero for being out.

Similarly, despite a decade of gay activism, there were sporadic anti-gay acts at MIT. A fraternity barred gays from a dance, a billboard was vandalized, and a newspaper ridiculed the idea of equal rights for gays. In 1981, a fraternity placed posters around campus calling for the death penalty for gays and they held a rally in Central and Harvard Squares calling for the extermination of gay people.[14] These and other severe acts prompted MIT to finally adopt a policy prohibiting harassment against gays.

One of the first signs that the Boston area was on the path towards spearheading what would become queer theory was the work of women belonging to the Combahee River Collective in 1977. The group was noteworthy because it represented black women (predominantly lesbians), asserting their voices at a time when the LGBTQ movement was dominated by white males. It produced one of the first major publications on intersectionality, the social doctrine that discrimination against one group was connected and related to discrimination against others and that minorities stood to benefit through united action against all forms of bias, oppression, and prejudice—social, economic, personal, and public—in order to create a better world.

The collective, based in Cambridge, grew out of the wave of leftist politics sweeping the country in the 1960s. Co-founder Barbara Smith first participated in anti-racism actions at Mt. Holyoke College in 1968 and realized that the movement had some serious problems. "We [Black feminists] were definitely marginalized. Anything that didn't look like it wasn't in support of the central politics of the male-defined Black Power movement was considered disloyal."[15]

Smith's twin sister, Beverly, was working at *Ms.* magazine when an editor invited the pair to attend a conference hosted by the National Black Feminist Organization in 1973. Energized, they tried to organize a Boston chapter, but the effort fell apart. So, the sisters and allies started the Combahee River Collective, named after the location in South Carolina where Harriet Tubman had led 750 enslaved people to freedom.

As they studied and debated the issues confronting them, the group developed a deep understanding of how these social problems were interconnected and they acted to make change by speaking out and creating their ground-breaking declaration, the "Combahee River Statement." By issuing the decree, the group boldly opposed not just racism and homophobia but the capitalist structure of the United States itself, proudly declaring "we are actively committed to struggling against racial, sexual, heterosexual, and class oppression, and see as our particular task the development of integrated analysis and practice based upon the fact that the major systems of oppression are interlocking."[16]

The Combahee River Statement has been a font of inspiration to people fighting for social justice since its release. It encouraged leftist activists during the dark Reagan years, influenced the environmental justice movement in the 1990s as it challenged the racist distribution of hazards and enforcement of anti-pollution laws, and it inspired the Black Lives Matter movement in the 2000s.

Boston's transgender community asserted itself in the 1970s with one of the most important organizations in the Boston area, the Tiffany Club of New England, forming in 1978. Many transgender people had been energized by the widespread publicity given to Christine Jorgensen when she had gender reassignment surgery in Copenhagen in 1952. She was a celebrity for undergoing hormone therapy and surgery and across the country, people who knew there was a difference between their assigned and real genders found her story heartening. At the time, however, getting medical personnel to affirm a person's real gender was nearly impossible.

In 1962, the Freedom for Personality Expression club was founded in Los Angeles. Restricted to heterosexual cross dressers, the club created chapters across the country including one in Boston, founded in 1968. This group evolved into the Cherrystone Club (the name was conceived when a group of its founding members, sitting in a bar, decided that they were a "bunch of cherries getting stoned"). That group met from 1973 to 1975 in the apartment of Dorothy Dean at 500 Columbus Ave. It was here that the famous Fantasia Fair, an annual weeklong celebration of gender diversity in Provincetown, was first organized.

The Cherrystone Club split in 1977 with some looking for a social group, while others wanted to focus on services and support. The support group became the Tiffany Club of New England. One of its unique features was its clubhouse, first located in Weston and now in Waltham. New members were recruited through ads placed in the Boston Phoenix and other papers as well as through the club's popular newsletter, Tapestry. New people were carefully screened. For example, when for a time the clubhouse was in Wayland, "[t]he potential member called the club from the legendary Wayland Public Library Telephone Booth. Two club members would then drive the three miles from the club to the telephone booth to interview the individual.

If they were found to be worthy and well qualified, they would be escorted back to the Wayland House."[17]

The courage of the group members and the impact they would have on thousands of people over the next several decades cannot be overstated. This was a time when transgender people had few rights and most of the cisgender public, including gay men and lesbians, either ignored them or were openly hostile. The era when anyone could be arrested for dressing in any clothes not meant for one's assigned gender had only just ended and most doctors and other professionals often treated trans people harshly, totally disregarding their dignity and needs. These brave pioneers opened the door for the generations of trans and non-binary people who would follow.

Harvard wasn't easy for everyone, as the experience of Elizabeth Bishop (1911-79) demonstrates. Born in Worcester to a prosperous family, Bishop's grandfather provided the granite for the MFA and the McKim Library. Her childhood was brutal. Bishop's father died when she was eight months old and her mother, mentally ill and suicidal, physically abused her as her mother moved the family back and forth between Nova Scotia and Massachusetts. After her mother entered a mental hospital when Bishop was five, she was sent to other relatives until she went to live with an aunt and uncle in Revere.

Bishop had a trust fund used to send her to summer camp where she had her first crush on another woman. By then the young Bishop had read Havelock Ellis and knew about same-sex attraction. Yet she did not consider herself a lesbian, only someone who was attracted to people like herself. Bishop attended the Walnut Hill School, a boarding school in Natick, graduating when she was nineteen. Here as well she had crushes on other girls. Bishop went to Vassar and when she couldn't get invitations to other students' homes for summers and holidays, she rented cheap rooms in Boston; anything to keep her away from her family. During this time, she had an affair with a man–he would commit suicide a year after graduation when she turned down his marriage proposal but was still mostly attracted to women. Bishop also began binge drinking, beginning a dance with alcoholism that would mark her life. Though she kept her sexuality low-key in public, in private she was most confidant, once telling her good friend and poet Robert Lowell that she had never met a woman she couldn't seduce. She had relationships with women decades younger than her as she spent many years traveling the world, living in Switzerland, Brazil, and many other places. Her time in South America amounted to more than a decade while she enjoyed a relationship with a woman there.

Eventually she returned to the United States and Lowell helped secure her a teaching position at Harvard. The love of the last decade of Bishop's life was Alice Methfessel whom she met when she was staying in the guest quarters at Kirkland House and Methfessel was secretary there. The two were very discreet and Bishop never referred to Methfessel as her lover or partner, calling Methfessel simply "her friend". This reluctance to advertise the relationship did not mean there was no passion, however. Bishop "loved the lock of hair that Alice allowed Elizabeth to smooth back from her forehead, and those nice satiny eyelids shut tight as Alice slept. She loved the coffee Alice brought to her now in bed, and looking out the window to see nothing but bare branches when Alice drew back the curtains, and the sound of Alice's voice, nice and loving cheerful. As she spoke the words that became their waking up ritual, good morning I love you."[18] All this makes her poetry even more remarkable in that she never wrote about her own romantic experiences.

Even though Lowell often assisted Bishop in private, publicly he was very homophobic; almost as if he was trying to make up for having pursued a career in poetry rather than law, business, or some other more masculine career. Looking at Bishop's experiences teaching at Harvard in the 1970s, it's difficult to distinguish between the bigotry of sexism versus that of homophobia. For example, the college limited Bishop's hours so as to avoid having to give her health insurance and the administration constantly belittled her. These experiences help explain why Bishop believed that any public hint of her being a lesbian would cause her ouster from Harvard and made an incident at a North End restaurant, Francesca's, all the more frightening. The petite, beautiful Bishop was dining with a much younger, more masculine woman when the two were screamed at by a drunk group. The situation defused short of violence but Bishop, increasingly fragile, was badly shaken.

Bishop internalized the bigotry. To defend herself, she attempted to build a psychological wall between her personal life and the world and did not participate in the women's or the gay rights movements. But the pressure she felt contributed to her alcoholism. She drank, quietly and regularly, unnoticed even if she was at a party until she'd pass out and when Bishop read her poetry she seemed to purposely diminish herself. "Quiet elegance. Discreet blondes, pearls. The protective coloration. In public. Miss Bishop presented herself in that way. When she read her work she wore a suit, yes, with a skirt! Clunky heels, a white blouse, little pearls." It was her mask to shield herself from the straight world. "In private, at home in Cambridge, Elizabeth Bishop wore the tightest leather pants, had her own flamboyance, and of course drank and smoked and hacked and coughed."[19]

At first, she first lived at 60 Brattle St. in Cambridge and then Lewis Wharf. When she moved, a friend asked her what she wanted for the place. "Closers, closets, and more closets," she replied, knowing that her gay friend would catch the double meaning.[18] She died there in 1979.

An extremely important institution that was founded in these years was the Fenway Community Health Center. In the 1970s, most mainstream medicine considered homosexuality an illness and many doctors treated LGBTQ patients with contempt. Not only did this marginalize people, but it encouraged doctors to perform electroshock treatment, chemical castration, conversion therapy, and other actions that actively harmed their victims. Thus it was rational that many feared seeking treatments for venereal and other diseases. At the same time, despite the great medical institutions in the city many of Boston's elderly, students, and poor residents found it impossible to access care. Physicians tended to have their offices in wealthier neighborhoods and the fees they charged made them unaffordable.

The Fenway was home to students and veterans of the antiwar movement. They organized their community to oppose urban renewal, promote affordable housing, and fight arson. One of the most prominent activists was David Scondras, who was the Director of Community Services at the Boston Center for Older Americans. Despite the fact the center was operated by the Christian Scientists (who eschewed conventional medical care), Scondras let a health clinic operate at the center after hours. They quickly found that the demand for services was greater than the little clinic could meet. Working with Linda Beane, a Northeastern University nursing student, Scondras visited a Black Panthers' health clinic that had combined health care with community activism. The two were inspired.

Along with others, they opened the Fenway Community Health Center. It relied on volunteer staff including doctors and nurses from the many nearby hospitals. The clinic served everyone: young, old, the poor, students, and gay men and lesbians. By the end of the 1970s, the Fenway was the most important provider of health care to the LGBTQ community in the state. In those early days, staffing was chaotic and many were unqualified or untrained for their responsibilities, but they were very passionate about serving their patients. For example, Ron Vachon, a bearded six-foot-three man with the most disarming demeanor, began working with the clinic after accompanying a date there to pick up a file. Vachon, a Vietnam War veteran and a physician assistant, became the clinic's first paid employee and part of the strong connection between the gay community and the clinic, welcoming all into the offices.[20] Lesbian health services were provided under the umbrella of the center's women health unit and eventually the Fenway established a department that focused on services for trans people.

Growing demands for professionalism altered the course of the Fenway later in the 1970s. Access to federal and state funds, vital to keeping the center open, meant that its freewheeling collective administration had to be transformed into a conventional community clinic. It was forced to use licensed doctors and nurses, comply with local building codes, and develop a standard operating and management structure as the price of receiving funding. The collective briefly thought about resisting professionalization and rejecting regulations, but without a license, the clinic couldn't apply for grants or bill patients. This didn't lessen the controversy over reform as many of the volunteers thought they should be immune from regulation; at one point, Scondras ripped up a letter demanding the center apply for a license. The staff thought they could easily rebuff regulators' pressure as no one in the state would allow it to close.

However, both state and federal authorities pressured the health center so that a full license was obtained in 1978. But more reforms were needed. Seeking to modernize the administration of the clinic in 1980, Sally Deane became Executive Di rector as financial problems again threatened to close down the clinic. Taking charge, she found there were no personnel standards and that the center's building required substantial renovations. Most serious, the clinic had deducted withholding taxes for its employees without forwarding them to the government because it had used the money for operating expenses. The IRS was on the verge of shutting down the clinic and going after its board of directors for the money. To keep the doors open, the clinic turned to the Deaconess Hospital for a loan which led to the Fenway's final transition away from a community-based management model to a professional-led clinic. All staff were required to have appropriate licenses and Deane was given large powers to make changes. The clinic began accepting Medicaid and private insurance as the center shifted from reliance on volunteers with close ties to the community to staff hired by the clinic itself. Even the board changed.

The transition was accompanied by controversy and soul searching. Over time, the Fenway's gay clientele became more middle class and whiter than the neighborhood's population and *GCN* attacked its lack of diversity.[21] By the early 1980s, however, the Fenway was run by a team of professionals (many of them LGBTQ people) who saw working at the center as a special way of contributing to their community. There was also a strong commitment to working to promote LGBTQ health and a close set of working relationships with other medical institutions in the city. All of these factors were to prove vital as an epidemic began to decimate Boston's gay male population in 1981.

Another enduring and important group founded in these years was BAGLY (Boston Alliance of Gay and Lesbian Youth). Its roots begin in New York City in early 1969 when Gay Youth New York was formed. Using the slogan "Youth Organized, Youth Run," chapters were organized in Boston and Worcester with the Boston chapter sponsored by HUB. In 1974, the state awarded the Charles Street Meeting House $52,000 to develop what was eventually called Project Lambda, a program to work with LGBTQ youth in the city. This may be one of the first grants of public money anywhere in the United States that went to specifically assist LGBTQ people. The young people of this project recruited others within their age cohort at the Sword and Stone Coffee Shop on Charles St., Ken's on Boylston St. and other places where young LGBTQ people congregated. The program was successful, but lost its funding in 1976, leaving Bridge Over Troubled Waters as the only group helping LGBTQ young people.[22]

In 1977, a group of adults came together to revive Project Lambda. Meeting at the Arlington Street Church, the group's supporters included Ann Maguire who hosted a series of spaghetti dinners at Somewhere Else to raise money for them. But Boston's youth felt mostly ignored by the adult LGBTQ population and by 1980, the youth were frustrated by its adult leadership. Robin McCormack helped the young people raise funds to open an office at 128a Tremont St. and a new twenty-two and under group, BAGLY, was formed.[22]

BAGLY's longtime adult administrator has been Grace Sterling Stowell (1957-), who has provided leadership not only to LGBTQ youth but to the trans community and other Boston activists as well. Growing up in Bedford, Massachusetts, she began as an adolescent to realize she was different in terms of gender and gender expression. Unfortunately, she was harassed and teased. It rarely got physical, but she often felt unsafe. The experience gave her great insight into the problems faced by many LGBTQ people as she remembered that "feminine males are often most marginalized–have no status in school, family, community. Often most at risk for violence."[23]

Stowell had begun to realize there were others like her around 1979 or 1981, but no one ever discussed those sorts of things. Fortunately she met LGBTQ people in college and began to go to bars, primarily the 1270, Napoleon's, and Buddies. She read about BAGLY in *GCN* and went because it seemed interesting and eventually, she was asked to be its adult advisor. BAGLY continues to serve LGBTQ youth, providing services and safe places for them to thrive. It sponsors a youth pride parade, many formal and informal events, and has kept thousands of young people safe in a world that is often difficult. Recognizing their vital service, BAGLY and Stowell were marshals of the 2010 Pride Parade in Boston.

The mixture of, and tensions between, politics and celebration at Pride continued. In 1975, some of the marchers tried to divert the parade to Post Office Square for a rally in support of Susan Saxe, the radical lesbian wanted by the FBI for her role in the death of a policeman during a bank robbery. Few marchers followed their lead, however. Reverting back to a celebratory spirit, in 1976 a group of lesbian motorcycle riders, eventually called Moving Violations but mostly known as Dykes on Bikes, began their tradition of leading the parade to great cheers.

The celebration at the conclusion of the 1977 parade proved to be the most inspiring and controversial of the decade. Part of the event, held at the historic Parkman bandstand on the Common, brought shouts of assertiveness and celebration. It featured Elaine Noble and Barney Frank (two politicians who had championed the concerns of the LGBTQ community) who gave rousing speeches. Bubbling with energy, when Ann Maguire boldly told the crowd: "I'm a dyke and I'm proud of it," they screamed in approval.

But 1977 was also the year that Shively burned a Bible on the podium of the Pride Celebration. He was imitating William Lloyd Garrison who had famously burned a copy of the constitution in Boston to protest slavery, but the historical reference was lost on the crowd. The lead up to the burning was dramatic. Shively wore his Harvard academic regalia to the podium. Next to him was another man, wearing just cutoff jean shorts and holding a giant wok filled with lighter fluid. Having carefully rehearsed ahead of time, Shively built to a crescendo talking about the repression holding LGBTQ people back. As he spoke he burned bank documents, college correspondence, an insurance certificate, and a dollar bill. Then a ripple of fearful anticipation ran through the crowd as they wondered what he would do for a finale. Shively turned to John Mitzel who was nearby, saying "[s]hould I just rip out the pages in Leviticus?" Mitzel responded, "Charley, after all the other stuff, that would look tame."[24]

Shively took out his copy of the King James Bible and threw it into the wok where it quickly caught fire. Though he knew it was coming, the man holding the wok was taken aback, wavered, and somehow, the burning bible fell to the ground. Others around him were in various stages of shock and anger. As chaos took over the stage, an older man jumped up and began stomping on the bible to put the flames out. Everyone agrees that Noble told Shively to leave the rally as fast as he could. Later, Mitzel claimed that Dignity members, led by Brian McNaught, charged the bandstand shouting, "Kill him! Get him off!" McNaught, however, offers a different description of the chaos. He says he was shocked by the burning bible but only went up on the stage at Noble's suggestion that he was the only person who could calm the crowd.[25] Supporting McNaught's version of the incident, while *GCN* reported there were shouts of "get off the stage" directed at Shively, it has no mention of anyone storming the bandstand. Though there were many letters about the incident and some play on television newscasts, it was eventually forgotten.

Provincetown's reputation as a roaring, anything-goes LGBTQ resort was by now long established. The A House had catered to gay men since at least the beginning of the century, but in the summer of 1976, owner Reggie Cabral decided that it was time for it to "go gay" and began to charge women vastly more to get in and drink than he did men to discourage them from patronizing his bars. The next year he converted the upstairs Macho Bar into a back room and employed a muscular body builder to guard its stairs. He used a riding crop to swat customers' posteriors as they passed by. The town police, determined to put a stop to this sort of ribald activity, staged a raid on July 22, 1977, where they arrested a town selectman who was using a belt to whip a bound man while another performed oral sex on the "victim." The crowd was so entranced by the performance that no one noticed the police had arrived until the arrests began and altogether, seven men were taken into custody.

Though the judge was unsure whether whipping was a sex act, the arrested men pleaded guilty and had their cases continued after paying court costs. The town suspended the A House's liquor license for two weeks. "For a town that hosted a convention of transvestites the last two years, the whipping/fellating combo apparently was a bit too much. Dressing up is one thing, bar sex is another."[26] However, not only was the selectman re-elected, but he went on to chair the board and its finance committee.

Cabral was only trying to keep up with the competition. The Crown & Anchor matched Cabral move for move, trying to outdo him. It featured a back room bar, hired top-rated drag entertainers, and opened a high-energy disco. The complex became a national legend as "once a year the Crown hosted a gala drag contest.

Queens would fly in from all over to compete, with many of them spending thousands on their gowns, their shoes, their hair, and their surgeries. Once the winner was announced, the fights would start, and the show's second part played itself out in the parking lot, where wigs were ripped off and punches thrown."[27]

In the afternoons was the famous tea dance at the Boatslip, an institution so integrated into the day-to-day life of the town that no one can remember when it first began (most likely 1975 or 1976). After last call at 7:00, the action moved to the Pied Piper for after-tea.

Though he would not publicly come out until more than a decade later, Barney Frank was elected to the state House of Representatives from Back Bay in November 1972, and quickly became one of the major forces for LGBTQ equality at the State House. Hiding his sexuality, he had marched in the 1972 pride parade not as an out gay man but as a politician seeking LGBTQ votes.[28] He was aided in staying in the closet by the press. None of the Boston media asked Frank if he was gay even though he was the sole sponsor of gay rights legislation in the state house until Elaine Noble was elected two years later. His anti-discrimination legislation lost 208 to 16 in 1973, a defeat he thought was such a disgrace that it was useless to try again unless some dramatic change occurred.

A native of Bayonne, New Jersey, Frank had moved to Massachusetts to attend Harvard. After Kevin White became mayor by defeating the racist Louise Day Hicks who had run on an anti-busing platform, the new mayor tapped a number of white Harvard men to help him run the city. Frank proved to be an excellent strategist and quickly rose in the administration, becoming one of the Mayor's key aides. But he and other liberals lost confidence in White's policies and governing style. Because of this Frank left after three years at City Hall. He earned a law degree from Harvard and worked for various politicians before running for office himself.

The first time Frank was publicly questioned on his sexuality was at a 1975 hearing before the Licensing Board during an effort to force Jacque's to have earlier closing hours. Owner Harry Vara had tried to rally LGBTQ people to support him, but years of bad treatment of patrons and dirty conditions in the bar had turned most away from him. In addition, though many Bay Village residents were gay, they were the most vocal against the bar because of the crime and prostitution that spilled forth from Jacque's into the surrounding streets. Frank was at the hearing when Vara's attorney asked if he was gay. Frank answered in the negative.

Frank planned to come out publicly in 1980 but deferred because of the sudden opening of a congressional seat. The Vatican decided that priests could not hold elective office, forcing beloved liberal Father Robert Drinan to step down as the representative from the western suburbs. Quickly jumping into the election, Frank overcame a crowded field to win the Democratic primary and then easily beat his Republican opponent.

After he arrived in Washington, Frank began to privately out himself but remained publicly closeted. Later he would write that "[t]he strain of living in the closet takes a heavy toll on your personality. And it is hard to keep the anger that is directed toward your own self-denial from spilling over to dealings with others."[28]

In the 1970s, Boston's demographics began to change. From an all-white city with an important black minority, it began to attract substantial numbers of Latino and Asian people. The place of Latinos in Boston's LGBTQ community parallels their complex relationship with the city as a whole. Far from Latin America and the American southwest, Latinos only began to have an important presence in the city in the late 1950s. Some came directly from Puerto Rico, while others first lived in New York or western Massachusetts before settling in Boston. Their first neighborhood was the South End; not the faded (yet beginning to be gentrified) row house blocks that were home to gay men, but rather a rundown section of the neighborhood near Blackstone Park that featured clusters of ramshackle wooden tenements, auto repair shops built in converted stables, and other incompatible land uses collectively known as Parcel 19.

Boston's Latinos quickly diversified. Its core of Puerto Ricans was joined by refugees from Fidel Castro's Cuba, exiles from the repressive US-backed regime in the Dominican Republic, and middle-class Mexican-American students and graduates who came from around the country to attend colleges in the area. Parcel 19 couldn't contain the growing population and hemmed in by the gentrification of the South End, many of the newcomers settled in Dorchester, Jamaica Plain, and beyond.

The city's plans for the South End were controversial. Aware that South End residents, many of whom were gay, would react in horror to the city's plan to demolish the neighborhood, a 1950s urban renewal proposal was discarded by Edward Logue (administrator of the Boston Redevelopment Authority) and a new plan was hastily drawn up. Attempting to appease the growing power of the South End gentry, Logue's 1962 plan mostly spared the rowhouse part of the neighborhood but concentrated demolitions along Shawmut Ave. and called for the creation of a twenty acre park where several thousand mostly-Puerto Rican tenants lived. This plan was still too radical and it was withdrawn as well.[29] Finally, in 1965 a third plan was released and after a carefully controlled (if not corrupt and oppressive) process, approved.[30] In any case, urban renewal in the South End was on. The row houses were mostly saved but the South End's Puerto Rican population was to be dispersed for ball fields and a new hockey rink.

Led by residents and clergy and assisted by community organizers, the people of Parcel 19 fought to keep themselves from being displaced. They agreed they needed new housing, but the land uses the Boston Redevelopment Authority were proposing did not meet their needs. Thus the residents created their own planning process and hired their own planners and architects. And after Kevin White was elected mayor this alternative vision for the heart of the South End triumphed.

It also resulted in a jarring juxtaposition of architectural styles. Many newcomers, unaware of the distinct architectural history of Parcel 19, bemoaned the destruction of row houses for what eventually became known as Villa Victoria. In reality, there never were rowhouses in the area and what was built in the 1970s and 1980s represents a Latino compromise with the surrounding area rather than a rejection of it. The development also represents a stark economic divide. Household incomes in the rowhouse district could be thirty times greater or more compared to inside Villa Victoria.

Though the community spread across the region, Villa Victoria was a center for LGBTQ Latinos. Efraim Barrados (1946-), author and professor, remembered a school teacher who hosted Saturday night parties at the Villa where all LGBTQ people were welcomed. There were house parties for Latinos across the city in part because most bars were unwelcoming to them. When they did go out, they tended to cluster together, often apart from other LGBTQ people.[31]

Villa Victoria was a rare victory for Boston Latinos. In a complex political situation dominated first by intense conflicts between the Irish and Yankees and later by the growing violence of the Irish establishment towards blacks, Latinos struggled to assert themselves and were mostly ignored. Those who had lighter skin colors could occasionally pass through the racial barriers imposed by Boston gay society. Those who were too dark were lumped together with blacks and faced similar, if not even worse, discrimination.

In the 1970s, the Boston Latino LGBTQ community dramatically expanded and changed. Increasing chaos in New York made tame Boston seem more welcoming and it became common to meet LGBTQ Latinos who had once lived in Miami, Philadelphia, and other more traditional centers of Latinos in the United States. Looking to become national and world forces, Harvard and other colleges began to admit more Mexican Americans as well as the children of the elite from Latin America. But as their numbers grew, so did the discrimination they faced.

In 1980, everything suddenly changed. First, Castro decided to relax emigration restrictions and over 125,000 Cubans moved to the United States. Most of these were peaceful working class straight people but there were enough homosexual, criminal, and mentally ill people included in the mix that the whole group of Marielitos was stigmatized. Second, deteriorating economic conditions in Mexico along with brutal US-initiated wars in Central America also sent a large wave of people into the US. Coupled with a high fertility rate, the Latino population of the United States as well as Boston exploded.

The first political awakening of Boston's Latino LGBTQ community had occurred in the 1970s. Boston and Cambridge saw a burgeoning Latino arts scene, many of the leaders of which were LGBTQ. At the same time, a few LGBTQ Latino were appointed to important government and nonprofit positions. Orlando Del Valle for example, worked for the Massachusetts Commissioner of Public Welfare and later helped found Club Antorcha, a group dedicated to fighting AIDS. He used his influence to help open doors for other LGBTQ Latinos, creating a network of activist across government and academia.

Compared to white LGBTQ activists, Latino and African American activists faced additional pressures. Coming from marginalized communities, LGBTQ activists of color had to confront housing, education, employment, and other types of discrimination that some white activists could avoid. Racist attitudes also spilled over into the LGBTQ world and many people of color felt unwelcome in bars and gathering places. Sometimes, competing issues pulled at them, forcing them to prioritize which problem they would address at a given point in time.

The most important LGBTQ Latino of this era was Jorge Hernandez (1951-86), the Executive Director of Inquilinos Boricuas en Accion (Puerto Rican Tenants in Action). Because of his ability to deliver votes for Kevin White, Michael Dukakis, and others, Hernandez was the most powerful Latino in the state. He moved to Massachusetts when he was ten and then went to Cornell and Harvard before leading Villa Victoria from 1977 to 1986. Good natured and brilliant, he was constantly on the lookout for people to recommend for government employment and other important jobs. He thrived on helping others and many of the people he assisted, both gay and straight, returned the favor by working with Hernandez to advance his agenda centering on fostering Latino rights and opportunities. There was even talk of Hernandez running for public office. The charismatic but closeted gay man (he liked to go to the Paradise in Cambridge) had a bright future.

A strange case of prosecutorial anti-gay bigotry in 1978 would result in the founding of two well-known organizations. Paradoxically, both the tremendously respected Gay and Lesbian Advocates and Defenders (GLAD)–later renamed GLBTQ Legal Advocates and Defenders – and the extremely controversial North American Man/Boy Love Association (NAMBLA) can trace their beginnings to the same problematic criminal case brought against several men in Revere, Massachusetts.

Then as now, Revere was a working-class suburb, accessible by public transportation and noted for its blocks of one-, two-, and three-family houses on postage-stamp-sized lots. It's also known for both political corruption and affordable housing. In the 1940s, gay men spent time at its beach. Frank O'Hara set part of his 1949 novel there, but eventually gay men began to frequent beaches further north or in Provincetown instead.

The criminal case began when a school bus driver was accused of raping two brothers aged twelve and thirteen. His arrest led police to another man who was accused of having sex with four boys under the age of twelve. Next, a search of his possessions led to a cache of over one hundred photographs of nude boys, additional charges against the two men involving other youngsters, and a rape charge against Richard Peluso of 242 Mountain Ave., Revere. Then on December 7, 1977, District Attorney Garrett Byrne triumphantly announced that a grand jury had issued indictments against twenty-four men who were members of a sex and drug ring involving under-aged teenagers at Peluso's apartment. Byrne went wild with his accusations, telling the press that the gatherings were part of an organized group that had ties to national pornographers. He boldly asserted that the group included prominent Bostonians and that the men involved would be tried for rape. He also set up a hotline for the public to report on any other homosexual related crimes. A witch hunt was on.

Byrne bragged that his hotline attracted 100 callers, but no arrests ever came from it. However, gay men in Boston were terrified that the Revere case and hotline were the start of a general crackdown on LGBTQ people. These fears were confirmed when the Boston police invaded the Copley Library and began to randomly arrest anyone they thought was gay. Suddenly almost a hundred men, many just reading or looking for books, were arrested for lewd and lascivious conduct. Panic spread across the city.

Mitzel, members of the Fag Rag collective, and others immediately responded by forming the Boston-Boise Committee, named after a similar anti-gay roundup in Idaho and the group picketed Byrne's office and the BPL, set up a fund to pay for the accused's legal fees, and held rallies and community education events. Meanwhile, John Ward put out a call for lawyers to help the accused, because most were afraid to do so. Not used to being challenged, the District Attorney's office grew furious and when Ward announced he was going to court to block the hotline, an Assistant District Attorney threatened him. "If you show up in court tomorrow, we'll make sure you never practice law in this town again." Part of the anger was posturing because the arrests were based on shaky legal grounds. Most of the library arrests were quickly dismissed and knowing that the hotline was illegal, Byrne quietly discontinued it.

The allegations regarding the Revere ring soon fell apart. Of the twenty-four indictments, four men did not exist and there was no pornography that featured the boys from Revere. Finding prosecution witnesses was difficult as the sex was generally consensual or was exchanged for money and most of the incidents had happened five to six years earlier. Not only was there no national connection, there was no local sex ring; many of the defendants had never even been to Revere, and many of the men did not know each other. In time, most of the youths who provided testimony said they were coerced and threatened with prosecution for perjury.[32] Byrne tried to get sixty-four boys and young men to testify but only thirteen were willing.

In the end, just one man went to trial, Donald Allen, who testified in his defense that he never had sex with the boys and was just there because he was researching male hustling in Boston for a scientific research paper (published in 1981). He was convicted on the testimony of Peluso and Prescott Clarridge, who pled guilty and appeared in court as part of a deal with the prosecutors. Clarridge had been the assistant headmaster of the Fessenden School until the charges were announced and decades later, Clarridge would be accused by former students of molesting them. The other men plea bargained for reduced charges and sentences. Except for one man who was returned to Bridgewater State Hospital, no one went to jail and most got off with probation, light sentences which even back then reflected that the cases against them were weak.

The aftershock of the Revere cases continued for several years. In a bizarre turn, Superior Court Chief Justice Robert Bonin was forced off the bench because he and his wife attended a talk by Gore Vidal at the Arlington Street Church that was a benefit for the Boston-Boise Committee. The rational was that a judge should not be seen as publicly supporting one side in a case that might be decided in his jurisdiction. Ward started GLAD by putting a notice in *GCN* and five people showed up at a meeting at the Old West Church, eager to help.[33] Still going strong over forty years later, GLAD provided the legal team which made same-sex marriage a reality in Massachusetts as well as working on important cases ranging from assisting people with AIDS to advancing trans rights. Mitzel and others soon left the Boston-Boise Coalition and it morphed over time into NAMBLA, the notorious and scorned advocacy organization of intergenerational love—with no more support in Boston than it had elsewhere. Byrne had hoped that his strong anti-gay actions would help him survive a tough electoral challenge but was voted out of office. Fortunately, the library arrests were the last large-scale police crackdown against LGBTQ people in Boston.

For all the rhetoric from the Boston-Boise Committee that there was something beneficial to the teenagers in these intergenerational meetups in Revere, there is scant evidence that the teenagers were given anything more lasting than marijuana and alcohol. None of the men helped the youngsters gain access to education, employment, or housing and they did not provide counseling, medical care, or other services to the boys. The men simply used the teenagers for sex.

Not surprisingly (but interestingly), some of the NAMBLA men tried to use to their advantage their association with the broader LGBTQ community. They alleged their legal problems were similar to those of the vast majority of LGBTQ people who would never touch a teenager. Mitzel and the other radicals, in their efforts to connect intergenerational sex to the gay rights movement, belittled those who rejected the sexual contacts that had happened in Revere.[34] There is no evidence that they partook in intergenerational sex themselves and no one then or later accused them of sex with minors, but their callousness is striking now that we know how these types of relationships are rarely totally consensual and can often leave victims scarred for life.

A final damning lesson from the case is the role of the heterosexual community in creating this group of teenagers who were involved in the Revere scandal, many of whom were homeless or in state custody. Most of these teenage boys were on the street and vulnerable because they had been thrown out of their homes for being gay or bisexual. Their families had internalized the hateful messages from clergy, lawmakers, the news media, and others and when they discovered their children were expressing same-sex desire or behavior, they cast them out. There would have been vastly fewer children to abuse if their families and communities had been less homophobic. As the 1980s progressed there were far fewer gay teenagers on the streets of Boston because it was less likely they would be tossed aside by their families and those that are on the streets had access to services: housing, education, medical care, and counseling that gave and still gives them alternatives to selling themselves on the streets or congregating in houses where they might meet men out to use them. Sadly, lesbian, gay and especially transgender teens are still at much greater risk of rejection and are more likely to be homeless on the streets of Boston today than straight youth and though their numbers are lower than what they were decades ago, LGBTQ youth remain the most likely to be victims of abuse.

A young man from nearby Rhode Island helped advance the rights of gay students everywhere in the early 1980s. Aaron Fricke (1962-) was born and raised in a suburb of Providence. He would have been like any other baby boomer if he was not gay; with two children and a stay at home mother, the family was indistinguishable from millions of others in the 1960s and 1970s. Fricke was aware of his sexuality early in his life. He was never abused and he had plenty of opportunities for sex with other boys in the quiet town of Cumberland, less than an hour from Boston. But along with a growing realization that he was gay, there were also many clues that who he was and what he liked doing were wrong. When he was around six, for example, he casually mentioned he liked the way Batman looked and his sister acted disgusted. Another time, a neighbor's mom caught Fricke and a boy in a closet together, becoming upset, and when Fricke touched another boy during a sleepover, the boy's mother beat him. Thus Fricke learned to repress any and all signs of homosexuality, but at the cost of being alienated from everyone around him. "Many of my feelings were stifled; there was no one with whom to communicate my innermost thoughts. Somewhere in my subconscious, fears were combining that would remain in my memory to haunt me later on. Would I be disliked? Was I dangerous?"[35]

For young people growing up in certain metropolitan areas such as the Boston/Providence region, there was ample evidence that LGBTQ people existed as well as positive examples of LGBTQ life. Fricke's family visited Provincetown during the summer where he saw same sex couples walking hand in hand. One Halloween, he accidentally knocked on the door of a house where a party of gay men, many in drag, was taking place. None of this helped him manage the pressures of junior high school, however.

The more his peers began to pair off or talk about the joys of heterosexual sex as only eighth graders can, the more isolated Fricke became. He began to eat lunch alone as he felt a need to carefully guard his every word and action. The psychological distress increased. "Once in a while somebody would call me a faggot when walking past a lunch table. This was scary, because I thought I was keeping my homosexuality a close secret. I hope that no one knew I was suspect but apparently there were rumors. Fortunately, I heard these remarks only occasionally and only from a limited number of students." Then he was physically attacked by other students for being gay, leaving him constantly on edge.

High school was even more difficult. "I had given up all hope of ever finding love, warmth or tenderness in the world. I did not lie to myself, but I did my best to keep other people from thinking I was homosexual." Trying to keep the world at a distance, the 5'7" Fricke turned to food and his weight ballooned to over 210 pounds. "it was confusion, not self-hatred, that drove me to this escape. Confusion about where to turn, about what my future would be like if I couldn't fit into the rest of society."

In his junior year of high school, things began to change. He made a few friends and then met a classmate who was open about being gay. He showed Fricke a copy of *GCN* and told him about Dignity and other gay people. In the spring of 1979, another gay student asked Fricke to be his date at the junior prom but Fricke was not ready for such a step. So the boy asked a Brown University student instead, but the administrators at Cumberland High School refused to let the couple attend. The student was unable to mount a legal challenge because he was only seventeen and for many reasons, including a deteriorating relationship with his parents because he was gay, the student dropped out of school. Yet some students were supportive of the idea.

Fricke's senior year began with the principal giving a speech promising a good year because "we no longer had to put up with the problem of the year before," referring to the prom. The prejudice energized Fricke. He became increasingly out, which meant he had to endure bouts of harassment: slurs, spitting, and threats of violence. The school administration was hostile, the principal refused to let him out of gym, and his English teacher tore up an essay on homosexuality, declaring it an unacceptable topic for an assignment. He began to realize that other students, male and female, also struggled to come to terms with their own LGBTQ feelings. Some days they would be at the edge of confessing they were gay only to retreat to say they were bi or straight.

In the spring of 1979 as the school geared up for Senior Prom, Fricke was eighteen and determined to go to the prom with another boy. First, he came out to his parents. His mother had already guessed he was gay but his father had no clue. However, both parents were supportive. Summoning his courage, he asked Paul, the boy who had wanted to bring him to the prom the year before, to be his date. Fricke then went directly to the principal, who flatly refused to let him attend prom with a boy. Showing courage, Fricke, with the help of the Providence office of the National Gay Task Force, sued. John Ward became involved and they decided to base their case on Fricke's first amendment rights. Responding to the suit, the school said it would not let a same-sex couple attend the prom because of the risk of violence to the couple and the dishonor and bad publicity it would create if word got out the school was accepting of gay students.

Meanwhile, the reaction of the student body to Fricke's intention varied from support to anger. Then he was physically assaulted by a group of students and suffered a cut below his eye that required five stitches. The principal had offered Fricke protection, but he had refused it because he thought it was hypocritical because when he had asked for help before, his pleas had been rejected. But now he accepted it.

A judge affirmed that going to the prom was an expression of free speech and that the fear of violence against a same-sex couple was not a valid reason for barring them, nor was fear regarding the reputation of the school. The school unsuccessfully appealed and Fricke attended the prom with his male date. The case received extensive coverage in the *Boston Globe* and Fricke's experiences, as well as his courage at speaking out, helped jumpstart the movement for safe schools for LGBTQ students in Massachusetts and elsewhere.

The hysteria of 1978 was the last large-scale police action against LGBTQ people in Massachusetts in part because within two years, the SJC effectively eroded the ability of police to arrest them. For decades, the definition of who was a lewd, wanton, and lascivious person in Massachusetts was very vague. For most of the period in which these laws were in effect, the police didn't even have to provide any details about what led to the arrest, giving them vast powers to harass anyone. Coupled with homophobic judges who were ready to condemn and convict without evidence, thousands were ensnared and imprisoned, their lives ruined. A few with resources and without a need to keep their sexuality secret contested their arrests and often saved themselves, but those who were poor or afraid of losing their jobs or families had no recourse. LGBTQ people of color and those who were gender non-conforming were particularly at risk from these loosely defined (but harshly enforced) laws. This mostly ended with an SJC decision in 1980.

The facts in *Commonwealth v. Sefranka* were not in dispute. At a rest stop along Route 24 in Brockton that was a popular cruising area, men would pull up in a car and flash their headlights. Another man would go up to the car and if both parties were agreeable, the men would either have sex there or drive someplace else to consummate their relationship. Determined to stop this activity, an undercover policeman in an unmarked car flashed his lights and Edward Sefranka got in his car. The policeman said he wanted to have sex there but Sefranka said no, he wanted to go elsewhere, and when the policeman refused, Sefranka left, got into his own car, and started to drive off. He was arrested as he left the parking lot.

Sefranka appealed his conviction and won when the SJC ruled that the term "lewd, wanton, and lascivious" was so vague as to be meaningless and not actionable by the police. Therefore, the law only covered acts or the solicitation of acts that would be public. But since Sefranka wanted private sex, the court ruled he was innocent. The decision signified the application of legal standards that had long protected heterosexuals in Massachusetts. While public sex was prosecutable, just about all heterosexual consensual sex between adults in private had been legal for over a hundred years despite the laws on the books against it. The state courts were beginning to apply legal concepts equally to everyone.

Police would continue to use disorderly and anti-loitering laws to ensnare LGBTQ people and homophobic judges would continue to harass LGBTQ people asserting their rights while the laws regarding same-sex relations were still on th books, but the police had lost their primary justification for the arrest and harm of LGBTQ people and for the most part, harassment began to fade, at least in Boston.

For many in the area, there seemed to be a freedom that was unimaginable elsewhere. Housing discrimination had mostly disappeared inside the gay ghettos. Some employers were open to hiring LGBTQ people while others were at least willing to ignore the sexuality of their employees. No one believed that life was perfect. Not everyone enjoyed this new atmosphere of tolerance and there was enough violence, rejection, and bigotry around to remind everyone how much work remained to be done; still, there was enough loosening of discrimination that most could dream of a day when there might be freedom for everyone. The community bubbled with palpable hope and optimism for the future as summer began in June 1981. No one saw the horror already embracing them.

Chapter 11

Desperate Times

BEFORE THE INTERNET, it was impossible for most people to find the *Morbidity and Mortality Weekly Report* (MMWR) published by the Centers for Disease Control, and few medical professionals bothered to go to their local medical library (if there was one) to read it. Naively, many thought the age of infectious diseases was over. The attention of most medical research in the 1970s focused on cancer, heart disease, and other chronic illnesses because doctors believed antibiotics stopped most bacterial infections and vaccines prevented most viral ones. The field of infectious disease was dull, a medical backwater.[1]

Everything changed on June 5, 1981 when the *MMWR* ran an Epidemiological Short on five young men, all gay, who had been treated for Pneumocystis carinii pneumonia at Los Angeles hospitals. By the end of 2016, over 650,000 people in the United States would be dead of what would be known as HIV-AIDS with the total world mortality exceeding 35 million. In Boston, as with the United States as a whole, most of those infected or dead were gay men or transsexuals. Deaths were agonizing, featuring high fevers, frantic gasps for air, and intractable pain; they were tragedies, with victims mostly people in the prime of their lives, dying at a time when living into one's old age was becoming a right; and they were heartbreaking as uncountable people lost friends, relatives, life partners, hopes, and dreams.

For a few months, it was easy to ignore the disease as there was little information about it. The *Globe* first covered the mysterious illness in a short front page story on August 29, 1981, that was a reprint of an Associated Press article. The story mentioned that the CDC had reported on a mysterious combination of Pneumocystis and Kaposi's sarcoma among gay men in June and July but provided little additional information.

Then on December 10, another front page article led off with, "A mysterious epidemic of rarely seen diseases, including a type of cancer endemic to Africa, is suddenly afflicting sexually promiscuous young men, most of them homosexual." The article went on to say that there had been one reported case of the syndrome in Massachusetts, a Provincetown man in his thirties who died of Pneumocystis in 1980. The article reported that, "The typical victim is a homosexual man in his 30s who has multiple sex partners. He suffers for months from fatigue, low fever, weight loss, swollen lymph glands and a yeast infection called thrush (cottony white spots in the mouth and throat); he may then get an aggressive form of pneumonia, spreading ulcers in the anal or genital area, a severe fungal infection of the throat or esophagus, and sometimes the purplish skin spots or other hallmarks of Kaposi's sarcoma."[2] The article noted that no one knew what was causing this new syndrome but suggested that it might be amyl nitrate, promiscuity, or some other environmental factor. It described the epidemic as "scary" and "fearful."

Regrettably, *GCN* failed to adequately take notice of the disease and though it ran an article on the developing epidemic every other month or so, it devoted at least three times more articles to intergenerational sex as it did on AIDS up through 1984. It wasn't until staffers and volunteers began to fall ill and die that it increased its AIDS coverage.[3] The reasons for this failure are complex. Based in Boston where AIDS took longer to break out than elsewhere, the collective that ran the paper simply may have not noticed the impact AIDS had in its early years. In addition, the staffers who put out the paper were out of touch with, it not openly disdainful of, the concerns of mainstream LGBTQ people and like straight conservatives, many thought it was just a promiscuous white cisgender gay man's disease. Thus, the paper's writers continued to focus on intergenerational sex (which was the priority of only an infinitesimally small percentage of the community) rather than AIDS (which would ravage almost everyone, infected or not).

Bay Windows, founded by Sasha Alyson in 1983 to be a mainstream and local alternative to *GCN*, covered AIDS from the beginning. But it had the advantage of not having started publication until after it became clear that the epidemic was going to hit gay men very hard. Overall, the coverage in the Boston LGBTQ press was high-quality. In contrast to some New York publications, *GCN*, *Bay Windows* and other Boston papers never devoted much space to spurious AIDS conspiracy theories and they focused on treatment, prevention, and the rights of those infected.

Across Boston, gay men whispered to each other about the new disease as word of it quickly spread through the bars, cruising areas, and other places they socialized. Some thought it would never come here, others vowed they would never get sick, and many thought it wasn't a real disease, claiming AIDS was just a weapon for homophobes to use against them. Even as they searched themselves for signs of the disease, no one publicly declared themselves at risk.

This heavy hand of denial kept gay men from panicking. At first. Michael Ward, writing a memoir of his lover's death from AIDS early in the epidemic, recalled one friend saying, "I'm too vanilla to get AIDS."[4] Even in the early 1990s, one hustler refused to get tested because "not knowing his HIV status also made it possible for [the hustler] to work at making it negative. He did this by making himself look and feel like a young god–someone who could not be seropositive, let alone someone who could have AIDS".[5] Limiting one's sex partners to those who seemed most robust was an early defense mechanism. It didn't work, of course, as people were infectious for years before they showed any sign of physical decline, but it was one way of denying one's risk.

But the disease eventually forced everyone to acknowledge its threat. Spread thin as the Kevin White era was ending, friends and colleagues noticed that Jorge Hernandez seemed fatigued. In addition to running Villa Victoria, no small task, he served on a multitude of boards and special committees, and few thought he had any issues that couldn't be solved by a vacation. Others told themselves that he was uncharacteristically uninvolved in the 1983 mayor's race because his heart was with Mel King while his head knew Ray Flynn was going to win. Hernandez was politically savvy, and he knew he would have to represent the Latino community going forward no matter who won. Thus, many were shocked when it was announced in April 1986 that the indefatigable Hernandez was dead. Among Boston's LGBTQ Latino community, word quickly got out that he had died of AIDS. Though the cause of his death was never publicly disclosed, for many this was the first inkling of how bad the epidemic would be in the gay Latino community. Villa Victoria eventually opened the Hernandez Cultural Center in a renovated church which would be the site of many AIDS fundraisers over the next decade.

The medical community was torn between compassion and spasms of fear. Patients were treated as if they were actively infectious and that any contact with them might be lethal. For example, on one occasion Ward walked to his lover's room at the Deaconess Hospital to find its door covered by large red stickers announcing PRECAUTIONARY ISOLATION, meaning visitors and attending staff had to wear masks, gloves, and gowns. Ward's lover, Mark Halberstadt, lamented, "I feel like a leper. They're frightened of me. Every time they come in, it looks like aliens are invading my room. I feel like I've awakened in a horror movie."[4]

It wasn't just straight people who treated AIDS patients cruelly. In the first several years of the epidemic when little was known regarding the virus behind AIDS or how it was transmitted, many LGBTQ people oscillated between denial and open terror. The disease was a death sentence that pushed waves of nausea and fear over the community, warping and distorting almost every aspect of LGBTQ life. Some men left their partners when they found out they had been diagnosed with AIDS, terrified they might catch it. Others abandoned their friends. Even thirty years later, when it was clear that a person whose viral load was undetectable was not infectious, gay dating sites routinely included comments that told anyone who was HIV positive not to respond.

In the years when there were no treatments, the shock of being diagnosed with a fatal illness could be devastating. When Alan Kukonis, who would later become a board member of AIDS Action Committee (AAC) and the National Coalition of People with AIDS, had a biopsy that confirmed he had Kaposi's sarcoma in 1985, he felt like his life suddenly stood still. "This can't be happening. This can't be happening to me,"[6] he thought. He had only recently moved back to Boston after living a decade in San Francisco, New York, and South Florida and he felt he was just getting his life together.

Dying and abandoned by the straight world, the LGBTQ community was on its own to confront the epidemic. Wondrously, the community pulled itself together, demonstrating courage that many never knew was in them. What became the AIDS

Action Committee of Massachusetts (AAC) grew out of meetings organized by Larry Kessler and others at Buddies and the Fenway Health Center. Mostly gay men, its first volunteers were from Cambridge, Back Bay, and the South End. When these meetings began in December 1982, there were only a handful of AIDS cases in the state and most of their gay male peers were either in denial or unaware of the doom approaching the community. Thus Kessler and the others found themselves with endless lofty but much-needed objectives, from educating gay men and medical providers to helping people with AIDS access medical insurance, health care, legal advice, counseling, housing, and many other services. They quickly needed to master their personal grief while helping others cope with tragedy. They learned how to raise money and organize a community.

Though he was well-liked, there was no reason to predict that Larry Kessler (1942-) would become one of the major figures in the effort against AIDS. He did have a long history of activism, working on peace and anti-poverty programs in Pennsylvania before coming to Boston where he helped create Project Bread's Walk for Hunger. For a brief time, he retired to run a card store, but the AIDS epidemic quickly brought him back to the non-profit world. A devout Catholic who had once considered becoming a priest, he used all of the personal qualities he could muster: patience, organizational abilities, focused attention, and determination to steer Boston through the worst days of the epidemic.

AAC staff assisted people with AIDS such as Kukonis in navigating their new lives, helping them to make the best of their life with the disease. Kukonis realized he could either feel helpless or empower himself. He learned that "coming out is like peeling an onion" and realized that hiding things, whether being gay or having AIDS, sapped energy and stole the spark from his life.[6]

By 1985, the epidemic was hitting Boston hard and Kessler stopped going to gay bars. "It's because I would just stand around and visualize these guys all in hospital beds," he said.[7] To those in the middle of the epidemic, it sometimes looked like everyone would soon be swept away. By the mid 1980s, panic was everywhere gay men and trans people gathered as all around them people were falling sick and dying. There was no end in sight.

Provincetown rallied around its ill residents. The first official cases of AIDS appeared in Provincetown clinics in 1982 but looking back at the late 1970s health workers realized that they had seen cases at that time. At first, the patients were undercover, keeping their illnesses a secret. The town nurse, Alice Foley was aware of what was happening and with Preston Babbitt, the owner of the Rose and Crown guesthouse, she and others organized the Provincetown AIDS Support Group (PASG).

Foley later recalled that "always we were looking for ways to make sure Provincetown residents with AIDS could live as well as possible and die with dignity, be in a circle of loved ones." The caregivers became close to their clients. She spoke of one. "A transsexual. She was beautiful. Gorgeous. But in her AIDS treatment, they took away her hormones and she went back to being a man. I think she died more of a broken heart than of AIDS."[8] Some people died after long illnesses, while others appeared healthy one week and were dead of pneumonia the next. The effort show-cased another impact of the epidemic in Provincetown, Boston, and elsewhere: con-fronting AIDS made the town's entire population closer as gays, lesbians, and straight men and women volunteered alongside one another. Women were as likely as men to step up and help.

AIDS was relentless, tearing through the community, killing victims, and leaving everyone else grieving and desperate. Across the state, patient numbers start-ed small but rapidly grew. There were just five diagnosed cases in Massachusetts in 1982, but three years later there were 400 with 165 dead. By 1985 there was a new case reported every 36 hours. Survival times were grim in the years before effective treatments were discovered. Looking at all people in Massachusetts diagnosed with AIDS from 1979 to 1988, a study found that the mean survival time was 406 days and only 3 percent of people were alive five years after their diagnosis. In all, there were 2,158 cases as of December 31, 1988 with thirty cases identified (retroactively) prior to the first recognition of AIDS in 1981. Of all cases, 196 were from out-of-state; 1,740 were male (non-binary and trans people were not identified–another example of how they were ignored in those years); 896 were Boston residents with another 503 from inside the metro area. Further demonstrating the explosion in the numbers of sick, 671 had been diagnosed in 1988.[9] The worst was yet to come. At that point in time, ten thousand more gay men in the state were still to die.

There was one small piece of good news when a 1985 study of gay men in Boston found that only 20 percent were HIV positive. In comparison, similar studies in New York and San Francisco found that as many as 70 percent of the men showing up at gay health clinics there were infected.[10] However, this suggested that there might be 20,000 gay men in Massachusetts who had the virus in them.

The plague settled down like a heavy thick miasma on the South End and other LGBTQ neighborhoods as people began to understand that the AIDS battle would not end quickly. Some reacted to the epidemic by giving up sex altogether while others slowed down how much sex they were having. "There are some people who say they have become celibate," said Dr. Kenneth Mayer, a longtime researcher at the Fenway. "Certainly more people are dating and taking a longer time before they become involved sexually. We've made more inroads into changing sexual behavior than we have in getting people to stop smoking."[7] Some of the wild ways of the 1970s became a thing of the past. Yet the bars were full, cruising areas showed no sign of abandonment, and the back pages of LGBTQ papers remained full of sex ads. The disconnect was maddening.

The Fenway Health Center, now with ten years' experience of providing care to the LGBTQ community, by necessity became one of the country's premier sites for AIDS treatment. As current patients grew ill and new ones passed through it doors desperately seeking help, the Fenway was straddling all sides of the epidemic. With large numbers of LGBTQ staff, some colleagues died of the disease while everyone else had family and friends suffering from its effects. The Fenway's staff simultaneously played the roles of health care providers, patients, community resources, researchers, educators, hand holders, survivors, and advocates; all without being torn apart by conflict or losing their human touch. This was a nigh-impossible set of tasks.

Other community institutions found themselves being pulled into the effort to assist people with AIDS. GLAD started an AIDS law project after Beth Israel Hospital began to require all personnel to don complete body protections, even shoe covers, whenever anyone entered a room where a person might have AIDS, even if it was a non-positive gay person there for an unrelated issue. GLAD focused on strategic legal issues, litigating or negotiating for victories that would translate to broad movement on AIDS rights. Most of the day-to-day lawyering for people with AIDS was provided by several non-profit groups and volunteers including a program at Jamaica Plain Legal Services supported by the downtown, high-end law firm Hale and Dore and run by Harvard Law School and lawyers at Aids Action Committee and JRI – the Justice Resource Clinic.

The hospital and other medical providers eventually recovered their professionalism and treated their patients with dignity. However, GLAD found that dentists remained a particular problem. It wasn't just individual dentists; Tufts Dental School stopped treating most AIDS patients. Dr. Chris Doku, chairman of Tufts' oral surgery department, said emergency cases were treated but that others would be refused until a special isolation facility was in place "so they won't contaminate the rest of the patients."[7]

The fight to get AIDS patients dental care resulted in a Supreme Court victory several years later, led by GLAD attorney Bennett Klein. A dentist in Maine not only refused to provide routine care to people with AIDS, he went out of his way to demonize LGBTQ people and sent homophobic messages to the Maine Dental Association. GLAD's lawsuit against him was enabled by the Americans with Disabilities Act (ADA), passed in 1989 but whose public accommodation provision didn't go into effect until 1994. It was a risky lawsuit as the ADA had not yet been tested at the Supreme Court, nor did anyone know for sure that it might cover people who were only infected with HIV and not yet symptomatic. But the court sided with AIDS victims in 1998, declaring they had a right to medical (and dental) care.[11]

As in other cities, there was a range of responses to the epidemic. Some people and agencies made a conscious decision not to serve AIDS patients because of fear and bigotry. Others rose to the occasion, becoming heroes when they were needed the most. Some people died alone because of a lack of family and friends to take care of them, victims of ignorance and fear. Some carried their denial of their disease to the grave and it was not uncommon to go to a "cancer funeral" because no one would admit to the deceased having AIDS. But many people fearlessly went to work.

Kessler decided early on his goal was to ensure no AIDS patient "is left feeling abandoned. They suffer such terrible fatigue. If they have trouble getting to the market or the doctor's office, or whatever they need, we have volunteers to help".[12] At first, this meant that Kessler himself often visited people in the hospital or at their homes. Soon the sheer numbers overwhelmed him and AAC organized a buddy system, with a partner assigned to anyone who requested one. These people provided emotional support and helped connect patients to other services.

Though there were a few grants, much of the work was done by uncompensated volunteers and most of the money to fund programs came from the LGBTQ community so afflicted by the epidemic. LGBTQ people constantly contributed to AIDS service organizations through increasingly elaborate fundraisers while LGBTQ business owners and professionals became prime sponsors of these events. The largest fundraiser was AAC's annual AIDS walk, held annually in early June, which since its beginning in 1986 has raised millions of dollars. The Fenway Health Center also needed donations as medical reimbursements, government grants, and research contracts did not cover all the work demanded of it. The Fenway hired a large fundraising staff, and along with volunteers, they hosted many events with some targeted to gay men and some to lesbians in order to raise unencumbered funds.

The full extent to which LGBTQ people contributed to the fight against AIDS is unknowable, but the numbers of people who volunteered to help people with AIDS, provided safe sex education, donated money to AIDS organizations, attended rallies or demonstrations, and comforted those ill or the friends, lovers, families, or survivors of the disease, is as close as possible to 100 percent. The disease attacked everyone. Despair was everywhere, but so was courage and compassion.

AAC and others ran education campaigns targeting gay men. This was new to public health, which had long ignored LGBTQ people. By the late 1980s, however, it was impossible to go into a bar and not see posters advertising safe sex. Condoms were passed out in bars, street corners, Pride parades, the Fens, and wherever else LGBTQ people gathered. Volunteers and agencies produced pamphlets, posters, and handbills to educate about the disease so that everyone would know what was current about transmission, prevention, testing, and treatment. Some of these efforts might seem silly in retrospect; there may not have been a great need to create comics or pornography to promote safer sex. But at the time, when the epidemic seemed unstoppable, anything and everything was tried. People were desperate to save themselves and others.

In the early years, no one could tell if they were ill unless they came down with symptoms (which themselves could be deceptive, as often the disease manifested in the form of other infections like pneumonia). Eventually, there was a test that could identify if a person was infected, but that led to new issues and worries. Did an infection mean that you would progress to AIDS and die? What good was knowing you were infected if there was no treatment? What would knowing your HIV status mean for your life? Your relationship? Your employment? What about housing? Everyone at risk had to address these concerns. Every gay, bisexual, and trans person had to find their own way to navigate the terror and uncertainties of those years.

AIDS revealed the chasm between middle- and upper-class white cisgender gay men and poorer gay men, LGBTQ people of color, and people who were trans or non-binary. Though in the first ten years race and class were no protection against the virus, it quickly became clear that those who had more resources were less likely to become infected, had longer times between infection and illness, and were more likely to have the financial and social resources to meet some of the challenges of their decline. Any remaining fiction that sexual or gender orientation might trump the other inequities of society and create a sense of equality within the LGBTQ community was dispelled.

Over time, AAC, an organization founded by white, middle-class men, found itself needing to devote more of its resources to trans people, those who were non-white, and people who became infected because of sharing needles rather than same-sex relations. To their credit, the middle-class and wealthier gay men who provided the bulk of funding to AAC have never wavered in their financial support, but AAC needed better outreach to those in need. This also included blacks and Latinos suffering from the disease. They made progress in this regard. One effort was the annual Bayard Rustin lunch, named after the gay African-American civil rights strategist. The first lunch in 1990 was just a few people at a gathering at Club Café in Back Bay but over time it grew to include hundreds of people. New AIDS service organizations were organized including Men of Color Against AIDS, the Multicultural AIDS Coalition, and other groups. AAC hired people of color and worked to ensure that non-white people were included on its advisory boards. But despite these efforts, the issue of inequality would only get worse.

In contrast to the experiences in New York and San Francisco, for the most part city and state agencies in Boston and Massachusetts quickly mobilized to meet the challenges of AIDS and there was less animosity towards local government officials here than elsewhere. With its long history of public health infrastructure and its close contacts between public health practitioners and the community (many LGBTQ people worked for the Massachusetts Department of Public Health (DPH)), Massachusetts had one of the first state health departments to create its own AIDS unit. Focusing on assisting people with AIDS, John Auerbach, a gay man, was the unit's first director, and his professional yet urgent demeanor helped build cooperation between the state and the community.

DPH also funded smaller AIDS organizations, particularly those focusing on communities of color. When Latino activists approached DPH, it provided a grant so quickly there wasn't infrastructure yet in place to receive it.[13] DPH was also instrumental in helping organizations focusing on the black community to begin providing services. But there was never enough funding for the work that was needed; neither the state nor the federal government provided sufficient resources to meet needs.

With its large number of LGBTQ employees and their close relationship with many community activists, the City of Boston also was a resource rather than an obstacle. Mayor Kevin White responded to the crisis early on by creating a task force from city agencies that might interact with people with AIDS including representatives from Health and Hospitals, the Boston Housing Authority, the Emergency Shelter Commission, and other key city agencies. It was chaired by Brian McNaught, the city's liaison to the gay community at the time.

After White left office in 1984, Mayor Ray Flynn appointed Ann Maguire to coordinate AIDS services in the city as part of her responsibilities as liaison. With his strong anti-abortion legislative record, LGBTQ activists were wary about how he would respond to the growing epidemic. Fortunately, these concerns did not materialize and when Flynn left office in 1993, the biggest complaints against him was that he had refused to require condom machines in bars or mandate AIDS education in the public schools.

Even before the first official cases, people at Boston City Hospital (BCH), the medical facility that proudly served the city's poor, had noticed something was happening. Cases were coming in that looked suspicious, particularly amongst the city's African-American, Haitian, and Latino communities, but there was no recognition of the disease yet. After the summer of 1981, however, they knew that anyone that came in with unusual symptoms had to be screened for immune problems. The first years of the epidemic were extremely difficult for health care providers who didn't understand the disease and didn't know how to meet the needs of their patients. But they tried to do their best, given the limited knowledge of AIDS at the time, and motivated by compassion, City Hospital began to create the infrastructure necessary to address this new disease with its many unique challenges. But it took several years. Responding to the crisis, in February 1984 the city's Department of Health and Hospitals hired a full time AIDS coordinator, Anne Marie Silva, and a full time AIDS epidemiologist. Silva was charged with presenting a plan to coordinate all city AIDS efforts to the Mayor's Task Force on AIDS. The city launched an information campaign to spread what was known about infection and treatment, as well as making sure services were delivered to those in need. "My job was to make sure City Hall was on board about people," recalled Maguire. "We went forward. Because that's what we are supposed to do. This is what you do."[14]

BCH had been seen as hostile to gay men prior to the AIDS emergency. Its sexually transmitted disease clinic, which previously focused on gonorrhea and syphilis, was thought to be judgmental, overcrowded, and unwilling to treat men without grilling them over their sexual contacts—taboo in an era where gay men needed to trust each other and medical staff to keep their identities confidential. Still, it offered free treatment and more anonymity than most other providers and for many, it was one of the few places they could get care. The epidemic forced the facility and its staff to morph into a more welcoming place.

Kessler pushed BCH to open a ward just for AIDS patients. Considering his proposal, BCH consulted with San Francisco General Hospital, noted for its AIDS expertise, and on its advice, declined to create an adult AIDS ward, though they eventually did open a children's AIDS ward. Partly as a result of the epidemic, the city, heavily dependent on state and federal aid to provide medical care to the uninsured, began to work with others to develop a coalition that would eventually make Massachusetts the first state in the country to have universal health care coverage.

Another reason that there was less animosity in Boston over AIDS care and prevention was that the battle between moralists (who blamed promiscuity for AIDS) and those who asserted their right to sexual freedom despite the mounting wave of sickness was less pronounced in Boston than elsewhere. There was, of course, a puritanical segment inside and outside the community who rose to say AIDS was a punishment for promiscuity and that the community needed to stop having sex; but the reality was that it was nearly impossible in Boston to have the thousands of sex partners that some men in New York and San Francisco notched. There was one sad bathhouse, but few had been there. There were few backrooms, no nightly orgies, and no non-stop sex venues. Even the action in the Fens was mostly what was now called safe sex. From the beginning it was clear that people who became infected in Boston had not overindulged; they were merely unlucky. Thus the debate that focused on bathhouses in San Francisco and debauched bars in New York failed to gain traction within Massachusetts.

Still another reason for the cooperative nature of Boston's anti-AIDS movement were the values of organizations fighting the epidemic. Because many of the people involved in activism for the fight against AIDS were veterans of LGBTQ, community development, and anti-war movements (among other progressive causes), there was a shared assumption that institutions must have boards, staffs, and members that were inclusive of the people they served, in this case people with AIDS. It therefore made sense that the non-profit organizations that spearheaded the response to the epidemic were mostly run by those who were most affected by the disease. The Boston Living Center, for example, was set up to be a home away from home for people with AIDS. There they could meet other patients and learn about services with a special mission to serve those too ill to work but not hospitalized. It was staffed by and for people with AIDS to help them get through their daily lives and it continues to employ people with AIDS to serve the community.

The cooperative nature of Boston anti-AIDS work does not mean there was no rage. The anger and bitterness were white hot and have yet to cool thirty years later. People died because of ignorance and bigotry; research dollars were parsimoniously distributed, promising treatments were slow to be adopted, and too many didn't care about a disease that only destroyed LGBTQ or addicted people. Those who survived these tragic years still carry within them a bitter fury that will never go away.

The AIDS crisis did not slow activism. Rather, it made political involvement more urgent. In 1980, Mayor White infuriated the LGBTQ community by laying off liaison Robin McCormack. Officially, he was dismissed because of the intense budget crisis overwhelming the city as White closed libraries and fire stations and laid off hundreds of municipal employees. But insiders knew the real reason for McCormack's dismissal was that he had angered the mayor by refusing to become part of his political machine. White bent everyone and every institution in the city to his political will and did not tolerate those who dared to be neutral.

As a result, Boston's LGBTQ activists saw a need to create a group focused on city politics. There were two very important political opportunities on the horizon that added urgency to the organizing effort. One arose when it became increasingly clear that White was not going to run for re-election when his fourth term was up in 1983. McCormack's layoff demonstrated the importance of access to the mayor, and the election promised the chance to influence White's successor. The other came after the passing of a 1981 charter amendment to establish a city council that was a hybrid of nine district and four at-large councilors, creating opportunities for LGBTQ influence and access. Under the old nine-member, at-large city council, it had been extremely difficult to elect minority or LGBTQ-friendly candidates. With district councilors, the ability of LGBTQ people to influence city policy was greatly enhanced. After months of outreach, the first meeting of the Boston Lesbian and Gay Political Alliance (called BLGPA or the Alliance) was held on September 20, 1982, at the U-Mass building in Park Square, next door to where the Punch Bowl once stood. In January 1983, Eric Rofes was elected chair of the Alliance and Ann Maguire was elected vice-chair.

11.1 Eric Rofes

As predicted, the 1983 mayor's race opened up in late spring when White went public with his decision not to run for re-election. The presumed front runner, David Finnegan, had no LGBTQ support and along with Suffolk County Sherriff Denis Kearny, was ignored by most LGBTQ voters in Boston. Three straight candidates vied for the Alliance's endorsement. Mel King, the African American state representative from the South End, was thought to be the easy victor of the Alliance's support. He had been a consistent proponent of the anti-discrimination bill and passionately believed in the humanity of LGBTQ people. More closely tied to the radicals than the assimilationists, he was respected by both.

One candidate was also well-known but very suspect. South Boston native Raymond Flynn had first made his political mark as an anti-busing activist and thus most LGBTQ people distrusted him. As a state representative and city councilor, he had been a fierce anti-abortion leader, alienating lesbians and their allies. Though many grudgingly admitted that he worked to create ties between black and white Bostonians (marking him as a moderate in South Boston) and though he promised to not interfere with women's reproductive rights at Boston City Hospital and city licensed neighborhood health centers, he had no more than a handful of LGBTQ supporters.

City Councilor Larry DiCara had a better reputation than Flynn. He had been a real-estate lawyer and many had relied on him to get building permits and negotiate the often-difficult approval process for business and development. In the years where the council was dominated by rabidly racist and anti-LGBTQ conservatives, DiCara had spoken out as a representative of liberal constituents and many admired the courage that took. Still, with most LGBTQ people tending to vote liberal, the excitement that racist-identified Boston might elect an African-American mayor, and the generally high level of love and admiration for King, everyone expected that DiCara did not have a chance to win the Alliance endorsement.

However, DiCara was a hard campaigner and in a city where politics was a one-on-one affair, he had an uncanny ability to remember names and people's personal details—at times it seemed that he knew nearly everyone including many members of the Alliance. He also had a number of gay men working on his campaign including his finance chairman, Vin McCarthy, and press secretary, Mark Johnson. Along with other gay male allies, these men worked to get DiCara's supporters to sign up as Alliance members and attend the midsummer endorsement meeting. It turned into a classic bare-knuckled Boston political battle but instead of fighting to win the support of a Dorchester neighborhood association or a Catholic parish council, the political wrestling match targeted the city's LGBTQ voters. No longer a scorned minority, politicians now openly courted their vote.

To almost everyone's surprise, DiCara won the Alliance's endorsement. The radicals were stunned, never believing that there could be support for anyone besides King, and many were angry that so many middle-class assimilationist LGBTQ people had shown up at the meeting. For many radicals, it was the first time they ever had been confronted with evidence that they were not a majority of the community.

Ultimately, the endorsement had little effect. King easily won the heavily-LGBTQ precincts in the South End, the Fenway, and Jamaica Plain. DiCara finished fourth and did not advance to the final election. King breezed through the endorsement meeting for the mayoral final as Flynn still had little support and many of the DiCara supporters did not show up. But King lost the final election and LGBTQ people had to figure out how to work with a mayor few knew or liked.

AIDS did not dent LGBTQ nightlife, which continued to thrive. The raids on Boston gay bars were for many a distant memory, if not forgotten. Still, there was an exception. The Loft, located on Stanhope St. around the corner from police headquarters, was repeatedly raided in the early 1980s. It operated beyond the law and without permits, only opening after 2:00 a.m. when other legal establishments closed. There would be a line, primarily straight African-Americans on Friday nights and gay men on Saturday nights, waiting to get into the three story tenement building. On Saturdays, the second floor was for dancing and the third was a popular and notorious bar and backroom with pornography playing on a big screen and dozens of men having sex at any one time under a makeshift thatch canopy hanging from a chain attached to the ceiling. The bathrooms were tiny and had such long lines that men often urinated off the fire escape and it was so crowded, if a fire had ever broken out it would certainly have been deadly. The primary owner, Joe D'Onofeo, openly taunted the police, daring them to raid the club because he thought that would spark a Stonewall-like riot. The liaisons to the LGBTQ community, first Brian McNaught and then Maguire, were frustrated by D'Onofeo. They wanted to help him make the venue legal, but D'Onofeo relished his renegade stance.[15]

Though D'Onofeo enraged the police, they had a hard time dealing with him. The Loft was cited for operating after hours in 1979, but the charge was overturned by a judge because it had been raided without a warrant. They raided it in March 1982 and again on May 9 the same year, this time arresting its two owners and several employees on charges that ranged from selling soft drinks—how the bartenders hid the liquor no one knew—to keeping a house of ill fame. Though the mainstream press focused on the pornography and group sex, no charges were filed regarding these. Even the ill fame charge was dismissed by a judge who found the law unconstitutional, though the other charges stuck for a fine of $1,600 on each of the two owners.

The Loft was raided yet again on April 10, 1983. This time police used sledgehammers to break into the office and seize records. For this round, the charges included the illegal selling of soft drinks and alcohol. In addition, two patrons were arrested for performing unnatural acts. All the charges were dropped after a court found the raid, which again took place without a warrant, was illegal and all evidence seized inadmissible. Police raided the Loft raided a final time in 1985 and this time destroyed so much of the club that it never reopened. But D'Onofeo would later get his revenge.

While most bars were now never subject to police actions, police were always ready to raid a club if they got wind of any wrong doing. The House of Quagmire at 520 Tremont St. briefly had a backroom downstairs. A raid put a stop to the action there even though the arrests that stemmed from it were thrown out by a judge. The bar renamed itself the Eagle and remained open more than thirty-five years later.

Boston never had a club that was dominated by African-Americans, though by the 1990s there were venues that hosted Latino nights featuring Spanish-language dance music from the Caribbean. Moreover, there was widespread discrimination against African-American LGBTQ people in the city's bars, prompting the Boston chapter of the nationwide group Black and White Men Together to undertake a systematic assessment of how Blacks were treated in 1984. What they found was disturbing. Buddies, Campus, Chaps, the 1270, and the Loft routinely denied entrance to minorities. The report noted that Buddies "is often referred to as a bar where men are more fashion conscious" a code word for excluding working-class whites and people of color.[16] Like the other clubs, Buddies sometimes let blacks in, sometimes not, following the whim of the door personnel at the moment and how many blacks were already inside. A few could be tolerated, more than that was a problem. Blacks were kept out by their carding policy–blacks were asked to produce multiple forms of identification while whites were not.

Though it sometimes denied entrance to people of color, Chaps was one of the few bars to have black employees and enough black patrons to have them be able to form groups in one corner of the bar. They tended to cluster by neighborhood: Roxbury, Mattapan, and so forth. In contrast, the Eagle was well-integrated, employed blacks, and freely let in people of color. The report also noted that none of the bars surveyed had many disabled people patronizing them.

In contrast to the thriving men's bars, Boston lesbian bars were fragile. Saints, loved by many women, closed in 1983 and Somewhere Else was destroyed in a fire that demolished the bathhouse upstairs in 1987. Women could rely on Marquee in Cambridge, Greystone's downtown, and a variety of women's nights at clubs across the city, but for the most part lesbian bars tended to be smaller and more transient; however, they also served a more diverse clientele than men's bars.

LGBTQ people continued to patronize restaurants after the bars closed. Ken's in Copley Square was the most popular with table-hopping and sequential lap-sitting now common. Big groups often went to the Moon Villa in Chinatown, where ordering "cold tea" resulted in beer being surreptitiously served in metal water pitchers. Some stopped for a slice of pizza at Little Stevie's on Boylston St. or Buzzy's Roast Beef at Charles Circle. There was nearly a twenty-four hour LGBTQ presence in the city.

Flourishing nightlife was not limited to Boston. Provincetown also matured as an LGBTQ resort in the 1980s. Eric Rofes gleefully described the scene in a *GCN* column: "[t]he Boatslip Man, as we call him, has disco in his blood. He knows the words to every current song and has his shirt off by 5:15. Anything by Donna Summer causes a packed dance floor. They dance with one another and with everyone and no one, in a mass celebration of music, men, and the summer season. The air fills, these days, more with sweat and steam than with poppers, and the sound of whistles, shrieks, and tambourines punctuate the beat of the music."[17] Men making noises on the dance floors of gay bars was common in the 1980s. At Chaps, for example, there was almost always at least one or two men with whistles and one man liked to bring a cowbell to Buddies. There was also a notorious clubber who liked to loudly bleat like a goat. Less noisy, but just as noticeable were the men with flags, one in each hand, who would spin, gyrate, and dance with them.

In addition to the many property owners, LGBTQ visitors rented rooms in Provincetown guest houses, many now owned and operated by gay men or lesbians. Some rented an entire house for a week, stuffing in as many as a dozen people into a rental. The guest houses provided opportunities for LGBTQ people to live and work in Provincetown, income for retired people, and a chance to live openly-gay lives. Often the owners would manage the bookings, check in guests, and socialize while much of the grunt work of cleaning was done by houseboys, usually men in their early twenties but sometimes older or younger. In return for their labor the boys earned a free room, and thus the chance to live in Provincetown for the summer. Beyond direct tourism LGBTQ people populated the town as summer residents, artists, municipal employees, retirees, writers, and colorful characters.

The fishing industry had shrunk to a very small fraction of the local economy compared to LGBTQ tourism, yet Provincetown had a problem adapting to its gay resort image. This led to infrequent, but bigoted, crackdowns. From August 15-17, 1986, for example, there were confrontations between crowds of gay and trans people and the Provincetown police. With the assistance of state troopers, the Provincetown police suddenly decided that the nightly crowds that gathered in front of Spiritus, a popular pizza restaurant with late hours, were a problem and insisted on keeping Commercial St. clear. They said they were responding to complaints from neighbors regarding noise, public urination, and trash, though the crowd was well-behaved. The police charged the crowd and randomly seized people, arresting ten.

Thousands of LGBTQ people had been gathering in front of Spiritus Pizza at 1:00 a.m. since the 1970s. In a town where bars had to close early, it was a place for people to get a bite to eat, talk to friends, and do one last bit of cruising before calling it a night. It also enraged some of the townspeople because the crowds were so big that they blocked the single lane of Commercial St. Even though few, if anyone, needed to drive down the street at that hour (or any other time for that matter), the idea that outsiders, LGBTQ people, were potentially blocking their way infuriated some of the town.

Confronted by this raw homophobia, the LGBTQ community was no longer willing to take harassment quietly. In years gone by, the crowd would have complained among themselves, but complied with the police orders. Instead they grew angry and stood their ground. The straight owner of Spiritus, Paul Yingling, noted the change. "If they're called 'faggot,' they'll jump out of a car. They are willing to fight."[18] When the police ordered the crowd to disperse, it turned on them. The crowd stopped short of violence but would not back down either.

A majority of the town was in favor of the crowd and Town Hall was flooded with complaints, some from owners afraid their businesses would suffer, others from LGBTQ people who felt threatened by the action, and some from people who were straight but pro-gay. The police chief backpedaled by saying that he had only wanted to keep the street clear and that the police had gone beyond his orders when they also cleared the sidewalks. Over and over he repeated, as if in a trance, "[t]he streets have got to be kept open."[19]

Stung by the backlash, the selectmen said it was not anti-gay bias that had led to the clearing of the street, but no one believed them. The next Monday, more than 250 people attended a town meeting on the police actions where they called on charges to be dropped and blasted the selectmen and police for being homophobic. The summer almost over, the police quietly backed down. Slowly the town relaxed and accepted its position as an LGBTQ destination.

As many hoped, when a new council and mayor were sworn in Boston City Hall became more welcoming to LGBTQ people. Flynn thought he was vulnerable to left-wing challengers and quickly reached out to the LGBTQ community, going to the first BLGPA meeting after his swearing-in to sign an executive order protecting lesbian and gay people from discrimination in city hiring and contracts (trans issues were ignored by both BLGPA and the mayor) and working with BLGPA and others to create a resume bank of potential hires. Soon there were many lesbians and gays holding important positions in his administration. He even marched in the Pride parade once, but only for a few blocks and without any publicity.[14]

For many years, the highest LGBTQ elected official in the city was Councilor David Scondras (1946-). Originally from Lowell, Scondras was a math lecturer at Northeastern University when he began to work towards protecting the people of the Fenway from arson, gentrification, and abandonment. He first attracted attention through his work organizing tenants to pressure law enforcement and insurance companies to stop the arson fires threatening the neighborhood; then his work with the Fenway Health Center and other groups made him one of the most respected organizers in the city.

Scondras ran for City Council in 1981, but its format at the time (nine members elected at large) worked against progressive candidates and he narrowly lost. As lines were drawn for new neighborhood-based districts, one new district stretched along the Charles River from Beacon Hill to Mission Hill, District 8. The South End, the most heavily gay neighborhood in the city, was placed into a district with conservative South Boston despite strenuous protests, negating the political voice of the South End. Scondras jumped into the District 8 race but his candidacy was problematic for many in the LGBTQ community. He had city-wide name recognition and the ability to rouse a crowd with his enthusiastic rhetoric, but was considered erratic, too far to the left, and simply too unfriendly by many, though no one was willing to openly confront or oppose him. His opponents in the race were straight and while King's loss to DiCara was a shock, no one was surprised when Scondras failed to secure enough votes to win BLGPA's endorsement. However, the district's many LGBTQ and progressive voters, who were drawn by the excitement of the King campaign to come out to vote, put him on the council.

Re-elected four times, Scondras was a key liberal member of a city council that at times could be very conservative. With a strong mayor, there wasn't a lot that a councilor could accomplish. Scondras' greatest successes were related to housing and LGBTQ issues, sponsoring legislation to promote the construction of affordable housing as well as the city's anti-discrimination ordinance and a measure to set up the city's human rights commission. But at times he seemed more focused on other issues, such as his work against President Reagan's initiatives in Central America, and his inability to work in coalitions with allies both on and off the council eroded his support.

Like other out politicians of the 1980s, Scondras had to overcome often brutal homophobia. Many criticized him for simply kissing his life partner (later husband), Robert Krebs, on the podium of his election party. He received hate mail and death threats, leading many to fear for his safety. In the face of this hatred Scondras was fearless.

He also faced several controversies, the most damaging in his early terms caused by two of his aides, French Wall and Gary Dotterman. While neither was a member of NAMBLA, the two created a non-profit organization to raise money to defend men accused of sex with minors. When the news of this work hit the press, the city council voted to fire them, as technically aides are employed by the council and not by any specific councilor. The two sued and regained their positions only to be let go by Scondras, who announced he was only firing them because he had not been informed of their work prior to its beginning. There was little public support for either the aides or Scondras' handling of the issue. As previously mentioned, only a small group of radicals supported intergenerational sex. Scondras survived the trouble, but from then on he was marked as vulnerable. Only the advantages of being an incumbent saved him, and even that only for a time.

In 1983, Gerry Studds (1937-2006) made history when he became the country's first openly-gay congressman, representing a district that stretched from Provincetown to New Bedford and the southern suburbs of Boston. Studds sounded very much like an old Yankee scion, but in fact he was born on Long Island and moved to Cohasset as a child. His ancestors did include Massachusetts roots (he was named after distant relative Eldridge Gerry, the politician immortalized in the word gerrymander) but his family included relatives in Tennessee and elsewhere.

Studds had some minor sexual contact with other boys while attending boarding school at Groton, but the general unspeakability of sex in the 1950s and the lack of contact with girls afforded by his living situation meant that his sexuality did not stick out. At Yale, Studds had a difficult time "knowing there was something that I wanted and needed, but not understanding it, I hinted, I suggested, I wondered, requested, and very often and in terror of the consequences, I begged it."[20] He was isolated and lonely. After graduating, Studds bounced around jobs—banking, teaching and the State Department (when asked, he said he preferred females to males). He dated women, even proposing marriage to one before breaking off the engagement just before the wedding. Still, he knew he was gay. Now teaching at St. Paul's in New Hampshire, Studds was approaching a nervous breakdown as he fought to keep his sexuality suppressed. "Like every other human being, Studds wanted to have sex and fall in love too, but he couldn't. He felt trapped."[20]

Studds was heavily involved in the anti-war movement. He helped get Senator Eugene McCarthy into the New Hampshire primary and was a delegate for McCarthy at the infamous 1968 Democratic Convention in Chicago before finally running for office himself. Arriving as a new Congressman in 1973, Washington provided Studds with more anonymity than Boston and more freedom to act upon his gay impulses. Yet Studds, now well into his thirties, was still unable to adjust to the exhausting mixture of freedom and repression around him. His attempts to connect with other men were often only made after he had too many drinks and because he was afraid of men his own age, he often felt more at ease with those much younger than him. It was in this context that he met a male page. Teenagers who worked for Congress who assisted with the day-day function of the House and Senate, many pages were away from home for the first time and mostly unsupervised. Page X, as he would be known later, was above the legal age of consent and did not work for Studds or his committee. However, he was underage for consuming alcohol and the relationship was highly inappropriate, though consensual. The two traveled through Europe together and when the page wanted to end the relationship, Studds complied. The two remained friends and Page X would be seated in the second row at Studds' memorial celebration at the Kennedy Library thirty years later. Studds' experiences highlight the problem many men of his generation faced. After decades of hiding their sexuality and repressing every and all potential private connection with another man of their age and circumstances, they had a hard time adjusting to the new world where these types of relationships were now considered the gold standard for LGBTQ people.

In the fall of 1975, Studds met a waiter while out to dinner with some of his staffers. Smitten, he felt he was "thirty-eight going on sixteen."[20] The affair ended after a few months, with the pressure on Studds to keep his love life out of the press contributing to its demise. The short-lived connection contributed to a change in the Congressman's lifestyle over the next several years. He quit smoking, started exercising, and paid more attention to his personal appearance. He continued to be deeply in the closet back in Massachusetts, though anyone who probed would have noticed that he lived with his mother, didn't date women, and was otherwise very private about his non-political life. The press cooperated by not outing him.

Studds purchased a home in Provincetown and began to spend time there. Emboldened by his large re-election margin in 1974, Studds signed on as a supporter of Bella Abzug's lesbian and gay anti-discrimination bill in Congress. This prompted a primary opponent in 1976 whom Studds easily defeated. To a certain extent, this allowed Studds to relax a bit, but he still feared that coming out would cause him to lose his seat.

By late 1979, Studds began to take small steps to come out in Massachusetts.

He met several gay Bostonians, including Brian McNaught, who took him to gay bars including Buddies. Others invited him to dinners and house parties and at times, he would even venture out to sample the nightlife in Provincetown. Still, the public and his voters had no clue he was gay. By 1982, he had had another intense relationship with a man, with whom he then grew apart, and dated another. While he was still very circumspect in his behavior in Washington, he was growing more visible elsewhere. His district driver was a gay man and every LGBTQ activist knew about his sexuality, yet his district still had no idea he was gay.

Then on July 1, 1982, news broke about Congressmen having sexual relationships with pages and the press quickly zeroed in on Studds, who was the subject of a Justice Department inquiry. Quickly, allegations swirled around Capitol Hill of Congressmen snorting cocaine, coercing pages to have sex, and giving preferential treatment to those who responded positively to advances. During the FBI investigation a number of pages stepped forward to say they were harassed. Suddenly, Studd's private bubble popped as reporters staked out his condo in Provincetown and his mother's home in Cohasset while news helicopters flew overhead. Meanwhile, Studds hid at McNaught's Brookline condo. Most of the early accusations against Studds proved false. In the end, both Studds and Representative Philip Crane of Illinois were censured for conduct that was not part of the initial accusations.

The result was a publicly-out Studds, and the question now became what would happen should he chose to run for re-election in 1984. Studds was determined to run again because he felt that he had been treated unfairly and wanted vindication. He said he regretted the relationship with Page X but refused to apologize.

The 1984 Democratic primary proved contentious and sensing a rare opportunity in liberal Massachusetts, a conservative former sheriff jumped into the race. With little thought about the voter's priorities, this opponent's platform rested on the fact that Studds was gay. Yet he had a hard time addressing the issue in a way that didn't reflect poorly on him. In contrast, Studds had the advantage that his constituents liked him and were grateful for his years of service to the district, being particularly helpful to New Bedford's fishing industry. Studds easily won the primary. 1984 was a strong Republican year, with Ronald Reagan defeating Walter Mondale in a landslide and even carrying Massachusetts. Yet Studds was reelected and history was made; an out gay man was elected to Congress.

Page X never wavered in his support for Studds and his contention that the relationship had been consensual. In 1984, he volunteered for Studds' campaign, becoming his driver, and they briefly renewed their relationship. Though the Reagan years were an infuriating time for Democrats and LGBTQ people, for Studds (now open and at peace with himself) they were personally happy. He dated prominent Boston publisher Sacha Alyson for a time and then had other relationships. His congressional colleagues accepted Studds for who he was and he even brought a man to a White House reception and danced with him there (another first).

Studds had vigorous and often homophobic opposition during his next several races, but he always beat them through a combination of hard campaigning and excellent constituent services. However, once Democrats were swept out of power in 1994, he lost his taste for politics and declined to run again. By now, Studds had reconnected with Dean Hara, whom he had met over a decade earlier and they married in 2004. When Studds died suddenly, Hara was denied rights to Studds' pension. He joined the suit that was eventually consolidated in the *United States v. Windsor* decision that secured the right to marry across the country.

Even as the assimilationists changed mainstream politics, radical LGBTQ Boston continued to influence national trends. Becoming focused on personal liberation, Amy Hoffman and Cindy Patton published a lesbian sex-positive magazine for several years in the mid-1980s. Their publication, *Bad Attitude*, was part of radical Boston's contribution to what became known as the lesbian sex wars. Up to this time, lesbian pornography was produced for the pleasure of straight men and it was generally felt that it caused the exploitation and dehumanization of women. At the same time, gay male pornography was seen by gay men as affirming their sexuality with little or no political baggage. Therefore, Hoffman and Patton sought to create a magazine that would celebrate the erotic potential of women with women in a manner that affirmed lesbian sexuality and avoided the problematic lesbian pornography produced for straight men.[21] This was not the only feminist pornographic magazine; at almost the same time a group of women in San Francisco started *On Our Backs*.

Bad Attitude was directly linked to the circle of radical lesbian and gay men working at *GCN*. It was meant to be the female answer to *Fag Rag* and many of its guiding principles parallel the writings of Shively and other Boston radical gay men. The two strains of sexual political theory intertwined and influenced each other and perhaps the only reason that the male writings were published first was that the men had greater economic resources.

The prominent sex-positivity of the magazine challenged many lesbians. At the time, some women said they were lesbians out of protest to mainstream patriarchal society rather than because of same-sex attraction.[22] Many of these women claimed that political action was a higher priority than sex and some radical feminists condemned lesbian sexuality altogether, linking it with the worst abuses by men. Though both had very political backgrounds, Patton and Hoffman aimed to counter this self-censorship of lesbian eroticism by saying that it was just as important for women to own and celebrate their sexuality. *Bad Attitude* was only published for a few years, but along with other lesbian-produced sex magazines it influenced how women thought of themselves.

Studds was not the only gay Massachusetts congressman. The first anti-gay political attacks against Barney Frank came in 1982 during a hard-fought campaign against fellow incumbent Margaret Heckler. Massachusetts lost a seat after the 1980 census and Frank's enemies at the State House, angry because he had consistently voted against the Democratic leadership rather than because he was gay, decided to sacrifice Frank by combining his district with hers. But he ran against Heckler even though the new configuration had mostly been in her old district. As polls tightened, she played up family values and made veiled hints that Frank was gay. However, the effort failed because conservative, working-class voters didn't understand such vague charges and were moving away from Heckler because of economic issues, while liberals thought the charges were either irrelevant, untrue, or unfair. Frank won by twenty points.

Because 1983 was dominated by Studds, Frank again delayed coming out. In 1984, Frank began a quiet two-year relationship with a lawyer he met during the Democratic National Convention in San Francisco. Feeling more confident about his sexuality, Frank came out to friends and colleagues, almost all of whom were supportive. However, Frank's straight political allies were against him making any public announcement because they thought it would ruin his career and jeopardize the precarious liberal agenda of the mid-1980s. Frank was still protected by the *Globe's* policy to not out a person unless there was a scandal or a reason to do so, but by that point Frank's sexuality was the biggest gay secret in Washington.

By 1986, Frank was bolder about his sexuality (at least inside the gay bubble of Provincetown), sometimes surprising LGBTQ residents and visitors. For example, determined to do something about the AIDS epidemic, one man devoted a Saturday afternoon to staffing a table at the Boatslip tea dance to ask people to write their congressman. He vividly recalled, "[o]ne person picked up the letter, and I said, 'Will you please sign this letter to your member of Congress?' And he said, 'I am a member of Congress.' And I looked up and it was Barney Frank."[23] Frank preferred to dance at the Gifford House rather than the A House and went to Herring Cove to sunbathe and look at other men. There was a rule against gays outing each other, and thus his secret was safe.

A disgraced Republican Congressman (Robert Bauman) finally forced Frank out of the closet. Bauman lost his seat after being arrested for soliciting a sixteen-year-old boy and was angered by what he thought was a double standard. He believed he was being unjustly punished for his conservative voting record, and in his exasperation wrote a book that included a passage about an unnamed liberal Democratic Congressman whom everyone knew was gay yet had never publicly admitted his homosexuality nor had been outed. Many immediately connected the passage to Frank.[24]

Frank finally came out in May 1987 via two carefully arranged interviews with the *Globe*. Both reporters, Kay Longcope and John Robinson, were gay and had known about Frank for decades. Their articles were a combination of Frank's comic personal style and a description of how he had long struggled with coming out. His disclosure was well accepted by both his colleagues and his constituents and Frank was reelected with 70 percent of the vote in 1988. He went on to become one of the great liberal leaders of Congress, never facing a serious electoral challenge again even after there was a scandal involving Frank and a male prostitute who lived in his

Washington condo.

Though Boston was changing, the police were still old-school. For generations there had been whispers of corruption regarding Boston's liquor and entertainment establishments that included payoffs to the police in return for protection of bar owners. In 1986, these rumors proved real as the FBI seized personnel records from the police as well as files on hundreds of bars. The probe involved thirty to fifty policemen and 249 establishments with eighteen gay bars part of the investigation. Later it was extended to the fire department which had its own shakedown problem, one that was run independently of the police department.

Many bars hired detail cops; uniformed, off-duty officers that helped deal with potential troublemakers. The practice seemed tightly-regulated with the department setting compensation levels, working conditions, and hours. In reality, bars were forced to pay detail cops beyond the rate established by the city because if they didn't make these under-the-table payments, their licenses were at risk. If they did pay, the police ignored violations of drinking laws and building codes, so the payoffs were a way to avoid getting fined for overcrowding, serving underage drinkers, or other problems. Almost all bars in the city were paying off the police, but gay bars were particular targets of corrupt cops and the ensuing FBI investigation. Evidence showed the corruption was brazen, with the standard payment being $100 per month to the officer controlling that area. Another issue was that paying off one policeman didn't guarantee security, as other cops would sometimes stop in to demand money for themselves.[25] When the FBI began to investigate many bar owners cooperated, feeling they had not been getting their money's worth from the corrupt system.

In 1988, eight policemen went on trial for corruption and Boston gay bar owners provided much of the testimony that convicted them. For example, Norman Chaletzky, owner of the 1270, testified that it was better to have the officers as friends than enemies. He was caught on tape saying "Once they get on the payroll, you can't get them off."[26] It cost him $1,000 per year but while he was making payments, the 1270 was never cited for any violations. Evidence included videotapes of the police taking cash from Chaletzky and his partner, Joe McGowan.

The man who made the cases possible was the owner of the Loft, D'Onofeo, who got his revenge on the policemen who kept raiding his bar by wearing a wire so that the FBI could gather evidence on McGowan. The two had been so close that whenever D'Onofeo was arrested during one of the Loft raids, McGowan would bail him out. Despite their friendship, he caught McGowan on tape admitting he was bribing the police. The FBI used these tapes to get McGowan to testify and the eight officers were convicted and sent to prison. The prosecutions ushered in a new era of freedom for bar owners. In the years from 1986 to 2001 when Brian Gokey owned Luxor in Bay Village, for example, he was never shaken down by the police.[27]

Though many straight Massachusetts Democrats were seen as liberal on LGBTQ issues, their acceptance could quickly dissipate. In one of the worst post-Stonewall examples of anti-gay government action in the state, Governor Michael Dukakis went after the rights of LGBTQ people to become foster parents. In doing so, he struck at the very idea that they were fit to have families, raise children, or have the same basic rights that straight people had. It was homophobia at its worst, with the issue provoked by a stray *Globe* article on foster parents colliding with Dukakis's political ambitions.

11.2 Foster Equality Demonstration

Don Babets and David Jean had been a couple for years and both were well-known and respected activists. They were noted for their easy going kindness and hard work as well as their toughness under pressure. In early 1984, they decided they wanted to become foster parents out of concern for the large number of children languishing in inappropriate housing situations. Living in Roxbury, they were at a time and place in their lives where they thought about having children of their own but were faced with the difficult logistics of adoption or surrogate childbearing.

Motivated by the belief that they were helping at-risk children in the foster care system, they applied to the Massachusetts Department of Social Services (DSS) to be foster parents. The first sign that something was wrong was that it took several months to receive the approval that was usually granted in a few weeks. However, in the professional opinions of the state's child welfare workers, the men were fit to be foster parents. After they were certified, they had two young boys placed in their home in April. The boy's mother approved of the placement and there were no initial problems.

That changed when a *Globe* reporter, acting on a tip by a neighbor in what may have been the worst case of anti-LGBTQ bias in the paper since it had unquestionably run articles on the Revere case five years earlier, published a story on May 8, 1984 about the two men and their foster children. The story strongly implied that the neighbors were concerned with the children's welfare, though most of the comments were from one man who later said he was misquoted. Regardless, the issue blew up. The couple had not wanted the story to run, afraid they would have the children taken away from them, but the reporter thought that wasn't likely. For a brief moment the reporter seemed correct. On the morning of the story, the DSS Commissioner personally assured Babets and Jean that the children would not be moved.

However, now that the *Globe* had created neighborhood opposition where none had existed, the state administration panicked. That afternoon, faced with an uproar, the children were taken away as Dukakis said he had been unaware that gay men were allowed to be foster parents. The next week, the Massachusetts House of Representatives passed a resolution against gay foster parents and with the exception of a few loyal politicians, most of the straight liberal establishment abandoned LGBTQ people. Proposed gay-rights legislation was declared dead that year and almost no straight person was willing to speak out that gay people could be respectable parents.

Pushing the anti-LGBTQ bigotry further, the state hastily published new placement guidelines that made it virtually impossible for same-sex couples to be foster parents (as well as making it very difficult for single people). Furthermore, the state put in a question in its foster care application form asking applicants if they were gay. Falsely claiming that the policy had been developed based on consultation with child-welfare experts, it was now the official policy of the Commonwealth of Massachusetts that LGBTQ people were not fit to be parents. It was the children in the foster care system who were most harmed by this new policy that was implemented a time when the state estimated that there was an immediate need for 25 percent more slots in the system, including placements for 750 children in inappropriate or emergency situations.[28]

The LGBTQ community, whether they were interested in being parents or not, rallied around this direct attack, pressuring the state for the next several years. A special task force was formed to organize rallies and public support while the Alliance and the Massachusetts Gay and Lesbian Political Caucus (known as the Caucus) worked to have voters contact their state representatives and senators to express their opposition to the new policy. GLAD, acting on behalf of Jean and Babets, sued the state and the full extent of the lack of valid child-welfare rationale for the policy became clear when documents released as part of the discovery process leading up to a trial showed that DSS was against prohibiting LGBTQ people from being foster parents. In fact, as Priscilla Golding (who worked at DSS at the time) recalled, there was widespread anger in the office regarding the new policy. There were many LGBTQ people working for DSS who, along with their straight colleagues, knew there was no valid reason that the children should have been taken from Jean and Babets.[29]

Furthermore, the Commonwealth went on to use the incident as an excuse to attack the civil liberties of all LGBTQ people in the state. Later, the State Police admitted it infiltrated meetings of the Caucus, the Alliance, and other organizations using the excuse they had to monitor these organizations because of the potential for violence in protest of the policy.[30] In their jaundiced eyes, all LGBTQ people were dangerous radicals capable of criminal activity despite the fact that in hundreds of demonstrations, meetings, and other events over the years of the controversy, there was not a single incident of law breaking, except perhaps by the police who were illegally surveilling the groups and individuals involved.

After Dukakis left office, the state settled with Babets and Jean and LGBTQ people were again allowed to be foster parents. Dukakis never apologized for his actions, though his Secretary of Health and Human Services, Phillip Johnson, later admitted the policy was wrong. "Although it was a very difficult political situation, the state should have ignored the ruckus, because the truth is, we know very well that gays and lesbians can be and usually are terrific parents," he said. "Those of us involved feel very bad about how it played out."[31]

Ironically, just as the Revere raids had an important legacy in that GLAD was founded in reaction to the anti-gay bigotry of District Attorney Byrne, so did the foster care scandal ultimately strengthen the community. The controversy created the working coalition that would push for and protect LGBTQ rights in Massachusetts over the next several decades. LGBTQ political organizations would lobby legislators and create a working group of influential straight, religious, business, and other institutions that added their weight to pro-LGBTQ rights; GLAD was the legal organization dealing with the courts, while the community itself raised money, attended rallies, provided human faces to the media, and energized multiyear struggles to advance their rights. After the foster care controversy, the tools and experience were in place to pass the statewide anti-discrimination law in 1989, defeat the anti-same-sex marriage constitutional amendment in 2007, and oppose the anti-trans rights referendum in 2018. Once again, LGBTQ people learned from adversity.

Chapter 12

Tears, Rage, Victories, Defeats

S IX YEARS INTO the epidemic and despite defiance, prayers, and hand-holding, people were dying of AIDS in ever increasing numbers. There was no cure and no therapy that could extend the lives of the sick. At times the fear, grief, and fury were so great it was hard to breathe. In New York City, anger over complacency in the gay community, the resistance of government on all levels to make AIDS a priority, and a lack of support for research and treatment prompted activists to start ACT UP, the AIDS Coalition to Unleash Power, in early 1987. Soon after, as one Boston man remembered, in "the relative quiet of the upstairs video lounge at Luxor. And there over a beer or two on a cold winter night, without any of us having met or ever heard of Larry Kramer, we held the first meeting of ACT UP Boston and planned the first demonstration."[1]

Boston's chapter of ACT UP formally incorporated in 1988 with its official address at the Lesbian and Gay Service Center at 338 Newbery St. Its Articles of Incorporation read "ACT UP/Boston is a coalition of outraged individuals united to bring public, scientific, and religious leaders into an earnest, unbigoted, search for a cure for Acquired Immunodeficiency Syndrome." Soon, the Boston LGBTQ community was flooded with ACT UP posters, buttons, and pamphlets.

With its large number of labs, pharmaceutical companies, and universities, Boston was a major center of medical research and one of the targets of ACT UP was the methods with which research was being conducted. Traditional drug research relies on double-blind protocols; half the patients in a study received treatment, half placebos, with neither doctors nor patients aware of who was receiving treatment and who was not. In this way, results were less likely to be biased by outside factors. With AIDS, this type of study was immoral because it denied drugs to the dying. The protocols also didn't work; it was easy to see who was surviving and who was declining. In addition, researchers often wanted patients who were still healthy and hadn't developed the opportunistic infections and cancers that would eventually kill them. Thus, those most in need of help were being systematically excluded from drug trials. Furthermore, desperate patients could not take the chance that they would end up in the placebo arm of a study as that would mean suffering and death, so researchers could not recruit patients. Despite these problems, researchers clung to their inappropriate methods. Access to experimental drugs, proclaimed ACT UP and AIDS patients, was a basic human right and denying them (and therefore ensuring that someone died) was murder. To end these types of trials ACT UP began to regularly stage protests at Harvard Medical School with the largest demonstration on September 27, 1988.

Much of ACT UP's anger was directed against the Massachusetts General Hospital (MGH) because of the hospital's relatively poor treatment of AIDS patients. Most indigent AIDS patients were treated at BCH, while those with resources tended to go to the Deaconess Hospital because of its partnership with the Fenway Health Center. Unfortunately, the AIDS ward at the Deaconess grew so crowded that the hospital would periodically stop admitting new patients and like most public hospitals, BCH was chronically underfunded and overcrowded. Both institutions for the most part offered state of the art medical care, though for the first fifteen years of the epidemic this could do little more than prolong life for a few months and perhaps alleviate just a fraction of the suffering. Still both BCH and Deaconess Hospital treated patients with compassion and respect.

12-1 ACT UP Demonstation

Much of the frustration centered on securing prophylactic treatment for sufferers of Pneumocystis carinii pneumonia. Reports out of San Francisco strongly suggested that regular treatment with aerosolized pentamidine prevented recurrences of the disease, which was often fatal for AIDS patients who had a second or third bout. But of the 400 people living with AIDS in the Boston area in 1988, only two to three dozen were getting the drug even though estimates suggested that up to 70 percent of late stage AIDS patients needed it. The Fenway and the Deaconess were trying to provide the medication, but a national shortage was slowing their response. As a result, people with AIDS were angry and desperate. "People are dying because of red tape," charged Lenny Malone, chairman of the Boston People with AIDS Coalition.[2]

At MGH, however, one of the best hospitals in the world and therefore a place that should have been providing the most up-to-date AIDS care, the hospital declined to even try to get aerosolized pentamidine for patients because it was waiting for additional proof that it worked. ACT UP mobilized a series of actions, but only after the hospital repeatedly refused to meet with ACT UP representatives regarding pentamidine and other issues. In one of their largest demonstrations, they staged a "die-in" (members lay on the floor, representing patients whose deaths were hastened by MGH policies) in the hospital lobby.

Another demonstration took place at the Cathedral of the Holy Cross on May 22, 1988, to protest Cardinal Bernard Law's opposition to sex education, condom use, and needle exchanges. This was one of the first of what would be almost weekly protests against the Cardinal that would continue through the early 2000s as victims of the local Catholic sexual abuse crisis challenged the church's response to that issue as well. As ACT UP became more vocal opposing Catholic policies, these protests at the Cathedral grew more controversial. For the next twenty years, conservative Catholics would accuse almost every Boston LGBTQ activist of having been at the May 22 protest.

Still another demonstration was a large rally in front of the Kennedy Federal Office Building on June 27, 1988, to protest the federal government's slow and inadequate response to the AIDS crisis. That same year on December 19, a demonstration at John Hancock Insurance Company demanded it cover aerosolized pentamidine. Seven people were arrested at this protest. Denise McWilliams of GLAD offered to find legal help for their cases, showing how the Boston ACT UP chapter was able to connect with resources throughout the community. The protestors also had the support of most LGBTQ people. These and other demonstrations reflected the fear, anger, and frustration of the LGBTQ community that there was no real treatment for the disease. While pentamidine might delay additional bouts of pneumonia, it did not stop the ultimate march towards death and while there was one approved treatment (AZT), it had numerous side effect (nausea, vomiting, headache, dizziness, fatigue, weakness and muscle pain) and the virus soon proved resistant. People kept dying and as mourners wiped away their tears after yet another funeral, rage grew alongside grief.

Sometimes desperation resulted in advocates and protestors pushing for drugs that in retrospect were not adequate solutions. Many in ACT UP Boston wanted access, drug trials, and approvals for Dextran Sulfate and Peptide T, drugs that were rumored to be helpful but were ultimately found to be worthless. Similarly, sometimes activists pushed back against measures that seemed to be wrong, but ultimately proved extremely valuable. For example, many opposed a BCH program that treated babies whose mothers were HIV positive with AZT. Given the often horrific side effects (caused in part by dosing regimens that were far too high) and short term effectiveness of AZT in adults, as well as the problematic and often cavalier drug treatments that some doctors were offering AIDS patients, to oppose this new protocol seemed rational at the time. In the end, however, giving newborns a short treatment of moderate doses of AZT was one of the best ways of preventing maternal-to-child transmission of the virus. Again, these protests reflected the widespread anguish and the lack of trust in medicine at the time.

Demonstrators, providers, patients, researchers, and advocates worked together in Boston to fight the epidemic. ACT UP was free to take direct action, leaving the others to look reasonable as they pressed for identical demands. Together they convinced insurance companies to provide funding for treatments, helped open up research programs to community input, and worked with patients to access what assistance was available. It was this kind of cooperation that resulted in the development of the innovative Community Research Initiative and laid the groundwork for the very rapid adoption of Highly Active Anti-Retroviral Therapy (HAART)–the practice of giving patients three or more drugs at a time–that would eventually save millions of lives. Working with the city, this coalition of activists and insiders created an AIDS housing initiative so that the disease would not result in homelessness (though the process of setting up this program included several boisterous demonstrations inside City Hall), and they used funds from the state to create educational campaigns to try to keep new infections from occurring. In another example of how the city was not perceived as an enemy, ACT UP's first anniversary open house was held in the Piemonte Room at City Hall.

The cooperation between LGBTQ activists and city officials continued under Mayor Flynn. Ann Maguire, who would hold many positions at City Hall under his administration, had the Mayor's ear and she used her influence to help people with AIDS. Flynn, despite his conservative Catholic politics, proved to be personally empathetic to the community and kept a range of formal and informal channels of cooperation open. The many out people who worked at City Hall helped as well so that Bostonians were able to devote energy and resources to fight the epidemic, not each other. Similarly, Mayor Thomas Menino had prominent LGBTQ people in his administration who had close contact with the community, including Maguire, now promoted to Chief of Staff. These connections proved priceless during the epidemic.

While some fought to stay alive, others examined how they lived. In the 1980s, Boston's LGBTQ population began to move out of the traditional strongholds of central Boston and Cambridge. Some moved to Dorchester, particularly the Jones Hill area, to take advantage of a new openness to LGBTQ households in that neighborhood. While not as gay as the South End or as lesbian as Jamaica Plain, the area was sought out for its cheaper housing, open space, and its quiet streets. One man said that in Dorchester he found "everything the South End seemed to lack. White picket fences. Open space. Space. Most of all, what he considered affordable housing stock, brightly painted Victorian-era homes on expansive manicured lawns."[3] The newcomers were well-received. One Irish bar owner, for example, boasted that twenty percent of his customers were gay or lesbian, while old timers saw gays and lesbians as just one more group settling in the neighborhood.

Some LGBTQ people were leaving the city altogether, though suburban conditions were more difficult because of the lack of ways to connect to others. "When you move out here, you can't exactly look in the phone book under G for Gay," said one young woman who had recently moved to Salem to take a teaching job but didn't know how to meet other LGBTQ people until she discovered a group called the North Shore Gay and Lesbian Alliance. There were other problems. "In Boston where people are exposed to much more, I feel free to walk arm in arm with a friend. If I did it here, I'd take my life in my hands," said a man who worked in Bridgewater and founded a rap-group for South Shore gays.[4]

The suburbs had their allure, however. They were cheaper and quieter. Real estate prices in the city were in a long-term boom and increasing faster than incomes, making housing unaffordable to many in core neighborhoods. In addition, many LGBTQ people wanted to get away from the nightlife as they felt too old for the bars while still others were fed up with the superficial aspects of bar culture. Some were raising families and simply wanted to settle down. "Many in their 30s and 40s say they traded in the sexually tense atmosphere of some Boston bars years ago for more low-key, stay-at-home recreation. Others said they had never enjoyed bar-hopping in the first place, and, like many suburbanites, spend much of their leisure time in outdoors activities–but ones organized by groups of gays, from volleyball tournaments at the beach to hiking trips in the mountains of New Hampshire." Boston's core neighborhoods and Cambridge were still central to the community, but it was spreading out.

The AIDS epidemic hit so hard and deep in an era when there were many political reversals that at times it was easy for many to be overwhelmed by despair and depression. But just when it seemed that the disease might win, two men rallied the community with grace, dignity, humor, and fashion. Known as the Hat Sisters, John Michael Gray and Tim O'Connor provided hope and reassurance in the dark days before new therapies hit the market. They continued working to rally the LGBTQ community around AIDS, legal rights, and other issues after that point, and were always present during the political battles in the decades that followed. In the years between their meeting in 1984 and Gray's death in 2016, the couple were known for their fabulous outfits and elaborate hats. They dressed stylishly and identically, but never showed up wearing an ensemble they had worn before. Together they made every event they went to a special occasion and they promoted as many causes as they could. They sparkled at more AIDS fundraisers than anyone could count, and their charitable support included aiding the homeless, LGBTQ rights, music, and the arts, as well as many other non-profits organizations in Boston and Provincetown. Therefore it was not surprising how beloved they were by the community. On summer afternoons, their car (with Hat Sister vanity plates) would pull up in front of the Boatslip and when they strutted onto the deck in their glittering dresses and hats, tea dance would go wild.

One of the saddest aspects of Gray's memorial service was that he wasn't present to join in its joy, as he loved a good party. Gray could work a room and make people smile. The Arlington Street Church was filled to standing room only as the program included hymns, a Broadway showtune singalong, and reminisces that ranged from the times they saved an agency facing financial ruin through their tireless fundraising to Gray's promotion of arts education in the Newton schools to the wild days of the 1980s when so many people had so much fun.

The couple was close friends with Mayor Menino and his wife, Angela (both of whom attended their wedding), and no Pride parade was complete without the four of them together and waving at the cheering crowds. The Hat Sisters were even immortalized in a nationally syndicated comic strip produced by Eric Orner. They symbolized the spirited resistance of Boston's LGBTQ community during some of its most tragic days.

The 1980s and 1990s were a time when LGBTQ cultural, athletic, and social institutions blossomed and proliferated. There were hiking groups, bowling leagues, choruses, theatre companies, softball leagues, hockey teams, neighborhood potluck associations, and even a country western line dancing group. There was a network of local political activists stretching across almost every core community and impromptu groups putting on dances and fundraisers for a variety of causes, some of which linked Boston and Provincetown together. Some wealthier same-sex couples' names began to appear as couples in donor lists in the back of programs of major cultural institutions.

How out these groups were to mainstream society varied. Some were proudly LGBTQ. The Boston Gay Men's Chorus left little to speculation with its title, though some members had to keep their names out of its programs in its early years. Other organizations were less open but eventually became known for their LGBTQ focus, despite the fact that they carried official, more cautious names that dated from their founding. Over time, many of the leaders and professionals associated with LGBTQ groups used their growing experience to work for mainstream institutions.

Boston also developed a large number of LGBTQ sports teams. Sometimes they played in straight leagues, but other times there were enough participants to enable an all-LGBTQ league to form. The sports ranged from hockey and football to soccer, swimming, and running. In one example of how society was becoming more accepting, LGBTQ teams in straight leagues rarely encountered homophobia. Lenny Poussard, for example, played on gay hockey teams for over twenty years against countless straight opponents and could only recount one anti-gay slur.[5] Though slurs and other anti-LGBTQ actions were still common in school sports, adults were more welcoming.

At first it seemed that the wave of outrage regarding AIDS would pass Provincetown by and even as late as July 1988, the town was peaceful. The Pride march that month featured a candlelight procession and the Boatslip hosted a fundraiser for the town rescue squad that raised over $5,000. AIDS patient Patrick Grace spoke at the parade. "In the midst of a crisis, we are pulling together and we are living love."[6]

Then ACT UP staged a die-in at the health clinic in Provincetown in August to protest the lack of aerosolized pentamidine, not knowing that the clinic was administering the drug to patients quietly as they were not licensed to do so. One clinic worker remembered, "[o]ur administrator didn't want to go public with this information until the Department of Public Health okayed it. In sub rosa fashion, however, we were making sure no one was going to die of Pneumocystis."[7] But there was no way the clinic could state on the record that it was breaking the law, so the ill feelings continued. The next summer, ACT UP held another protest march down Commercial St. to take the town to task for not doing enough to combat AIDS. Providers were dismayed by the protests but did not break their silence.

For a while, there was a split as many people with AIDS felt that the Provincetown AIDS Support Group (PASG) was too medical and process oriented. These men created a new organization because they wanted more control over their lives and treatment decisions. Eventually the two organizations again grew close and the Provincetown Positive People With AIDS Coalition shared office space with PASG.

In the years after the disease was first identified, AIDS's impact on the LGBTQ community continued to evolve. Early on, there were noticeable attitude shifts among younger men who came of age after the disease was killing people. For middle-class cisgender gay men born after 1955, AIDS had a large impact on their social lives. Reaching the age of peak sexual activity as the AIDS epidemic was roaring, they had different attitudes toward sex than older men ever experienced. There was now danger in casual sex; relationships and safe sex were important, while one-night stands and sex were approached cautiously. Many young gay men wanted monogamy, a concept often openly scoffed at by older radicals.

Outside these middle-class safe zones was a different matter. Young working-class men as well people of color were still more likely to be isolated and faced pressures that worked against stable, safe relationships. Almost all teenagers were also at increased risk. Coming out in high school was still difficult and potentially dangerous: "[f]ear and furtiveness have often reduced youthful encounters to quick sex."[8] Living at home, and thus with family made same-sex dating difficult and for those unable to come out, the risks continued.

There are no surveys or data on how LGBTQ relationships changed because of AIDS, but many feel that the epidemic brought an end to what had been a golden age of promiscuity and contributed to new trends of settling down. In part this was just all a matter of stereotypes; LGBTQ people had been in couples for centuries. But many argue that monogamous couples became more prevalent in the 1990s.

Same-sex dating could be intense, yet so discreet as to be invisible to the straight world around it. For example, when *Bay Windows* columnist David Valdes met Jason Greenwood in 1993 their first several months of dating included long dinners at cheap restaurants in the Back Bay, strolls along Newbury St., and discreetly holding hands at jazz concerts. "It was lightly snowing when, quietly, he kissed my head. Not my lips or cheek—that would have been too direct—just the top of my head. And I, the one who had craved this so long? I bolted away like a cow that has backed into an electric fence, then fled into the building," remembered Valdes.[9] The two men were grad students and gay activists at the time and out to their families.

On the other hand, romance came easy to many people and at times during the years around 1990, it seemed that love affairs were seizing the hearts of LGBTQ people everywhere in the city. Veteran lesbian activists Priscilla Golding and Barbara

Burg fondly remember their courtship which involved movies, baking, and a cuddly cat named Max. Neither had grown up thinking they would settle down with one partner for life, but after more than two decades together, they have a contentment that permeates their lives.[10]

Many relationships endured and deepened, only to hit tremendous social and legal walls. Signing a lease, buying a car or house, trying to provide health insurance to a partner, even figuring out how to introduce the person they've spent decades with, were all difficult. LGBTQ relationships were not legally recognized, and thus disaster was always a close possibility. A sudden death could leave the survivor destitute and homeless, and there were no rights to see the love of one's life at the hospital if they were ill. Financial protections were non-existent.

Despite a city anti-discrimination ordinance, LGBTQ people still faced tremendous prejudices that continued to warp their daily existence in part because they were often so unpredictable. Sometimes it seemed there was no prejudice and life was easy. Then suddenly, anti-LGBTQ bigotry jumped out and a person, couple, or family was refused housing, someone was fired, or a group was thrown out of a restaurant. In addition, the threat of violence loomed ever near. Then, just as suddenly, acceptance reasserted itself. As early as the 1980s, many large Boston companies became supportive of their LGBTQ employees. Slowly, the major banks, law firms, and other institutions in the city earned reputations as safe places to work. For the most part this was an informal process, one that depended on internal company policies that had no force of law behind them. Still, this represented progress from decades gone by when LGBTQ people were almost unanimously in the closet. Enough discrimination still existed in employment, housing, and other situations that LGBTQ people were always on edge and knew that if discrimination happened, there would be no recourse. A particular exception to the rising acceptance was some of the city's many religious institutions, which continued to openly discriminate against LGBTQ people. For example, after working for seven years at the *Christian Science Monitor*, reporter Christine Madsen was fired for being a lesbian in 1982. The Church declared that no open LGBTQ person could be an employee, teacher, or practitioner. The paper also placed a memo in her employment file stating, "[t]his employee is not recommended for rehire unless radical change in views on homosexuality takes place."[11] Though Madsen sued, the courts ruled she had no right to keep her job. The need for legal protections remained acute.

Over time, the Massachusetts courts put into some protections for LGBTQ people. For example, the SJC affirmed the right of lesbians to have custody of their children in a 1980 divorce case. This encouraged women to use new reproductive technologies to become mothers in the decades afterwards, increasing the number of children who needed legal recognition of their parents' same-sex relationship. Despite these small advances, however, there was still need for an anti-discrimination law.

It took seventeen years of trying, but the Massachusetts legislature finally approved a gay rights bill on November 7, 1989, that included protections for lesbian and gay people in employment, housing, credit, and public accommodation. When it was passed, Massachusetts was only the second state to have an anti-discrimination law (Wisconsin being the first), though eleven states and eighty cities had executive orders.

Part of the delay in passing rights legislation was that all bills needed to clear three votes in both chambers to be enacted with the major hurdle being the Committee on Bills in the Third Reading in each chamber. The official purpose of these committees was to check legislation for legal accuracy and compliance with the state constitution, but in practice they were used to stop or delay bills unpopular with the legislative leadership or influential law makers. To make passing a law even more difficult, bills do not carry over from one legislative term to the next; they die at midnight on the last day of that term. After that, the process has to start from the beginning.

By the mid-1980s, a majority of legislators in both houses were in favor of the anti-discrimination bill, so anti-gay law makers used parliamentary maneuvers, including killing it in the Third Reading, to stop it from reaching the governor's desk for signature. The only good to come of these efforts was that it taught LGBTQ advocates how to use legislative rules to stop measures they opposed, a lesson they relied on when anti-LGBTQ people tried to stop civil unions and same-sex marriage after 2000.

The key group that advanced rights at the State House was the Massachusetts Gay and Lesbian Political Caucus. Founded in 1973 during the first push for the anti-discrimination bill, the Caucus relentlessly lobbied the legislature to pass this and other important legislation. The Caucus had started as a small group meeting at Somewhere Else that included Martha Jones, Steven Tierney, Ann Maguire, Joe Martin, and others. They worked closely with State Representative Barbara Gray of Framingham and Elaine Noble, but it was Barney Frank who encouraged them to focus on lobbying the legislature. In the early years the Caucus had no money and most of its members were in low-paying jobs; Tierney was working at Boston University as a resident hall director for $11,500 a year, for example. When the Caucus put out a mailing, members had to dip into their own pockets in order to pay for it. Then Harry Collings stepped in to raise money and used his extensive rolodex to throw an annual party to fund the Caucus's budget.[12] Collings would use this experience to raise money for the Fenway and other groups during the AIDS years and Mayor Menino appointed him to be head of the Boston Redevelopment Authority. During most of the 1980s, there were no out LGBTQ legislators and thus the Caucus was forced to reach out to straight allies on Beacon Hill and elsewhere to keep the legislation alive. Though the effort suffered multiple setbacks, the Caucus slowly gained support and improved its effectiveness.

A pivotal move to advance the anti-discrimination bill had come when the Caucus hired the polished lesbian and brilliant political tactician Arline Isaacson as its lobbyist in 1983, though the money that the Caucus paid her never came close to compensating her for the countless hours she put in. A seasoned lobbyist for the Massachusetts Teachers Association who already knew many people on Beacon Hill, she led the fight for LGBTQ rights at the State House for the next several decades. Without her skills, contacts, and sacrifice, the legislative victories to come might never have happened.

Though it offended the radicals, the key to the Caucus's assimilationist strategy was convincing legislators that LGBTQ people were just like straight people. Isaacson and other advocates never threatened; they quietly requested support for bills and they avoided coverage in the mainstream press as they sought to cultivate personal relationships with lawmakers. The Caucus relied heavily on Mel King and his successor from his South End district, Byron Rushing, to move its agenda forward. Royal Bolling, the only African-American state senator, also was very important as the Caucus built a coalition to support the bill. This political alliance included women's groups, welfare rights groups, and other progressives. The coalition was put to good use in the battle to pass legislation for domestic partner benefits, protect same-sex marriage, and approve trans rights.

Another important coalition consisted of religious institutions that came together as key allies of the LGBTQ community. The state still had some of the strongest Unitarian and Congregationalist churches in the country and these were almost unanimous in their support for LGBTQ issues. They were joined by Reform Jewish congregations and other left-leaning institutions to create solid support among their clergy. At the same time, Massachusetts had few evangelical and conservative-Christian churches, leaving the powerful Catholic Church as the only religious opposition to LGBTQ rights in the state. This created a unique situation: the preponderance of religious leaders was pro-LGBTQ and could be relied upon to add their moral force to the conflicts ahead.

One very influential congregation that provided political support and welcomed LGBTQ people to its services was Temple Israel. Located on the Riverway, it was the largest Jewish synagogue in the city and a prominent member of the Reform Jewish movement. An LGBTQ group, Am Tikva, had been holding Shabbat and holiday services for LGBTQ Jews since 1976. But many people wanted the community provided by a large mainstream congregation and Jewish LGBTQ people with children needed access to religious schools and other services. Some LGBTQ people were already members of Temple Israel but the clergy and temple leadership wanted to do more. They invited several current members as well as outside LGBTQ people to a meeting to ask what it would take to persuade others to join the congregation. The pivotal suggestion was to allow same-sex couples to join as families, recognizing their relationships long before there was legal marriage. Through this and other efforts, Temple Israel became known for its LGBTQ participation and even began holding workshops for other congregations wanting to be more open.[10]

Despite the heroic work by the Caucus, Isaacson, supportive religious institutions, and others, the battle to pass the anti-discrimination bill was a long and difficult fight. When they weren't openly hostile, opponents denied that there was discrimination against gay and lesbian people and asserted that current laws were sufficient to protect them. At the same time, they argued that homosexuality was inherently wrong and immoral and thus the state should do nothing to promote it. At times the homophobia was intense. In 1983, for example, one legislator declared, "[t]he worst thing the state ever did was to let the gays out of the closet. The only thing they've ever offered to culture is AIDS and herpes."[13] Yet 1983 represented a milestone in that it was the first time the Senate passed the anti-discrimination bill. It subsequently died in the House.

In 1984, there were twenty votes in favor of the bill in the forty-member Senate, but most of these supporters were not in leadership positions. Therefore, advocates couldn't prevent opponents from stopping the bill by using the parliamentary maneuver of asking the SJC for a review—a procedure established by the state constitution. By the time the court handed down its opinion that the bill was indeed constitutional, the year was almost over and Senate President William Bulger, the brother of the infamous (and former male hustler) Whitey Bulger, was absent. There would be no action on the bill that year. Again, the near-success flushed out homophobic comments; at least two senators were " screaming faggot and dyke all over the place and saying the most ridiculous things" on the floor of the Senate.[14]

In 1985 the bill was defeated because of the uproar caused by the gay foster parent controversy as well hysteria over the growing AIDS epidemic. As before, opponents demonstrated that they were motivated by prejudice as the notoriously anti-gay House Speaker, Thomas McGee, did his best to defeat any and all pro-LGBTQ legislation. Later in 1985, George Keverian built a coalition of progressive representatives that included the sponsors of the bill. They led a revolt that drove McGee out of the speakership. Keverian and his new leadership team were pro-LGBTQ, but they didn't assume office in time to influence the 1985 vote.

The House passed the bill in 1986, shifting the effort to the Senate where the legislation again bogged down. It took six months to even bring it up for first consideration but the bill was approved on a 20 to 15 vote. Opponents had to use procedural maneuvers to stop it, adding dozens of amendments that each forced a new twenty-four hour delay. On December 31, the bill died in the Committee of the Third Reading of the Senate as the legislative term came to an end without it coming up for its third vote.

In the next session, it seemed that the bill would again fail to come to a vote, but this time the Caucus was quietly working to ensure that it would not be defeated by manipulating the rules. As the weather turned cooler, there was much angst and an expectation of another defeat. But because of Isaacson's lobbying, Bulger finally decided not to squash the bill and at last prohibited opponents from filing amendments or using the Committee of the Third Reading to kill it. The bill easily passed.

Governor Dukakis signed the bill in front of 200 people at the State House.

This was followed by a public signing at Faneuil Hall with a thousand people watching. The spectacle was capped by a jubilant party at the Boston Opera House with over two thousand cheering, dancing, and jumping celebrants. Tierney remembered that "[p]eople were on top of the furniture and running up and down the lobby's ornate stairs" as they celebrated.[15] Once the rights bill was passed, opponents vowed to put the new law to a referendum; however, the bill had been drafted to include an exemption for religious institutions and the Massachusetts constitution prohibits referendums on religious issues, so the entire bill was off-limits regarding a vote. There was nothing opponents could do to overturn the law and it remains in effect today.

Despite AIDS and the dispersal of LGBTQ people outside the city, nightlife continued though it certainly evolved as bars began to move out of Back Bay. The most popular venue for young gay men, Buddies, was destroyed by fire. Though it was crowded when the fire broke out in a first-floor bakery, no one was injured in the orderly evacuation of the basement nightclub. Unfortunately, some checked their keys with their coats and couldn't retrieve them for over a week. Buddies would long be mourned. "Some years later a queen wrote an article in the local gay paper saying that if you were gay in Boston in 1985, you'll always remember where you were at the moment you heard that Buddies burned, like our parents used to tell us about Kennedy's assassination."[16] Buddies reopened on Kneeland St. and eventually changed its name to Buzz. Chaps was displaced by a condominium project and moved to Warrenton St. in the Theater District, where it remained popular for another decade.

By 1990, the South End and Bay Village combined to be the center of LGBTQ nightlife. Though Playland was still open, it was mostly ignored, but Jacques and Napoleon's continued to attract large numbers of customers, securely anchoring the eastern end of the area. Buzz and Chaps moved the action into the Theatre District while Club Café, Luxor/Mario/Jock's (the venue had three bars), Fritz, and the Eagle represented the western edge of this group of bars. Club Café was part of a large complex that included a disco, a cabaret room, a restaurant, and a health club downstairs that was owned by the same group. Jock's and Fritz were sports bars with large numbers of televisions showing competitions that ranged from ice dancing to football. Club Café and Luxor were video bars, featuring elaborate music videos and comedy clips.

Further out, the Ramrod expanded to include Machine (a disco) while the 1270 began to decline, changing its name to Quest before finally closing. Cambridge had the Paradise near MIT and Campus-Manray and Marquee (a women's bar) in Central Square. In the suburbs were Fran's and the Randolph Country Club, both still popular decades after they first opened.

For the most part, there were few arrests of gay men in this time period, at least in Boston itself, and it hadn't been a crime to cross dress in public for decades. But there were still periodic crackdowns in suburban cruising areas; the State Police made it very clear that arresting men at rest stops along highways in Massachusetts was a priority. For example, using undercover decoys they arrested ten men in Norwell in June 1989. Despite immediate protests, the police announced they would tow unoccupied cars and place decoys at rest stops again if cruising did not stop. GLAD stepped in and most charges were dismissed if the men appealed, but the intermittent harassment continued.

With private sexual relations legal as was soliciting them, there was little risk of arrest. However, the police still shut two private clubs. In 1990, the Thunderhead Club (a private S&M group on Dorchester Ave.) was raided. The charges included prostitution (which was really charging a $5 cover for food and refreshments) and possessing dangerous weapons (S&M toys). All charges were eventually dropped, but the club was disbanded.

12.2 The Back Bay Fens in 2018

In 1992, a party of the Boston Jacks, a safe sex group, was raided in the South End. Again, asking for money at the door was cited as evidence of prostitution and again, charges were eventually dropped. There were debates as to whether these raids were signs of homophobia or were instigated because the events were in residential neighborhoods. In any case, few dared open their homes to large sex parties that charged for entry and thus they were no more.

The Fens, with its secluded paths in the reeds, suffered from periodic vicious attacks on gay men. The violence escalated in 1989 and the police put decoys in the park that summer. Boston Police Supt. Joseph C. Carter said at a news conference that the department had assigned the Community Disorders Unit to serve as liaison to the lesbian and gay community. Community representatives hailed the action, which placed Detective Sgt. William Johnston, who commanded the unit, at the center of the response to anti-gay incidents based on civil rights violations. It marked the first time that a whole police team, rather than an individual, were designated as liaisons. Also important, the police publicly acknowledged that homophobia was involved.

In response to these attacks, the Fenway Health Center established the Victim Recovery Program. Targets of assault were no longer on their own; the LGBTQ community was working together to meet the violence they faced. In addition to homophobic attacks, LGBTQ people were often victims of violence at the hands of intimate partners. This had been a serious problem for years but ignored by LGBTQ advocates because they saw it as a heterosexual problem.

The Fenway began to collect statistics on violence and though most believed its numbers were too low, they demonstrated that the police had severely underestimated the degree to which LGBTQ people were under attack. In 1989, for example, the Fenway reported there had been eighty-four anti-gay incidents involving 128 persons and three LGBTQ organizations across the state, including one homicide in the Fens. This compared with thirty-four incidents in 1988, involving sixty-two victims.[17] That year was not an outlier. In 1993, there were twenty-one violent incidents reported in the Fens alone including a stabbing and a hammer attack.[18] In response, lights and a telephone were installed and there were calls to remove the reeds. However, there was little additional action taken and within a few years the popularity of the area for outdoor cruising faded as new technologies began to influence how gay men met each other.

Violence, AIDS, and political losses increased anger. Tapping into the same fury that created ACT UP, LGBTQ people started Queer Nation. The founders were fed up with the bigotry of straight society; but Boston's chapter, like its ACT UP group, was less contentious than organizations in other cities and had closer ties to the LGBTQ and straight establishment. For example, the group held many of its meetings in City Hall and proved very influential as it provided energy and fueled assertive resistance at a time when it seemed there was little momentum for advancing LGBTQ rights. Much of its activism focused on anti-LGBTQ violence, which seemed to be increasing in the early 1990s (though the lack of data makes the reality of this perceived resurgence of muggings and assaults difficult to assess). At the time, however, many people felt that street assaults were becoming more frequent and in response to a series of gay bashings in the South End, Queer Nation held rallies calling for an end to the violence and increased police protection. They even held a "kiss-in" to highlight the lack of acceptance of LGBTQ people in straight bars. Though some of the anti-gay leaders of South Boston were convinced Queer Nation was behind the effort of LGBTQ veterans to march in the Saint Patrick's Day Parade, that was not the case. Initially very energetic, by the mid-1990s, Queer Nation had ceased to be a major force in Boston.

By the early 1990s, male street prostitution appeared to be winding down in Boston though much of the trade was simply pushed to Providence where it continues to thrive to this day. The factors for the decline of male sex work in Boston included the decline of the Combat Zone, the redevelopment of Park Square, the gentrification of neighborhoods around the Common and Public Garden, and a change in social norms that both reduced the demand for male prostitutes (men could more easily meet other men and there was less repression that kept men in denial of their sexuality) and reduced supply (fewer boys and young men were thrown out on the streets when their sexuality was revealed).

High-end male hustling continued. The experience of Roger Brown (1925-97), a famous Harvard psychologist, sheds light on this type of prostitution. Brown met his lifelong partner, Albert Gilman, when both were graduate students at the University of Michigan in 1947. The two considered themselves married and when Albert died of cancer in 1989, Brown was devastated and turned to renting male prostitutes. He blamed his behavior on loneliness and age discrimination in the gay community, but other issues (including alcoholism) affected him.

His favorite company to procure the services of young men was Dream Boys, where a phone call to its downtown offices brought a young man to his door for ninety minutes at a cost of $220. The young men were vague about their backgrounds, which added to their allure. "Perhaps strangeness or anonymity is simply an aphrodisiac," mused Brown.[19] The young men were mostly working class, squeaky clean, and willing to please. Brown told of one young man who thought he would be meeting "hot babes." But when informed of the true gender of the clients, he quickly accommodated them. They received half of the fee plus tips.

Despite the arguments of some lesbian friends who pointed out that these young men were vulnerable and could have been coerced into these jobs, Brown believed the men were willing participants who just wanted some additional cash. Some worked through agencies, while others worked independently. In either case, their ads could be found in the back pages of *The Phoenix*, *Bay Windows*, or other gay papers. Again, the men involved in both sides of these encounters were ostracized by other members of the community, but they continued to be part of it.

Transvestite and transsexual sex work remained robust. Night found them in Bay Village, particularly in the block around Jacques. With employment discrimination particularly severe, many trans people were very poor and economic necessity continued to drive many to prostitution despite the dangers. Though it had a large number of LGBTQ residents, Bay Village spent decades trying to stop prostitution on its streets. Members of its neighborhood association took down license plate numbers of johns looking for sex, demanded police crackdowns, and tried to close Jacques. Though the bar was slapped with an early closing time, the conflicts persisted.

Though he signed the anti-discrimination bill, Governor Dukakis's rocky relationship with LGBTQ activists continued until his term ended in 1990. Then the ties of LGBTQ community with the state Democratic Party were further strained when Boston University President John Silber secured the party's nomination for governor that year. For decades, the party had been split between liberals and conservatives with Dukakis, for example, losing the governorship in the 1978 Democratic primary to conservative Ed King before beating him in the 1982 rematch. In 1990, between disillusionment with Dukakis and a gathering recession in the state caused by the collapse of the minicomputer industry and overbuilding in the region's housing market, conservative Democrats came out in force and voted for Silber.

John Silber's supporters admired his harsh treatment of women, minorities, and others they did not like. He regularly attacked women, once calling his university's English Department a "damn matriarchy" because it employed too many women, and he fought LGBTQ students at BU, denying them the right to have an official club and going out of his way to denigrate them.[20]

In contrast, Republican gubernatorial candidate William Weld was a patrician Yankee with a style that was reminiscent of old-style Northeastern liberal Republicans. During the election Weld said he did not like the 1989 anti-discrimination law but that he would not work to overturn it and would do his best to make sure it was enforced. Though Silber had a gay son who would die of AIDS in 1994, Silber was vitriolic in his rejection of the law and made LGBTQ people uneasy. As a result, many worked for Weld.

David LaFontaine, a longtime activist who played an important role in making Massachusetts schools safe for LGBTQ youth, and Vin McCarthy, a prominent lawyer and onetime Democratic candidate for Congress, were two of the first gay men to come out for Weld. LaFontaine stood on the steps of the Statehouse to announce "[n]ow that the Democrats have nominated an autocratic bigot for governor . . . large numbers of gay people are looking to the Republican party as a place where we will seek inclusion and advocacy for our equal rights struggle."[21]

Other activists were willing to give Silber a chance to explain himself. Alliance leader Don Gorton, for example, said that "the community has not had a chance to assess how candidates stand on our issues. Most gay men and lesbians remain in the undecided column." Many were just uncertain, afraid to appear pro-Republican because the national party was so virulently anti-gay. "It's clear the community doesn't have the luxury of writing off any candidate or party until we sit down with both, discuss issues of concern, and see where we stand," said Isaacson. "Either could be governor for eight years and ruin lives or give equal status under the law. Never has it been so unclear as to what we will do," she added. "Within each party, there are those who hate us and there are those who support us."[21]

Some LGBTQ activists claimed that the community was responsible for Weld's 75,000-vote victory over Silber. That is unlikely given how Silber had managed to alienate so many of Massachusetts' liberal and minority constituencies. But the damage was done, and four years later when Weld ran for reelection, liberal Democratic opponent Mark Roosevelt still had a problem bringing LGBTQ voters back into his coalition.[22]

There was a group of white cisgender gay men who were high-profile Republicans for the next fifteen years, many of them members of the Log Cabin Republican Club. An exception because he was African-American, Abner Mason (1962-) grew up in North Carolina and his parents were Jessie Jackson delegates to the Democratic National Convention in 1988. Mason came north to attend Governor Dummer Academy, a private school in Byfield, before matriculating to Harvard University. After graduation, he owned a series of small businesses and quickly rose in gay conservative politics. He unsuccessfully ran for city council in 1991 and then worked for Governors Paul Celluci and Jane Swift, culminating as Swift's patronage secretary. Later he was appointed to the National AIDS Advisory Board by President Bush. During his career, he was noted for his sharp elbows and fierce conservative rhetoric. Frustrated as Massachusetts moved to the left, leaving him marginalized in both the LGBTQ and African-American communities, he eventually moved out of the state.

One gay man who tried to have a political career as a Republican was Mike Duffy (1963). He and his fellow conservative gay Republicans positioned themselves as being socially progressive and fiscally conservative, an easy stance for them as most came from white, middle-class, suburban backgrounds and many had attended prestigious colleges. This combination of beliefs was off putting to LGBTQ people who strongly believed in the economic and social justice issues important to communities of color as well as those who supported an activist government that funded social services.

These gay Republican men represented the apotheosis of the best-little-boy syndrome: trying extremely hard to meet an ideal they believed would save them from discrimination even if it caused them to experience scorn from their LGBTQ peers. A fawning Harvard case study on his political career called Duffy, "young, energetic, personable, well-educated, and ambitious" as the authors wondered why he never achieved greater respect from other LGBTQ people.[23] It is debatable, however, whether the community was ever ready to be led by white prosperous gay men who rejected most of its political values, but by the 1990s the increasing visibility of diverse elements of the community along with the angry realization that the prime opponents of LGBTQ rights were Republicans made these men outcasts. Their power base would always be in the straight, moderate wing of the Massachusetts Republican party, a group that was steadily declining in numbers and influence.

Duffy was born in New York and grew up in Florida. At Trinity College he was energized by Ronald Reagan, ignoring the president's terrible AIDS policies, and he co-founded a conservative newspaper. It was only after he graduated in 1985 and entered the Kennedy School of Government at Harvard that fall that he began to come out. He vowed to keep his private life separate from his public persona, but by his second year at Harvard that became difficult and he was out enough to be asked by a fellow student to help organize an LGBTQ group at the Kennedy School. They were scared to meet in the building and convened at an off campus location. The fear was not that they would be expelled–the Kennedy School had hosted a seminar on gay and lesbian politics, taught by Eric Rofes, back in 1984–but that students and professors might discover they were gay and somehow shame them. Even off campus, Duffy felt "sick to his stomach with anxiety" at those meetings. Over time, however, the student group helped him to become more comfortable in his own gay skin. As with many young people of this era, the more LGBTQ he met, the easier time he had accepting his sexuality, though he never developed sympathy for others not as fortunate as he.

Graduating from the Harvard, Duffy returned to Connecticut to be finance chair of liberal Republican Christopher Shay's campaign to fill Stewart McKinney's seat after he died of AIDS. But Duffy couldn't stay in Connecticut because it was too isolated. Upon returning to Massachusetts he worked for the state Republican Committee then run by Raymond Shamie, a conservative with very homophobic positions. In 1989, Duffy worked for a private nonprofit organization that served the elderly. Though he was not previously noted for his political work in Massachusetts and his community involvement was fairly modest, Duffy decided to run for state representative against Byron Rushing in 1990. The Ninth Suffolk District probably had the largest number of gay men in the state and at the time there were no out LGBTQ legislators in Massachusetts. But 40 percent of the neighborhood was black, 10 percent Latino and the remainder a highly-mixed group of people, mostly liberal. Democrats made up 55 percent of the voters, with Republicans just 12 percent. Another Log Cabin Republican, Richard Tafel, became Duffy's campaign manager. Attending the Divinity School, Tafel had been introduced to Duffy by a straight friend who thought they were the only two gay men at Harvard.

Many LGBTQ people were upset that he challenged Rushing. Scondras called the race a lose-lose situation, as either an openly gay man or the staunchest ally of the LGBTQ community would be defeated while Isaacson, like many others, were troubled by the potential of toppling one of the few Black politicians in the state. In addition, because Rushing had been in the house since Mel King had stepped down in 1982, Rushing was close to the House leadership and many believed he would be essential to advancing LGBTQ interests in the legislature (a prediction that would prove true in the fight to protect same-sex marriage). Thus the community split. Frank, Studds, Noble, and Scondras supported Rushing while Franco Campobello of Club Cafe, Alliance Chair Rosemary Dunn Dalton, and LaFontaine backed Duffy. To try to get the Alliance endorsement, large numbers of gay Republicans became members and though they couldn't deliver enough votes to secure the Alliance's nod, they succeeded in denying it to Rushing at a meeting that featured shouts and heated arguments. 1990 was a good year for Republicans as the Alliance endorsed Weld while *Bay Windows* endorsed Duffy. However, LGBTQ voters in the South End, like their straight neighbors, remained strong supporters of Rushing and he easily defeated Duffy as most voters strongly favored Democrats.

The Log Cabin Republicans were always a marginalized group. The vast majority of LGBTQ people despised them, Barney Frank famously called them Uncle Toms, and most of the South End shunned and openly mocked them. Their reception by their straight Republican colleagues was even crueler. While for many years the Massachusetts Republican party ignored or quietly tolerated them, the national party repeatedly humiliated and rejected them, prompting some to wonder while any rational adult would put up with such abuse. Yet they kept on trying to gain minimal acceptance from the national party. They never succeeded and as the national Republicans became increasing anti-gay, most of these men would leave the party after 2000.

Over time, the Massachusetts Log Cabin Republicans chapter withered. As Republicans held the Massachusetts Governor's Office for the next sixteen years they grew increasingly conservative. In addition, it was clear that the small group of

Republicans in the legislature were more rabidly anti-LGBTQ than the remaining conservative Democrats and by the time Mitt Romney was elected Governor in 2002, the idea that the state Republican Party offered a safe pro-gay alternative to the Democratic Party was ludicrous. The Log Cabin Republicans were mostly invisible during the fight over gay marriage, though they were on record as opposing Mitt Romney's efforts to stop marriages from happening. The Massachusetts chapter eventually disbanded and though it would later be revived, it has ceased to be a factor in Boston's LGBTQ community.

Despite the increasing acceptance of homosexuality in adult society, many children continued to be terribly harassed. In response to advocacy by and for young people, Governor Weld convened a commission to investigate the problems faced by LGBTQ youth. What they found was horrifying. One gay student, for example, testified that he "was spit on, pushed, and ridiculed. My school life was hell. I decided to leave school because I couldn't handle it."[24]

Though many parents now affirmed their love when a child announced they were gay, many did not. One young lesbian told the Commission, "I got kicked out of my house in July, and at that point there was violence involved. My mother went nuts and came at me with an iron."[24] Nearly every adult LGBTQ person remembered their personal traumas as adolescents and there was a broad push to address the violence and abuse directed at young people. Advocacy was building, but many youths continued to be terribly at risk.

In the later part of the 1990s, the state began to implement a number of programs that would ultimately help make some LGBTQ youths lives more tolerable. The state convened a task force to oversee its LGBTQ youth initiatives and its reports led to the development of gay/straight alliances at schools across the state, training for teachers and administrators, funding for LGBTQ youth programs, and other important initiatives. The abuse problem remains, particularly for trans and non-binary youth, but for some LGBTQ young people, there are resources in place to help keep them safe and enable them to thrive. One of the most-favored aspects of Boston Pride has been its student marchers. Almost every LGBTQ adult carries the physical and emotional scars from the abuse they endured when young.

Though there were still places out adults could not safely visit, most central neighborhoods in Boston were openly welcoming of LGBTQ people by the 1990s. Even East Boston, still heavily working-class Italian (but soon to attract thousands of Brazilian and Latino immigrants) had many out residents who lived in peace alongside their neighbors. The two exceptions to this welcoming attitude were Charlestown and South Boston. Most LGBTQ people, like people of color in the city, feared to visit South Boston. Many remembered the decades of vicious gay bashing that youths from the neighborhood had committed and there were many who could not forgive the violent anti-busing riots of the 1970s. For most, going there didn't seem worth the risk. Of course there were LGBTQ people who lived in South Boston (both those born there and newcomers), but they remained largely invisible. There were rumors that the parking lots near Carson Beach were cruisy at night and debates around whether the L St. Bath House, the famous beachfront facility built by Mayor Curley that was noted for its nude beaches (men strictly segregated from the women, of course), was a gay friendly place but few chose to investigate these spaces.

Similarly, most LGBTQ people avoided the annual St. Patrick's Day parade (in which no openly LGBTQ person had ever dared to march), the largest public event in Boston and a drunken mess that was and still is accompanied by numerous assaults and arrests each year. Many Irish LGBTQ people lamented being excluded the parade, however, because they were proud of their heritage. "Our grandfather and cousins who came to Boston to work had heavy County Cork accents. We grew up listening to the Clancy Brothers and the Irish Rovers. We learned about the role our grandfather and great aunts played in the struggle for Irish independence."[25] Quietly, some began to attend the parade but they remained invisible.

In 1992, the homophobia of South Boston exploded into the open when a group of LGBTQ Irish people, the Irish American Gay, Lesbian, and Bisexual Group of Boston (GLIB), later Outvets, applied for permission to march in the parade and were refused. The parade was produced by the South Boston Allied War Veterans Council, a loosely organized group of current and former residents. Mayor Flynn tried to arrange a compromise and held meetings between Parade leaders and LGBTQ representatives, but the Council rejected any effort that meant inclusion. GLIB sued, winning an injunction allowing them to march.

Twenty-five brave LGBTQ people marched in the face of some of the worst violence in South Boston since the busing crisis two decades earlier. The episode was also the most extreme public violence against LGBTQ people in Boston history despite the large police presence deployed to protect the marchers. Some of the parade watchers wore t-shirts that read "90 years without queers: Keep St. Patrick's Day straight." Some in the crowd threw food and beer at the marchers while others screamed obscenities; still others turned their backs as the group marched by.[26]

GLIB marched in 1993 after securing another injunction, suffering once again from violence and abuse. In 1994, the Council canceled the parade rather than let LGBTQ people march and it filed suit in federal court asserting their right to hold a parade without them. The Council succeeded in temporarily winning legal relief for the 1995 parade, allowing them to discriminate based on the First Amendment to the Constitution—excluding LGBTQ people was considered free speech by the court. In retaliation, the city cut off funding for the parade and Mayor Menino banned city employees from participating as part of their public duties. Boston firefighters and police in full uniform had marched in the parade for decades but could no longer do so. Then on June 19, 1995, the US Supreme Court ruled in favor of the Council and LGBTQ people were out of the parade. Most politicians avoided the parade; only conservatives participated. Most LGBTQ people refused to go into the neighborhood and for the next twenty years, LGBTQ people were denied the right to be in the parade.

In contrast, the Pride parade adapted to new times. During the early years of Pride, Beacon Hill was the center of LGBTQ life and a march down Charles St. was the natural route for the parade. Many marchers felt energized by balloons and banners on the street, but twenty years later, the center of the community had shifted to the South End. Yet the parade had never more than touched a corner of that neighborhood and it was time to change the route. After consultations with a number of people both inside and outside of Pride, a new route was announced for 1993, one that went down Clarendon St. to Tremont St. and then back up Berkeley St. The high point of the parade was thus in front of the Boston Center for the Arts with the idea that a reviewing stand (abandoned after a year or two) would allow marchers to show off as they passed. There have been minor variations in the route since then to accommodate construction projects or other needs, but for the most part, the parade now begins in Copley Square, bows through the South End, and then ends at Government Center Plaza.

Between troubled management and worse finances, Pride often skated on thin ice. But it was public actions that brought the most unwanted attention. The 1996 Pride parade was the year of a controversy that became known as Bedgate when one man exposed himself while walking on stilts and a group of women simulated sex on a bed lashed to a truck. Most of the crowd in the parade or watching it either let them pass or jeered them but the incidents were widely covered in both the straight and gay press, sparking outrage from many people. Technically, the open display of genitalia in Boston was a misdemeanor (indecent exposure) not a felony (open and gross lewdness) and the police would have had to witness the acts to make arrests. Topless females were not against the law in Boston. That didn't stop conservative straights including City Councilor James Kelly from demanding arrests.[27]

Once again, it was a controversy rooted in debate around the fundamental meaning of Pride. This time there was an additional position in the political vs. party debate: should Pride be a celebration of LGBTQ sexuality? A variant of the radical position, some held that Pride needed to remind LGBTQ people and educate straights that the community was not only made up of cisgendered people who just happened to do things differently in the privacy of their bedrooms but that sexuality and gender expression were at the center of what made a person gay, lesbian, bisexual, or transgender—positions that had been advanced by advocates such as Hoffman and Shively for decades.

Not everyone agreed such openness was needed or helpful and the controversy boiled inside the community for months. *Bay Windows* editor Jeff Epperly called it an "idiotic act of guerrilla theater gone bad."[28] Some pointed out that LGBTQ families often included young children who should not see open displays of sex. Others thought it brought shame on everyone. The women involved, however, offered no apologies as they insisted that they were making a political point about the centrality of sex in LGBTQ life. One wrote to *Bay Windows*, saying, "[t]o be pro-sex, lesbian and unashamed is difficult in a sex-phobic and sexist society. Hence, The Bed was a perfect outlet for my pride and politics."[29] In part because of the controversy and increasing fears that an outsider might seek to disrupt the event through violence, after that year security was tightened. People marching had to pre-register and sign agreements that banned nudity or sexual acts. These measures are still in effect over two decades later.

Controversy also undermined LGBTQ politicians. After ten years in office, Scondras' time as a city councilor came to a sad end. At his height, Scondras was one of the main progressive voices in the city, championing protections for renters and LGBTQ people as well as fighting for more funding for AIDS services and other important programs. Over time, his influence waned. Some thought he was ignoring his constituents while his allies found him unreliable and could never count on Scondras showing up at a rally or hearing.

In February 1993 Scondras made a series of late night phone calls to the police. Released just before the final election, they featured "a rambling and clearly distressed Scondras making demands" on the 911 dispatchers.[30] As a result, many of his LGBTQ supporters quietly began to consider his straight opponent. He still had the endorsement of major unions and many progressive organizations, but *Bay Windows* withheld its endorsement and in the final election, Scondras lost by twenty-seven votes. His political career was over. In 2007, he was arrested for soliciting sex with a minor. Scondras claimed it was harassment and a made up charge, but he was convicted and ordered to register as a sex offender.

Reflecting straight society's complex pattern of acceptance and repression violence against LGBTQ people shifted away from gay men towards trans women Murders of gay men seemed to decline as murders of trans women appeared to increase. Deborah Forte was found dead of multiple stab wounds in Haverhill on May 15, 1995. Trans activists were determined to see justice done and they held a vigil outside the courthouse when her murderer went on trial the next year. The trans community was organizing to protect itself as worse was yet to come.

In November 1997, Chanelle Pickett met William Palmer at Playland. Late that night, Palmer strangled Pickett, choking her neck for over eight minutes after beating her face and body and stuffing bedding down her throat. One of the thing that made the vicious murder sting so much was how the press treated the victim and her murderer. Showing absolutely no respect to Pickett, The *Herald* kept referring to her as a he and repeatedly used her dead name (the one that reflected her assigned rather than real gender). In contrast, the paper said the murderer was "polite and clean-cut, wears khaki pants and sports coats, drives a blue sport utility vehicle and was often seen by neighbors walking his German Shepard, Max, around the well kept neighborhood." They even called him preppy.[31] The *Globe* and *Bay Windows* also disrespected Pickett by misgendering her pronouns. Adding to the anger of the trans community, the jury at Palmer's trial only convicted him of assault and battery, the least possible charge that carried a maximum sentence of two and a half years. There was no respect or justice for trans women and the trans community was fearful and angry.

Chapter 13

To Marriage

I N 1996, RESEARCHERS finally developed an effective treatment for AIDS: "cocktails" of drugs that if taken with almost complete adherence to a daily schedule promised to restore or preserve a person's immune system such that opportunistic infections and otherwise rare cancers were prevented. Boston institutions, including the Fenway and several area hospitals, were part of an international consortium of providers that tested the new drugs and protocols that proved so lifesaving and doctors around the region quickly put their patients on the new regimens. For many (but not all) AIDS was suddenly transformed into a chronic disease with stories told of people on their deathbeds who miraculously rose up and regained their health.

There would be no celebrations or victory parades, however. For one thing, the numbers of dead were shocking. Because of poor record keeping and the stigma around the disease, it is impossible to know how many people died of AIDS in Massachusetts during the fifteen years between when it was first identified in 1981 and when effective treatments became available in 1996. But even using the official statistics that undercounted the people who were lost, the numbers are heartbreaking.

In Provincetown alone there were 384 recorded deaths from AIDS by 1996; over 10 percent of the year round population had died of AIDS. Many had not been residents for long but chose to live out their final days in the town.[1] Some long-term residents left for their last days; still others stayed until the end. Provincetown may have the largest death rate from AIDS in the entire United States.

For Massachusetts overall, using an estimate (based on official statistics) of about 12,000 AIDS deaths among men who had sex with men and an adult gay male population of about 120,000 (approximately 4 percent of the total male adult population), roughly 10 percent of the gay men in the generations born between 1920 and 1970 died of HIV/AIDS. Another 10,000 gay men were infected with the virus. Thus, almost everyone who was part of the community was touched by the epidemic and everyone had to deal with its effects: loss, anger, and indescribable grief.

Some of the most prominent and well-regarded gay and trans people of the era died in the epidemic. To name just a few, there was Stephen Davies, famous for dressing up on Sunday nights at Boston-Boston as Rocky from *The Rocky Horror Picture Show*; Ron Doyle, media critic for the *Middlesex News*; Paul Everett, the director of the first production of the *Ten Percent Review*; Roberto Colon, a cofounder of the Bayard Rustin Breakfast; Tim Bennet, cofounder of the Boston Living Center; Kent Anderson, a singer with the Tanglewood Festival Chorus; Peter Maroon, the "Mayor of Kilmarnock Street"; Fred Mandel, the author of Boston's Human Rights

Ordinance and veteran of dozens of social justice causes; and Michael Smith, cohost of the radio show, *One in Ten.* There were many others, not as well-known but just as important, who were taken long before their time and who meant so much to their families, friends, and the others they touched before dying. Some of them include:

> Kevin Flynn. Died in 1991 at age 31. Born in Brockton and lived in the South End and Dorchester. "Kevin's passing leaves a hole in the lives of those who knew and loved him."

> James d'Anjou. Died in 1991 at 29. "He danced for fun, sometimes losing himself in music for hours."

> John Van Etten. Died in 1990. "John was extremely proud of his students who often sang during the holidays at the Prudential Center, City Hall and Quincy Market. He was devoted to teaching music to inner city children."

> Raymond Nadeau. Died in 1994 at age 45. "Ray knew the seductive power of talk. Ray knew how to make even Jean-Paul Sartre exciting, erotic—to anyone."

> Rhael Rafik, also known as Aroma Lamour, was renowned for his "sense of humor, the lilt of his walk, his outlook on the world and, of course, the Mother's Day brunches."[2]

Another reason not to celebrate the medical breakthrough was that the treatments didn't work for everyone. Many found the drug regimens too unforgiving; if patients skipped doses, some treatments would thus fail to keep the virus from breaking out. There were just a handful of regimens to choose from and many had already used up some options by trying drugs the old way, one at a time. Some found the side effects so overwhelming they had to stop treatment. For people without health insurance, and many with health plans of marginal quality, the drugs were cruelly unaffordable. Though some of these people were able to secure treatment through government or drug industry programs, others died because they lived in a country that didn't believe in universal health insurance.

Sill more died because of the way society treated the poor, non-white people, and those who did not conform to society's strict ideas about gender. Reflecting other health inequities, the disparities in death rates due to AIDS between whites and blacks and Latinos remains large, while trans people have also continued to be hard hit by the disease. Overall, the drugs proved to be highly effective for higher-income cisgender white men with good health plans and strong social support systems. Black and Hispanic men, transgender people, and the poor continued to face an awful epidemic.

AIDS did not slow LGBTQ activism in Boston; in fact it added urgency to many issues, especially Domestic Partner Benefits (DPB). In the absence of universal access to health care, having insurance to pay for doctor visits, hospitalizations, drugs, and other medical costs was essential. Though there were some programs to assist the poor, for the most part adults under the age of sixty-five relied on employer-provided insurance to pay for their health care. But this was only available to employees, their legally recognized spouses, and children. Many dependents of LGBTQ people, with marriage closed to them, were excluded. Though health insurance was the most important, there were other important marriage-related benefits that were not available to same-sex spouses and dependents including the right to make medical decisions when a partner was incapacitated, inherit property, access bank accounts, and a host of other privileges.

In response to this problem, LGBTQ people in West Hollywood, California and those who obtained their health insurance through the Screen Actors Guild pushed to have Domestic Partner Benefits, an administrative procedure that allowed an employee to register their partner with their employer who would then grant the partner the same benefits they were giving married spouses. These benefits allowed an employee to put their partner on their health insurance and often included them in family leave and other human resource policies.

The first prominent company to adopt DPB was Lotus Development, a software company headquartered in Cambridge. Hearing about the work in California, a group of LGBTQ employees approached their human resources department who then hired an outside consultant, Andrew Sherman, to create a DPB program that included procedures for signing up and verifying partner status, an outline of benefits provided, and the accompanying forms and brochures to make the program possible. Lotus, like many other employers, extended DPB not just to same-sex couples but also to opposite-sex couples who for whatever reason, were not married. There was speculation, never tested in court, that to provide DPB to same-sex partners without also making them available to opposite-sex couples would be discriminatory. After they were implemented by Lotus in 1991, DPB spread across the country and by the time same-sex marriage was legalized in Massachusetts in 2003, most large private companies and many state and local governments outside of Massachusetts were allowing their employees in same-sex relationships to access the program, many based on the Lotus example.

There were major problems, however. The federal government did not recognize these programs and many states and private entities did not either. Thus, a couple might have a domestic partner agreement recognized by their employer, but if one partner was suddenly hospitalized unconscious in another state, the other partner might not be allowed to see them, even if their insurance was paying for their health care. Another problem was that not every employer agreed to implement a DPB program. The federal government did not and many smaller employers also were against it as were some very large companies. Those opposed included one of the largest companies in the country at the time, EXXON. DPB did not change federal or state laws nor was there an established legal right to them. They were policies adopted by the entities that granted them and they could be rescinded at any time.

Another difficulty was that the federal government considered the portion of the health insurance premium that covered partners to be taxable income. Since World War II, health insurance premiums have not been considered income, sparing both employees and employers from payroll taxes and making the benefit tax-free to the employee. In contrast, insurance premiums paid for DPB health care were taxable and as premiums grew, so did tax bills. Changing this was problematic as the tax implications were embedded in the basic laws governing insurance. Eliminating the tax would take a sympathetic majority in Congress and a pro-LGBTQ president, something still extremely remote.

Activists in Boston naturally wanted the city to provide DPB but they ran into another legal issue: Massachusetts law, written decades earlier to prevent corruption, did not allow cities and towns to give insurance coverage to anyone they wanted. Instead, the state limited coverage to a select list of potential beneficiaries. Led by the Mayor's Gay and Lesbian Liaison at the time, John Meunier, the city convened a series of internal meetings to figure out how to implement DPB in the context of this law. One of the key events of this planning was a secret meeting, held in a conference room at the Fenway Health Center that included Mayor Flynn, his key LGBTQ aides, outside activists from the Alliance, and the consultant to Lotus, Sherman, who was volunteering his time and expertise to the city. There was quick agreement that benefits that the city could legally grant should be included in an immediate program. But though some pressed the city to go ahead and provide health benefits and dare a lawsuit, Flynn was unwilling to do this, reasoning that it would be worse to dangle the prospect of health insurance that they knew would most likely be taken away.

Even this limited set of benefits faced opposition. A head count indicated that the proposal would win City Council approval, but conservative councilors still savaged the idea. At one point, Sherman was testifying before the Council about the proposed ordinance setting up the DPB program and Councilor Dapper O'Neil, vehemently opposed, pressed him as to who was paying for his work. Sherman replied that the work was pro bono, setting off a several minute long exchange between the two as O'Neill repeatedly asked who this Mr. Bono was while the puzzled Sherman kept trying to explain he was working as a volunteer.

The ordinance approved, in 1993 the city set up a process for registering domestic partnerships, including opposite-sex couples. These recognized partnerships did not entitle people to health insurance but did give city employees certain rights, including bereavement leave prompting one wag to suggest that at least same-sex relationships were recognized at death. The new policies also guaranteed the right of partners to visit patients at Boston City Hospital.

Soon after, Flynn resigned to become Ambassador to the Vatican and was replaced as Mayor by Thomas Menino, who made Ann Maguire his chief of staff. This prompted a more aggressive approach to the issue and in 1995, the city filed a home-rule petition with the legislature asking to be granted the right to give health insurance to same-sex couples. As with the anti-discrimination bill, the legislature did not act on it and kept putting up procedural road blocks to keep the petition from passing. In 1998, for example, Thomas Finneran, the anti-LGBTQ Speaker of the House, asked the SJC if the city even needed a home rule petition to grant DPB and whether the city could create its own definition of what was a domestic partner.

The legislature eventually passed the DPB home-rule petition but it was vetoed by Governor Paul Cellucci because of the complicated reasoning that though he was in favor of same-sex partnerships, he believed that allowing heterosexual DPB would undermine marriage. Frustrated, Mayor Menino signed an executive order offering health benefits for unmarried spouses of city employees effective November 1, 1998.

A group funded by a coalition of conservative organizations and the Catholic Church sued, pointing out that state law prohibited the city from giving health benefits to domestic partners. The group made it very clear that not only did it oppose giving health benefits to same-sex partners, it was opposed to any and all benefits, recognition, or tolerance of LGBTQ people. As predicted, a judge granted the opponents an injunction prohibiting the city's domestic partner health insurance benefits from going into effect and on appeal, the SJC upheld the opponents. The July 9, 1999 decision, written by Justice Margaret Marshall, was sympathetic to the needs of same-sex couples but held that Boston did not have the authority to give health insurance to domestic partners. Only the legislature could do so.

Returning to the legislature brought frustration as Finneran continued to use every possible legislative maneuver to block passage of laws that would give health benefits to the unmarried partners of state and local public employees. As with the anti-discrimination bill, opponents killed legislation by sending it to the Committee on Third Readings, asking the SJC for rulings on parts of the law, or simply refusing to hold votes. Soon it was 2003 and the law was no closer to being passed than it had been four years previously. LGBTQ lobbyists on Beacon Hill seethed, but they were getting refresher lessons on how to stop bills. They were about to get an opportunity to show how much they had learned.

The legislature continued to block pro-LGBTQ legislation but the Massachusetts courts were more supportive. The long history of sodomy laws in the state finally came to an end on February 21, 2002, when the SJC ruled that people who "engage in sodomy in semipublic places such as parking lots, wooded areas, and public beaches cannot be prosecuted as long as they make sure they cannot be seen by others."[3] This was based on the right to privacy when it came to sex that had been extended to heterosexual people back in the nineteenth century. Now same-sex couples had the same rights as opposite-sex couples, eviscerating what was left of the sodomy law.

GLAD had hoped to use the lawsuit to obtain a complete overturn of the sodomy and lewd and lascivious laws but the court said that since there was no evidence that that private same-sex activity had been prosecuted in the past several decades, there was no standing for GLAD to sue. In one sense, the SJC left open the issue of whether the laws were constitutional at all. Yet just as it had made slavery impossible without actually ruling on slavery itself back in 1781, the SJC had done the same thing to sodomy. Massachusetts was the only New England state with a sodomy law still on the books, but now it was unenforceable and would most likely have been overturned had anyone ever had a chance to appeal it. The decision demonstrated that the SJC was sympathetic to LGBTQ people. The question, soon to be put to the test, was how far would the SJC go to affirm their rights?

Compared to the rest of the country, the late 1990s were a golden age in Provincetown. The writer EJ Graff happily recalled, "[y]oung women in swimming trunks and bikini tops swaggered along the water, some tossing footballs back and forth, 'doing their community service,' as one friend of mine used to quip, so the rest of us could watch their impressive shoulders and forearms in action, invitations for later on, if you had the chutzpah and charm to approach."[4]

Many women used the economic freedom offered by Provincetown to operate small businesses. Coupled with the town's longstanding openness to live out one's sexuality without fear of prejudice, many lesbians saw the years around 2000 as a special time and place. "Women are buying houses and businesses, and opening restaurants. Where once there were five inns run by women, today there are 15. What began as an annual women's weekend in October 12 years ago now lasts a week. More than 7,000 women from around the country gather for events that include a prom, community dinner and golf tournament run by Ms. Maguire, a devoted golfer."[5]

LGBTQ people found the town to be a wonderful place to live or visit. Though the winter population was small with many places closed (particularly between New Year's and the end of March), each spring the town revived as businesses reopened and seasonal residents returned. Soon the tourists and part-timers arrived, at first mostly on the weekends and then by Memorial Day, the town appeared bursting at the seams. The spirited times, slowly diminishing after Labor Day, continued to the end of the year.

Many enjoyed a comfortable summer routine. Some would rise early for a walk along the beach, a quiet stroll through town, or a coffee at one of the many shops along Commercial St. In the afternoon, the LGBTQ section of Herring Cove beach (to the left of the parking lot as one faced the water) would be packed with sun bathers lying towel to towel, some running off to play in the ocean, others watching their neighbors show off, and a few slipping off into the dunes to see if there was any action there. There were a number of decisions about how to spend the day that sometimes seemed to dominate conversation. One was what time to go to tea dance at the Boatslip. Every afternoon, rain or shine, the deck at the Boatslip was full of LGBTQ people. Some preferred to show up early, shortly after tea began at 4:00 p.m. Others were dedicated latecomers, preferring to arrive after 6:00 p.m. just before the Hat Sisters, the most well-known couple in Boston/Provincetown LGBTQ society, made their entrance to wild applause. But everyone left when the music stopped at 7:00 p.m.

At that point there were other choices: which of the dozens of restaurants to dine at and which drag or cabaret act to catch. Next there was the most important decision of the evening: A House or the Crown and Anchor? Maybe one of the other bars and dance spots? In any case, the end of the night would be a meetup in front of Spiritus. There was one final decision: call it a night or venture down to Dick Dock, under the deck of the Boatslip, for a final nighttime adventure. The decision hinged on the need for sleep, as for years the police ignored the action as long as it was contained there.

13.1 The A House in 2018

All of this might have seemed frivolous to outsiders living in progressive areas, but for many LGBTQ people this was their only chance to live in complete freedom and feel the basic human comfort of holding hands, the euphoria of being among the LGBTQ community, or the ability to express their true gender without fearing that someone might physically or verbally abuse them. No one in Provincetown cared about gender or sexuality, who someone was sleeping with or what people wore, provided that outfits were smart, sexy, and stylish. Outrageous and experimental outfits were applauded while conservative dress was booed. One of the town's most popular residents was Ellie, a speedo-clad trans septuagenarian father of five who dazzled the crowd with her renditions of Sinatra favorites. There was also economic freedom; Provincetown was still inexpensive and retirees could live in a place they could afford, college students out for the summer or high-school drop outs could support themselves, and many LGBTQ entrepreneurs could build the businesses of their dreams.

The summers were also punctuated by a number of special events with many taking place the same weekend or week annually. There was baby dyke weekend over Memorial Day, the film festival in June, while the unofficial circuit twink party was Fourth of July week, and Bear Week, Girl Splash Week, and Carnival Week later in the summer. The fall brought the Fantasia Fair, Spooky Bear Weekend, and Women's Week.

The week that often brought the most comment was Family Week because it highlighted some of the most important diversity of the LGBTQ community. Begun by two men who brought their daughters to Provincetown in 1996, it grew into a major summer activity, attracting hundreds of children and their parents. "It was a magical event, [one man] recalled, at which children of gay parents—many of whom didn't know other families like theirs—suddenly felt less alone."[6] At first the week was overwhelmingly composed of female couples, but over time the number of male couples, as well as single people raising children, increased. The event today is full of children getting their faces painted, impromptu parades, smiling (and sometimes howling) toddlers, and all the wonders and issues that families confront.

The peak of the summer was Carnival, an event created by business owners to keep the season going near the end of August. A cross between Mardi Gras, New Year's Eve, and Pride, its crowning event was its Thursday parade featuring wild floats, elaborate costumes, and people dancing in the street simply because they were carried away by the excitement. The only complaint was that there were lines everywhere, sometimes extending down Masonic Place around the corner to Commercial St. to get into the A House or along several blocks near the Boatslip for Wednesday's tea dance. In addition to the official events (a pool party, nightly dances, and a legendary drag lunch at The Patio) there were many unofficial parties and gatherings: dinners among friends, cookouts at the beach, and a mudslide party (named after its featured drink) on Pearl St. that was famous in its own right for its dashingly handsome hosts and good-looking guests.

Beginning in the late 1990s, Boston experienced dramatic change as it grew into one of the most prosperous cities in the country. Powered by technology, medical science, money management, and other high-paying industries, the city of abandoned housing and decaying neighborhoods found itself with a housing shortage as an influx of wealthy newcomers pushed out the poor, the elderly, and the middle class. The South End, once shunned by the well-to-do as a place for young poor gays, was now the location of million-dollar condominiums for straight households. Many LGBTQ people who would have once lived in Boston now found themselves priced out. Low-income people of color were the most likely to suffer from the prosperity of the "New Boston."

In Boston's hyper-segregated landscape, gay men of color continued to be marginalized. Yet two leaders emerged to empower Boston's gay black community and to educate white LGBTQ people. One of these was Gary Daffin (1964-). Born in Alabama, almost as soon as he arrived in Boston to go to college he became a major force in the region, respected by both the LGBTQ and straight communities. The charismatic and hardworking Daffin co-chaired the Caucus in the late 1980s as it was marching towards victory over the gay-rights bill and he went on to run the Multicultural AIDS Coalition. In one sense, he represented a new generation of LGBTQ people who came of age after the time of guilt. "I think black, LGBT folks didn't feel safe to be out. I decided I was gay when I was five, so I never had all the baggage of thinking there was something wrong with being gay. For me, it was never really a choice. It was who I am."[7]

Full equality remained elusive, particularly for LGBTQ people of color and thus they made efforts to change the community. Founded in September 2009 by Corey Yarbrough, the Hispanic Black Gay Coalition (HBGC) sought to create a safe place "where people of color would feel welcomed and accepted, without bias or question."[8] Yarbrough and his lover, Quincey Roberts, like many other Black and Hispanic people, felt alienated from the white LGBTQ people and they were motivated by a need to connect social justice and advocacy work with their daily lives. Focusing on AIDS prevention, anti-discrimination, and other issues very important to people of color, the organization grew to employ five people with a budget of $250,000. It created outreach programs for queer and trans women of color and worked to empower LGBTQ people of color.

After Flynn left office, City Hall continued to be open to LGBTQ people. Mayor from 1993 to 2013, Thomas Menino was noted for his compassion for people with AIDS and his willingness to advance the interests of LGBTQ people. This did not come late in his career, it was part of who he was. When Ann Maguire was with BLGPA in 1984, she had introduced Menino to LGBTQ people in his Hyde Park council district, an area not known for its high numbers of LGBTQ voters. Menino contacted her to set up a meeting saying he wanted to represent all of his constituents: "I hear there is a gay group in my neighborhood. I'd like to go meet them," he told her.[9] He was not one think first about whether a decision was politically expedient; he approved a needle exchange program, for example, simply because it would save lives. Maguire was Menino's campaign manager and then his chief of staff. Strongly supported by her boss, at one point she was one of the most powerful women in the state.

Despite better health outcomes, people with AIDS continued to face discrimination, at times being forced to fight society around them more than the virus. By 2001, it was clearly possible for people to live with AIDS. Life expectancies for many afflicted approached that of those who were not infected. But insurers and some health care providers continued to treat people with AIDS as if they were on their death beds, undeserving of the care that others received. A particular problem faced by people with AIDS was the risk of contracting Hepatitis C, a liver disease that is spread in ways similar to HIV. In those days before a drug treatment, many who were infected with the Hepatitis C virus eventually succumbed to liver disease for which the only treatment was a transplant. AIDS patients suffering from Hepatitis C were routinely rejected for new livers.

Belynda Dunn had been one of AAC's most effective organizers, almost single handedly persuading Boston's African-American churches to confront the crisis that was tearing through their congregations. But Dunn was dying, needing a liver transplant at a time when her insurance company called such a treatment for HIV-positive women risky and experimental. GLAD tried to use federal court to force her insurer to pay for her transplant, but time was too short. Mayor Menino, who knew Dunn and was angered by her insurance problems, called the head of her insurance company and convinced him to pay for the transplant.[10] Unfortunately, the transplant didn't work and Dunn did not survive. Soon after GLAD was contacted by a man who had been rejected by his insurance, the state-run Medicaid program MassHealth. They represented him before the board that ran the program and for the first time in the country, a state authorized a transplant for an HIV positive person. Now these medical services are routine for HIV positive people everywhere (if they have insurance).

After twenty-five years, Pride continued to have successes and controversies. To illustrate Pride's vulnerability, despite having attracted over 100,000 people to its parade and post-parade gatherings over each of the past several years, when heavy rains forced the cancellation of the 1998 parade and festival the organization behind Pride teetered on bankruptcy. It was only the intervention of Harry Collings and Vin McCarthy that prevented it from going under.[11] Just as great a threat, however, were the many in the community, both radicals and assimilationists, who openly questioned whether a parade and week of festivities and ceremonies were still necessary. The radicals believed that too many Pride events were frivolous and overrun by cisgender gays and lesbians who were too quick to condemn anyone they thought was disturbing their carefully crafted image of respectability. The assimilationists were angered by media coverage that inevitable focused on drag queens and scantily clad marchers. They were bored by the many Pride events that they felt targeted overly narrow segments of the community. Both sides thought the event was becoming dull. In spite of this, Pride marched on.

Though there were annual battles between those who saw Pride as a celebration and those who relied upon it for political expression, the conflicts never created an irreconcilable schism. Sometimes the two sides came together in ways that combined political expression with fun. The 1999 parade is a great example of how the natural creativity of LGBTQ people could be harnessed to assert their rights.

Though the parade almost devolved into another dispute over sexual expression, it was most remembered for the many people who wore items related to Tinky Winky, a character from the children's television program, *The Teletubbies*. For reasons known only to him, Jerry Falwell, the notorious homophobe who founded the radical conservative group, The Moral Majority, had decided earlier in the year that the purple, purse-carrying fictional character with a triangle antenna on his head was teaching America's preschoolers that being gay was okay. He spoke out several times against this innocent children's show. In response, "Tinky Winkys of various sizes appeared all along the parade route—cuddled by toddlers, dangling from drag queens' ears, and perched atop trucks. There was even a human-sized Tinky Winky in the crowd."[12] The parade also featured Candace Gingrich, the lesbian sister of the Republican Speaker of the House, and Randy Price, a local newscaster who had recently come out as gay. Both were well-known advocates of LGBTQ rights.

The problem of how to pay for Pride surrounded the event each year. By the early 2000s, Boston Pride was 90-95 percent corporate funded via sponsorships and fees. "If not for corporations there would be no pride," declared Sylvain Bruni, the chair of the Pride committee.[13] Insurance expenses alone were $10,000 for the week and individual donations were insufficient to meet the $100,000 - $120,000 it cost to put on all Pride events each year. These corporate donations saddened some radicals and enraged others who equated corporate capitalism with anti-LGBTQ prejudice as well as oppression of women and people of color. Many thought the extras that were part of Pride were irrelevant. In their view, if the community simply put on a parade and held a rally, there would be no expenses. But the parade needed insurance, security, and a full-time, year-round staff to organize everything. The tensions continued unresolved.

There were limits to what Menino and the city would tolerate. Boston never had the rich bathhouse culture of other cities. Lundine's and the Irvington Hotel had been popular up until the 1960s when they were replaced by the Club Baths, the Boston outpost of a national chain that was housed in a glorious Henry H. Richardson building in the Combat Zone and the seedier Regency Baths in the Financial District. Both of these were gone by 1990 as was Sauna 294, located upstairs from Somewhere Else. There was an attempt to open a bathhouse on upper Boylston St. near Fenway Park but neighborhood opposition stopped that. Thus it was surprising that the Safari Club opened in the industrial part of the South End in 1993. Most of the controversy surrounding the bathhouse was inside the gay community, with some AIDS activists against it because they saw it as a place where unprotected sex might flourish. Others believed that unsafe sex could happen anywhere and that gay men still had a right to promiscuity despite the epidemic around them.[14]

After the police ignored it for years, they finally raided the Safari Club on October 6, 1999. Stating action on two written complaints, the raid found used and unused condoms, popper bottles, and a vodka bottle—a major legal infraction. Other violations were a lack of licenses for being a lodging house (renting rooms for up to six hours), music, and televisions. The club would never reopen.

The city's AIDS establishment kept quiet about the raid. Others were angry. Bay Windows said "I've been trying to think of a more stupid use of municipal enforcement powers, and darned if I can come up with one."[15] Others blamed it on the puritanical city ethos of Boston. But the city would never again have a sex club.

Though murders of gay men declined,[17] Boston was not safe for everyone.

There had been a number of tragic years for Boston's trans community as the violence continued. However, trans people organized to fight the oppression as well as the way the cisgendered community treated them. On February 24, 1997, they convinced the Cambridge City Council to pass an amendment to the city's Human Rights ordinance to prohibit discrimination based on gender identity or expression. Three days later, there was a vigil and demonstration in memory of Chenelle Pickett in front of the Cambridge Court House protesting the legal system's lackadaisical treatment of the murderers of trans women. There would be additional demonstrations meant to achieve justice for her death. Despite this activism, the violence continued with Monique Thomas murdered in 1998.

After still another brutal murder (that of Rita Hester), the anger sparked a national movement to protect trans women. One woman recalled that "Rita Hester was statuesque and glamorous. Usually clad in her favorite colors, black and purple, perhaps in a slinky tube dress adorned with ruffles, she was a familiar figure both at Allston bars such as the Model Café and the Silhouette Lounge and at Jacque's Cabaret." Another friend fondly remembered that Hester "liked to wear opera-length gloves with rings on top, big pieces of costume jewelry."[16] On November 28, 1998, this beautiful black woman whose talent and kindness brought joy to so many people was stabbed twenty times and died at the hospital. Her murderer was never found and the grief over her loss was tremendous.

Adding to the shock of losing a prominent member, the trans community was further brutalized by the lack of respect for Hester in the press. As with previous murders of trans women, The *Globe* insisted on calling her a he, as did *Bay Windows* while The *Herald* piled on its disrespect by using her dead name. Sad and angry, trans people and their allies held a series of memorials and protest marches to honor Hester and her generous spirit. They held a candlelight vigil outside the Model Café on December 4, 1998, attended by over 200 people. A week later they demonstrated outside the offices of *Bay Windows*, showing their anger over the poor treatment of trans people by the LGB community in general and that newspaper in particular. The trans community and their allies had had enough. Though Boston later passed an amendment to its Human Rights ordinance prohibiting discrimination based on gender identity and expression, they demanded a state law. But their needs were ignored as same-sex marriage occupied most of the LGB community's attention.

The rallies became the genesis of what is now the annual Trans Day of Remembrance, honoring all the trans people who have been murdered each November 20th. In part, the national movement to remember the many transgender people slain in cold blood is something for Boston to be proud of. It is one more example of activism that originated in the city which continues to transform the country. On the other hand, the movement still exists because trans women continue to be murdered and the Day of Remembrance is necessary because it is a reminder of the hatred and bigotry that continues to mark cisgender society's treatment of trans people.

Perhaps the most important contribution of Boston's LGBTQ community to the country was same-sex marriage. Before 2003, LGBTQ people were second-class citizens and their relationships officially invisible. After that pivotal year, any LGBTQ youngster could dream of finding a special someone, accessing the contentment of a permanent relationship, and knowing the security of legal marriage. Before same-sex

13.2 Arline Isaacson (center) with Steven Tierney and Urvashi Vaid

marriage was legalized, young LGBTQ people were forced to remain onlookers while their adolescent and young adult peers paired up, dated, and married. Being able to marry meant that LGBTQ were able not only to love but to officially and publicly declare it.

One very large problem for same-sex couples was the lack of legal standing in family, tax, and probate law. Unless same-sex couples completed an elaborate set of legal documents including wills, durable powers of attorney, medical proxies, and so forth (items only the well-off could afford) they could find themselves powerless during personal crises such as hospitalizations, inheritances, separations, or simply picking up a child after school. Even if a couple completed all the necessary paperwork to comply with Massachusetts law, they could still run into trouble if a problem happened out of state, as these documents had no interstate validity nor were they recognized by the federal government.

The lack of marriage directly harmed LGBTQ couples, creating a rising demand for action. For example, Martin Friedman had been with his partner, a Boston firefighter, for over forty years when he died. "Martin cared for his partner during a long battle with throat cancer and related surgeries, swabbing out his throat so he would not choke on mucus plugs. But as a non-spouse, he lost the family's major source of income when John died and the pension died with him. Not only would Martin have retained his economic security had he been eligible for survivor benefits, but he would have had access to health insurance (a major expense paid from the monthly pension) and been spared the high taxes that came from inheriting the home they shared."[18]

The devastation caused by the AIDS epidemic demonstrated the need for marriage. Partners often found they had no legal rights, even to physically be with their loved ones as they died. Families, hostile to their sons' and daughters' sexuality, could deny property to widowed loved ones, evict them from lifelong apartments, and even bar them from attending funerals.

Another important reason for making gay marriage a priority was the large number of lesbians raising children. Despite an SJC ruling affirming some rights, women found they could not rely on the law to integrate their partners into their child's lives. Schools refused to let mothers not recognized by the law pick up children, doctors wouldn't let women take their children in for treatment, and the day-to-day indignities thrown at same-sex families wore them down.

These experiences caused the issue of marriage to grow in importance. Contrary to what opponents inside the LGBTQ community would later contend, marriage in Massachusetts was a grassroots issue from the bottom up, and one that had the support of the great mass of LGBTQ people long before the fight was taken up by major LGBTQ organizations.

The woman who led GLAD's legal challenge to the prohibition against same-sex marriage was Mary Bonauto. A graduate of Northeastern Law School, Bonauto had a number of traits that leant themselves to the marriage lawsuit: she was brilliant, tireless, media savvy, and personable. A lesbian in a long-term relationship, she knew firsthand how important this case was. By the year of the suit, GLAD had grown into a multistate organization, litigating and negotiating on behalf of LGBTQ clients throughout New England with access to similar LGBTQ legal organizations across the country as well as some of the best legal minds anywhere. They also had close connections to top Boston law firms and law schools.

The Massachusetts push for same-sex marriage began in 1993 when the Hawaiian Supreme Court ruled that gay couples were being illegally deprived of the right to marry. That ruling was eventually overruled by a state constitutional amendment but not before Congress approved and President Bill Clinton signed the notorious Defense of Marriage Act (DOMA) that prohibited the federal government from recognizing same-sex marriages. It also set in motion a series of state DOMAs that similarly targeted LGBTQ people. These laws made the late 1990s a dark age for LGBTQ rights.

The unsuccessful effort to secure same sex marriage in Hawaii convinced Bonauto and others that time had come to advance it in New England. They began in Vermont, creating the first state-sanctioned civil unions in the country. This prompted serious discussions among Massachusetts couples: should they go to Vermont to get a civil union even though it was legally moot in Massachusetts? Were symbolism and social implication so important that it was worthwhile? Some (but not many) couples thus went to Vermont.

Relying on the legislature to approve same-sex marriage was not an option. Though there was a clear majority in both houses in favor of DPB, it had not been sufficient to break the lock of anti-gay leaders. Furthermore, though polls suggested that a majority of Massachusetts voters were in favor of marriage, it was not clear whether there would be enough legislators in favor a bill legalizing it. The only way to get same-sex marriage in the Commonwealth would be through a court case.

Bonauto and her allies considered trying to enact civil unions in Massachusetts, but the Vermont experience demonstrated that these would be as strongly attacked by conservatives as marriage itself. So why, Bonauto reasoned, should she get so many people to invest so much time and energy for an outcome that would not produce as many rights and would be attacked just as vehemently as marriage?

An alternative strategy advocated by many Boston radicals, also not pursued, would have been to extend the range of legal, social, and economic benefits bound up in marriage to those not married. Given the tremendous burden posed by traditional heteronormative marriage and patriarchal society, why not get rid of marriage and create a new, more equitable legal structure that recognized all relationships? But this would have run into the same roadblock at the State House that thwarted all other pro-LGBTQ legislation. Conservative lawmakers who refused to let DPB pass would not have allowed the creation of an alternative legal structure, particularly one that was open to LGBTQ people. Through their absolute opposition to any LGBTQ rights, conservatives forced advocates to fight for same-sex marriage. Still another problem was that these marriage alternatives would not have extended across state boundaries. While Massachusetts marriage would also be stopped from having an impact beyond state lines by DOMA, at least there was the hope that federal and state DOMA laws might eventually be overturned as the full-faith provision of the US constitution mandated that a legal marriage in one state must be recognized in all others as well as by the federal government. A marriage alternative, on the other hand, would have required action by Congress and the president, a very remote possibility.

But when to file a lawsuit? Feeling pressure, Bonauto and others saw the movement towards pro-LGBTQ rights at the SJC but the central concern was whether there was now a majority of justices who would be in favor of same-sex marriage. There would only be one chance to succeed because if GLAD sued too early and lost, it might delay same-sex marriage for generations.

But waiting to sue also had a cost. There were thousands of LGBTQ people across the state in long-term relationships and they had thousands of children in need of the legal protections of marriage. GLAD studied state and federal laws and regulations and found that several hundred Massachusetts and over a thousand federal laws referenced marriage. With an anti-discrimination law in place, the lack of marriage represented the single most widespread set of issues confronting the Massachusetts LGBTQ community at the time. Furthermore, Bonauto's compassion had been moved by the stories of people who were coming into GLAD looking for help. She later recalled that "the most searing calls I received came from men who had just been turned out of their own homes by a deceased partner's biological family, or were left with nothing because their partner had died without a will, or were not permitted to say their final goodbyes at a hospital once the 'real family' showed up."[18] Delaying a marriage case tore at Bonauto's emotions.

Even so, GLAD was very careful not to go to court for same-sex marriage too quickly and passed up cases that might have resulted in adverse decisions. For example, working with a lesbian plaintiff, the organization decided not to appeal a 1995 decision of the Massachusetts Commission Against Discrimination that allowed a private school to both require its teachers to live on campus and prohibit same-sex couples from living together, effectively keeping the woman out of a job. The lawyers and the plaintiffs felt that the courts were not yet ready to make same-sex marriage a right.

Events soon forced GLAD to file suit. Conservatives were moving towards a referendum banning gay marriage. In 1999, conservative law makers began to introduce anti-same-sex marriage bills, but none made it out of committee thanks to the work of Isaacson and the Caucus. One effect, however, was to boost organizing in the LGBTQ community and the membership of the Freedom to Marry Coalition, founded in 1996, grew rapidly. Then an anti-gay group, the Massachusetts Citizens Alliance (MCA), was organized in 2000 to oppose same-sex marriage with the goal of putting a referendum on the ballot in 2002 or 2004. Isaacson, Bonauto, and other strategists, veterans of the fight to pass the anti-discrimination bill and domestic partnership legislation, thought it would be easier to defend same-sex marriage if there were people already married than if the referendum happened first. It is harder to take away a right, they reasoned, then to add one on. It was time to file suit.

The case for marriage was cautiously constructed. The language selected was "freedom to marry" and the couples selected to be plaintiffs were carefully screened to ensure they were sympathetic with lives that were close to people in opposite-sex marriages. The couples presented tended to be higher income middle-aged professionals. This had the negative effect within the LGBTQ community of reinforcing the view among radicals and others that marriage was an assimilationist goal that didn't affect the lives of many LGBTQ people. But GLAD thought it was vital that the couples in the case be non-threatening and appealing to straight people.

The lead plaintiffs were Julie and Hillary Goodridge. Hillary worked for the Unitarian Universalist grants making program. Julie was a financial advisor who specialized in socially responsible investments. They had met in 1985, had been a couple since 1987, and had a daughter in 1996.[19] The six other plaintiff couples, all of them middle class and photogenic, had also been carefully screened by GLAD and advised that they potentially faced hostility or even violence. In Massachusetts, marriage licenses are issued by clerks in each of the state's 351 cities and towns but the process is overseen by the state Department of Public Health. Therefore the case, filed on April 11, 2001, became known as *Goodridge v. Department of Public Health*.

As predicted, the MCA announced its referendum campaign to amend the state constitution that July, targeting the legislature to pass a measure that would not only have stopped same-sex marriage, but would have also outlawed civil unions and DPB. In May 2002, a lower court ruled against marriage. Though this had been predicted and GLAD was ready to file their appeal, the judge's words still stung. He downplayed the rights that accompanied marriage and suggested that since same-sex couples couldn't procreate, there was no need for them to seek relief from the law. He suggested that they petition the legislature for the right to wed, not the courts.

The anti-marriage constitution amendment was rejected 15-0 at its first hearing at the legislature and was killed 137-53 at the July 17, 2002 constitutional convention. At that point, it was too late to have a ballot question before 2004. However, the number of anti-marriage votes suggested that opponents had enough support to advance their amendment by collecting signatures for a referendum.

From the beginning, everyone knew the lawsuit would be decided by the SJC, presided over by Chief Justice Margaret Marshall, a native of South Africa who hailed from a family opposed to the deeply racist apartheid policies there. She was appointed Chief Justice by Republican Governor Paul Cellucci over the opposition of conservatives who believed her to be anti-Catholic because of some of her earlier rulings. Oral arguments before the SJC were made on March 4, 2003. Then people on both sides of the issue had to wait.

The SJC delayed releasing a decision, a not unusual action as the court frequently did this when considering complex, controversial cases. But conservatives grew nervous and for the first time, there was talk of the legislature passing some sort of civil union bill that would also prohibit marriage. There were even a series of secret meetings that included Finneran and Liz Malia, the lesbian State Representative from Jamaica Plain, but nothing came of these talks.

The court handed down the historic *Goodridge* decision on November 18, 2003 declaring "Civil marriage is at once a deeply personal commitment to another being and a highly public celebration of the ideals of mutuality, companionship, intimacy, fidelity, and family." It said, "Because it fulfills yearnings for security, safe haven, and connection that express our common humanity, civil marriage is an esteemed institution, and the decision whether and whom to marry is among life's momentous acts of self-definition." These words resonated across the country's LGBTQ community and even are sometimes incorporated into straight wedding ceremonies. The ruling was 4 to 3 in favor of marriage, with the justices opposing same-sex marriage mostly discounting the need for couples to wed or suggesting it was something th legislature should fix, not the courts.

As was customary, the SJC gave the state 180 days to put the ruling into effect, meaning that unless something drastic was done, same-sex marriage would become legal for the first time in the United States on May 17, 2004. Getting the SJC to declare the right to have a marriage with a person of the same sex turned out to be the easy part, however. Defending same-sex marriage proved to be much more difficult.

Chapter 14

Queer New World

THE REACTION OF the LGBTQ community to the SJC ruling for same-sex marriage included a wide range of emotions. There was everything from surprise (many thought the outcome of the court case would be another bitter disappointment) to happiness bordering on euphoria because for the first time in the United States, for the first time in the life of Massachusetts LGBTQ people, they had equal opportunity to be married. Some couples knew immediately they would get married, with many wanting to wed as soon as possible. Others sat down and discussed the matter, carefully laying out the pros and cons to come up with the solution that best met their needs. Some sadly anticipated that this new world would ruin everything by making LGBTQ lives more like straight lives. A few thought this might be the beginning of a golden age of freedom. But perhaps the most common emotion was fear. Would the right to be married be taken away? Would other courts interfere? Would the legislature or the government stop it? Six long months had to pass before marriage became legal and anything could happen in that time.

These fears were rational. As soon as the decision was released, a battle began in the courts and legislature that would last for the next several years. At any point, events could have turned against LGBTQ people, dashing their new dreams and perhaps delaying same-sex marriage for a generation or more. Even longer would be the federal effort to make same-sex marriage equal in standing to straight marriages across the nation. The barriers at the federal level were daunting: DOMA, the issue of whether any other state would accept same-sex marriages from Massachusetts despite the constitutional duty of states to do so, and a political climate that was often brutal. That uncertainty would not end until nearly ten years later when the United States Supreme Court ruled in the *Windsor* case that all people in the country had the right to same-sex marriage.

Now defeated in court, some marriage equality opponents suddenly had a change of heart regarding civil unions. Isaacson remembered that "[l]egislators who were previously opposed to all gay rights were suddenly tripping over themselves to give us civil unions, and we said, 'Thank you very much, but we just want marriage.'" Most anti-marriage advocates were unwilling to compromise, however, because they wanted to deny all rights for LGBTQ people and rejected civil unions as being too affirming of same-sex relationships.

After years of blocking all pro-LGBTQ legislation, House leader Finneran laid out three options: letting the ruling stand, creating civil unions as a replacement for marriage, or passing a constitutional amendment outlawing same-sex marriage as well as prohibiting all marriage alternatives. He did not say where he stood, but marriage advocates predicted he would back the most bigoted alternative possible. At the same time, Governor Romney also came out against same-sex marriage. The opposition of Romney, preparing to run for president, was not a surprise. He had become increasingly conservative since taking office and the few remaining gay men in the state Republican Party were looking to exit it. Romney was not just opposed to LGBTQ rights, he was cruel even when face to face with LGBTQ people. For example, a meeting was arranged between the *Goodridge* plaintiffs and Governor Romney in a vain attempt to convince him to tone down his increasingly strident opposition. One of the plaintiffs found the governor to be "cold as ice" and so dismissive of Julie Goodridge when she pleaded to the governor to protect her marriage and the rights of her daughter that she burst into tears.[2]

Another disappointment was Senator John Kerry. He had courageously voted against DOMA but now balked at supporting same-sex marriage. Once divorced and twice married, Kerry was planning to run for president in 2004 and suddenly distanced himself from the LGBTQ community that he once relied upon for votes and campaign contributions.

There were two ways the legislature could intervene to prevent same-sex marriage. One would be to pass a law to create civil unions that would simultaneously abolish same-sex marriage. The other was to approve a constitutional amendment to overturn the court decision. Both actions faced obstacles. Though a civil union law would only need a simple majority to pass, it was not clear that the SJC would agree that civil unions were equivalent to marriage. If they were not the same as marriage, then the court would rule that this alternative did not adequately meet the conditions of equality imposed in its ruling. In addition, no one knew if there were enough votes to pass a civil union law. Conservatives opposed it because it legitimized same-sex relationships, while LGBTQ allies were against it because it was not as good as marriage. Nor was it clear that Governor Romney would sign the bill because it would link him to tolerance of LGBTQ people.

On the other hand, passing a constitutional amendment in Massachusetts is very difficult. There are two procedures, both dependent on votes of the combined Senate and House (200 members total) meeting in a special session as a constitutional convention. One route is to have the legislature approve an amendment submitted by legislators with at least 101 votes in two succeeding terms (a term covers two years). If successful, the amendment then goes to the voting public. The second path is through an initiative process that begins with a gathering of signatures of registered voters for the amendment. If a sufficient number are collected and certified, then fifty-one votes are needed in two consecutive terms to send the amendment to a referendum. Isaacson and other LGBTQ people fighting to protect the court decision nervously tallied the votes they could depend on, those who would be consistently against them, and those whose votes were unknown or perhaps open to persuasion. Seeing the strength of the anti-marriage forces, anxiety levels were extremely high.

Of major concern was how black and Latino (there were no Asian or Native

American representatives or senators) would legislators vote. While many straight white supporters were wavering, minority legislators had been consistently dependable pro-LGBTQ votes since the days of Mel King in the 1970s. But complicating the issue, many prominent black clergy came out against marriage, particularly Eugene Rivers, head of the city's influential Black Ministerial Alliance. Fortunately, not only did black and Latino legislators hold firm, they took the lead in defeating anti-marriage amendments and over the next several years, African-American elected officials, including Representative Byron Rushing and Senator Diane Wilkerson, would be major voices for marriage.

The anti-marriage forces were strong with the most organized and well-funded opposition coming from the Catholic Church. Its political arm, the Catholic Action League (CAL), spelled out its position in a brief filed with the SJC. It noted that the Massachusetts penal code had long included laws against same-sex acts, indicating that for centuries it was the custom and intent to treat same-sex relations differently from opposite-sex relations. The legacy of Puritan anti-sodomy laws continued to haunt LGBTQ people three hundred years later. CAL argued that sexual relations were at the core of marriage and that to place love, commitment, and sharing at the center of marriage was a radical shift. In addition, CAL's brief to the court suggested that child rearing was best left to opposite sex couples, that denying marriage did not cause any harm to LGBTQ people, and that the court had no right to change thousands of years of understanding of what marriage was. These arguments would be constantly repeated over the next three years as the battle to protect same-sex marriage raged.

Fortunately for marriage advocates, the reputation of the Archdiocese of Boston was in tatters, its political power destroyed. At one time, the influence of the Catholic Church had been extremely strong. Though the nineteenth century had been marked by anti-Catholic rhetoric and much of the twentieth-century regional political scene was a battle between Catholic Boston and its Protestant suburbs, by the middle of the twentieth century the church's political influence was at its zenith. At one time, a phone call to the legislative leadership could kill a proposed law, and as late as the 1990s, the church had thrown its weight to successfully defeat an assisted suicide referendum.

The Church had nearly destroyed itself, however, by ignoring the sexual abuse of children by its priests for decades, moving accused men to other parishes while ordering families to remain silent. When the *Globe* finally exposed the extent of the abuse, the Boston Archdiocese (once one of the most powerful in the country) was financially and morally bankrupt.[3] Still trying to influence state politics and destroy same-sex marriage, the Catholic Church held information meetings in parishes and organized a rally on the Common that attracted several thousand people. It announced a parish-based voter registration project and heavily lobbied legislators while it threatened to defeat pro-marriage supporters at the next election. But the laity no longer listened to its priests and the Cardinal's ability to rouse voters had dissipated

The hierarchy opposed it, but most Catholics were in favor of same-sex marriage.

The Catholic Church further compromised itself by joining a coalition that included partners such as Focus on Families and other extreme anti-LGBTQ organizations. Showing its homophobia, the Archdiocese tied itself to groups who compared homosexuality to bestiality and suggested same-sex marriage would lead to the end of civilization. Even worse, the church began adopting some of the horrendous rhetoric of these groups. Even as Cardinal Patrick O'Malley called for treating gays and lesbians humanely, the paper he controlled (*The Pilot*) said that the approval of same-sex marriage world lead to the legalization of incest and child molesting.[4]

Many Catholic opponents and most of the church hierarchy said they were not anti-gay bigots, but these arguments rang hollow as they hurled anti-gay vitriol at LGBTQ people. Some Catholics tried to say they hated the sin yet loved the sinner but given that same-sex attraction and gender non-conformity were part of their core being, these attacks were aimed at the very existence of LGBTQ people. Furthermore, the church had little positive history regarding LGBTQ people. For centuries it had condemned all same-sex behavior and though the church operated some hospice services, it had provided little comfort to those dying of AIDS. In addition, the church strongly condemned sex outside of marriage while at the same time opposing same-sex marriage, leaving celibacy as the only option for LGBTQ people. The bishops said they were upholding a thousand-year tradition, not opposing civil rights. Yet the church was against any compromise and threatened legislators who suggested that civil unions be established in lieu of marriage. As a result, those who remained faithful to the church, just a fraction of those who once did, mostly ignored the bishops' teaching on the issue. A few brave priests even spoke out in favor of same-sex marriage, only to be punished by the Archdiocese.

Fortuitously, Massachusetts had relatively few evangelicals and the network of conservative Protestants who worked to defeat LGBTQ rights in other states did not exist here. In contrast, the largest and most powerful alliance of religious institutions in the state was a group formed to advance LGBTQ rights, the Religious Coalition for the Freedom to Marry. Made up of Reform Jewish congregations, Unitarians, Congregationalists, Episcopalians, and other liberal religions, it helped funnel contributions and volunteers into the fight to protect marriage. The coalition formed in 1997, just as the LGBTQ community was getting ready to go to court and it provided a strong religious counterpoint to the bigotry of the Catholic bishops.

As the battle over same-sex marriage heated up, national money poured into the state as both sides began holding rallies that attracted some of the largest crowds the State House had seen in years. On January 8, 2004, a thousand supporters of same-sex marriage demonstrated at the State House. The Catholic Church held a large rally on Sunday, February 8, and two days later, the pro-marriage forces packed over 3,000 people into the State House before police shut down access to any more.

On February 5, 2004, the SJC rattled the opposition by declaring that civil unions would not be an adequate response to its ruling, saying they would establish "an unconstitutional, inferior, and discriminatory status for same-sex couples." This meant a simple law to create civil unions and outlaw marriage, requiring just a majority of legislators, would not pass constitutional muster. The state could still create this alternative, but the only way to do so would be by amending the constitution itself.

Same-sex marriage advocates slightly relaxed. Though they had been confident that the court would rule this way, they could not be sure, and though many thought they could win a vote against civil unions in the legislature, no one wanted to put that to the test. At the same time, anti-LGBTQ forces didn't particularly care about the ruling; they opposed civil unions as strongly as they did marriage. It was the moderates, who had held out hope for civil unions as a compromise and who found themselves a shrinking sliver between the two opposing sides, who were upset. They now had no cover.

Normally an event with just minor newspaper coverage, the entire country intently watched as the Massachusetts constitutional convention began on February 11 with all its traditional pomp including a parade of the state's forty senators into the House chamber led by the Sargent at Arms whose attire included a top hat and ornamental staff. Once again, John Winthrop's words, that Boston should be "a city on the hill, looked at by all for its communal charity," were on people's minds. Advocates and opponents knew that if same-sex marriage could not be defended in liberal Massachusetts, then it would not be possible in any state. The political fight grew in intensity as once again, Massachusetts was the central battleground of a great moral issue.

At that moment, pro-marriage advocates could only count on fifty supporters. What was unknown was how many of the remaining 150 legislators would vote against civil unions because they were against any legal recognition of same sex couples and how many were in favor of a civil union compromise.

The pro-marriage forces were led by an informal "group of groups" that included Isaacson, Bonauto, Holly Gunner, Josh Freitas, Robert Debenedictus, Norma Shapiro, Mark Solomon, Stan Rosenberg, and Gary Buseck. The group had been meeting every four to six weeks since the *Goodridge* suit had been filed. Including both veteran activists and newcomers with special skills, they were terrified. Looking back on the struggle, Holly Gunner (representing the ACLU) believed this fear helped make them more effective. "You had to be scared to have a shot at winning," she said.

On the morning of the first constitutional convention, the State House crackled with emotion as it filled with people from both sides. From the moment the convention opened with a recitation of the Pledge of Allegiance, emotions were high. Former city liaison John Affuso remembers how pro-marriage people shouted the pledge's final two words, "for all," so loudly that startled legislators looked up at the gallery.[6] One marriage supporter recalled that "[t]he building was packed, people on both sides of the issue jammed together, occasionally pushing and shoving. Small groups of fundamentalist Christians were sitting together, holding hands, kneeling and praying, some with eyes closed and hands to the sky making noise, speaking i tongues. Some were loudly praying for us, putting their hands over our heads. As Mary Bonauto walked through the corridors, some followed her around, chanting at her in an eerie tone, "eeevil, eeevil!"[2]

Showing his hand as the convention began, Finneran introduced a constitutional amendment to ban same-sex marriage without substituting civil unions–a complete repeal of the *Goodridge* decision. After hours of debate, the vote began at 4:55 p.m. with many in the audience and halls exhausted as some had been in the building since it had opened at 8:00 a.m. Finneran's amendment lost 98-100. Then a civil union compromise failed 94-104. The convention ran into a second day with opponents again proposing to outlaw same-sex marriage without civil unions, but they still lacked enough votes to move it forward.

Now applying the lessons learned in the long, frustrating effort to secure the anti-discrimination bill and DPB legislation, pro-marriage proponents decided to stall and filibuster the convention because at midnight, it would take a unanimous vote to extend it. But the pro-marriage crowd, lobbyists, and their legislative allies were near collapse, having been working without rest for nearly eighteen hours. As the evening grew late, they sent word to Club Café that they needed reinforcements to keep up the pressure to preserve the right to marry. In perhaps the most emotional and important outburst in the centuries-old history of LGBTQ Boston, people called friends, relatives, and acquaintances to tell them it was an emergency, imploring them to rush to the State House. From across the region, hundreds of LGBTQ people and their allies ran to Beacon Hill and soon the somber corridors and historic spaces of the building, whose cornerstone had been set by Paul Revere, reverberated once again with chanting, singing, and praying people, enthusiastically united in their support for marriage. The anti-marriage forces had gone home for the evening. The sudden outpouring of grassroots activism revived the spirits of exhausted legislators and lobbyists and re-energized the pro-marriage forces to maintain the filibuster. When the hour hit midnight, the convention adjourned and marriage was still on track. But the legislature had agreed to reconvene the constitutional convention in March.

The gold dome of the State House physically and symbolically dominates Boston. In a region that is steeped in history, the Charles Bulfinch-designed building is the physical embodiment of its rich past and both sides in the marriage debate tried to use this history to bolster their arguments. The state constitution, written by John Adams, predates the U.S. Constitution. What would John Adams have felt about same-sex marriage, both sides pondered? Byron Rushing, one of the most scholarly members of the House, pointed out that the authors of the state constitution hadn't allowed black people to vote, so expanding its protections to include LGBTQ people was not inconsistent with other changes over time.[2]

Meanwhile, five lawsuits were filed against the SJC decision, the most serious being the one by Jerry Falwell in federal court. Other lawsuits were filed by straight people, including former mayor Ray Flynn, that claimed same-sex marriage hurt their opposite-sex marriage. Fortunately, the courts quickly rejected these arguments and the state suits were defeated. Falwell's suit was also dismissed as the federal government traditionally played no role in how states framed their requirements for marriage.

Over the next month, advocates adopted a controversial and risky strategy: encourage supporters to vote yes on the proposal to replace marriage with civil unions, substituting the total marriage ban amendment with an alternative unpalatable to most opponents. Then they would marshal all their resources to oppose it at the second constitutional convention. Senator Stan Rosenberg, a gay but not yet publicly out legislator, proposed this strategy. Members of the coordinating group were skeptical, however, and it was only because of the great trust they had in Isaacson, who had guided LGBTQ forces on Beacon Hill for several decades, that they adopted Rosenberg's suggestion. The first phase of this strategy worked and on March 29, the constitutional convention reconvened and passed a civil union amendment 105-92. The yeas included eighty-three legislators who were pro marriage. The battle for marriage would resume with a new legislature in 2005.

As the day of marriage approached, anxiety increased even as many couples began planning their weddings, deciding where to apply for a license, how to solemnize their union, who to invite, whether to have a reception, and all the other trappings of wedding planning. Preparations were mostly low key and easily cancellable because no one knew if they might be some last-minute roadblock to this anticipated day. Part of the fear stemmed from Governor Romney, who to the very end kept saying he would do everything in his power to stop the marriages from taking place. Fortunately, the governor's threats were not backed by actions.

May in Boston can be dismal, with cold rains and raw winds. But Sunday, May 16, 2004 was unseasonable sunny and warm with low humidity and just a light breeze. Cambridge opened City Hall at midnight to enable same-sex couples to apply for marriage licenses at the first possible moment it was legal, deciding that LGBTQ people had waited long enough. Living just a few blocks away, Senator Jarrett Barrios and his longtime partner Doug Hattaway hosted a small dinner to celebrate the event. After dessert and some toasts, the party walked down to a closed off Massachusetts Avenue where there were 5,000 chanting and cheering people waiting for the doors to open. The first couple in line, the first same-sex couple to receive a marriage license in the United States, was Susan Shepherd and Marcia Hams.

Across the state, Monday was filled with joy bordering on euphoria. Couples applying for licenses in Lexington were greeted with hugs and balloons. Similar crowds cheered same-sex couples on in other towns. Mayor Menino made sure that there was adequate staff to accommodate the 213 couples who showed up at Boston City Hall that first day. There were another 268 marriage license applications in Cambridge and hundreds more in other cities and towns. Because of a quirk in Massachusetts law, there is a default wait time of three days between the application for a license and its issuance unless the couple petitions a judge to waive the waiting period, which several couples did.

Mary Bonauto was in tears even before plaintiffs David Wilson and Rob Compton walked down the aisle at the Arlington Street Church. "It's beyond overwhelming. I just didn't have any idea how I would feel. It's a day for joy," she said.[7] Plaintiffs Mike Horgan and Ed Balmelli planned their jazz serenaded wedding at the Marriott Copley Place in just ten days. Julie and Hillary Goodridge had their daughter as their ring bearer after they applied for and received a waiver to allow them to be married that Monday. When their minister asked if there was anyone present who had a reason why the couple should not be married, the crowd broke out in laughter. The clergy at Temple Israel were so excited about same-sex marriage that two of the weddings that first week included three rabbis and two cantors. These were events not to be missed.

The 2004 elections were a disaster for LGBTQ people in most of the United States as the court ruling in Massachusetts prompted a new wave of state DOMA laws to be passed. Many pro-gay politicians were defeated and it seemed that Massachusetts might be the lone state with same-sex marriage. In the wake of these losses, some, including a few people at the national offices of the Human Rights Campaign (HRC), believed the moment too soon for marriage equality. They suggested that the effort for marriage be put on hold. The opposition from HRC was particularly worrisome because it had channeled significant funds to MassEquality, one of the organizations working to preserve same-sex marriage, despite not having been initially supportive of the Massachusetts effort. But Bonauto and others convinced national LGBTQ leaders and organizations to remain supportive.

On the other hand, the situation inside the state was becoming more promising. Anti-marriage Tom Finneran resigned as Speaker of the House. Though disheartening for LGBTQ people nationally, the 2004 elections were positive for same-sex marriage in Massachusetts. Several anti-gay incumbents were replaced while everyone who voted for marriage was reelected. One furiously homophobic representative from Somerville was replaced by the young, erudite Carl Sciortino, an openly gay man. After a distinguished career in the legislature, Sciortino would become the Executive Director of AAC. In Massachusetts, at least, being openly gay was better for getting elected than being publicly anti-LGBTQ.

Demonstrating that the support for same-sex marriage was strong at the ballot box was the priority of the grassroots arm of the pro-marriage forces during this election cycle. MassEquality began almost spontaneously in response to attempts to pass DOMA legislation in Massachusetts in the late 1990s. Though these efforts never made it out of committee, it pointed out the need for a large-scale movement, based in the LGBTQ community but including any and all straight allies, which would reach out to districts across the state. MassEquality started small; it only incorporated in 2001 and hired its first employee in 2003 but it was able to muster thousands of volunteers to advocate for marriage. MassEquality was helped by Freedom to Marry, a national organization that devoted large amount of resources to protect same-sex marriage in Massachusetts. That group was led by Evan Wolfson, who had made a case for same-sex marriage in his law school thesis back in 1983.

Pro-marriage groups pivoted to prepare for the 2005 constitutional convention, going through state lists of marriage certificates to identify same-sex marriages. The goal was to find constituents in each district to help change the votes of sixteen legislators so that the civil union amendment would be defeated. Fortunately, the anti-marriage forces fell into the trap laid for them when marriage opponents announced they would vote against the amendment because they could not endorse civil unions, making the prospects for the amendment poor. Unfortunately, opponents also decided to attempt to pass a signature-initiated amendment banning both marriage and civil unions, meaning that they would only need fifty votes in the constitutional convention to send the amendment to the voters. The only positive aspect of this was that it meant the earliest the amendment could get on the ballot would be 2008. Against this impending amendment, Mass Equality and other organizations met with legislators to introduce them to same-sex couples in their districts. There seemed to be progress, but the final outcome was very much in doubt.

When the constitutional convention convened on September 14, 2005, the civil union amendment was defeated 39 to 157, but that included anti-gay legislators who were opposed to civil unions because they were against any and all efforts to make the lives of LGBTQ people better. A close look at the vote suggested that 120 legislators were now in favor of same-sex marriage but that left more than enough to pass the signature-initiated amendment.

Motivated by anti-LGBTQ animus, opponents now went out to collect signatures for a constitutional amendment to ban civil unions and same-sex marriage. They submitted over 125,000 to the Secretary of State, more than twice as many as needed. This meant there would be another showdown at the next constitutional convention and so the battle continued even as more LGBTQ people wed.

The 2006 state elections yielded four more supporters in the legislature with no one who had voted in favor of gay marriage defeated. It also brought in pro-LGBTQ and pro-marriage Deval Patrick as governor. The election proved that Massachusetts, unlike elsewhere, supported marriage at the polls. This helped convince some borderline legislators that a pro-marriage vote would not hurt their careers.

On multiple occasions in the past, the constitutional convention had defeated amendments with less than majority support simply by adjourning before a vote was taken, so this became the pro-marriage strategy. On November 9, the convention voted to adjourn until January 2, 2007, the last day of the legislative term. It looked like the amendment would be defeated until lame-duck Governor Romney intervened and convinced the SJC to issue a ruling that though it could not force the constitutional convention to act, there should be a vote. The pro-marriage forces reeled and despite the work of governor-elect Patrick and others, the amendment passed 62-134, twelve votes more than necessary. One more vote in the new legislative term, which began the next day and would last for two years, and the amendment would go to the ballot.

Within a few weeks, pro-marriage forces persuaded three legislators to switch their votes. That still left a need to convert nine more legislators before the next constitutional convention, scheduled for June 2007. Changing votes was becoming increasingly difficult as the remaining legislators were mostly hardcore opponents. Additionally, pro-marriage advocates were seeing resistance inside the LGBTQ community. Radicals, never happy with the marriage push to begin with, were becoming increasingly uneasy with the public face of a marriage campaign that stressed the normalcy of same-sex couples. They felt insulted and abandoned by this strategy and began to openly oppose marriage as a patriarchal institution, worrying advocates who were afraid that anything less than a united front would hurt their cause. In the trenches seeking to convert the votes of individual legislators, pro-marriage advocates continued to stress the unremarkable qualities of same sex couples. Though this was insulting to some LGBTQ people, the group managing the fight saw no viable alternative strategy.

Marriage advocates were able to draw on the Massachusetts Democratic establishment that didn't want a 2008 referendum that could potentially boost Romney's presidential campaign, an argument that won three more votes. But just a week before the constitutional convention, the pro-marriage forces were still six votes shy of defeating the amendment. Desperate, they used all the resources it could muster, from Log Cabin Republican Patrick Guerriero to Senator Ted Kennedy and Representative Barney Frank.

14.1 The march through the Common

More legislators flipped but the night before the convention, pro-marriage forces were still three votes down as LGBTQ lobbyists and their opponents desperately worked to win votes. LGBTQ people did not fight this frenzied battle alone; progressive allies from across the state joined to help them. The morning of the convention began with a gathering of the Religious Coalition for the Freedom to Marry at St. Paul's Episcopal Cathedral, where in 1971 Pride marchers had stopped to protest religious bigotry against LGBTQ people. Now the church was open and affirming. After a rousing prayer service in favor of marriage, this large gathering of pro-LGBTQ clergy from across the region marched through the Common to the State House singing a

South African freedom song that had the powerful line, "We are marching in the light of God."[2] Inside, the lobbying continued. Both sides were now frantic as no one was sure which way the vote would go.

The Senators walked into the House chamber at 1:01 and the convention convened at 1:08 with an immediate call for a vote. The Senators voted by roll call and at 1:13 the vote stood at thirty-four no, five yes. If just 45 of the 158 representatives voted yes (two seats were vacant), the anti-marriage amendment would go to a public referendum. The House votes electronically and for the next several minutes, the world seemed to stop. Across Boston, Massachusetts, and the country, LGBTQ people held their breath. The consequences of this vote were enormous. Either same-sex marriage would be preserved with the hope it might spread across the United States or it might be eliminated, with the dreams of millions of LGBTQ people destroyed. Neither side was sure how the vote would go.

When the Senate and House votes were tallied, the amendment lost 45-151. Same-sex marriage was saved and was never again at risk in Massachusetts. That night, gay bars across the state were packed with joyous LGBTQ people and their allies. There was a line to get into Club Café, a group of LGBTQ people were seen dancing in front of Sister Sorel restaurant on Tremont St., and happy bears (burley gay men) spilled out into the street outside of Fritz as they raised victory toasts. Strangers hugged each other on the sidewalks of the South End and a crowd gathered in Copley Square to celebrate. In Provincetown, Commercial St. was a mass of deliriously happy people. There were parties in Jamaica Plain, Medford, Northampton, and other places as a new queer world was at hand.

The fight for marriage was successful because it used coalition tactics tested in the legislative battles of the past several decades. At its core was a steering committee of seasoned LGBTQ activists. GLAD was the legal arm: Bonauto, Buseck and their allies coordinated strategies that culminated in the SJC rulings of November 2003 and February 2004 as well as the legal analysis of the various bills and amendments filed afterwards. The Caucus, with its lobbying effort led by the brilliant Isaacson, was the point group that worked with allies in the legislature to focus on individual lawmakers to flip them to support marriage. The outside organizations also kept constituent pressure on legislators to help the effort.

The success of same-sex marriage was built on the activism that began in the 1970s. This work produced a victory in several ways. First, it trained multiple generations on how to work with elected officials, honing their skills at lobbying and organizing and produced longstanding relationships with allies outside the LGBTQ community. Second, it gave LGBTQ activists a sense of their ability to win legislative and policy battles. They could advocate for same-sex marriage with optimism that their efforts had a reasonably-strong chance of succeeding. Finally, each policy debate and victory helped energize the community and boost public support for LGBTQ issues. A strong majority of the Massachusetts public grew accustomed to supporting LGBTQ rights. "In Massachusetts it was more difficult to demonize lesbian and gay people as shadowy 'strangers in our midst' because Massachusetts activists had been at the forefront in creating a culture where LGBT people were visibly embedded in communities."[1]

Same-sex marriage began as technology greatly transformed LGBTQ life. Up until the 1960s there was almost no way to know of the existence of other LGBTQ people except through face-to-face contact, creating a heavy reliance on bars and cruising areas for information. In the 1970s, anyone looking for evidence of other LGBTQ people had to read the back pages of the *Boston Phoenix*, tune in to the few weekly radio programs, or read one of the several LGBTQ newspapers that sprang up in those years. Even *GCN* felt compelled to occasionally run directories of bars, though it often refused ads it thought were too explicit. The 1980s in Boston, like elsewhere, were a golden age for the LGBTQ press with papers and magazines proliferating constantly.

A major change in how people found each other was the introduction of phone sex lines in the late 1980s. Primarily aimed at gay men with a few lines for transsexuals, lesbians, and bisexuals, these services allowed anyone to call and anonymously talk one-on-one or in groups with likeminded people. Thus a new form of interaction entered people's repertoire, phone sex. It was no longer necessary to go to a bar or cruising area to meet sex partners. An added bonus was the lack of danger of violence, arrest, or catching a sexually transmitted disease, though some men openly stated they were looking for unsafe sex (whether this was just a way of playing out fantasies during the AIDS epidemic or a true request is unknown). Boston businessman Larry Basile, the owner of Fritz, made millions off this new technology as he set up lines across the country. (He would donate a significant percentage of the profits to LGBTQ causes.) The only downside was the cost of these services. At ten cents per minute, some users ran up large bills and if they were not out to families or roommates, these could lead to awkward conversations.

In the mid to late 1980s, the development of the Internet created another technology-based alternative to bars, newspapers, and cruising. At first access relied on slow, clumsy dial-up services that were not much more than bulletin boards. Users could post messages and pictures and read others' postings. These boards quickly acquired the capacity for group forums, chat rooms, private email, one-on-one messaging, and more. Ultimately, the Internet was a tremendous resource, particularly for young people or those in isolated communities. However, the immediate casualty was newspaper advertising revenue. Coupled with a late-1980s real estate boom that crushed many LGBTQ bars, many newspapers disappeared.

For a brief time, the Boston area had its own LGBTQ Internet bulletin board service, the Bear's Den, but it quickly folded with rumors that it was shut down because it allowed minors to log on. More durable were chat rooms and private messaging via America on Line (AOL), Gay.Com, and others. At its height, AOL would feature 3-4 Boston focused chat rooms (technology limited the number of participants to just two dozen or so per room). Initially, these chat rooms complemented bars. Luxor, for example, held AOL nights where users sported tags featuring their screen names. Over time, however, the technology further reduced the community's reliance on bars and cruising areas. Bars began to empty out and close while the Fens and other cruising areas ceased to be popular places to meet.

The latest disruptive technology is the addition of apps that allow people to talk, send messages, and hook up via their phones. Now people can connect anywhere at any time and there is no need to go to a bar or cruising area, no tether to one particular place. Many in the LGBTQ community consider these apps to be the final death of LGBTQ bars.

But it wasn't just technology that changed nightlife and cruising in Boston. New social norms transformed the LGBTQ community as well. When they were a disreputable minority, bars and house parties were the only places LGBTQ people could relax free of hatred and condemnation, while cruising areas were the only place many could have sex; discovery by families, roommates, and landlords meant ruin. As a result, many who came out before 1990 believed that sex in cruising areas was part of their liberation and activists such as Charley Shively and John Mitzel declared it was their right to cruise anywhere they wanted. Eric Rofes told friends that one of the reasons he stepped down as Chair of the Alliance was that he wanted to be an advocate for sex in the bushes of the Fenway. Though many looked down on these free-wheeling habits, few openly condemned them before the advent of AIDS.

Public cruising was almost always a male activity as women and trans people were more at risk from assault or police actions. But as gay men acquired social respectability and became open about their sexuality, their way of life changed. The prominent male-male couples of the early twentieth centuries rarely dared to live together. Piatt Andrew and Henry Sleeper, for example, maintained side by side houses. As time went on, however, couples moved in with each other and many had children. While many did not practice monogamy, it was still awkward, if not impossible, for one partner to announce they were leaving the house to go to a bar or cruising area to find other sex partners.[8] Thus, living together, marriage, and childrearing reduced the number of people who visited bars and cruising areas and as both depended on volume, the loss of patrons resulted in their decline and closing.

Another problem was gentrification. As high housing costs reshaped the region, Boston's LGBTQ population dispersed around the metropolitan area. While the South End remained heavily gay, its population was older, more affluent, and less likely to go out. Beacon Hill and Back Bay were no longer gay neighborhoods and the Fenway was now mostly students. Young LGBTQ adults were now living in Allston/Brighton, Mission Hill, Somerville, and Medford. This meant traveling to a bar in Boston now took more time and money.

The same rise in property values hurt gay bars, which historically opened in low-rent areas. The legislature still controlled liquor sales in the city, keeping the number of bars well below what the market could support. This caused the value of liquor licenses to rise and made it more difficult to secure one. As a result, gay bars found it difficult to compete for the few open licenses available. Finally, some straight bars and restaurants now welcomed LGBTQ people. Almost every establishment in the South End was welcoming as were many other city venues. This made it hard to draw a line between gay and straight establishments. Elsewhere, the acceptance of LGBTQ people varied. In some bars, non-binary people could be very open and same-sex couples could be seen holding hands. In most parts of the region, same-sex couples could never touch and trans people had to be extremely cautious. But there was enough acceptance in the post-marriage equality world that LGBTQ people now had other options.

Some gay bars reacted by becoming more welcoming to straight people. At some point after 2000, it became popular for straight people to go to gay bars and for the most part they were welcomed unless their numbers become so large the bar no longer felt gay. The venerable Jacques, for example, began to cater to bachelorette parties. The impact of these bachelorette groups, many of whom have been accused of drunk and inappropriate behavior by LGBTQ patrons, was and is hotly debated in Boston, Provincetown, and elsewhere. Rowdy groups of drunk straight women were known to walk into bars, demand free drinks from bartenders, order DJs to play a favorite song, and try to kiss gay men or grab their genitals.[9] On a Saturday night in Provincetown, the entry of a bridal party into a bar could be like a bomb going off as LGBTQ people would quickly leave. This was not just a problem for gay bars; across the country many straight bars were banning these groups.[10]

In all, there were twenty-one bars in and around the Boston area in 1971. There were sixteen in 1996, but only seven full-time bars in 2007. With fewer places to go to begin with, women and non-binary people were particularly hit by the lack of venues. Mourning the end of the long running and very popular dyke night, one woman lamented "[e]very time a gay bar or a gay night closes, I weep for us, as a culture, and as a community. Because I don't want to be–I don't want to be assimilated," she says. "Because that's what gave us power. That's what gave us life."[11] For many, there is a void that can't be filled.

By the mid-2000s, just about every college had an LGBTQ student group. Harvard was at last open to LGBTQ people, but there could still be problems, particularly for lesbians. As one 2012 Harvard sophomore complained, "I think the gay male population is much more visible than the lesbian community, and I don't know why that is. It's something I've always thought about, but I'm just not sure...I don't think it's something Harvard talks about a lot."[12]

Lesbians at Harvard would often try and fail to find other gay women at the university. The struggle was made more difficult because many did not fit the stereotypes thrust on them while for some, their sexuality was fluid. A few seemed to envy their gay male counterparts. "I guess I feel like if I were a gay guy, I could go home with a different guy every night of the week if I really wanted to, whereas as a lesbian you can't really do that because you end up going back with the same people,"[12] reported one lesbian. Though the student body had more or less equal numbers of male and female students, LGBTQ parties were disproportionately male and one student estimated that out of every ten same-sex couples, eight were men.

There was an organization called Girlspot, but it has not been active in several years and as a result many women sought dates elsewhere. One woman lamented that "[t]he options end up being: room parties, final clubs, or a movie in the dorm–in any case, trapped in the heteronormative (and, from that structure, homonormative) walls of Harvard that seem unapproachable and unfriendly from the outside."[13]

The effort to protect same-sex marriage had been substantially boosted by the presence of out LGBTQ legislators. One of the most important was Liz Malia (1949-). The youngest of five children in an Irish Catholic family where her father was a doctor and her mother a nurse, she grew up in an upstate mostly-Republican New York town. But her family was heavily influenced by progressive Democratic politics and Malia learned her liberal values early. Malia entered Boston College in 1967 and after graduating, became an organizer of health-care workers.

Jamaica Plain was represented for many years by the anti-gay Senator Arthur Lewis, who was used by Senate President William Bulger to employ the parliamentary tactics that killed the anti-discrimination bill so many times. In this political environment, Malia became the administrative assistant to progressive Jamaica Plain Representative John McDonough in 1989 and when McDonough stepped down to work on health-care issues, Malia ran for the seat. She quickly became the favorite in a three-way special election. She easily won the race and has held it since 1998. Malia was out from the beginning, thanking her partner in her swearing in speech. As the most senior out LGBTQ member of the legislature, she was central to the efforts to protect same-sex marriage.

Another important LGBTQ voice in the legislature was Jarrett Barrios (1969-). He was proud to be Latino. "'I grew up in a Cuban family, both my mom and my dad, born in Fort Lauderdale, raised in Tampa, Fla.," Barrios said. "Coming out as a gay man in Tampa when I was in high school I guess it was hard, but it was hard, perhaps, for everybody. But a big, loving Cuban family probably made it a little easier at the end of the day."[14]

He moved to Cambridge to go to Harvard and after graduating and earning a law degree from Georgetown University, Barrios worked for Councilor Scondras. He was elected State Representative in 1998 and then to the Senate in 2002 representing Cambridge, Chelsea and other nearby areas. In addition to being a progressive voice in the legislature, he made a moving speech during the marriage debate when he told of the problems his family faced when he had to take a sick child to the hospital. He married his long-term partner soon after marriage became legal.

Barrios left the Senate in 2007 and a few years later he sadly went public regarding his divorce. He wrote in the *Globe*, "[i]n part because there were so many naysayers, we worked to be a model couple—with each of us trying be the perfect husband. Like other lesbian and gay couples, we hoped to show our relationships for what they are: loving partnerships that deserve the possibility of 'happily ever after' that marriage promises." He added, "Just as gay and lesbian couples share the joys of marriage, we will share the pain of divorce, something for which we have no template."[15]

The push for same-sex marriage both in Massachusetts and nationally tremendously alienated trans people as it sidelined their need for anti-bias legislation and anti-violence protection. One trans man noted, "we made a deal early on to be silent about our lives so we weren't muddying the waters for other people to have same-sex marriage and the truth is many of us need same-sex marriage, too. So we were asked to be quiet about our identities, but also about a movement that many of us are part of and that was very painful and we're left out, overtly and by negotiation."[16] This bitterness increased when Congressman Barney Frank betrayed the trans community by stripping trans protections out of the federal anti-discrimination bill. His stated reason was that it was necessary to pass the bill, yet he knew he still lacked the votes, making the gesture politically pointless but cruel.[17] He hurt the trans community without advancing gay and lesbian rights.

Doubling down on his betrayal, Frank blamed transgender activists for not educating and lobbying Congress. In doing so he ignored the years of effort that trans people had put into advancing their rights. In 2004, for example, transgender advocates targeted HRC, Frank, and Senator Kennedy to include gender identity in the ongoing effort to pass hate crime and other legislation in a campaign called, "civil rights for who?" They gathered thousands of pink postcards and sent them to HRC, which then betrayed them by supporting Frank's move.

There were rumors that some LGB leaders were dismissive of trans activists and accused trans people of riding on their civil rights efforts. There were whispers that some even said trans people were not really part of their community. Frank and others argued that once LGB protections were in place, the needs of trans people could then be addressed. But trans people did not accept this need to wait. Meanwhile, there is still no federal anti-discrimination bill for any LGBTQ people.

The first trans protection bill was even not introduced in the Massachusetts legislature until 2007. This delay contributed to the feelings of many that trans people were being sidelined until marriage equality was settled. In addition, some trans people felt betrayed; while millions of dollars poured into Massachusetts and then other states to promote same-sex marriage, only a small fraction of that amount was available for trans civil rights. One trans man sadly remarked that "[i]n some ways I think this experienced mimicked the experience of being shut out by your family of origin, because of your gender identity, but instead, our chosen family, the LGB community, was shutting some of us out."[16]

Unfortunately, the bill stalled in the legislature for several years because opponents had crafted a powerful political message that resonated among anti-trans bigots: the bill would let criminals into women's bathrooms. This transphobic argument was successful and it wasn't until the public accommodation clause was taken out of the bill that it moved through the approval process. This reduced bill was approved by the legislature on November 17, 2011 and signed by Governor Patrick six days later. It went into effect July 1, 2012, making Massachusetts the twelfth state to have a trans non-discrimination bill. After that point, trans people had protections regarding housing, employment, credit, and post-secondary education. Yet they lacked legal standing when it came to public accommodation—the right to go into stores, restaurants, and other public places as well as the right to use bathrooms corresponding to affirmed gender.

Trans rights activists went back to work and in 2016, Governor Charlie Baker signed into law a bill that outlawed discrimination based on gender identity in public places. Opponents quickly announced a signature drive to put a referendum to overturn the new law on the ballot. Because this was a proposed change to a law rather than the state constitution, it would not be subject to a vote in the legislature and could go directly to the ballot.

Opponents submitted enough signatures to get a rollback on the ballot, but they failed to secure enough signatures to put the law on hold, a good omen for protecting trans rights, but no one was willing to express confidence that the referendum (known as "Question 3" due to its position on the ballot) would be defeated. Another reason to be hopeful was the depth and breadth of support for protections for trans people. A broad coalition, Freedom for All Massachusetts, was quickly formed with trans people in the lead. Lesbians and gay men rallied around the effort to defend the law in a spirited, if very belated, payback for the work of trans people to win and protect same-sex marriage. Almost every important corporation and institution in the state supported trans rights including all four of Boston's major league sports teams most large employers, many faith organizations, labor unions, and others. Still, given the poor fate of LGBTQ issues at the ballot box, no one was taking the effort to oppose the rights bill lightly and as the summer began, there was a lot of fear about what might happen in November 2018 when the initiative would be put to a vote.

Despite signs of a more welcoming society, many trans people continued to face intense obstacles. There was a high rate of poverty in the transgender community because of discrimination, and violence remained a tremendous problem. Discrimination was deeply rooted in the prejudices of the cisgender community, which included many gay men and lesbians. One woman said that "people need to stop thinking that trans people are disordered. They just are people".[16] Among the challenges trans people faxed were sexist ideas of what was acceptable male or female behavior. A middle school youth questioning his female gender assignment, for example, had to fight to be allowed to join a football club. Fortunately, there were clubs and support groups, both locally and online, that he could reach out to.[18] Many people courageous ly rejected the pressure to be male or female, celebrated being non-binary and used pronouns that were not explicitly male or female. Many now use pronouns such as they or xi rather than he or she, for example.[19]

Many transgender people came to Boston because of its liberal reputation. Particularly in its colleges and universities, it was possible to avoid some of the worst episodes of bigotry that happen elsewhere. Outright harassment is, for the most part, not accepted here. But there are the small everyday affronts that add to stress. One person recalled that "I haven't experienced any kind of classic textbook harassment or meanness or bullying. On the other hand, there are the everyday things that really grind you down. Pronouns are a big one, being misgendered by strangers, accidentally misgendered by people who know my pronouns, being called 'sir' at the burrito truck."[19]

This transphobia was dangerous. The Fenway surveyed 452 trans people in 2013 and found that 65 percent experienced discrimination because they were non-gender conforming or trans, 25 percent reported that this discrimination occurred in a health-care setting, and 5 percent said that a health-care provider had refused to treat them because they were trans or gender nonconforming.[20]

In 2001, Massachusetts added anti-trans crimes to its list of hate crimes and mandated that they be reported. Yet by 2011, no crimes had been reported to the state. This reflected the extremely difficult position in society for trans people and the problems of working with the police, not that the state was a safe place. Trans people are afraid of the police, their efforts to reach out to cisgendered people are often rejected, crimes against them are considered to be not important or brought upon by themselves, and they are vulnerable because of discrimination.[21]

Much work remained to be done. The Boston Foundation and the Fenway collaborated on a 2018 report on the status of Massachusetts's LGBTQ population relying on a variety of surveys and sources for its data. Despite having the second highest LGBTQ percentage of any state and decades of social and political progress, the results were sobering. 65 percent of trans people reported discrimination against them in a public place (unchanged from the 2013 number), 17 percent lived in poverty, 24 percent experienced discrimination in a health-care situation while 61 percent experienced housing discrimination, and 75 percent of LGBTQ people who were murdered were trans.[22]

For nearly a decade after same-sex marriage was legal in Massachusetts, it remained unrecognized by the federal government and though the number of states that allowed same-sex marriage slowly increased, many couples found themselves in a legal twilight zone, not sure what rights, if any, they had. However, the LGBTQ community basked in a glow of new possibilities. Marriage made life easier and more peaceful for some couples with children. "This Valentine's Day," one couple said, "we will likely enjoy a nice quiet dinner at home, once the kids are in bed."[23]

The reactions of the straight world towards same-sex couples changed. One

woman noted that "[i]f you're introduced as someone's wife versus their girlfriend, there's a different meaning." Others said that before marriage, "their relationships felt invisible. Despite being in a relationship they were treated as if they were single. Marriage gave LGBTQ people and others the language to describe their relationship."[24]
There were fundamental improvements to people's lives that likely stemmed from the new legal status afforded to LGBTQ people. A study of gay men who received healthcare from the Fenway, for example, found that legalizing same-sex marriage had a profoundly positive impact on the health of Boston gay men, reducing clinic visits for physical and mental health issues by 13 percent. Visits for HIV/AIDS related issues were stable, indicating that these men were still receiving care, but it appeared that overall health improved. The benefits were the same for both partnered and single men.[25]

Changes in attitudes towards LGBTQ people began to extend to places formerly very hostile. South Boston was caught up in the city's widespread redevelopment and gentrification and the neighborhood began to lose some of its conservatism. Some of the most rabidly anti-LGBTQ people died or moved out of the area while those that remained were more supportive of LGBTQ rights. But they were mostly silent, however.

After twenty years of exclusion, Mayor Marty Walsh tried to broker a deal to allow LGBTQ veterans to march in 2014 St. Patrick's Day Parade but the effort broke down. However, LGBTQ people marched as members of several South Boston community groups that year. Suddenly, almost anti-climatically, the LGBTQ veterans group was allowed in the 2015 parade. The change in how they were received by the crowd was dramatic. "When Boston Pride walked past Dorchester Street and onto East Broadway, spinning rainbow umbrellas and wearing 'wicked proud' shirts, the crowd yelled loudly in support. Some of the marchers said 'thank you' in response, while others just waved in happiness"[26] It seemed that the world, or a small corner of it, had been reborn.

Then in 2017, the Council suddenly reversed itself and again voted to keep LGBTQ groups out of the parade. As previously mentioned, however, Southie was different now. For the past several years, Kiki beach (a gathering of LGBTQ people at the M Street beach on summer Saturdays) had attracted scores of people who were not shy about their gender and sexuality. No one cared. In 2017 Edward Flynn, the son of Mayor Ray Flynn who had once joined a lawsuit against same-sex marriage, campaigned for city council in the South End, a neighborhood that Southie politicians had ignored since district elections had been implemented. He actively campaigned for LGBTQ votes.

Demonstrating Southie's new attitude, the reaction of most people in the neighborhood was disgust at the Council's homophobia. Many thought it was time to move on, let LGBTQ people march in the parade, and focus on other issues, while others were proud of diversity. Facing overwhelming condemnation, the anti-gay elements of the Council backed down and again allowed LGBTQ people in the parade. More changes were still to come. In an astounding turn of events in 2018, the Council hired an out gay man, Bryan Bishop (a leader of the LGBTQ veterans group), to organize the parade. He now oversees the parade he was once banned from.

Provincetown changed as well. It began to attract visitors from across the country with tourists from as far away as Los Angeles buying up summer homes. In part, this was the result of better transportation. During the summer, Provincetown was linked to Boston via high speed ferries; but this priced out the young people who came to work in the summertime and explore the wonders of an openly gay resort. As longtime-writer EJ Graff sadly noted, "[n]o longer do the Smith College girls get jobs as servers for the summer, sharing a run-down house for Memorial Day (known as 'baby dyke weekend'), roiled with romance and breakup drama."[27] Young people still visited the town, but only for a weekend or a week.

The young American LGBTQ workers were replaced by straight college students from Eastern Europe, who took advantage of a special visa program that allowed them to work in temporary jobs over the summer followed by the chance to travel across the country for an additional three months. As a result, Bulgarian is now the second most spoken language in the town in the summertime with many Jamaicans and Brazilians also working during high season.

In addition, the number of guest houses fell dramatically as there was more money to be made by converting them to condominiums. Many owners rented these units, keeping the summer population high, but the gay houseboys who once flocked to the town are gone. Similarly, the year-round population, never large, shrank. It was a fight over space between affluent LGBTQ people and those who were working class. "What makes the battle for Provincetown unusual is that it is largely a class struggle within a gay world."[28] However, LGBTQ people dominated the town to the extent that in 2005, the entire Board of Selectmen was gay or lesbian.

Provincetown also greatly benefited from same-sex marriage, adding to the resort atmosphere. One caterer remarked that "I have nine weddings to prepare menus for. I'm building a Web site and revamping my brochures. And I have to reserve chairs, glasses, dishes and silver now, or they'll be all booked up."[29] Some weddings were low-key; the new couple might simply have drinks at the Red Inn after a modest ceremony at Town Hall. Others were lavish. In 2018, one couple celebrated their nuptials by holding a catered reception at the Monument that included fireworks over the harbor.

Provincetown continues to be a popular LGBTQ resort with open displays of affection on the beach and LGBTQ people involved in almost all aspects of daily life. The crowd may be older and wealthier than before, but there are still people of color and younger folks among the visitors, and there remains an air of freedom that is rare outside the town. A Saturday night still finds Commercial St. packed at 1:00 a.m. and the town's drag shows and outrageous, yet entertaining, street life continues.

Well past its one hundredth year as an LGBTQ resort, the community is strong.

14.2 Crowd outside Spiritus Pizza, July 4, 2018

Also reflective of the new queer world, out LGBTQ politicians were no longer remarkable in Massachusetts. Though the number of out legislators remains small (presently just five) gay men and lesbians running for higher offices are routine and their sexuality is not a campaign issue. Richard Tisei (1962-), a longtime popular Republican state representative senator was repeatedly reelected even though the number of Republicans in the legislature was very small. He came out to the public in 2010 when candidate Charlie Baker picked him to be his running mate. The two were unopposed in the primary but lost to Deval Patrick and his running mate in the November elections. Tisei's sexuality was not an issue.

Encouraged by the political troubles of the Democratic congressman who represented his district, Tisei unsuccessfully ran against him in 2012 but was not able to overcome the general distaste for Republicans in the state even though the district was one of the few in New England with significant Republican presence. When the congressman retired at the end of the term, Tisei tried running again but was soundly defeated by a straight Democrat who more closely represented the political values of the voters–the electorate did not automatically dismiss LGBTQ candidates, but neither were they willing to support them if they were too conservative.

Republican Patrick Guerriero ran into a similar problem. He was a popular state representative and then Mayor of Melrose, a small suburb the north of Boston. Ambitious, he became Governor Jane Swift's deputy chief of staff and then her running mate in 2002. But when Mitt Romney entered the governor's race, Swift withdrew and though Guerriero continued to run for Lieutenant Governor, he was defeated in the primary. He went on to become head of the national Log Cabin Club in 2003 and subsequently became a political consultant.

Being more in tune with the increasingly liberal Massachusetts electorate, lesbian Democrats have had more success. Maura Healey (1972-) was born in New Hampshire and attended Harvard. With a law degree from Northeastern, she was a clerk for a federal judge and then an assistant district attorney for Middlesex County. She spent seven years working for the state Attorney General before running for the office herself when the incumbent ran for Governor. She easily secured the Democratic nomination and won nearly two thirds of the vote against her Republican rival. Her sexuality has never been a problem and her political future is bright.

Stan Rosenberg's experience (1949-) highlights the ways being gay is both a non-issue and something that can create problems. He was a native of Massachusetts and had a difficult childhood, being raised in foster homes. Poor but bright, he supported himself while attending University of Massachusetts - Amherst and then worked for a variety of politicians, culminating in serving two years as Executive Director of the Massachusetts Democratic Party. He was a State Representative for four years and then successfully ran for the Senate in 1990. In 2015, he became Senate President, the first to be gay or Jewish.

Rosenberg, a lifelong bachelor who was the subject of rumors about his sexuality, came out publicly in 2009. His decision to come out, which despite the year still took courage, was prompted by his growing relationship with Bryan Hefner (1987-). Hefner also had a troubled childhood, spending years with abusive parents that included multiple bouts of homelessness before being permanently removed from his family. Yet Hefner was also successful, attending, but not graduating from, Lesley University before landing a string of well-placed political internships, including one in the Rosenberg's Senate office.

The two soon became romantically involved despite their great differences in age. Many were put off by Hefner; he had an edge that made even LGBTQ people in state politics uneasy. No one knew, however, just how problematic he would prove to be. "There is almost universal agreement on Beacon Hill that Hefner, a Tasmanian devil of inflated ambition and emotional instability, caused considerable wreckage."[30] The two married in 2016. Rosenberg encouraged Hefner's ambitions as the young man styled himself to be a politically savvy consultant who ran Rosenberg's political operations.

For decades there had been an ever-changing cadre of young gay male political aides around the State House and City Hall. They shared many traits: they were usually single, worked long hours, tended to not have much money, and for the most part, were quiet but involved members of the LGBTQ community. Thus, they bonded while standing in the back of candidates' forums, fundraisers, and other political events. Few lasted in the group for long. Some, like John Meunier, once Gerry Studd's driver and later an aide to Mayor Flynn, married his longtime partner when it became legal, started a family, and became a successful businessman. Others succumbed to alcoholism or just grew tired of the high-pressure work.

Hefner was different. His "indiscreet behavior—unsolicited dick pics, incessant sexual come-ons, and wanton groping—became a wide-open secret on Beacon Hill. Gay culture can be permissive, but Hefner's behavior was extreme by any standard."[30] He was often drunk and carried on several affairs with or without Rosenberg's knowledge. He seemed to want raw power, not to influence policy, and as a result had a hard time finding or holding a job. Hefner was also mean, making crude remarks about other politicians and completely lacking empathy.

Hefner also didn't care if his sexual advances were welcome or not. In November 2017, four men reported that they had been sexually harassed by him including sexual assaults and unwanted groping. Rosenberg claimed he had kept Hefner separate from his official business in the Senate but soon it was discovered that Hefner had access to Rosenberg's official Senate email and sent out messages under his name. Hefner was accused of threatening men with ruin if they did not accept his advances, including lobbyists and legislative aides. Under pressure, Rosenberg first took a temporary leave as Senate President and then stepped down permanently and retired from office. An investigation cleared Rosenberg of any law breaking but severely criticized his ethics. Hefner was indicted by a grand jury. The case had not yet gone to trial as of 2018. As the scandal slowly unfolded, there was no blanket condemnation of LGBTQ people, though one homophobic *Boston Herald* columnist decided that Rosenberg and Hefner were a worse pair than Whitey Bulger and his brother, Senate President William Bulger. The columnist's bigotry led him to overlook Whitey's nineteen murders.[31] Most were sympathetic to Rosenberg even as they criticized the latitude he had given Hefner.

Boston Pride continued to experience conflicts over its meaning and its proper commemoration. Reflecting the diversity of LGBTQ people, many come to it with incompatible expectations. Some, connected to other social justice movements, want the parade to be primarily a political event. Some people feel that "the corporate presence at Pride is unwelcome, even unethical".[32] Others go to Pride to celebrate being an LGBTQ person and have fun. They want loud music and colorful costumes as they experience the sheer exuberance of LGBTQ life. Mindful of decades of repression, they welcome the marchers who represent the openness of their employers. Pride Committee Chair Sylvain Bruni state that "we believe that this is a good thing. It is good to have corporate America backing gay rights and being supportive of the LGBT community. We think that it is important to have companies that show their support both for the community in general, and for their employees."[32]

Some disagreed. In 2015, a small group stopped the parade at the corner of Boylston and Charles Streets to demand the removal of police and shift attention to issues raised by the Black Lives Matter movement. Leader Diva Williams argued that "[t]he Stonewall Warriors are here to bring Pride back to its roots. The Stonewall Riot was a riot against police brutality [of] black and Latinx queer people," she said. "It's been hijacked by mostly cisgender white men and turned into this commercial circus. Anyone with a political or radical message is segregated to the back of the parade."[33] In 2016, a Woburn police officer was selected to be parade marshal, but his criticisms of Black Lives Matter led to his replacement.

In 2017, a group staged an action at the start of the Pride Parade for fifteen minutes to protest the lack of attention to the number of trans women murdered in the past year. "The direct action group in Boston Pride criticized organizers for lacking sufficient leadership of queer and trans people of color. They also criticized parade organizers for their relationships with large corporations and the police, which both contribute to the oppression of LGBTQ people."[34] One of the organizers asserted that "Capitalism is antithetical to queer and trans people of color liberation."

In the last several years, the loudest cheers in the crowds have been for the survivors of the Pulse nightclub shooting in Orlando, Florida, trans people marching in support of the public accommodations bill, and a group of LGBTQ police. Despite its problems, many LGBTQ people still look forward to Pride and celebrate the dancing drag queens, phalanxes of out high-school students, and the many politicians who march to show their solidarity with the community. At the 2018 rally and festival on City Hall Plaza, there were so many people it was difficult to walk through the crowd.

Over the many years of LGBTQ activism in Massachusetts, the community and its political allies always tried to avoid a ballot question on their civil rights. Most were confident they would win any referendum against them, but none were willing to put this optimism to the test and suppressing ballot measures had been a central strategy of the Caucus and others since the 1980s.

Therefore, the 2018 anti-trans rights referendum was extremely troubling for all LGBTQ people and a special nightmare for the trans community. Adding to the anxiety, trans people were under assault by the federal government and President Donald Trump, who sought to erase their existence and extinguish their rights. To make matters more difficult, because of obtuse wording, the referendum required a yes vote to support trans rights, potentially confusing voters.

Mason Dunn, the trans man who ran the "Yes on 3" campaign, had an extremely difficult job in keeping the progressive coalition in support of the referendum together. Trans people and cisgender gay men and lesbians had been publicly feuding for almost twenty years as the bitterness over same-sex marriage festered. Trans people continued to feel rejected and marginalized, but they needed gay and lesbian cisgender contacts and support to get money, endorsements, and votes.

Dunn was a longtime leader of a New Hampshire trans political group before coming to Boston to lead the final push for the accommodations bill. He (his preferred pronoun) never forgot the tremendous obstacles stacked against trans people. As trans people and their allies grew fearful as the election drew near, Dunn was a strong, calm voice. Paradoxically, the fear was made worse by the lack of a public anti-trans campaign. Except for a few Internet ads, there was no sign of the opposition. Were they planning a last-minute television blitz? Did they have a secret weapon ready to unleash on the electorate? What was the opposition up to?

On November 7, it became clear that there was no organized opposition. There was an official anti-trans group, but they raised less than a quarter of what the pro-trans coalition raised. National money stayed out of the election and there was no last-minute media campaign as the anti-trans people had no money. As trans people and their supporters filled a room at the Copley Plaza Hotel on election night, it was clear that Question 3 would win. The only uncertainty was how big the margin of victory would be.

Trans people won a landslide victory, gaining just over 70 percent of the vote. The public-accommodation rights of trans people were affirmed and just as important, Massachusetts demonstrated to its trans neighbors, friends, and loved ones that they were honored, cherished, and welcomed. As Michelle Samuels, a trans woman at Boston University wrote soon after, "We found a way to defend transgender rights, we won by a landslide, and along the way, we made a space where trans, gender nonconforming, and other queer people could feel confident, safe, and strong enough to announce who they really were."[35] The queer new world embraced everyone.

Epilogue

THIS BOOK ENDS on election night, November 6, 2018, when Massachusetts voters overwhelmingly affirmed the public accommodation rights of transgender people. With the trans community in the lead, it was night for all LBGTQ people to celebrate and many filled a ballroom at the Copley Plaza hotel to savor the victory. It was too much to dream that all of the LGBTQ people who have lived in or visited Boston and Provincetown over the years could have been there to share in the triumph. So instead I wished there were three people who could have come back to life for that one night. First, I wished for Rita Hester because one of the things that make LGBTQ people special and an asset to the world is their ability to combine glamour with politics and style with protest. Who better represents this than Ms. Hester?

Second, I wished for Prescott Townsend. Nearly one hundred years ago he was at the State House, advocating for the rights of LGBTQ people at a time when no one else had the courage and ability to do so. He is a symbol of the great urge for freedom and dignity that unites those from the present with the past.

Last but not least, I wished for Katherine Bates in the hope she'd recite a poem that gives a soaring voice to the suffering and triumphs of the past four hundred years. To be an LGBTQ person is to have poetry in one's soul.

But I hated to limit those who could have seen that victory. I wished for all the transgender people who have been murdered to be up on that stage as they are our martyrs. I wished for the chance to see the more than 12,000 Massachusetts LGBTQ people who died of AIDS. If they could come back for a night, they could be hugged and remembered one more time and perhaps the suffering of those who died and those who were their friends and loved ones could be somewhat eased for a moment. I wished for all those bullied and those whose lives were ended by despair to come back so that they might know that we feel their pain and that their experiences have fueled generations of activism. I wished that every young person who struggled to come to terms with their sexuality and gender to have been able to stand arm in arm together because on that night they would know that millions had affirmed their dignity. Everyone who ever held a protest sign or someone else's hand, everyone who simply asserted their right to be who they knew themselves to truly be, deserved to be on the podium that night. This was their time.

Notes

Chapter 1

1. Heath W. Thomas Morton: From Merry Old England to New England. *Journal of American Studies.* 2007; 41(4):135-168.
2. Robinson JD. Thomas Morton Abandoned at Isles of Shoals. http://www.seacoastnh.com/history/history-matters/thomas-morton-abandoned-at-isles-of-shoals/. Accessed September 17, 2017.
3. Morton T. *Revels in New Canaan* 1637.
4. Bradford W. *Of Plymouth Plantation 1620-1647.* New York: Alfred A. Knopf; 1984.
5. Todd AL. "Holy Experiments and Unholy Acts: Sex, Law, and Religion in Colonial Massachusetts, Rhode Island, and Pennsylvania" Honors Thesis. University of Southern Mississippi. 2013.
6. Tobias A. *Gay Like Me.* 1998; http://harvardmagazine.com/1998/01/tobias.html. Accessed August 12, 2017.
7. Warner M. New English Sodom. *American Literature.* 1992; 64(1):19-47.
8. Oaks RF. "Things Fearful to Name": Sodomy and Buggery in Seventeenth-Century New England *Journal of Social History.* 1978; 12(2):268-281.
9. Godbeer R. "The Cry of Sodom": Discourse, Intercourse, and Desire in Colonial New England *The William and Mary Quarterly.* 1995; 52(2):259-286.
10. Salem Quarterly Court. Records. The History Project; 1641.
11. Painter G. The Sensibilities of Our Forefathers. 2001; https://www.glapn.org/sodomylaws/sensibilities/connecticut.htm. Accessed January 1, 2018.
12. Foster TA. Defiant Husbands: Manhood, Sexual Incapacity, and Male Sexual Incapacity in Seventeenth-Century New England *William and Mary Quarterly.* 1999; 56(4):723-744.
13. Talley CL. Gender and Male Same-Sex Erotic Behavior in British North America in the Seventeenth Century. *Journal of the History of Sexuality.* 1996; 6(3):385-408.
14. Seventeenth Century Transgender People. 2011; http://transgenderlawpolitics.blogspot.com/2011/05/seventeenth-century-transgender-people.html. Accessed December 6, 2017.
15. Adams J. *Legal Papers of John Adams* Cambridge, MA: Harvard University Press; 1965.
16. Bouvier L. History of LGBT Boston. In: Stein M, ed. *Encyclopedia of Lesbian, Gay, Bisexual, and Transgendered History in America.* New York: Charles Scribner's Sons; 2004.
17. The History Project. *Improper Bostonians: Lesbian and Gay History from the Puritans to Playland.* Boston: The Beacon Press; 1998.
18. Kokai JA. Even In Their Dresses The Females Seem to Bid Us Defiance: Boston Women and Performance 1762-1823. Thesis. Austin, TX, University of Texas; 2008.

Chapter 2

1. Mass.gov. Massachusetts Constitution and the Abolition of Slavery. www.mass.gov/guides/massachusetts-constituion-and-the-abolition-of-slavery. Accessed February 14, 2018.
2. National Park Service. The George Middleton House. https://www.nps.gov/boaf/learn/history-culture/george-middleton-house.htm. Accessed September 18, 1017.
3. The History Project. *Improper Bostonians: Lesbian and Gay History from the Puritans to Playland.* Boston: The Beacon Press; 1998.
4. Scupham-Biltman T. Extraordinary Lives 4. 2011; http://queerstoryfiles.blogspot.com/2011/10/extraordinary-lives-4.html. Accessed September 18, 2017.
5. Lopata J. Yankee Doodle Dandies. MySecretBoston.com. Accessed September 18, 2017.

6. Rotundo EA. Romantic Friendship: Male Intimacy and Middle Class Youth in the Northern United States, 1800-1900. *Journal of Social History*. 1989; 23(1):1-26.

7. Callow JT. Kindred Spirits: Knickerbocker Writers and American Artists, 1807-1855. Thesis. Chapel Hill, NC: University of North Carolina Press; 2012.

8. Lloyd P. Washington Allston: American Martyr? *Art in America*. 1984; 72(3):145-179.

9. Mr. Price. Flyer. The History Project archives, Early 19th Century.

10. Levesque GA. *Black Boston: African American Life and Culture in Urban America, 1750-1860*. New York: Routledge; 2018.

11. Jobson B. Sex in the Marketplace: Prostitution in an American City, Boston, 1820-1880: Thesis. Graduate School, Boston University; 1982.

12. Lane R. *Policing the City*. Boston 1822-1885. Cambridge, MA: Harvard University Press; 1967.

13. Thompson G. *Venus in Boston: And Other Tales of Nineteenth-century City Life*. Amherst, MA: University of Massachusetts Press; 1950.

14. Shand-Tucci D. *The Crimson Letter*. New York: St. Martin's; 2004.

15. Edelstein T. *Strange Enthusiasm: A Life if T. W. Higginson* New Haven, CT: Yale University Press; 1968.

16. Merrill L. *When Romeo Was a Woman: Charlotte Cushman and Her Circle of Female Spectators*. Ann Arbor, MI: University of Michigan Press; 2000.

17. Rapp L. Charlotte Cushman. 2015; http://www.glbtqarchive.com/arts/cushman_c_A.pdf. Accessed November 15, 2017.

18. Leach J. Harriet Hosmer: Feminist in Bronze and Marble. *The Feminist Art Journal*. 1976:9-13.

19. Green P. Overlooked No More: Edmonia Lewis, Sculptor of World Wide Acclaim. *New York Times*. July 25, 2018: on line.

20. Kesterson D. Hawthorne and Melville. http://www.hawthorneinsalem.org/ScholarsForum/HawthorneandMelville.html. Accessed December 15, 2017.

21. Parker H. *Herman Melville: A Biography, Volume 1; Volumes 1819-1851*. Baltimore, MD: JHU Press; 2005.

22. Seasholes NS. *Gaining Ground: A History of Landmaking in Boston*. Cambridge, Massachusetts: The MIT Press; 2003.

23. Lopez R. *Boston's South End: The Clash of Ideas in a Historic Neighborhood*. Boston: Shawmut Peninsula Press; 2015.

24. New England Historical Society. Emma Snodgrass, Arrested for Wearing Pants. http://www.newenglandhistoricalsociety.com/emma-snodgrass-arrested-wearing-pants/. Accessed December 10, 2017.

Chapter 3

1. Bendroth ML. *Fundamentalists in the City: Conflicts and Divisions in Boston's Churches, 1885-1950*. New York: Oxford University Press; 2005.

2. Deutsch S. *Women and the City: Gender, Space and Power in Boston 1870-1940*. New York: Oxford University Press; 2000.

3. Faderman L. *Surpassing the Love of Men*. New York: William Morrow and Company; 1981.

4. Handlin O. *Boston's Immigrants: 1790-1880*. Cambridge, MA: Belknap Press of Harvard University Press; 1941.

5. Sarna JD, Smith E, Kosofsky S-M. *The Jews of Boston*. New Haven, Connecticut: Yale University Press; 1995.

6. Ballou RA. *Even in "Freedom's Birthplace"! The Development of Boston's Black Ghetto, 1900-1940*. Ann Arbor, Michigan, University of Michigan Press; 1984.

7. Woods RA. *The City Wilderness: A Settlement Study*. Boston: Houghton, Mifflin and Company; 1898.

8. Hartley BL. *Evangelicals at a Crossroads: Revivalism and Social Reform in Boston, 1860–1910*. Durham, NH: University of New Hampshire Press; 2011.

9. Wegmann J. *What happened to the three-decker?*, MIT; 2006.

10. Mousseau DL. *Anne Whitney: Her Life, Her Art, and Her Relationship with Adeline Manning*. Doctoral Thesis. Fresno State University; 1992.

11. Fryer J. What Goes on in the Ladies Room? Sarah Orne Jewett, Annie Fields, and Their Community of Women. *Massachusetts Review*. 1989; 30(4):610-628.

12. Shand-Tucci D. *The Art of Scandal*. New York: HarperCollins; 1997.

13. Cheney ED. *Memoir of Susan Dimock*. 1875.

14. Lopez R. *Boston's South End: The Clash of Ideas in a Historic Neighborhood*. Boston: Shawmut Peninsula Press; 2015.

15. Leopold E. My Soul is Among Lions": Katharine Lee Bates's Account of the Illness and Death of Katharine Coman. *Legacy*. 2006; 23(1):60-73.

16. Fisken BW. Alice Brown (1857-1948). *Legacy*. 1989; 6(2):51-57.

17. Fisken BW. Within the Limits of Alice Brown's "Dooryards": Introspective Powers In Tiverton Tales. *Legacy*. 1988; 5(1):15-25.

18. Guerrier E. *An Independent Woman: The Autobiography of Edith Guerrier*. Amherst, MA: The University of Massachusetts Press; 1991.

19. Johnson VS. *The Other Black Bostonians: West Indians in Boston, 1900-1950*. Bloomington, Indiana: Indiana University Press; 2006.

20. Palmieri PA. *In Adamless Eden: The Community of Women Faculty at Wellesley*. New Haven, CT: Yale University Press; 1995.

21. Jones A. *She's That Way": Female Same-Sex Intimacy and the Growth of Modern Sexual Categories in the U.S., 1920-1940*. Thesis. New Haven, CT: Graduate School of Yale University, Yale University; 2013.

22. Lynn Archives. Spinsters Gathering. The History Project; 1896.

23. Rollins H, Parrish S. Keats and the Bostonians. Cambridge, MA: Harvard University Press; 1951.

24. Rollyson C. *Amy Lowell Anew: A Biography*. Lanham, MD: Rowman and Littlefield, Publishers; 2013.

Chapter 4

1. Bouvier L. History of LGBT Boston. In: Stein M, ed. *Encyclopedia of Lesbian, Gay, Bisexual, and Transgendered History in America*. New York: Charles Scribner's Sons; 2004.

2. Shand-Tucci D. *The Crimson Letter*. New York: St. Martin's; 2004.

3. McCormick J. *George Santayana - A Biography*. New York: Alfred A. Knopf; 1987.

4. Green M. *The Problem of Boston*. New York: Norton; 1966.

5. Strouse J. *Alice James: A Biography*. Boston: Houghton Mifflin Company; 1980.

6. Califano SK. *The Comradeship of the "Happy Few": Henry James, Edith Wharton, and the Pederastic Tradition*. Thesis. University of New Hampshire; 2007.

7. James H. *Beloved Boy: Letters to Hendrik C. Andersen*. Charlottsville: University of Virginia Press; 2000.

8. Corsano K, Williman D. *John Singer Sargent: Painting Love and Loss*. Lanham, MD: Rowman & Littlefield; 2014.

9. Burdett O, Goddard EH. *Edward Perry Warren: The Biography of a Connoisseur*. London: Christophers; 1941.

10. Stewart IJ. *Putting the Pieces in Place: The Collecting Practices of Edward Perry Warren (1860-1928) and the Museum of Fine Arts, Boston*. Thesis. Concordia University; 2003.

11. Colman C. About Ned *New York University Public Law and Legal Theory Working Papers*; 2016.

12. Green M. *The Mount Vernon Street Warrens: A Boston Story, 1860-1910*. New York: Charles Scribners and Sons; 1989.

13. Doyle DD. "A Very Proper Bostonian": Rediscovering Ogden Codman and His Late-Nineteenth-Century Queer World. *Journal of the History of Sexuality*. 2004; 13(4):446-476.

14. Harvard Crimson. *Boston Athletic Club-House*. 1889; www.thecrimson.com/article/1889/1/3/bos-

ton-athletic-club-house-the-new-athletic/. Accessed October 21, 2017.

15. Doyle DD. *The Dandy and the Aesthete: Middle and Upper Class Homosexual Identities in Late Nineteenth Century America*, Thesis. New York University; 2004.

16. Jobson B. *Sex in the Marketplace: Prostitution in an American City, Boston, 1820-1880*: Thesis. Graduate School, Boston University; 1982.

17. Fanning PJ. Fred Holland Day: Eccentric Aesthete. *The New England Quarterly*. 1980; 53(2):230-236.

18. Fanning PJ. *Through an Uncommon Lens: The Life and Photography of F. Holland Day*. Amherst, MA: University of Massachusetts Press; 2008.

19. Norton R. *Letter: Herbert Copeland to F. Holland Day*, January 24, 1910. http://rictornorton.co.uk/day.htm. Accessed November 1, 2017.

20. Shand-Tucci D. *Ralph Adams Cram: An Architect's Four Quests*. Amherst, MA: University of Massachusetts Press; 2005.

21. Howe MAD. *A Partial Semi-Centennial History of The Tavern Club*. Boston: The Tavern Club; 1934.

22. Knight E. *Charles Martin Loeffler* Chicago: University of Illinois Press; 1993.

23. Shand-Tucci D. *The Art of Scandal*. New York: HarperCollins; 1997.

24. Theodore Dwight to Isabella Stewart Gardner, undated, *Isabella Stewart Gardner Papers*, Archives. Isabella Stewart Gardner Museum, Boston.

25. New England Historical Society. *Female Impersonator Julian Eltinge Gets His Start in Boston's Gay '90s.* http://www.newenglandhistoricalsociety.com/female-impersonator-julian-eltinge-gets-his-start-in-bostons-gay-90s/. Accessed November 12, 2017.

26. Gomez C. *What A Drag! America's Most Famous Impersonator*. 2016; https://www.huffingtonpost.com/chuck-gomez/julian-eltinge-jules-broadway_b_1484153.html. Accessed November 12, 2017.

27. Hirschler E. *Sargent's Daughters: The Biography of a Painting. Boston*: MFA Publications; 2009.

28. Toibin C. *The secret life of John Singer Sargent*. 2015; http://www.telegraph.co.uk/art/artists/the-secret-life-of-john-singer-sargent/. Accessed February 20, 2018.

29. Fairbrother T. *John Singer Sargent: The Sensualist*. New Haven, CT: Yale University Press; 2000.

30. Stern E. Diary September 1897 to June 1899.

Chapter 5

1. Garland J. *The North Shore*. Beverly, MA: Commonwealth Editions; 1998.

2. Tharp LH. *Mrs. Jack*. Boston: Little, Brown, and Company; 1965.

3. Sleeper HD, Andrew AP. *Beauport Chronicle. The Intimate Letters of Henry Davis Sleeper to Abram Piatt Andrew, Jr. 1906-1915*. Boston, MA: Society for the Preservation of New England Antiquities; 1991.

4. Beaux C. *Background with Figures*. Boston: Houghton Mifflin; 1930.

5. Smith N. *Banned in Boston*. Boston, MA: Beacon Press; 2010.

6. Krahulik KC. *Cape Queer? Journal of Homosexuality*. 2006; 52(1-2):185-212.

7. Egan LR. *Provincetown as a Stage*. Orleans, MA: Parnassus Imprints; 1994.

8. Vorse MH. *Time and the Town: A Provincetown Chronicle*. New Brunswick, NJ: Rutgers University Press; 1942.

9. Murphy L. Cleaning up Newport: The U.S. Navy's Persecution of Homosexuals after World War I. *Journal of American Culture*. 1984; 7(3):57-64.

10. Murphy L. *Perverts by Official Order: The Campaign Against Homosexuals by the United States Navy*. New York: Huntington Park Press; 1988.

11. Chauncey G. Christian Brotherhood or Sexual Perversion? Homosexual Identities and the Construction of Sexual Boundaries in the World War One Era. *Journal of Social History*. 1985; 19(2):189-211.

12. *Proceedings of the Navy Courts of Inquiry. Newport, Rhode Island*. United States Archives. Washington DC 1918.

13. Zane SL. *The Newport Sex Scandal and the Early-Twentieth-Century Origins of the U.S. National Security*

State, Thesis. University of Connecticut; 2012.

14. Franke PM. *Prides Crossing*. Beverly, MA: Commonwealth Editions; 2009.

15. Vice Crackdown. Order "Powder Puff" Youths to Jail. *Boston American*. June 14, 1918: 6.

16. Stevens S. Urge Reform Campaign to Save Girls Taken in Vice. *Boston American*. June 13, 1918: 3.

17. Court. 11 Are In Court to Answer to Vice Charges. *Boston American*. June 17, 1918: 3.

18. Massachusetts Supreme Judicial Court. *Commonwealth v. Lee Porter*. Massachusetts State Judicial Archives; 1920.

19. Bernardin CW. John Dos Passos' Harvard Years. *The New England Quarterly*. 1954; 27(1):3-26.

20. Paley A. *The Secret Court of 1920*. 2000; http://www.thecrimson.com/article/2002/11/21/the-secret-court-of-1920-at/. Accessed November 13, 2017.

21. Office of the Dean. *Court of Inquiry Files*, Harvard University Archives. 1920.

22. Meyer TR. *Frat Boys Called Fags: Queer Fraternity and Honosocial Culture in the Secret Court of 1920*, Thesis. Harvard University; 2011.

23. Wright W. *Harvard's Secret Court: The Savage 1920 Purge of Campus Homosexuals*. New York: St. Marin's Griffin; 2006.

Chapter 6

1. Shively C. Prescott Townsend. In: Bullrough V, ed. *Before Stonewall: Activists for Gay and Lesbian Rights in Historical Context*. New York: Harrington Park Press; 2002.

2. Beebe L. *Boston and the Boston Legend*. New York: D. Appleton-Century Company; 1935.

3. Office of the Dean. *Court of Inquiry Files*, Harvard University Archives. 1920.

4. Bar on Trial. Owners of "Lighted Lamp" Put on Trial. Boston Globe. April 14, 1922: 9.

5. *Letter from Stewart Mitchell to Richard Hillyer*. Boston Athenaeum: Stewart Mitchell Correspondence; 1924.

6. Kantor SG. *Alfred H. Barr, Jr. and the Intellectual Origins of the Museum of Modern Art*. Cambridge, MA: The MIT Press; 2002.

7. Tommasini A. *Virgil Thomson: Composer on the Aisle*. New York: W. W. Norton and Company; 1997.

8. Watson S. *Prepare for Saints*. New York: Random House; 1998.

9. Gaddis E. *Magician of the Modern*. New York: Alfred A. Knopf; 2000.

10. Duberman M. *The Worlds of Lincoln Kirstein*. New York: Alfred A. Knopf; 2007.

11. Kirstein L. *Diary*. New York Public Library at Lincoln Center; 1927.

12. Cowan R. *Unpublished diaries*. Boston Athenaeum Archives; 1929-33.

13. Trinward S. Spectacles and Speakeasies: Gay life in the '20s and '30s. *Esplanade*. November 12, 1976: 10.

14. Wicker R. Boston's Bohemian Blueblood: An Immodest Interview with a Happy Old Man. Boston Athenaeum: Prescott Townsend Collection. 1969:8.

15. Townsend. Beans, Cod, and Libido: The Life of Prescott Townsend 1894-1973. *Manifest Destiny*. 1973.

16. Minor F. Women in Bars. *Esplanade*. June 17, 1978: 14.

17. Closed B. Licenses of two clubs revoked. *Boston Globe*. July 25, 1934.

18. Inspections. New Checkup by Officials of Local Spots. *Boston Globe*. December 3, 1942: 14.

19. Shand-Tucci D. *The Crimson Letter*. New York: St. Martin's; 2004.

20. Terrell MH. *Some Kind of Social Doctor: Historical Study of Martha May Eliot's Policies for Maternal and Child Health*: Florence Heller Graduate School, Brandeis University; 1990.

21. Harvard T.H. Chan School of Public Health. *Child health pioneer Martha May Eliot: A woman ahead of her time*. 2018; www.hsph.harvard.edu/news/centennial-martha-may-eliot/. Accessed June 7, 2018.

22. Hyde L. *Rat and the Devil: Journal Letters of E. O. Mathiessen and Russell Cheney*. Hamden, CT: Anchon Books; 1978.

23. Donaldson S. *John Cheever: A Biography*. New York: Random House; 1988.

24. Bernstein A. *Millions of Queers (Our Homo America)*. Unpublished manuscript; 1940.

25. Landlady A. Takes A Diplomat Nowadays To Manage A Rooming House Well: Also Patience, Good Taste, a Business Head and Personality, says One Woman Who Goes In For Light and Real Home Feeling. *Boston Globe.* January 4, 1931.
26. Calkins G. *Interview.* The History Project, 1991.
27. Freedman E. *Maternal Justice.* Chicago: University of Chicago Press; 1996.
28. Murphy L. The House on Pacific Street. *Journal of Homosexuality.* 1986; 12(1):27-50.
29. O'Toole D. *Outing the Senator: Sex, Spies, & Videotape.* New York: James Street Publishers; 2005.
30. Vidal G. Interview.. The History Project Archives; 1973.
31. Kaplan D. *Tennesse Williams in Provincetown.* New Brunswick, NJ: Hansen Publishing Group; 2007.
32. Krahulik KC. Cape Queer? *Journal of Homosexuality.* 2006; 52(1-2):185-212.
33. Williams T. *Tennessee Williams' Letters to Donald Windham, 1940 – 1965.* Athans, GA: The University of Georgia Press; 1976.
34. Williams T. *Memoirs.* New York: Doubleday; 1975.
35. Smith N. *Banned in Boston.* Boston, MA: Beacon Press; 2010.
36. Reed R. Interview. The History Project. 1997.
37. Lord J. *My Queer War.* New York: Farrar, Straus, Giroux; 2010.
38. Snupin I. Charge Beacon Hill "Twilight" Man Member of Queer Love Cult Seduced Young Man. *Mid-Town Journal.* January 29, 1943: 1.

Chapter 7

1. D'Emilio JA. *Out of the shadows: The Gay Emancipation Movement in the United States, 1940-1970*: Thesis. Graduate School of Arts and Sciences, Columbia University; 1982.
2. Freedman E. *Maternal Justice.* Chicago: University of Chicago Press; 1996.
3. Clarridge AP. *Gay Harvard in the 1940s.* 2009; http://harvardmagazine.com/2009/01/cambridge-02138. Accessed October 17, 2017.
4. Clarridge P. Interview. The History Project. Not dated.
5. Boland Murder. Sailor Admits Bludgeoning Boland to Death. *Boston Globe.* December 13, 1953.
6. Shand-Tucci D. *The Crimson Letter.* New York: St. Martin's; 2004.
7. Gooch B. *City Poet: The Life and Times of Frank O'Hara.* New York: Alfred A. Knopf; 1993.
8. O'Hara F. *The Fourth of July,* Folder 1. Located at: Donald Allen Collection, University of California, San Diego. Unpublished (1951).
9. Roffman K. *The Songs We Know Best: John Asbery's Early Life.* New York: Farrar, Straus and Giroux; 2017.
10. Krone M. Gay Boston in the 1940s. *Spirit Magazine.* 2014:34-37.
11. X M, Haley A. *The Autobiography of Malcolm X.* New York: Random House; 1964.
12. Marable M. *Malcolm X: A Life of Reinvention.* New York: Viking; 2011.
13. Carr H. *The Brothers Bulger: How they Terrorized and Corrupted Boston for a Quarter Century.* New York: Grand Central Publishing; 2006.
14. Krone M. *1950s Gay Boston.* Boston Queer History 2014; https://markthomaskrone.wordpress.com/2014/11/21/1950s-gay-boston/#comments. Accessed December 9, 2017.
15. Cathcart A. *Unpublished memoir.* Boston Athenaeum Prescott Townsend Archive. 1995.
16. Vacca R. May 23, 1954: "Rum-Saturated" Silver Dollar Bar Under Fire. *The Troy Street Observer* 2013; https://www.troystreet.com/tspots/2013/05/31/on-may-23-1954/. Accessed November 13, 2017.
17. Sydney S. Interview. The History Project; Not dated.
18. Grant J. Intrerview. The History Project; 1995.
19. D'entremont J. *Pilgrims' Progress: Boston's Gay History.* 2007; http://archive.guidemag.com/magcontent/invokemagcontent.cfm?ID=211D6820-56B6-41CB-8DF1503C48C70284. Accessed November 12, 2017.
20. Trinward S. Boston's gay bars – a history. *Esplanade.* November 26, 1976: 14.
21. Robinson J. Napoleon Club: still fabulous after 41 years. *Boston Globe.* October 12, 1994: 27.

22. Trinward S. Gay bars: A history. *Esplanade.* December 10, 1976: 10.
23. Trinward S. Paradise. *Esplanade.* December 9, 1977: 11.
24. Foley A. *Oral History.* The History Project; 1995.
25. rinward S. The Women's Bars. *Esplanade.* December 25, 1976: 15.
26. Murray L. *Stonewall and Me.* 2009; http://gayberkshires.blogspot.com/2009/06/forty-years-since-stonewall-1969-2009.html. Accessed November 13, 2017.
27. Trinward S. Gay Bars: A history. *Esplanade.* January 14, 1977: 12.
28. Vacca R. May 22, *1955: The Legendary Latin Quarter Closes.* 2013; https://www.troystreet.com/tspots/2013/05/31/on-may-22-1955/. Accessed November 15, 2017.
29. Keblinsky J. 11 Boston Night Spots Off-Limits to Servicemen. *Boston Globe.* January 13, 1955: 1.
30. McHenry B. *Oral History.* The History Project; 1985.
31. Shively C. *Oral History.* The History Project; 2008.
32. Dewhurst RS. *Ungrateful city: The collected poems of John Wieners,* University of Buffalo; 2014.
33. Jonas S. *Selected Poems.* Hoboken, NJ: Talisman House, Publishers; 1994.
34. Kahn EJ. Bottoms up. Public Sex in Provincetown Bars. *Provincetown Magazine.* 1977:9.
35. Krahulik KC. Cape Queer? *Journal of Homosexuality.* 2006; 52(1-2):185-212.
36. Happenings. To Fellows and Friends Afar and Near. *Provincetown Advocate.* May 26, 1955: 1.
37. Birthday Party. To Fellows and Friends. *Provincetwon Advocate.* August 28, 1958: 1.
38. Trinward S. Twelve Carver. *Esplanade.* December 10, 1976: 9.
39. Faderman L. *Odd Girls and Twilight Lovers: A History of Lesbian Life in Twentieth-Century America.* New York: Penguin; 1991.
40. Hoffman B. *Interview.* The History Project; 1997.
41. Toohey F. The First Beaux Arts Ball. November 12 *Esplanade,* 1976: 7.
42. Mansour G. *Interview* by author. 2017.
43. Bronski M. *Drag Lad Tells All.* 2003; https://www.glapn.org/sodomylaws/usa/massachusetts/manews018.htm. Accessed Noember 26, 2017.
44. Baker H. Sex Offenders in a Massachusetts Court. *Journal of Psychiatric Social Work.* 1950:102-107.

Chapter 8

1. Kennedy L. *Planning the City upon a Hill: Boston since 1630.* Boston: University of Massachusetts Press; 1994.
2. Lopez R. *Boston's South End: The Clash of Ideas in a Historic Neighborhood.* Boston: Shawmut Peninsula Press; 2015.
3. Keyes L. *The Rehabilitation Planning Game: A Study in the Diversity of Neighborhood.* Cambridge MA: MIT Press; 1969.
4. Werth B. *The Scarlet Professor.* New York: Doubleday; 2001.
5. Martin RK. Scandal at Smith. *Radical Teacher.* 1994; 45(Winter):4-8.
6. Soares M. LH*A Daughters of Bilitis Video Project: Lois Johnson and Sheri Barde*n. 1989; http://herstories.prattinfoschool.nyc/omeka/document/MV-59. Accessed November 1, 2017.
7. Willowroot A. *Maxine Feldman ~ Memories of Max from 1964 on.* 2007; http://www.spiralgoddess.com/MaxineFeldman.html. Accessed November 8, 2017.
8. Kiritsy L. *Lesbian trail blazer Maxine Feldman dies.* 2007; http://www.edgemedianetwork.com/news///36268. Accessed November 8, 2017.
9. Krone M. *On the Cusp of Liberation. Boston Queer History* 2015; https://markthomaskrone.wordpress.com/2015/05/17/on-the-cusp-of-liberation/. Accessed December 8, 2017.
10. Lesbian Party. Butch Balls Baffle Bulls. *Mid-Town Journal.* November 15, 1957: 1.
11. United States Navy. *Survey of Commericalized Prostitution Conditions.* 1960.
12. United States Navy. *Survey of Commericalized Prostitution Conditions.* 1961.
13. Trinward S. The Shed: Rustic Roundevouz. *Esplanade.* February 11, 1977: 8.
14. Zipper J. *Interview.* The History Project; 1985.
15. Krone M. 1950s *Gay Boston. Boston Queer History* 2014; https://markthomaskrone.wordpress.

com/2014/11/21/1950s-gay-boston/#comments. Accessed December 9, 2017.

16. Dole R. Homosexuality and Madness at Harvard. *Harvard Gay and Lesbian Review*. 1994:31.

17. Holleran A. 1994. *Harvard Gay and Lesbian Review*. 1994.

18. Gambone P. Beyond Words. In: Merla P, ed. *Boys Like Us: Gay Writers Tell Their Coming Out Stories*. New York: Avon Books; 1996.

19. Frank B. Frank: *A Life in Politics from the Great Society to Same-Sex Marriage*. New York: Farrah, Straus and Giroux; 2015.

20. Marotta T. *Sons of Harvard: Gay Men from the Class of 1967*. New York: Quill; 2003.

21. Tobias A. *Gay Like Me*. 1998; http://harvardmagazine.com/1998/01/tobias.html. Accessed August 12, 2017.

22. Tobias A. *The Best Little Boy in the World*. New York: Random House; 1973.

23. Stein J, Plimpton G. *Edie: An American Biography*. New York: Pimlico; 2006.

24. Nichols T. *Coming out in Boston in 1969*. 2016; https://www.huffingtonpost.com/thom-nickels/coming-out-in-boston-in-1969_b_3567428.html. Accessed November 13, 2017.

25. Maegher D. *Crushes Lovers Boyfriends Tricks*. Boston: Self-published; 2017.

26. Kahn EJ. Bottoms up. Public Sex in Provincetown Bars. *Provincetown Magazine*. 1977:9.

27. Cathcart A. *Unpublished memoir*. Boston Athenaeum Prescott Townsend Collection. 1995.

28. Manso P. *Ptown: Art, Sex, and Money on the Outer Cape*. New York: Scribner; 2002.

29. Conn SR. New Pilgrims in Provincetown: Cape Cod Village Is the Site of 'Beatnik' Beachhead That Is Angering the Local Residents. *New York Times*. July 25, 1966: 29.

30. Peary G. *John Waters and his Dreamlanders in P-Town*. http://www.geraldpeary.com/interviews/wxyz/waters-p-town.html. Accessed December 4, 2017.

31. McNeil L., McCain G. *Partying with John Waters in 1970s Provincetown*. 2016; https://www.vice.com/en_us/article/jmkdgy/of-bourbon-and-black-beauties-nan-goldin-and-cookie-mueller-in-provincetown. Accessed November 1, 2017.

32. Unknown. Beans, Cod, and Libido: The Life of Prescott Townsend 1894-1973. *Manifest Destiny*. . 1973.

33. Lucas DS. *Letter*. Boston Athenaeum Prescott Townsend Collection. 1959.

34. Bouvier L. History of LGBT Boston. In: Stein M, ed. *Encyclopedia of Lesbian, Gay, Bisexual, and Transgendered History in America*. New York: Charles Scribner's Sons; 2004.

35. Shively C. *Oral History*. The History Project; 2008.

36. Shand-Tucci D. *The Crimson Letter*. New York: St. Martin's; 2004.

37. 37. Krone M. Prescott Townsend: The Brahmin Who Became A Gay Rights Pioneer. 2013; https://markthomaskrone.wordpress.com/2013/10/. Accessed December 8, 2017`.

38. Doherty B. *Harassment of Gays at MIT: A Clash of Sexual Roles*. William Canfield Papers: Northestern University; 1982.

Chapter 9

1. Maguire A. *Interview* by author. 2017.

2. Graves J. *Many Roads Traveled: The Autobiography of John Graves*. Fort Lauderdale, FL: Self Published; 2000.

3. McNaught B. *Telephone Interview* by author. 2018.

4. Morgan F. *Interview*. The History Project. 1995.

5. Downs J. *For Charley Shively, Gay Liberation Was About Sex and Rebellion, Not Equality*. 2017; http://www.slate.com/blogs/outward/2017/10/12/remembering_charley_shively_a_gay_liberation_activist_who_rejected_equality.html?wpsrc=sh_all_dt_fb_top. Accessed December 11, 2017.

6. Streitmatter R. *Unspeakable: The Rise of the Gay and Lesbian in America*. New York: Faber and Faber; 1995.

7. Cobb N. Gay liberation pushes social, political action. *Boston Globe*. March 14, 1971.

8. New Hampshire. U. N. H. Wins? *Gay Community News*. January 26, 1974: 1.

9. White E. *States of Desire: Travels in Gay America*. New York: Dutton; 1980.

10. Accardi P. Gay student groups defy 'inbred guilt'. *Boston Phoenix*. April 16, 1970.

11. Willenbecher T. Martin Duberman. *Esplanade*. June 3, 1977: 9.

12. Hoffman A. The Mystical Hiring Committee of Life. *Prairie Schooner*. 2007;51(2):166-179.

13. Whitaker J. *Women's restaurants*. 2013; https://restaurant-ingthroughhistory.com/tag/bread-roses-restaurant/. Accessed July 12, 2018.

14. Krone M. *Cambridge Women's Center Began With a Building Takeover in 1971*. Rialto. 2014.

15. Gay AN. *The View From the Closet: Essays on Gay Life and Liberation, 1973-1977*. Boston: Union Park Press; 1978.

16. Eisenberg MA. *The process of homosexual identification and the effect of the homosexual subculture on the lifestyle of the homosexual*, Thesis. University of Massachusetts; 1974.

17. Wolf S. Anger in the Gay Ghetto. *Boston Phoenix*. July 10, 1970: 9.

18. Soares M. LHA *Daughters of Bilitis Video Project: Lois Johnson and Sheri Barden*. 1989; http://herstories.prattinfoschool.nyc/omeka/document/MV-59. Accessed November 1, 2017.

19. Johnson L. *Interview. Boston's Other Voices*. The History Project. 1989.

20. Indiewire Team. *Heaven is Working with John Waters in a Low-Budget Hell: A Crew Member's Memoir*. 2011; http://www.indiewire.com/2011/09/heaven-is-working-with-john-waters-in-a-low-budget-hell-a-crew-members-memoir-52036/. Accessed November 27, 2017.

21. O'Rourke W. The Return of the Benches. *New York Times*. August 25, 1973: 23.

22. Manso P. *Ptown: Art, Sex, and Money on the Outer Cape*. New York: Scribner; 2002.

23. Brill D. Boston's Alliance of the Alienated: Will It Work? *Gay Community News*. August 27, 1975: 3.

24. Fitzgerald K. Provincetown's Ann Maguire to be honored for creating breast cancer research institute. *Wicked Local Truro* 2014; http://truro.wickedlocal.com/article/20140509/News/140506157. Accessed August 7, 2018.

25. Ring T. *Queer Women Who Paved the Way: Political Pioneer Elaine Noble*. 2017; https://www.advocate.com/women/2017/3/08/queer-women-who-paved-way-political-pioneer-elaine-noble. Accessed October 20, 2017.

26. Davis W. Pols Jump on Lavender Bandwagon. *Boston Phoenix*. October 22, 1974: 27.

27. Hoffman A. *An Army of Ex-Lovers*. Amherst, MA: University of Massachusetts Press; 2007.

28. Frank B. *Frank: A Life in Politics from the Great Society to Same-Sex Marriage*. New York: Farrah, Straus and Giroux; 2015.

29. Brill D. Investigation Bares Anti-Gay Police Report. *Gay Community News*. June 8, 1974: 2.

30. O'Brian D. The Police and the IFOs: Watching Crooks – Or Intimidating Gays. *Boston Phoenix*. June 3, 1975: 4.

31. Longcope K. The Homosexual, the Catholic Church and Dignity. *Boston Globe*. July 22, 1973: D22

32. Pomfret S. *Since My Last Confession*. New York: Arcade Publishing; 2008.

33. Lopato J. *LGBT Catholics celebrate 40 years of Dignity/Boston*. 2012; http://archive.boston.com/lifestyle/blogs/bostonspirit/2012/11/gay_catholic_group_dignity_cel.html. Accessed December 12, 2017.

34. Trinward S. Gay Media. *Esplanade*. June 3, 1977: 9.

35. Peterson D. *Oral History Project*. The History Project. 2010.

36. Burns R. Interview. In: Schulman S, ed. *ACT UP Oral History Project*. 2012.

37. D'entremont J. *Pilgrims' Progress: Boston's Gay History*. 2007; http://archive.guidemag.com/magcontent/invokemagcontent.cfm?ID=211D6820-56B6-41CB-8DF1503C48C70284. Accessed November 12, 2017.

38. Meunier J. *Interview* by Author. 2017.

39. Mansour G. *Interview* by Author. 2017.

40. Brown N. Gays seek Fenway protection. *Boston Globe*. June 24, 1980: 9.

41. White D. *Personal Communication*. 2018.

42. Allen D. Young Male Prostitutes: A Psychosocial Study. *Archives of Sexual Behavior*. 1980; 9(5):399-426.

43. Anderson H. Teenage Hustlers. *Gay Community News*. March 30, 1974: 3.

44. *Election Time Again – Stop Hassling the Queers* [press release]. The History Project. Undated but

early 1970s.

45. Anderson H. Hustling... *Gay Community News*. April 13, 1974: 2.

46. Brill D. The Block: Complaints Spur Police. *Gay Community News*. June 1, 1974: 1.

47. Vitti P. *The Passage: Memoir of a Boston Undercover Cop in the '60s*. New York: AuthorHouse; 2012.

48. Sullivan RD. Marching Through History. *Boston Phoenix*. 1995: 14.

Chapter 10

1. Scott B. *Personal Communication*. 2017.

2. Meunier J. *Interview* by Author. 2017.

3. Eisenberg MA. *The process of homosexual identification and the effect of the homosexual subculture on the lifestyle of the homosexual* Thesis. University of Massachusetts; 1974.

4. Pomfret S. *Since My Last Confession*. New York: Arcade Publishing; 2008.

5. Graves J. *Many Roads Traveled: The Autobiography of John Graves*. Fort Lauderdale, FL: Self Published; 2000.

6. Nichols S. *Interview*. The History Project. 1995.

7. Maguire A. *Interview* by Author. 2017.

8. Gay AN. *The View From the Closet: Essays on Gay Life and Liberation, 1973-1977*. Boston: Union Park Press; 1978.

9. McLaughlin J. Gay Boston is a Reality. *Boston Globe*. February 18 1979: 87.

10. Rofes E. *Socrates, Plato, and guys like me: Confessions of a gay schoolteacher*. Boston: Alyson Publications; 1985.

11. Tissot S. *Good Neighbors: Gentrifying Diversity in Boston's South End*. London: Verso; 2015.

12. White E. *States of Desire: Travels in Gay America*. New York: Dutton; 1980.

13. Faludi S. *Gay Rights: The Emergence of a Student Movement. 1981*; http://www.thecrimson.com/article/1981/6/4/gay-rights-the-emergence-of-a/?page=single. Accessed November 16, 2017.

14. Doherty B. *Harassment of Gays at MIT: A Clash of Sexual Roles*. Northeastern University - William Canfield Papers; 1982.

15. Price K. *Black, Feminist, Revolutionary: Remembering the Combahee River Collective*. 2014; http://www.ebony.com/news-views/the-combahee-river-collective-405#ixzz50WJjnGD4 Accessed December 6, 2017.

16. Collective CR. *The Combahee River Collective Statement. 1977*; https://americanstudies.yale.edu/sites/default/files/files/Keyword%20Coalition_Readings.pdf. Accessed December 6, 2017.

17. Grange L, Hoff J. *A brief history of the Tiffany Club of New England. 2004*; http://tcne.org/club-history/. Accessed August 14, 2017.

18. Marshall M. *Elizabeth Bishop* Boston: Houghton Mifflin; 2017.

19. Spivack K. *Talents in a Teapot: Robert Lowell, Elizabeth Bishop, and Boston Confrontatio*n. 2011; 109(Spring):238-256.

20. Martorelli T. *For People, Not For Profit: A History of Fenway Health's First Forty Years* New York: Arthur House; 2012.

21. Batza CP. *Before AIDS: Gay and lesbian community health activism in the 1970s*, Thesis. University of Illinois - Chicago; 2011.

22. Opposition. West End Renewal Project Stirs Tumult at Hearing. *Boston Globe*. April 25, 1957.

23. Stowell GS. *Interview*. The History Project. 1999.

24. Mitzel J. *Interview*. The History Projec. 2012.

25. McNaught B. *Telephone Interview*. 2018.

26. Kahn EJ. Bottoms up. Public Sex in Provincetown Bars. *Provincetown Magazine*. 1977:9.

27. Nightlife P. Out on the Cape. *Boston Magazine* 2006; http://www.bostonmagazine.com/2006/05/15/out-on-the-cape/. Accessed December 11, 2017.

28. Frank B. *Frank: A Life in Politics from the Great Society to Same-Sex Marriage* New York: Farrah, Straus and Giroux; 2015.

29. Lopez R. *Boston's South End: The Clash of Ideas in a Historic Neighborhood*. Boston: Shawmut Peninsu-

la Press; 2015.
30. Keyes L. *The Rehabilitation Planning Game: A Study in the Diversity of Neighborhood.* Cambridge MA: MIT Press; 1969.
31. Barrados E. *Interview.* The History Project, 1999.
32. Rowland M. The Revere Case. *Boston Phoenix.* August 5, 1978: 18.
33. Burns R. *Interview.* ACT UP Oral History Project 2012.
34. Mitzel J. *The Boston Sex Scandal.* Boston: Glad Day Books; 1980.
35. Fricke A. *Reflections of a Rock Lobster.* Boston: Alyson Publications; 1981.

Chapter 11

1. Shilts R. *And the band played on: Politics, people, and the AIDS epidemic.* New York: MacMillan; 1990.
2. Knox RA. Mysterious disease afflicts gays. *Boston Globe.* December 10, 1981: 1.
3. Burns R. *Interview.* ACT UP Oral History Project 2012.
4. Ward M. *The Sea is Quiet Tonight.* New York: Querelle Press; 2016.
5. Brown R. *Against My Better Judgement.* New York: Harrington Park Press; 1996.
6. Kukonis A. Interview with Alan Kukonis, Boston's Other Voices Person of the Year In: Stickel P. *Other Voices:* WROR; The History Project. 1989.
7. English B. Boston gays try to come to grips with AIDS. *Boston Globe.* December 5, 1985: Metro 1.
8. 8.   Braham J, Peterson P. *Starry, Starry Night: Provincetown's Response to the AIDS Epidemic.* Cambridge, MA: Lumen Editions; 1998.
9. Seagel GR, Oddleifson S, Cam E, et al. Survival with AIDS in Massachusetts, 1979 to 1989. *American Journal of Public Health.* 1993; 83(1):72-78.
10. Knox RA. Hub study shows lower incidence of AIDS-linked virus. *Boston Globe.* March 11, 1985: 1.
11. Klein B. *Interview* by Author. 2017.
12. McLaughlin L. AIDS victims' anxieties grow. *Boston Globe.* May 18, 1983: 1.
13. Amaro H. *Interview.* The History Project, 2006.
14. Maguire A. *Interview* by Author. 2017.
15. McNaught B. *Telephone Interview.* 2018.
16. Black and White Men Together. *Boston Bar Study.* 1984.
17. Rofes E. First Tea Dance of the Season. *Gay Community News.* May 21, 1983: Summer Supplement Page 3.
18. Longcope K. In AIDS era, Provincetown emotion high scuffle shows tensions. *Boston Globe.* September 9, 1990: 67.
19. Steele P. Selectmen Ponder Next Moves. *Provincetown Advocate.* August 21, 1986: 11.
20. Schneider MR. *Gerry Studds: America's First Openly Gay Congressman.* Amherst, MA: University of Massachusetts Press; 2017.
21. Hoffman A. *Bad Attitude: A Lesbian Sex Magazine.* Boston: The History Project; 2017.
22. Ginsburg K. *On Our Backs With A Bad Attitude* [Internet]; 2013. Podcast
23. Aurigemma M. *Interview.* ACT UP Oral History Project. 2014.
24. Longcope K. Why a gay politician came out: Frank tells how a book prompted his decision. *Boston Globe.* May 31, 1987: A25.
25. Alters D, Paz-Martinez E. Charges leveled of illegal payoffs to Boston police. *Boston Globe.* December 21, 1986: 33.
26. Kenney C, Elizabeth Neuffer. Good cop, bad cop. *Boston Globe.* April 2, 1989: Sunday Magazine Page 18.
27. Gokey B. *Personal communication.* 2018.
28. Clews C. 1984. *Boston Globe campaign brings gay/lesbian foster ban.* 2013; www.gayinthe80s. com/2013/05/1984-boston-globe-campaign-brings-gaylesbian-foster-ban/. Accessed April 26, 2018.
29. Burg B, Golding P. *Interview* by Author. 2017.

30. Fehrnstrom E. Capitol cops spy on gays. *Boston Herald*. May 26, 1988: 1.

31. Ramos JT. How same-sex couples got the right to adopt in Massachusetts. *Boston Globe*. June 21, 2015: R16.

Chapter 12

1. Wychules, P., Letter to the Editor, *Bay Windows*. December 19, 1991. p. 6.

2. Knox, R., Drug divides AIDS patients, researchers, *Boston Globe*. March 24, 1988. p. 1.

3. Diaz, J., The south South End, *Boston Globe*. December 8, 2002. City Weekly p. 1.

4. Constable, P., Metropolitan briefing; suburbia's bars for gays, *Boston Globe*. November 6, 1982. p. 1.

5. Poussard, L., *Personal correspondence*. 2018.

6. Margolin, A., Hundreds celebrate gay pride with march, rally, *Provincetown Advocate*. July 28, 1988. p. 1.

7. Braham, J. and P. Peterson, *Starry, Starry Night: Provincetown's Response to the AIDS Epidemic*. 1998, Cambridge, MA: Lumen Editions.

8. MIller, N., Will AIDS lock the closet door for gay youth?, *Boston Phoenix*. May 1, 1987. Section 2 p. 6.

9. Greenwood, D.V., *Homo Domesticus : Notes from a Same Sex Marriage*. 2007, Cambridge, MA: Perseus Books Group.

10. Burg, B. and P. Golding, *Interview* by Author. 2017.

11. Clark, J., Lesbian Journalist Fired by Christian Science Monitor, *Gay Community News*. March 20, 1982. p. 1.

12. Tierney, S., *Telephone Interview*. 2017.

13. Cicchino, P.M., et al., Sex, Lies and Civil Rights: A Critical History of the Massachusetts Gay Civil Rights Bill. *Harv. C.R.-C.L. L. Rev*, 1991. 36.

14. Goldsmith, L., Legislating Liberation: Talk with a Lobbyist, *Gay Community News*. January 28, 1984. p. 3.

15. Tierney, S., *Telephone Interview*. 2018.

16. Rubenstein, W., My Harvard Law School. *Harv. C.R.-C.L. L. Rev*, 2004. 39: p. 317-333.

17. Longcope, K., City police unit assigned to curb attacks on gays, *Boston Globe*. June 2, 1990. p. 25.

18. Kiley, R., Gardens crimes stir action, *Fenway News*. 1993. p. 1.

19. Brown, R., *Against My Better Judgement*. 1996, New York: Harrington Park Press.

20. Loth, R. and S. Lehigh, Weld says Silber Holds "Sexist Attitudes", *Boston Globe*. October 11, 1990.

21. Longcope, K., Gay activist says he will back Weld but others want to hear more about issues, *Boston Globe*. September 27, 1990. p. 64.

22. Aucoin, D., Gays split in governor race. Both Weld and Roosevelt are laying claims for support, *Boston Globe*. October 17, 1994. p. 13.

23. Case Program, *An openly gay man in politics: the story of Mike Duffy*. 1992, Harvard Kennedy School of Government.

24. Governor's Commission on Gay and Lesbian Youth, *Making Schools Safe for Gay and Lesbian Youth*. 1993.

25. Cahill, S. "Cherishing Everyone Equally:" *My Gay Irish American Journey*. 2016 [cited 2017 November 30]; Available from: http://www.therainbowtimesmass.com/cherishing-everyone-equally-gay-irish-american-journey/.

26. Meunier, J., *Interview* by Author. 2017.

27. King, L., Pride Parade Marred by Lewd Incidents, *Bay Windows*. June 13, 1996. p. 1.

28. Epperly, J., Gross Stupidity at a Great Parade, *Bay Windows*. June 13, 1996. p. 6.

29. Janules, H., Letter to the Editor, *Bay Windows*. June 13, 1996. p. 16.

30. Bresslour, L., District 8 Council Race: Tapes, Issues, and Trends, *Mission Hill Gazette*. October 29, 1993.

31. Johnson, J.B. and D. Talbot, 'Preppy' allegedly kills date in drag, *Boston Herald*. November 25, 1995. p. 1.

Chapter 13

1. Braham, J. and P. Peterson, *Starry, Starry Night: Provincetown's Response to the AIDS Epidemic.* 1998, Cambridge, MA: Lumen Editions.
2. The History Project, *Catalog of AIDS Obituaries.* 2018.
3. Ellement, J., SJC Limits Prosecution for Sodomy, *Boston Globe.* February 22, 2002. p. 1.
4. Graff, E. *Equality is Changing Provincetown's LGBTQ Scene.* 2017 [cited 2018 January 4]; Available from: https://www.vice.com/en_us/article/a3wa5j/straight-people-are-taking-over-an-lgbtq-resort-town-v24n5.
5. Rimer, S. *Resort Where Lesbians Can Feel Right at Home.* 1996 [cited 2017 December 11]; Available from: http://www.nytimes.com/1996/08/05/us/resort-where-lesbians-can-feel-right-at-home.html.
6. Bernstein, F.A., Gay Parents, a Big Week in the Sun, *New York Times.* 2July 27, 017. p. Travel 1.
7. Lopata, J. *Black and Gay Today.* 2012 [cited 2017 November 20]; Available from: http://archive.boston.com/lifestyle/blogs/bostonspirit/2012/02/black_and_gay_today.html
8. Ocasio, G.M. Breaking *TRT Exclusive: Corey Yarbrough Bids Adieu to HBGC.* 2015 [cited 2017 November 13]; Available from: http://www.therainbowtimesmass.com/15171/.
9. Maguire, A., *Interview* by Author. 2017.
10. Klein, B., *Interview* by Author. 2017.
11. Bouvier, L. and M. Krone, A History of Gay Pride, *Boston Pride Guide 2015.* 2015.
12. Abraham, Y., Tinky Winky a favorite in Gay Pride parade, *Boston Globe.* June 13, 1999. p. B1.
13. Davis, A., *Interview*, The History Project. 2004.
14. Flint, A., Sex club debated in gay community, *Boston Globe.* September 25, 1995.
15. Epperly, J., City powers where they don't belong, *Bay Windows.* October 14, 1999. p. 6.
16. Fox, J.C. *Transgender Day of Remembrance to honor Rita Hester, other victims of violence.* 2012 [cited 2017 August 12]; Available from: http://archive.boston.com/yourtown/news/downtown/2012/11/transgender_day_of_remembrance.html.
17. White, D., *Personal Communication.* 2018.
18. Bonato, M., Goodridge in Context. *Harv. C.R.-C.L. L. Rev.,* 2005. 40: p. 1.
19. Weddings/Celebrations, Hilliary Goodridge, Julie Goodridge, *New York Times.* May 23, 2004. p. 10.

Chapter 14

1. McCauley J. *On the Right Side of History,* Thesis. University of Windsor; 2012.
2. Solomon M. *Winning Marriage* Lebanon, NH: University Press of New England; 2014.
3. Lawler P. *The Faithful Departed.* New York: Perseus; 2010.
4. Cunningham MT. Catholics and the ConCon: The Church's Response to the Massachusetts Gay Marriage Decision. *Journal of Church and State.* 2005; 47(1):19-42.
5. Gunner H. *Telephone Interview.* 2018.
6. Affuso J. *Interview* by Author. 2018.
7. James E. Four who Fought for Marraige. *Bay Windows.* May 20, 2004: 3.
8. Brown R. *Against My Better Judgement.* New York: Harrington Park Press; 1996.
9. Vellner T. No, We Won't Sandwich the Bride: On Handling Gay Tokenism. *The Toast* 2015; http://the-toast.net/2015/02/05/no-we-wont-sandwich-bride/. Accessed November 20, 2017.
10. 10. Levitz J. The Bachelorette Party's Over: Venues Snub Bridezillas and Their Entourages. *Wall Street Journal.* July 27, 2018.
11. WBUR. *With The End Of Dyke Night's Second Saturdays At Machine, An Era Comes To A Close.* 2017; http://www.wbur.org/artery/2017/11/09/second-saturdays-end-at-machine. Accessed December 20, 2017.
12. Bercovitch S. *Gay and Female, Out and Alone.* 2015; http://www.thecrimson.com/article/2012/10/25/scrut-gay-and-female/.
13. Elrod E. *Random Acts of Gayness.* 2011; http://www.thecrimson.com/article/2011/5/9/lesbi-

ans-harvard-out-queer/. Accessed December 15, 2017.

14. GLAAD President. *GLAAD's new president has Cuban roots.* 2009; www.miamiherald.com/living/article1933679.html#storylink=cpy. Accessed December 11, 2017.

15. Barrios J. *Equal right to marry, and divorce.* 2010; http://archive.boston.com/bostonglobe/editorial_opinion/oped/articles/2010/09/02/equal_right_to_marry_and_divorce/. Accessed December 3, 2017.

16. Scott G. Boston Area Transgender Community Leaders and the "ENDA Crisis" *An Oral History Project* Goddard University; 2009.

17. Frank B. Frank: *A Life in Politics from the Great Society to Same-Sex Marriage* New York: Farrah, Straus and Giroux; 2015.

18. Moyer C. *Spoken Stories: A Narrative Inquiry Of Transmasculinities And Women's Colleges.* Thesis. Oakland, CA, Mills College; 2016.

19. Brown J. *Transgender at BU.* 2015; http://www.bu.edu/today/2015/transgender-at-bu/. Accessed November 27, 2017.

20. Reisner S, White J, Dunham E, et al. *Discrimination and Health in Massachusetts: A Statewide Survey of Transgender and Gender NonConforming Adults Fenway Community Health Center*, 2014.

21. Gorton D. *Anti-Transgender Hate Crimes: The Challenge for Law Enforcement.* The Anti-Violence Project of Massachusetts; 2011.

22. Cahill S, Geffen S, Vance A, Wang T, Barrera J. *Equality and Equity: Advancing the LGBT Community in Massachusetts.* The Fenway Institute and The Boston Foundation;2018.

23. Scagel E. *Valentine's Love Stories from New England Power Couples.* 2013; http://www.therainbow-timesmass.com/valentines-love-stories-from-new-england-power-couples/. Accessed November 13, 2017.

24. Raymond JM. *From our house to the State House: Understanding the impact of Goodridge v. Department of Public Health on lesbian, gay and bisexual individuals in Greater Boston.* Public Policy Program, University of Massachusetts, Boston; 2009.

25. Hatzenbuehler ML, O'Cleirigh C, C CG, Mayer K, Safren S, Bradford J. Effect of same-sex marriage laws on health care use and expenditures in sexual minority men: a quasi-natural experiment. *American Journal of Public Health.* 2012; 102:285-291.

26. MacQuarrie B, Krantz L, Hanson M. Strife forgotten amid inclusive St. Patrick's Day parade. *Boston Globe.* March 15, 2015.

27. Graff E. *Equality is Changing Provincetown's LGBTQ Scene.* 2017; https://www.vice.com/en_us/article/a3wa5j/straight-people-are-taking-over-an-lgbtq-resort-town-v24n5. Accessed January 12, 2018.

28. Colman D. Rich Gay, Poor Gay. *New York Times.* September 4, 2005: 27.

29. Leland J. *Gay-Marriage Ruling, Boom for Provincetown.* 2004; http://www.nytimes.com/2004/01/21/us/in-gay-marriage-ruling-boom-for-provincetown.html. Accessed December 2, 2017.

30. Zuyland-Wood SV. *Love, Power, and the Downfall of Stan Rosenberg.* 2018; https://www.bostonmagazine.com/news/2018/05/04/stan-rosenberg-downfall/. Accessed June 21, 2018.

31. Carr H. Stanley Rosenberg, Bryon 'Pee Wee' Hefner Brought Chamber to New Lows. *Boston Herald.* May 4, 2018.

32. Mason A. *Are Pride Parade's Corporate Ties Undermining Its Original Queer Activist Message?* 2016; http://www.wbur.org/artery/2016/06/10/pride-paradess-corporate-ties. Accessed November 20, 2017.

33. Gentile A, Givens M. *Boston Pride Under Fire as Accusations of Transphobia, Racism, Censorship Loom.* 2017; http://www.therainbowtimesmass.com/boston-pride-fire-accusations-transphobia-racism-censorship-loom/. Accessed November 23, 2017.

34. Boston PSL. *Radical anti-capitalist contingent reaches thousands at Boston Pride.* 2017; https://www.liberationnews.org/without-justice-there-is-no-pride-stonewall-warriors-reclaim-boston-pride-parade/. Accessed November 23, 2017.

35. Samuels M. *The 'Yes on 3' Fight Showed Us We Are Not Alone.* 2018; www.bu.edu/sph/2018/11/15/the-yes-on-3-fight-showed-us-we-are-not-alone/. Accessed November 21, 2018.

Index

Luxor 245, 249, 260, 302
Lynn 57, 97

Machine (bar) 260
Madsen, Christine 256
Maegher, Dermot
Maguire, Ann 177, 189, 203, 211, 212, 232, 234, 236, 252, 257, 276, 277, 280
Maine 9, 10, 17, 102, 229
Majestic Theatre 88, 99
Male prostitution 88, 99, 125, 143, 148, 171, 175, 196-198, 214, 218, 225, 244, 259, 261, 262-263
Malia, Liz 288, 304
Malin, Gene 119
Malone, Lenny 250
Manchester-by-the-Sea 50
Manchester, CT 121
Mandel, Fred 272
Mann, Horace 34
Manning, Adeline 47-48, 49
Manray (bar) 201, 260
Mansour, George 149, 157, 196
Maplethorpe, Robert 76
Marblehead 19
March Hare 110
March, Elsie 24
March, Frederic 87
Mario's (bar) 143, 144, 145, 167, 260
Marks, Jeannette 56
Maroon, Peter 272
Marquee (bar) 237, 260
Mars, Ethel 92
Marshall, Francis 172
Marshall, John 68-72
Marshall, Margaret 276, 289
Martin, Joe 257
Mason, Abner 264-265
Massachusetts Citizens 287
Massachusetts Gay and Lesbian Political Caucus (Caucus) 133, 247, 248, 257, 258, 259, 279, 287, 300, 313
Massachusetts General Hospital 250
Massachusetts Supreme Judicial Court (SJC) 22, 23, 41, 222, 256, 259, 276-277, 285, 286, 288-289, 290, 291, 292, 293, 295, 298, 300

MassEquality 297, 298
Masturbation 13, 14, 17, 18, 44, 105, 106, 140, 191
Mathiessen, F.O. 121-123
Mattachine Society 136, 164, 173, 174, 175, 178, 194
Mayer, Kenneth 228
Mayflower 7
Mayflower Compact 7
McCarthy Eugene 241
McCarthy, Vin 235, 264, 281
McCormack, Robin 203, 211, 234
McDonough, John 304
McDowell, Eiliot 136, 137, 138
McGee, Thomas 259
McGowan, Joe 245
McKeller, Thomas 84
McMurray, Laura 195
McNaught, Brian 177, 192, 213, 232, 236, 242
McWilliams, Denise 251
Mead, James 172
Measure (magazine) 151, 152
Medford 82, 300, 302
Melrose 311
Melville, Herman 36-37
Men of Color Against AIDS 231
Menino, Angela 253
Menino, Thomas 252, 253, 257, 268, 276, 280, 281, 282, 296
Mercer, Sallie 34
Merlo, Frank 131
Merrimack River 11
Merrymount 8-10, 36, 75
Meteyard, Thomas 75, 77, 90
Methfessel, Alice 208
Metropolitan Museum of Art, New York 68, 71
Meunier, John 200, 275, 312
Michell, Edward 16
Middleton, George 23-24
Midtown (bar) 145, 146, 148
Miller, Neil 195
Milne, Robert 132
Mingo of Charlestown 18
Mission Hill 151, 239, 302
MIT 102, 175, 180, 196, 206

CPSIA information can be obtained
at www.ICGtesting.com
Printed in the USA
LVHW091718010519
616263LV00012B/586/P